ALL ABOUT
TROPICAL FISH

ALL ABOUT
TROPICAL FISH

DEREK McINERNY
GEOFFREY GERARD B.A., F.R.S.E., M.I.E.E.

Revised by

Dr Chris Andrews

FOURTH EDITION
COMPLETELY REVISED

With over 140 illustrations in colour and
200 illustrations in monochrome and line drawings
by D. McInerny in the text.

Facts On File
New York • Oxford

First published in Great Britain 1958
by Harrap Limited (formerly George G. Harrap)
19/23 Ludgate Hill, London EC4M 7PD

Reprinted: 1960; 1962
Second Edition Revised 1963
Reprinted 1965
Third Edition Revised and Enlarged 1966
Reprinted: 1967; 1969; 1970; 1971; 1974; 1974; 1980
Fourth Edition Completely Revised, 1989
© Geoffrey Gerard and The Estate of Derek McInerny 1958, 1963, 1966, 1989

ISBN 0-8160-2168-6

Facts On File books are available at special discounts when purchased in bulk
quantities for businesses, associations, institutions, or sales promotion.
Please contact the Special Sales Department at 212/683-2244.
(Dial 1-800-322-8755, except in NY, AK, HI)

Printed and bound in Singapore

10 9 8 7 6 5 4 3 2 1

Foreword

It was with great pleasure that I revised this latest edition of *All About Tropical Fish*, a book first published in 1958 and faithfully referred to by aquarists ever since.

The practice of ornamental fishkeeping is indeed an old one, dating back to Roman times, if not before. However, the last thirty years have seen a tremendous change in the hobby, both in the type and variety of fishes that are available and in the huge proliferation of aquarium equipment. Not that the answers to all fishkeeping problems lie in purchasing the latest filter or water-testing device, and hence throughout this edition every effort has been made to complement established methods and procedures with relevant advances in aquarium know-how and technology. As will be seen, wherever possible the fish have been arranged in each chapter in alphabetical order by their scientific names. Current scientific thinking on fish taxonomy has been employed where most relevant, although the exact taxonomic status of certain groups is under continual review.

The aquarium hobby will continue to develop and advance, and the amateur aquarist has an important role to play in recording his or her observations and communicating with other hobbyists via magazines and local aquatic clubs. It is this involvement of the dedicated amateur that allows the pursuit not only to sustain its popularity but also to grow, and constantly to recruit new enthusiasts.

I hope that the original authors' enthusiasm and attention to detail will in this, the fourth edition of *All About Tropical Fish*, continue to act as an inspiration to another generation of aquarists, who will be responsible for taking fish-keeping into the twenty-first century.

Dr Chris Andrews

Regent's Park, December 1988

Acknowledgments to First Edition

This book would not have been started but for the encouragement and enthusiasm of my wife, and certainly would never have been finished had it not been for the unceasing hard work and help given me by Miss Jean Christie.

I wish to express my thanks to my co-author Geoffrey Gerard and his wife for all their help, and to Mrs C. Gale for typing and corrections.

To Brian Barratt all praise for his patience and skill in producing the majority of the photographs. I am indebted to the Zoological Society of London for permission to photograph the following species: *Caecobarbus geertsi*, *Hemichromis bimaculatus*, *Hippocampus brevirostris*, *Leporimus fasciatus*, *Malapterurus electricus*, *Pterois volitans*, and *Serrasalmus spilopleura*; also to Dr E. Trewavas, of the British Museum (Natural History: Fishes), for help in identifying some of the rarer species. To the following, thanks are due for the loan of specimens: Mr H. Axelrod, New York, *Monodactylus sebae*, *Pelmatochromis guntheri*; Mr R. Chandler, Cambridge, *Jordanella floridae* (and for help in chemistry); Mr K. Fawcett, Reigate, Veil-tail Angel; Mr A. Gale, Dulwich, *Mollienisia velifera*; Mrs G. Hollis, Wandsworth, *Epalzeorhynchos kallopterus*; Mr J. Hunter, Maidenhead, *Aequidens curviceps*; Wing-Commander L. Lynn Courtrai, *Heniochus acuminatus*; Mr R. Mealand, Putney, *Hydrocoty'e vulgaris*, *Naias microdon*, *Samolus floribundus*, and *Saururus cernus*; Mr P. Phillips, Tottenham, *Tilapia mossambica*; Mrs K. Robertshaw, Edgware, *Aphyosemion sjoestedti*; Mr H. Russell-Holland, Totteridge, *Barbus vittatus*; Mr R. Skipper, Hendon, *Symphysodon discus*; Mrs I. Smith, Kingsbury, *Telmaterina ladigesi*; Mr E. Smykala, Friern Barnet, *Rasbora kalachroma*; Mr C. Stoker, Sutton, *Barilius christi*, *Cichlasoma biocellatum*, *Herichthys cyanoguttatus*, *Metynnis schreitmelleri*, and *Phenacogrammus interruptus*.

Acknowledgments are also due to Mr R. Clegg, Haslemere Museum, for photographs of water insects, to Mr L. Perkins, Dulwich, for photographs of *Abudefduf uniocellatus*, *Amphiprion bicinctus*, *Angelichthys cilaris*, *Chaetodon vagabundus*, *Dascyllus aruanus*, *Dascyllus trimaculatus*, *Gymnotus carapo*, and *Holocanthus annularis*, and to Mr W. Pitt, Walton-on-Thames, for photographs of *Mesogonistius chaetodon* and *Polycentrus schomburgki*.

That this book should ever have been published is entirely due to Miss Juliet Piggott, and to her I give my sincere thanks. Lastly I must express my appreciation to my publishers for the kindness and consideration shown to me throughout.

DEREK McINERNY

Ewhurst
1958

Contents

Acknowledgments

The publishers are grateful to the following for allowing them to reproduce new photographs in this edition:

Dr Alan Beaumont: *Gymnocorymbus ternetzi* (Black widow), p. 221; Clown Anemone Fish, p. 467; *Balistoides conspicillum* (or *niger*) (Clown triggerfish), p. 457; *Cichlasoma nigrofasciata* (Convict cichlid), p. 385; *Trichopsis vittatus* (Croaking gourami), p. 373; *Hemichromis bimaculatus* (Jewel cichlid), p. 391; *Serrasalmus natteri* (Natterer's piranha), p. 271; *Astronotus ocellatus* (Oscar's cichlid), p. 379; *Betta splendens* (Siamese fighting fish), p. 354.

Liz Bomford: *Melanochromis auratus* (Malawi golden cichlid), p. 392; *Pseudotropheus zebra* (Zebra cichlid), p. 412.

Picturepoint: *Platax orbicularis* (Redface batfish) (photo: Sim), p. 462; *Paracanthurus hepatus* (Regal tang) (photo: Sim), p. 456.

Planet Earth Pictures: *Chaetodon* species (Butterfly fish) (photo: Scoones), p. 458 and cover; *Colisa lalia* (Dwarf gourami) (photo: Paul Oliveira) (cover); *Betta splendens* (Siamese fighting fish) (photo: P. J. Palmer) (cover).

Introduction

The remarkable increase in the number of aquarists (the general term for those who keep fishes) shows the growing popularity of a hobby which transcends national frontiers and provides a common interest among men and women all over the world. Why is it that in so many homes there are to be found aquaria, and that of these, many contain tropical fish?

Advantages of Tropicals
In comparison with cold-water fishes, most tropicals are smaller, more dainty, and more colourful. They are accustomed to warmish water, which naturally contains less dissolved oxygen, so they need less of this gas. The warmth speeds up metabolism, making them more active than cold-water fishes. This has the advantage that in a given-sized tank more tropicals can be kept than cold-water species.

Interior Decoration
Once an illuminated aquarium has been installed, it becomes the focal point of the room. It is a fascinating sight to watch the brilliantly coloured exotic fishes weaving in and out among the rocks and aquatic plants. There is something intriguing in this living picture which gives a glimpse of the mysteries of the underwater world, and brings nature right into the home.

Expression of Individuality
There are many ways in which a tank can be set up; no two aquaria are likely to be identical. Some people prefer to keep fish of one species only; others like diversity, and their tank may harbour fishes from many parts of the world. But, whatever form the aquarium may take, the arranging of the various plants, with their different types of foliage and varying shades of green, and the placing of the rocks in position, gives plenty of opportunity for artistic expression.

Educational Value
Another aspect of an aquarium is its educational value. The study of the habits of fishes and their methods of breeding is both interesting and instructive. The owner soon begins to differentiate between different types of fish and learns about their methods of reproduction. Some fishes give birth to live young; others produce

eggs. But, since most tropicals breed frequently, the aquarist who keeps some live-bearers is bound sooner or later to have the opportunity of seeing the mating and eventual birth of some of these species in his aquarium. With the aid of a small breeding tank he can watch the spawning, hatching, and development of egg-layers. Moreover, the simple manner in which fishes mate affords a natural method of introducing children to the ways of nature.

Finally, it might be mentioned here that, both for children and for adults, looking after, and having regard for, other living creatures helps to develop a good trait in the human character. Where larger pets are out of the question, fishes may help to compensate for their lack. Strange as it may seem, even fishes soon learn to recognize their owner and treat him as a friend, coming fearlessly to his hand at feeding-time. In some hospitals, particularly those for children, fish tanks in the wards have proved to be most beneficial as they create an interest and help to take their mind off their circumstances.

Economy of Space and Freedom from Restrictions
A great advantage of the tropical aquarium lies in its economy of space. With 2 or 3 cubic feet one can keep 30 to 60 fishes; this means that even the smallest room can accommodate the fascinating hobby. Again, on owning an aquarium there are no restrictions such as apply in some blocks of flats, where dogs and other animals are prohibited on grounds of noise. Few people are likely to complain of the aquarist, with his tank of silently swimming fishes.

Initial Cost and Maintenance
What does it cost? Here is a fundamental question asked by everyone who wishes to keep an aquarium. Fortunately, the tank and equipment is not an unduly expensive piece of apparatus; the handy amateur who is prepared to do his own glazing can minimize the drain on his pocket. Rocks and water cost practically nothing; the common plants are inexpensive; fishes can be purchased from about 50 pence upward; heating and lighting costs are reasonable, as in a tropical tank the water is only lukewarm. Upkeep is low; if properly kept all that is necessary is an occasional scraping of the front glass, and perhaps siphoning away a small amount of sediment, filter maintenance and topping up with water. These operations require only a few minutes, and involve little expenditure. The skilful aquarist can even organize the feeding so that it costs practically nothing. With experience it is possible to breed certain fish whose sale not only will recover the annual expenditure on the aquarium but may even show a profit.

Social Aspect
The aquarist will soon find that his hobby is helping him to make a widening circle of friends whose interests coincide with his own. Almost certainly his enthusiasm will inspire other people to follow his example and become aquarists. Moreover, we must not forget to mention that in many parts of the country there are fish clubs

10

where newcomers are welcomed. Here for a very moderate subscription a member can attend periodical meetings, join in discussions, see films, and hear talks on various aspects of his hobby. The clubs organize shows, and perhaps the aquarist will win a coveted prize. The club brings him into touch with those who are more experienced fish-keepers than himself; this gives him opportunities of gaining valuable information which will help him to avoid making mistakes. In many countries there are fish magazines; these link together enthusiasts the world over. Through correspondence in the columns aquarists get in touch with one another, and friendships are formed. Contacts such as these contribute something towards building up a better understanding among men, and perhaps even help to establish peace and good-will.

Chapter One

The Aquarium

The first thing to bear in mind is that the aquarium should be as large as space and money will allow; the greater the volume of water, the more stable will be the water conditions (especially temperature). Again, sooner or later most aquarists wish to expand their hobby; the person who initially installs a large tank can extend with relatively little additional expense or equipment.

A vital point is that the surface area of the water exposed to the air should, for reasons discussed later, be as large as possible. To achieve this the tank should be long, and not too narrow compared to its height.

TYPES OF AQUARIA

Fish can and have been kept in a huge variety of receptacles, including bowls, battery jars and metal-framed glass tanks. However, the advent of rigid clear plastics, and silicone sealer for making strong but frameless glass-to-glass joints, has revolutionized the size and shape of home aquaria.

Plastic tanks tend to be small, and to scratch very easily. However, they are relatively inexpensive to buy, and are ideal as a hospital, quarantine or small rearing tank.

Most good aquarium shops now stock a range of all-glass aquaria, with the panes of glass joined together with aquarium silicone sealer. Properly constructed, these tanks are at least as strong and reliable as their old-fashioned and metal-framed equivalents, although they may incorporate a thin plastic frame for aesthetic reasons. Such tanks are also ideal for a salt-water (marine) aquarium, where metal-framed tanks may corrode and can even poison the fish. Since all-glass aquaria do not have a supported frame, it is always recommended to sit them on a layer of expanded polystyrene (e.g., ceiling tilings); which will even out any irregularities in the supporting stand or base.

Unless the tank is very small, it must never be moved once it is full of water – not only is an aquarium filled with water very heavy, but moving it when it is full may result in damage to the silicone-sealed joints. It must first be at least three-quarters emptied.

CONSTRUCTING AN AQUARIUM

Nowadays it is quite feasible for the aquarist to construct his own all-glass aquarium, using five sheets of glass and silicone sealer.

Let us assume that you wish to construct a 24"×12"×15" aquarium. An aquarium slightly taller than it is wide can look quite imposing. You will need five sheets of ¼" plate glass as follows:

Base measuring 24″×12″;
Back measuring 12″×14¾;
Front measuring 24″×14¾″;
Side 1 measuring 11½″×14¾″;
Side 2 measuring 11½″×14¾″.

To this must be added two strips, which will form ledges at the top of the front and back pane, measuring 23½″×¾″ and two cover glasses to sit on these ledges measuring 11″×11½″. Both the cover glasses and their supports can be made of thinner glass, say 3/16th″ thickness. Do note that if tanks taller or longer than this particular size are constructed, thicker glass will have to be used for the main panes, and expert advice should be sought.

Before construction can begin, it is important to smooth all the edges of each pane and then clean each one thoroughly. Smoothing the edges can be time-consuming, and is best approached using medium-grade wet-and-dry abrasive paper and plenty of clean water. When smoothing down the edges of the glass, the abrasive paper should be wrapped around a piece of wood — to avoid the danger of cuts to the aquarists' hands.

Once the edges have been smoothed, each pane of glass must be thoroughly cleaned in warm, soapy water, rinsed in clean water and then allowed to dry.

Tubes of silicone aquarium sealant are now available from most aquarium shops. Do not be tempted to use bathroom sealer from a DIY shop, as this may contain a fungicide which can cause problems for fish in aquaria.

To construct the tank you will also need a large, flat work-surface, a roll or two of plastic insulation tape and a heavy object to lean the panes against while they are drying. One or two clean house bricks can be used for the latter.

To begin with, the five main panes are joined with a thin layer of sealer along each edge, and then allowed to dry for 24 hours or so. The silicone sealer is applied to each of the internal joints (as a continuous bend) to make the tank completely watertight.

Starting with the base, a thin line of sealer is applied to the upper surface of one of its long edges. Next the back panel is placed carefully on top of the line of sealer, and leant against one of the bricks for support. Now a continuous line of sealer can be run down one of the vertical edges of the upright pane and across the side edge of the base pane. One of the side panes can now be placed on this line of sealer on the base, and the two upright panes brought together vertically. These two panes can be held in place with a piece of insulation tape. The process is now repeated for the other side pane and (in turn) the front pane, and throughout it is important to ensure that the upright panes sit squarely on the base pane, and that the corners are square.

After about 24 hours a continuous bend of sealer should be applied to the internal joints (including the corners), perhaps smoothing it with a damp finger. About 24 hours later the ledge on to which the cover glasses will sit can be sealed into position, about an inch from the top edge of the front and back panes. Then 24 to 48 hours later, all the supporting pieces of tape can be removed, and the tank well rinsed with clean water.

Tanks constructed in this fashion should always be sealed on a layer of

13

polystyrene. As mentioned above, this evens out any irregularities in the supporting base. Various 'sticky-backed plastics' are now available from DIY stockists and can be used to form an attractive trim to the tank, and a couple of glass marbles, glued into place with sealer, can be used to form handles for the cover glasses.

Further ideas for tank designs and improvements can be obtained by inspecting the tanks on sale at local aquarium shops, but it is worth bearing in mind that home-made tanks are not necessarily any cheaper than professionally constructed, shop-bought equivalents.

REPAIRING A LEAKY TANK

Many aquarists still have the metal-framed 'putty and glass' tanks, either in use or sitting disused in a garden shed or garage. Such tanks can if necessary be reglazed, using good-quality aquarium putty and replacing scratched or cracked panes with new ones. After a coat of non-toxic paint has been applied to the metal frame, this type of tank can then be as good as new, or at least usefully employed as a spare breeding or hospital tank. Where reglazing is not necessary, and perhaps where the old putty seals are a little suspect, silicone sealer can be used to seal up the internal glass-to-glass joints, making an old tank new again. When using silicone sealer to repair leaky tanks it is important to ensure that all the areas to be sealed are clean, even, free from loose material and completely dry. Tanks repaired using silicone sealer can be ready for use in 24 to 48 hours, following a good rinse in clean water.

METHODS OF HEATING

A variety of methods have been used to heat aquaria, including gas, paraffin and electricity. Generally speaking, an amateur hobbyist with a small number of tanks will heat his tanks individually, whereas anyone with a large number of tanks may find it easier and cheaper to heat the room in which the tanks are kept.

Gas burners beneath slate-bottomed tanks have long since been replaced by electric heater-thermostats specially designed for aquarium use. These are available from aquarium shops in a variety of different wattages. As a rough guide, allow 5 to 10 watts per gallon of water to be heated to the required 76° to 80°F. Large tanks or tanks in an unheated room will require nearer 10 watts to the gallon, whereas very small tanks or tanks in a relatively 'warm' room will require only 5 watts per gallon (or even less).

Do not, however, rely on room heating to maintain a steady tank temperature if, for example, that heating goes off overnight. To enable you to check easily if the tank water is being kept at the correct temperature, a reliable thermometer (also available from aquarium shops) should be obtained and placed in a prominent position.

Very large tanks (more than 3 or 4 feet in length) should be heated using two or three heater-thermostats which add up (in total) to the wattage required by a tank of that size. This ensures a more even distribution of the heat, and if one heater-thermostat should fail, the remaining one(s) will prevent the tank temperatures falling too low until a replacement can be obtained.

To heat a room containing a number of fish tanks, or even to heat a specially set-up 'fish house', paraffin heaters have been used. Although they are relatively cheap to run, they can be somewhat unreliable, and they do give off rather unpleasant fumes. This will result in an oily film showing on the surface of the water in the tanks, and this film should be removed by drawing a piece of newspaper across the surface of the water.

A cleaner and much more convenient method of heating a fish room or fish house is to utilize an electric fan-heater connected to a room thermostat and to minimize heating costs by effective insulation.

LIGHTING

An essential factor in keeping an aquarium is light. Not only does it enable the fish to be seen, but it also enhances the beauty of the tank, and stimulates plant growth by allowing photosynthesis to occur (see later). Whereas the commercial fish-breeder may house his tanks where they can receive natural light from a glass roof, the average hobbyist has to supplement his tank lighting by artificial means.

Most aquariums now come complete with a lid or hood that will accommodate tungsten (bulb) lighting or fluorescent (tube) lighting. Light bulbs are cheap to install, require quite frequent replacement and can add rather a lot of heat to the upper layers of the aquarium water. By comparison, fluorescent tubes are more expensive to install (though cheaper to run), last longer, and do not add very much heat to the aquarium. Fluorescent lighting is recommended rather than tungsten bulb lighting for the average home aquarium, and a number of different types of tubes are now available (some of which are very similar to natural daylight). The light output of fluorescent tubes does, however, decrease gradually with time, so they should always be replaced every 9 to 12 months.

As a rough guide, each foot length of aquarium will require about 20 watts of fluorescent lighting, left on for 10 to 12 hours per day. Tanks less than 24″ in length will require rather less light than this, and tanks deeper than 18″ will require considerably more.

These figures assume that the aquarium will be well planted with living plants. If plants are omitted, or if plastic plants are used, artificial lighting can be used for just a few hours a day – to view the fish. Should natural sunlight be available to the tank, these lighting figures (wattage and/or duration) can be reduced.

Various types of high-intensity spot lamps are now available for aquarium use, and these are of benefit in large, deep tanks, and to provide the large amounts of light required by tropical marine invertebrates.

It is suggested that during darkness the room light is switched on before the aquarium lights, so that the fish can adjust gradually. Ideally, the aquarium light should be switched off first, the room one later.

It is also important to position the aquarium lights properly (Fig. 1 overleaf). The fish generally show better if the light strikes them from the same side as the viewer (i.e., the front of the tank, see Fig. 1A). If the light is positioned too far towards the rear of the aquarium it may cast shadows towards the viewer, with a loss of attractiveness to the fish (Fig. 1B).

15

A   B

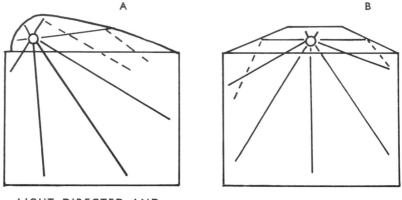

**LIGHT DIRECTED AND
REFLECTED BACKWARD**   *Fig. 1*

COVER GLASSES

Between the water surface and the lights is normally a cover glass or clear plastic condensation tray. This prevents the fish jumping out, and also prevents the water from condensation, splashes, etc. coming into easy contact with the electrical connections for the lights. Algae and other material builds up on the cover glass, and hence it will require regular cleaning.

POWER CONSUMPTION

The lighting, heating and aeration/filtration for the average home aquarium uses very little electrical power, and will not add much to the electrical bill for a household. Fluorescent lighting for a two or three foot aquarium is less than 100 watts per hour for 10 to 12 hours per day, and even the 100 to 200 watt heater is unlikely to be on for most of the time. Similarly, air pumps and filters have very low power-consumption.

Most tanks will require access to a single 13-amp wall socket, and various 'aquarium cable boxes' are now available to tidy up and simplify turning the various appliances on and off. Naturally, before carrying out any major tank maintenance the current to the aquarium should be disconnected at the wall socket.

STANDS AND CABINETS

When no suitable piece of existing furniture is available on which to place the tank, a stand can be obtained from an aquarium shop. These now come in a variety of designs and finishes, and will suit most situations in the home. Alternatively, aquarium cabinets (with or without the tank) can be purchased, turning the aquarium into a very attractive piece of room decor.

Bear in mind that stands with sharp feet may cut into carpet or floor coverings; this can be prevented by placing rubber or wood discs underneath the feet.

Chapter Two

Siting and setting up an Aquarium

SITING AN AQUARIUM

Weight

As an aquarium once set up is heavy and difficult to move, it will pay to give careful consideration to determine the best site so as to avoid having to undertake a difficult removal.

Bearing in mind that a cubic foot of water weighs approximately 62·5 lb., the water in a tank 36″ × 12″ × 12″ will weigh about 188 lb. To this must be added the weight of the tank, sand, gravel, rocks, etc., and the stand, so we arrive at a total of about 2 cwt., which is not an easy load to move about the room. From what has been said it will be appreciated that the aquarium should stand on a strong floor, which is well supported with substantial joists.

Size and Shape of Tank

As far as the fishes are concerned, a good shape of tank is the one referred to above. But it may not be convenient to hold rigidly to these dimensions, as the aquarist may wish the aquarium to occupy a special site in the room, such as a narrow mantelpiece or a particular cabinet. Size and shape, therefore, will depend on local conditions.

Height

This is not easy to determine, as it is difficult to be able to see straight into the front of an aquarium from both the standing and sitting positions. If the tank is situated in a hall it will need to be placed sufficiently high to avoid undue stooping. On the other hand, in a living-room where people are mostly seated a convenient height of stand is 3 ft., and this will be the height of the bottom of the tank.

Windows and Power Plugs

As has been previously mentioned, it is a bad plan to place an aquarium with its back to a window. A tank standing at right angles to the window will get the benefit of some natural light, and thus save some artificial illumination, which otherwise would be necessary. A good north light is preferable to a window facing south, where much direct sunlight will enter the tank and cause green water.

When artificial light is to be the sole means of illumination even a dark corner is quite suitable, and here one may be guided mostly by accessibility to power plugs, or electric outlets. It is advisable to use as short a cable as possible, and it is best to have the tank circuit connected to a plug point or outlet used solely for the aquarium so as to avoid inadvertent switching on and off.

Accessibility for Feeding and Cleaning

The tank should be placed so that it is easy to raise the lighting hood for feeding. There should be enough space in front to enable the aquarist to move about comfortably with jugs, jars, buckets, and siphon tubing.

Splashing and Spilling

Where there is water even the most careful aquarist will occasionally spill some, and it is unwise to place the tank on a highly polished or valuable piece of furniture. Even cloths laid down for protection sometimes become soaked, and can cause trouble.

SETTING UP AN AQUARIUM

Any new aquarium should first be given a thorough test to ensure that it is watertight.

If there are no leaks it may be emptied and placed in its final position. Should the test reveal a very small leak it is possible that this will seal itself, as the weight of water tends to bed down the glass. A large leak, however, must be repaired, or, if the tank has been purchased, it must be exchanged for one that is sound.

Now all is ready to set up the aquarium; for this work we shall require various items such as sand, rocks, etc. These will be dealt with in order. Do not forget, however, that if you wish to have a decorative backcloth on the back pane, this must be added to the outside before the tank is filled with water.

Sand or gravel should be purchased with care, but most pet stores sell the right material. It should be of the nature of fine gravel or flint, and not contain too much limestone or other minerals soluble in water. Too coarse a sand allows particles of food to fall into the crevices and give rise to decomposition, bacteria, and fouling of the water. On the other hand, too fine a material, such as silver sand or sea-shore sand, packs too tightly to allow the roots of the plants to spread and flourish. The most suitable is called in Britain 1/16th grade; it is about the size of the average pinhead, or, perhaps a little larger if an undergravel filter is used (see p.22). The amount required is approximately 12 lb. per square foot of aquarium base.

Washing Sand or Gravel

The sand must be washed thoroughly; it is surprising how much dirt can be removed. The method is as follows:

Half fill a bucket with sand, place it in the sink, and fill up with tepid water. With one hand dig right down to the bottom of the bucket and stir every grain of sand for two or three minutes. Now gently pour off the dirty water. Do this 10 or 12 times until the water poured off is quite clean. Dump the cleansed sand in the aquarium and repeat the process until sufficient is obtained to cover the whole base at an even slope. This should be from 2½″ at the back to 1″ in the front.

It is advisable at this stage to leave a small pocket in the centre front of the tank. This depression can be made by building a semicircular retaining wall of rocks which hold back the sand and leave a sump. Here the sediment will collect, and can easily be siphoned away.

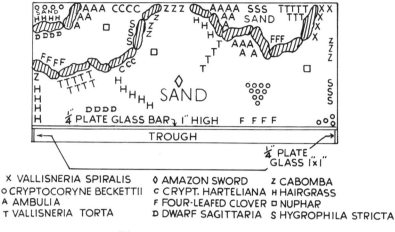

X VALLISNERIA SPIRALIS	◊ AMAZON SWORD	z CABOMBA
o CRYPTOCORYNE BECKETTII	c CRYPT. HARTELIANA	H HAIRGRASS
A AMBULIA	F FOUR-LEAFED CLOVER	□ NUPHAR
T VALLISNERIA TORTA	D DWARF SAGITTARIA	S HYGROPHILA STRICTA

Fig. 2 (Tank seen from above)

Another way of achieving the same object is to hold the sand away from the front of the tank by a long strip of ¼″ glass, 1″ wide (Fig. 2). This runs the entire length of the front of the aquarium, and is prevented from falling forward by placing in each front corner of the tank, flush with the side glasses, two small 1″×1″ squares of ¼″ glass. Now we have a long trough into which sediment collects, and where it can be siphoned away. All sharp edges of glass must be filed down to prevent the fishes cutting themselves.

Rocks and Rock-work

Well-designed and carefully laid out rock-work can enhance the appearance of the aquarium. It is important that the right kind of rock be chosen: natural water-worn stone is best. Flint, or other rock free from lime, is satisfactory, but artificial objects and lumps of coloured glass are not to be recommended. As the rock-work in many aquaria is badly arranged, it is worthwhile to consider briefly the technique of rock setting.

The method of haphazardly placing large clumps of rock has serious objections. Rarely is the appearance natural, and the fishes tend to stay out of view behind the rocks much of the time. Sediment, uneaten food, and even a dead fish can lodge behind a stone, decompose, and brew trouble for the aquarist.

A better method is to set up the rock-work in a series of steps. This is done by

19

building an irregular line of rocks standing on end and embedded into the sand near the front. The entire area behind is filled with sand level with the top of the rocks, which should lean slightly backward to increase the stability. Now about 4″ behind the front step a second irregular line of rocks is built, raising the level another 4″ or 5″; the space behind is filled with sand as before. There are now three levels (Fig. 3). If the work is done properly only the front face of the rocks will be seen, and there will be nowhere for dead fishes or sediment to lodge. When the three levels are planted a background of green plants stretches from top to bottom of the aquarium. On each layer the tops of the plants just reach to the bottom of those behind. With the exception of a few low ones in front, this system does away with the old idea that no short plants can be used at the back of the aquarium; see Fig. 3.

Fig. 3 (Side view of tank)

The tiers need not stretch the full width of the tank. Some aquarists may prefer two tiers, one in each back corner, leaving the centre back low; others may like to see a single tier with the summit at the centre of the back of the aquarium descending towards the sides. In either case, tall growing plants are used in the deeper parts. There will be small crevices through which the sand tends to pour, and these must be dammed up with rock fragments. The artistically minded aquarist has plenty of scope to create a most beautiful effect, and when the fish are introduced they prefer to swim in the foreground, and the undulating background is most natural and pleasing.

Ornaments

On the market there are miscellaneous coloured ornaments such as reclining mermaids, castles, treasure caskets filled with jewels, sunken ships, divers, starfish, etc. For those who like these, and perhaps in a children's nursery, they may add colour and amusement. But surely there is nothing more attractive than a natural under-water setting where the colours of the fish mingle with the various shades of the plants and the tints of the rocks? If the aquarist aims at giving the effect of having swum under water and literally scooped up, complete as it stood, a section of the pond or river's edge, the aquarium will appear natural and beautiful.

Filling the Aquarium with Water

Generally speaking, an aquarium may safely be filled with tap-water, providing it has not been drawn from a copper cylinder or through new copper piping; this can be very poisonous. Proprietary tap-water conditioners exist, which remove copper, chlorine and the like from fresh tap-water, thus making it safe for fish.

Once the rock and sand work has been completed, all is ready to fill the tank. Do not pour in water haphazardly from a jug; the force will destroy the artistic setting built up, and despite the careful washing of the sand innumerable particles will appear and cloud the water.

A good way to fill the aquarium is as follows: on the sand near the front place a saucer, and on this sit a clean jam-jar. Then, aiming carefully, slowly pour lukewarm water from a jug into the jam-jar. This fills rapidly, spills into the saucer (which breaks the fall), and trickles over the edge. Continue to pour gently until the saucer is covered, after which the pouring can be more rapid, as the curved lip of the saucer directs the stream of water upward, and not a grain of sand need be disturbed. The tank is filled to within 2″ of the top, and the water will be quite clear.

Now the heater-thermostat should be placed horizontally about half-way up the rear pane of the tank, and attached by using the polythene suckers which either come with the unit or may be purchased from a good aquarium shop.

Before planting, the filter should also be put into position, and then both the heater-thermostat and filter can be disguised using plant thickets. Of course, for safety reasons neither the heater-thermostat nor the filter should be switched on until the aquarist has finished setting up the tank.

AQUARIUM FILTRATION

Filters for use in the aquarium are now available in a vast array of shapes and sizes that is often bewildering to new hobbyists. However, they are all linked by their common purpose; that is, to pass water through one or more types of filter material, thereby making it more suitable for the maintenance of healthy fish and plants.

There are three basic methods of aquarium filtration — mechanical, chemical and biological. *Mechanical* filtration is the simplest, and occurs when the aquarium water is passed through nylon filter wool, a foam cartridge, or the like. Suspended particulate matter is trapped and effectively removed from the water. As a result this type of filter medium becomes clogged eventually, and hence must be regularly cleaned or renewed. *Chemical* filtration utilizes the absorptive properties of activated carbon. Each granule of activated carbon contains many tiny cracks and crevices, giving it an enormous surface area. The surfaces of activated carbon can attract and remove from aquarium water certain dissolved organic fish waste products and certain other compounds (including chlorine and some disease treatments). However, the absorptive powers of activated carbon are soon exhausted, and if chemical filtration is to continue in the long term the carbon must be removed every two or three weeks. Heating in an oven can to some extent regenerate activated carbon, but it is usually better to replace old with new. *Biological* filtration speeds up the decomposition of uneaten food and organic fish wastes. Harmless bacteria, which occur in large numbers on the surfaces of aquarium gravel, foam cartridge, carbon granules, etc., attack the organic wastes, converting them from potentially toxic ammonia, through nitrate, to much less toxic nitrate. Nitrate may be used as a food by aquarium plants and algae.

Several of the more commonly used aquarium filters are described below. While it is not essential to utilize a filter in an aquarium, a well-maintained filter will enhance water clarity, help stabilize water conditions, provide important water circulation and improve aeration. In fact, when a filter is in use additional aeration from any air-stone is usually unnecessary.

Undergravel filters utilize a 2″ to 4″ layer of fine washed aquarium gravel on the tank floor on a filter medium. With the aid of an air-pump and a porous filter plate (beneath the layer of gravel), a rich population of bacteria soon develops and carries out biological filtration. Naturally, the gravel also acts as a mechanical filter for suspended matter. While they are cheap to install and easy to maintain, some aquarists have found that undergravel filters may adversely affect plant growth. However, this may be offset by growing the plants in pots buried in the gravel. If an undergravel filter is to be used the filter plate and uplift tube must, of course, be put in position before the gravel, rocks, water and plants are added to the tank. To ensure efficient filtration using an undergravel filter, the gravel bed must be gently disturbed every two to four weeks, and the accumulated debris removed with a siphon tube.

Foam cartridge filters, when joined to an aquarium air-pump, draw water through a durable foam cartridge, and carry out both mechanical and biological filtration. Ideally suited for tanks of less than 20- or perhaps 30-gallon capacity, these filters can be easily disguised by plants in one of the rear corners of the tank. As routine maintenance, every two to four weeks the foam cartridge needs to be removed and gently rinsed in lukewarm running water. Then the cartridge can be slipped back on to the filter tube, cleaned and able to filter efficiently again. Foam cartridge filters are also very useful for breeding or hospital tanks.

Power filters are now available in a range of sizes to suit just about every size of aquarium. Powered by an electrically driven water pump, models are available that are placed either inside or outside the tank. The body of the filter is often packed with two or three different types of medium (e.g., filter wool, gravel, carbon), and as the water is passed through, mechanical, biological and even chemical filtration is carried out. While large power filters may be a little unsightly (whether placed inside or outside the aquarium), the small in-tank (internal) power filters are ideal for most home aquaria. A model which turns the tank volume over every few hours is sufficient for most community-type fish, although more powerful models are ideal for large messy fish like cichlids. As with other types of filters, the media in a power filter will require regular cleaning or renewing — if efficient filtration is to be maintained.

Whichever type of filter is used (and a local aquarium shop should be able to help aquarists with their initial choice), it must be left running for at least 18 or 20 hours out of each 24 hours. Turning a filter off for long periods will affect its performance, as will unnecessarily long periods between maintenance.

While undergravel filters can be used in tanks of any size, foam cartridge filters are ideally suited to small to medium tanks, and power filters are particularly useful in medium to large aquaria.

Plants

Plants are described fully under the chapter of that heading. Here we are concerned only with the method of planting. The main object to bear in mind is to form an attractive background, leaving ample space in front where the fishes can swim unhampered, and be seen. The tall, grassy type is best planted at intervals in rows, whereas the feathery ones look better when they are bunched into small clumps, which makes them appear like branching bushes.

Method of Planting

If the plants have roots hold the tip of the bunch of roots between the thumb and second finger and rest them on the sand. Now with the first finger push the upper

Fig. 4

part of the roots (where they join the stem) half an inch into the sand. Without moving this finger, scrape with the thumb and second finger some sand over any uncovered portion of the roots. Fig. 4 on page 23 shows the method. The roots now lie horizontally just under the sand, and are firmly held down.

When putting in rootless plants in bunches the method explained above is repeated, but this time the lower ends of the stems are placed together and treated exactly as if they were roots.

Some authorities advise aquarists to carry out their planting when the tank is only half full of water, but this method has disadvantages. The leaves of the plants tend to lie flat on the surface of the water, and so obscure the view of the roots. In addition, the foliage is liable to catch on the aquarist's hand, which when withdrawn from the water pulls the plants out of the sand.

Once the planting is completed top up the aquarium by pouring the additional water from a jug into one's hand, cupped beneath the surface so as to break the fall and avoid a disturbance. It is important that the water surface should be right up to the lower edge of the top of the tank, so that looking from the front the water surface cannot be seen, and the viewer gets the impression that there is no water in the aquarium. If the level is allowed to fall below the top the tank looks like a container holding water.

Lighting
As described in Chapter 1, the tank lighting system can now be installed in the aquarium hood. To encourage plant growth, this should be turned on for about 10 to 12 hours per day.

Settling Period
No doubt the beginner will be anxious to see fishes swimming around in his tank, but before stocking the aquarium it is advisable to allow a settling period of of 5 to 7 days. This permits the water to age a little, and gives time for particles in suspension to settle. Furthermore — and this is the most important factor — a settling period allows the new plants to anchor their roots, and to get a hold before they are subjected to the buffeting of the fishes, and for the filter(s) to begin to mature.

Temperature
For the aquarist who is going in for tropicals the settling period provides an excellent opportunity to adjust the temperature which is to be maintained in the tank. Install, as previously described, the heater thermostat, and switch on. Watch the thermometer now and then for a day or two. If it ranges between 76° and 80°F. all is well, but should the temperature vary much above or below this the thermostat must be adjusted accordingly.

Introducing the Fishes

Assuming that from 5 to 7 days have elapsed since setting-up the tank and planting, the aquarium should now be crystal-clear and the plants showing signs of growth. All is now ready for the great moment when the inhabitants take possession of their home. But here is a word of caution to the budding aquarist: until he has gained some experience, he will find it better to keep a few of the cheaper fishes. Many enthusiasts, through expensive initial losses, have become disheartened and given up; if only they had gained a little knowledge first, aquarium-keeping might have become a great interest.

When purchasing fishes it is essential to be quite certain that they come from a reliable source, and show no signs of disease. Good-quality stock may be a little more expensive, but is well worth the initial outlay. When buying fishes, look for lively behaviour, well-spread fins, plump stomachs, with no signs of sluggishness, droopping fins, or fungus anywhere on the body.

Your local aquarium shop will probably pack your fish into polythene bags for the journey home. Correctly packed, and prevented from chilling or overheating, they can survive several hours like this. On arrival at home, the bag containing the fish should be floated in the set-up tank for about 15 minutes. This will allow the temperatures to equalize, whereupon the fish can be safely released. Feeding the other tank inmates, and leaving the aquarium lights off for a few hours immediately after 'new' fish have been introduced can help reduce initial territorial squabbles.

Whatever happens, do avoid adding too many fish too soon into a recently set-up tank. Once the first stocking of (say) five or six hardy barbs or danios have survived and settled for a week or two, the stocking level in the tank can be *gradually* increased over six to eight weeks. Adding large numbers of fish into a new tank over a short period of time can result in unnecessary problems and losses. A guide to the safe stocking level which can be eventually attained in a tropical aquarium is discussed in Chapter 3.

Community Tanks

This expression is commonly used when several species of fish are housed together in one tank. For the aquarist wishing to have a number of fishes of different shape and colour, and intending to use the aquarium purely for decoration and interest, the community tank is perhaps the best type of aquarium to keep. Remember that some species prefer to swim about at different depths. This means that to fill the aquarium evenly it is necessary to have some fishes that normally swim in the top strata of water, others that prefer the middle strata, and some that are at home in the deepest water. It must be borne in mind that not all species will live together peacefully in a community tank; size is usually the governing factor, but where an exception arises it will be mentioned.

Those who own several aquaria and intend to breed may prefer to have only one species to one tank. Certain fishes have the habit of swimming in shoals, and undoubtedly these seem to be happier and look better than when kept with others.

Chapter Three

Some Important Rules

In fish-keeping rigid rules are few. Except for the essentials, quite a wide latitude is permissible. One aquarist following a certain line is successful and believes his theory to be correct, expounding it to everyone he meets. Another aquarist, holding views which are practically the opposite, meets with equal success, and is convinced that *he* is right. The fact is that fishes are adaptable, and in time become acclimatized to the prevailing conditions. Nevertheless, certain rules must be observed, otherwise failure is inevitable. Below are listed vital factors which no aquarist may ignore for long.

  (i) Oxygen, other gases and stocking level.
 (ii) Temperature variations.
(iii) Light and its functions.
 (iv) Plants and their actions.
  (v) The influence of animal life.
 (vi) Feeding and fouling.
(vii) Cleanliness and balance.

Each of the above will be dealt with under a separate heading.

OXYGEN, OTHER GASES AND STOCKING LEVEL

Just as human beings require to breathe, so do fishes; their gills, like our lungs, extract oxygen, and this vital gas is distributed through their entire system by the blood-stream. Remember, therefore, that the fishes do not merely aerate their gills: they need oxygen throughout their whole body.

The lungs of a man standing still extract enough oxygen to supply all parts of the body. But when he starts to run more oxygen is required to feed the muscles in operation. If he continues to run the demand for oxygen increases, until finally a stage is reached where the muscles require a greater supply of the gas than the lungs can furnish to the blood-stream. At this point he is forced to stop or slow down, otherwise he will collapse. In the same way fishes, which are practically continuously on the move (thereby using their muscles), must have an adequate supply of oxygen. Starve them of this, and they will become sluggish, lack the energy to move about, be unable to eat or digest their food, become liable to disease, and may die. From the foregoing it will be appreciated that oxygen is of supreme importance.

Water is a compound of two gases – hydrogen and oxygen – and normally contains in addition dissolved oxygen and other gases; it is this dissolved oxygen that fishes require to survive. Clearly, they can only extract the gas as long as it is

26

present in the water. Oxygen from the air is absorbed into the water at the surface, where this comes in contact with the atmosphere. If, therefore, the surface area is small the intake of oxygen is also small; a large surface area will allow a more rapid absorption of oxygen. Nevertheless, there is a saturation point beyond which water will not absorb more oxygen. Normally, the proportion of dissolved oxygen is not very high: roughly it can be taken at 5·8 parts per million, at 78°F.

Now, what happens when the fishes are introduced? Immediately they start to consume the dissolved oxygen in the water; at the same time the water replenishes its supply from the air above. As long as oxygen is replaced as fast as it is consumed by the fishes all will be well. But once the demand exceeds the supply, either by the fishes growing bigger and requiring more oxygen, or through a greater number having been introduced, troubles begin. Suggestions vary with regard to how many fish can safely be accommodated in an aquarium, but one guideline which appears to work very well is to allow 10 square inches of water surface for each inch of fish (excluding tail fins). This is the allowance for tropical freshwater fish kept at around 77°F; coldwater aquarium fishes actually appear to need a greater allowance than this, and marine fishes more still.

To calculate the surface area of an aquarium, multiply the length by the breadth (in inches) and the result will be the surface area in square inches. Divide this figure by 10 to give the number of inches of fish which can be safely accommodated.

Thus in a 24″ × 12″ × 12″ aquarium, the surface area will be 24″ × 12″ = 288 square inches which will accommodate 288/10 = 28 or 29 inches of fish. That is 28 one-inch fish, 14 two-inch fish, etc.

Aeration and Filtration
Aeration via an air-pump and air-stone and/or filtration both result in water circulation and turbulence, which helps replace the oxygen used by the fishes, and drives off the potentially dangerous carbon dioxide which they produce. Do not forget that other gases and fumes (e.g., carbon monoxide from some stoves, paint fumes, household sprays) can be toxic to fish, and so care must be exercised in a room with an aquarium.

Contrary to popular belief, it is not the bubbles rising through the water from an air-stone which dissolve into the water to increase the oxygen level but rather the increased turbulence and gaseous exchange at the water surface. Of course, as described in Chapter 1, filtration does far more than just aerate the water, and filtration (along with additional aeration, if needed) can permit the maintenance of perhaps 50 per cent more fishes than indicated above (i.e., 1½ inches of fish per 10 square inches of water surface). None the less, an aquarist setting up a new aquarium is advised to build up gradually to a stocking level of one inch of fish to 10 square inches of water surface over several weeks, and then if filtration and/or additional aeration is provided this stocking level may be increased further (up to a maximum of 1½ inches of fish to 10 square inches of water surface). Both these figures allow a safety margin for fish growth, and even for short-term pump or filter failures. Regular filter and tank maintenance is still of vital importance, though.

A word of warning. Over-vigorous water turbulence will upset some plants and fishes and should be avoided. Generally speaking, the fish should not be swept across the tank by the water from the filter or air-stone, but rather a steady but gentle flow should be produced by the air-pump or filter. Gentle disturbance of the plants can be an advantage, but vigorous movement is usually best avoided. Since water circulation will disturb any debris in the tank, it will helpfully highlight the need for tank and/or filter maintenance.

TEMPERATURE VARIATIONS

Most tropical fishes can withstand a fairly large variation in temperature, provided the increase or decrease is gradual and does not go to extremes. In nature the fluctuation can be very considerable; for instance, in India the temperature of a natural pool containing killifishes was found to be 66°F. at 10 p.m., and 109°F. in the afternoon. But it is not wise to take these liberties under artificial conditions. Here the extremes should be 68°F. to 90°F.; this range may allow a margin of safety for some species.

It is advisable to keep the average tropical fish at 78°F.; this means that with a reliable thermostat the temperature will fluctuate between 76°F. and 80°F. Some authorities recommend a lower temperature, but the authors disagree on the grounds that their fishes, kept within the above temperature range, are more lively, have a greater intensity of colour, eat better, grow quicker, and breed sooner than they would under lower temperature conditions. True, the speeding up of the fishes' metabolism may shorten their life by a week or two, but since the average fish lives 2 to 3 years, the curtailing of life by a relatively small span is unimportant, especially as we have avoided sluggishness and drabness of colour.

A sudden change of temperature either way causes discomfort to fishes. If they are suddenly introduced into cooler water considerable harm may be done; a chill can bring about a loss of resistance and make them susceptible to disease. A slight increase of temperature is unlikely to cause trouble, but a decrease must be avoided. When changing fishes from one container to another equalize the temperatures slowly.

LIGHT AND ITS FUNCTIONS

Light can be used as a means of enhancing the beauty of a tank. But light has a much more important rôle to play than this; it is a fundamental factor in the life-cycle of animal and vegetable matter. Without light most life would cease; this applies in an aquarium just as much as anywhere else.

Light is essential to plants, enabling them, through the process of photosynthesis, to absorb carbon dioxide, which they break down into sugar and starches for food. It is through the action of light that the plant is able to survive, feed, and reproduce. Just like fishes, plants 'breathe' (or more correctly, respire) constantly. That is to say, they are constantly taking in oxygen and producing carbon dioxide. However, under strong illumination photosynthesis occurs, and plants take in carbon dioxide and give off oxygen. Under favourable conditions, plants can produce much more oxygen by photosynthesis than they require for respiration, and hence plants can be useful for adding oxygen to the water for the filter. Sometimes you can actually see tiny bubbles of oxygen rising from the leaves of aquarium plants.

From the foregoing it will be seen that plants need light for their existence; if there is insufficient they will die. Too much light will cause green cells to develop until there are millions which can be seen collectively in the form of a green haze. If excess light continues, blanket and thread algae suspended in the water may attach themselves to rocks, plants, or the sides of the aquarium, on which they grow as a fur. Some cells cling together and form a mat of dark green algae, smothering leaves, rocks, sand, etc.; others may collect in a slimy mass near the surface of the water. While a small amount of algae is good as vegetable food, too much becomes unruly, unsightly, and can be harmful.

Strange as it may seem, plants can die from a lack of light resulting from over-illumination of the tank. The explanation is that the excess amount of light immediately causes algae to grow on the plants, forming a dark green or almost black covering over each leaf. So thick is the growth that light cannot penetrate it; as a result the smothered plant-leaves beneath become pale and weak. This process is seen if, say, a tin or a piece of wood is left for several days on a patch of grass. When the object is removed the grass underneath will be found to be weak and of a pale yellow tint compared with its surroundings. The black-green algae clinging to the leaf of a plant can be peeled off, when it will appear like a strip of leather.

The correct illumination of an aquarium is a major factor in keeping it clean and clear. Just the right amount of light maintains the plants growing healthily, but leaves nothing over for the formation of algae cells; as a result it should not be necessary to have to scrape green deposits off the walls of the aquarium.

For an illustration, let us suppose that x watts burning for 10 hours will supply the needs of 100 plants. Now, if the number of plants be halved there will be a surplus of light, and nature will quickly see that this is utilized by growing algæ. On the other hand, if we have 200 plants they will have to share the x watts available; each plant will now receive approximately half the illumination it really needs, and growth will suffer accordingly. If one must err it is far safer to have an excess of plants rather than a deficit. Some fish (e.g., certain *Labeo* species, mollies and some catfish) will feed on algae, and proprietary algae treatments exist. Getting the tank lighting and planting right is, however, a better long-term aim.

Having referred to the effects of light on plants, we will now consider its importance to the fishes themselves, and to certain other forms of aquatic life. In the first place, fishes, with the exception of the naturally blind species, require light to enable them to find their way about and search for food. Development and growth are influenced by light, which has a stimulating effect, causing the fishes to swim around, and exercise themselves; and it helps their bodies to perform the natural functions.

Strong light destroys bacteria, and this naturally helps to keep the tank healthy and prevent fouling. In cases where the sand has become polluted and blackened by bacteria it need not be discarded, but should be taken out, washed thoroughly to remove suspended matter, and then spread out thinly on a tray or ground-sheet, and allowed to stand for several hours in bright sunlight. This treatment will

29

destroy the bacteria, and the light will bleach the sand, so that it regains its natural colour and can be returned with safety to the aquarium.

PLANTS AND THEIR ACTIONS

As has been already mentioned plants play a vital rôle in an aquarium.

During daylight hours, they take in carbon dioxide and give off a little oxygen; by absorbing light they discourage the growth of algae; the roots feed on sediment from the bottom of the tank. If there are sufficient plants to absorb all the sediment being formed they assist the aquarist by relieving him of the necessity to siphon off the excess. Where there are insufficient plants, there is generally an excess of sediment.

Besides beauty, plants also provide shade and a natural setting for fishes, and may induce spawning; their foliage serves as supports for the eggs deposited by some species, and affords protection for the hatching fry. Even when larger fishes are concerned, plants act as a refuge for sick or bullied individuals, and for persistently pursued females. In some cases pieces of plant are bitten off by the fishes and used as nesting material. Furthermore, by absorbing carbon dioxide from the fishes, plants help stabilize water conditions, and prevent an increase in acidity (fall in pH – see p.33).

THE INFLUENCE OF ANIMAL LIFE

In an aquarium all forms of animal life require oxygen to survive. By releasing carbon dioxide they affect the nature of the water, tending to change the pH (hydrogen ion content), which in turn increases the acidity. Morover, the droppings contain organic matter, and this also affects the composition of the water. Not only fishes, but snails, *Daphnia*, mussels, etc., can create overcrowded conditions, by lowering the oxygen content and increasing the carbon dioxide in the water.

Another factor to bear in mind is the effect of a dead creature. Although a single dead body, even if uneaten by the other inhabitants of the aquarium, may not cause much trouble, a number can quickly foul the water due to mass decomposition; this applies especially to snails and *Daphnia*.

FEEDING AND FOULING

The commonest cause of trouble in an aquarium is due to over-feeding. Overfed fishes become bloated, lazy, and unhealthy; uneaten food which drops to the bottom of the tank decomposes, and sets up a chain of undesirable reactions. Fortunately, tropical fishes do not need large quantities of food. They are, when circumstances make it necessary, capable of existing without being fed for several days, even weeks. This is because they are able to live on nourishment stored up in their bodies. It is much safer to under-feed slightly than to over-feed grossly; the latter causes fouling, which leads to far more trouble. Fouling, if allowed to persist, will necessitate the changing of the water, cleansing of the sand, replacement of

30

plants and fishes. As a rough guide, tropical aquarium fish should be fed 2 to 4 times per day, but with no more food than can be eaten within a few minutes. Small fry will require small but more frequent meals, while large predatory fish such as some catfish, piranha, etc., can be fed every 2 or 3 days with relatively large meals. By exercising common sense aquarists will soon realize how much food their fish require.

If the aquarist has to be away for a period of (say) 2 weeks and has no friend sufficiently experienced in feeding aquarium fishes, it is better to leave them unfed. For a period exceeding 2 weeks, an inexperienced friend should be left small portions of dried food screwed up in tiny pieces of tissue paper. These can be laid out in a row, and instructions left that no more than one packet be fed to the fishes every other day. As a further safeguard hide away all other food, or the temptation to a kindly but inexpert assistant is often to augment the rations, which undoubtedly he will consider far too meagre.

CLEANLINESS AND BALANCE

The water in an aquarium kept under natural conditions should be clean, clear, and practically odourless; it should not need changing (save for a 25% partial water change every month or so), as the life-cycle and bacterial activity are functioning naturally, and should not be interfered with. Any major interruption will disturb the cycle, and there will need to be a period before readjustment is established again. Cleanliness is natural to the healthy aquarium, just as it is in nature. But if through over-feeding, over-stocking with fishes, under-planting, or some other cause, dirt, foulness, and bacteria are created in excess much trouble and even disease may result.

There are aquarists who claim that a dirty aquarium is healthy. The authors do not agree. True, due to plant-leaves dying and fishes excreting waste products in an aquarium, a sediment inevitably appears. It is generally called mulm, and a little is to be found even in the cleanest tank. Mulm, however, is natural and harmless; it is a factor in the life-cycle. Since the roots of plants feed to a certain extent on mulm, it is gradually drawn down below the surface of the sand; a little, therefore, is good. But if the aquarist has too many fishes, or insufficient plants in his tank, an unnatural excess of mulm will result; this should be siphoned off occasionally, though, better still, the cause of its formation should be rectified.

Although an excess of mulm may be unsightly, it rarely causes trouble. Rotting food, decaying plants, dead fishes, and decomposing snails cause bacteria and innumerable troubles. A clean aquarium is a healthy aquarium.

Copper Salts
Copper salts are deadly to fish, and they can stand only a very minute quantity. If the aquarist has no other source of water than tap-water, then he should allow the taps to run for several minutes before using any water in his fish tanks.

Because water evaporates, all aquaria have occasionally to be topped up. To do this always with water drawn through copper piping will gradually build up the copper salts in the aquarium until they reach toxic level. Fish which have lived healthily for months suddenly begin dying, with no signs of disease, no fin rot or other observable complaint. Some species can withstand a little more copper than others, so not every fish in a community tank dies at the same time. Nevertheless, they all will, once the toxic level reaches their toleration limit.

Should the aquarist suspect copper poisoning the remedy must be immediate, and all the water in the tank changed for rain-water, or at least water from a copper-free source. Copper salts are equally poisonous to aquatic plants.

Other Poisonous Metals

Brass alloy and aluminium are sometimes used for the making of aquaria and light-hoods. These metals can form poisonous salts, and so they should be coated to prevent this occurring. It is a wise plan to paint the interior of aluminium light-hoods with white paint once every year.

Nowadays there are a number of tap-water conditioners available from aquatic shops, which can be used to age new tap-water and safely remove poisons like chlorine, copper, zinc and the like.

Chapter Four

Water and its Components

Water, as previously mentioned, is a compound of two gases, hydrogen and oxygen, in the proportion of two volumes of hydrogen to one volume of oxygen. Water has great solvent powers, and owing to this, perfectly pure water is not found in nature. The purest natural form is rain-water, but even this while falling from the clouds dissolves gases and impurities present in the atmosphere. Moreover, on reaching the earth the rain starts to dissolve various minerals with which it comes in contact.

MINERALS

The minerals held in solution in water vary according to the nature of the ground through which the water percolates. That differs considerably: for instance, in moorland districts where peat prevails the water will contain dissolved acids. In places where there are considerable deposits of chalk the water will be alkaline. The alkalinity or acidity of the water is expressed in terms of what is known as the hydrogen ion concentration (or pH).

HYDROGEN ION CONCENTRATION

To understand fully about pH one would need to be a chemist. But for the aquarist it is only necessary to appreciate that by the theory of ionic dissociation an acid when dissolved in water does not exist entirely as molecules. Some of the molecules are dissociated into (*a*) positively charged hydrogen ions (H+) and (*b*) negatively charged hydroxyl ions (OH−).

The acid properties of a solution are entirely due to the hydrogen ions, and the degree of acidity expressed by the concentration of these. Sörensen introduced the symbol pH to denote the hydrogen ion exponent, and drew up a scale. This scale was graduated from the strongest acid solution pH 0·0 up to the strongest alkaline solution pH 14·0. Distilled water, being neither acid nor alkaline, is midway on the scale, and therefore has a pH value of 7·0, and is termed neutral. It follows that the more acid the solution, the lower is the pH. (It must be remembered that the pH grading *varies inversely* as the H concentration. The pH is, in fact, the log of the reciprocal of the H ion concentration.) Conversely, the greater the alkalinity of the solution the higher the pH. Some species of tropical fish come from water which is naturally slightly acid or slightly alkaline, and do better in an aquarium where the water approximates to the pH of their natural habitat. For the aquarist who wishes to breed certain species it is advisable to determine the pH of the water he intends to use, and adjust if necessary.

TESTING FOR pH

To obtain the correct pH value it is advisable to carry out certain tests, and three methods are referred to below:

Indicator Papers

These papers are obtainable in the form of small booklets, rolls or strips, and can be purchased from chemists. The material is available in a number of ranges, depending on the particular scale of pH values required. From the aquarist's point of view, short-range papers varying from pH 6·0 to pH 7·8 are the most suitable, as they cover the entire range from slightly acid, through neutral, to slightly alkaline. With each set of papers there should be a chart; this takes the form of a band of various colours, each marked with the relevant pH reading.

When one of the papers is dipped into the water the paper will change colour, and when this is compared with the corresponding colour on the chart the pH reading will be obtained. Litmus paper serves as only a rough guide for ascertaining the pH.

Test Kits

Test kits for measuring pH (and a number of other water chemistry parameters) are available from aquarium shops. A sample of water to be tested is usually added to a small vial, and a given number of drops of an indicator solution is added. The resultant colour is compared to a colour chart, and the pH noted. Test kits are probably more accurate than indicator papers, are easy to use and relatively inexpensive.

Electrical Method

This is the most accurate method, but the equipment required is often costly, and is beyond the pocket of the average aquarist. Also, absolute accuracy with regard to pH is probably unnecessary where fishes are concerned.

ADJUSTING pH

When altering the pH value of water strong acids such as sulphuric acid, or alkalis like caustic soda, should never be used. Weak acids or alkalis may, however, be employed. The most usual of these are sodium bicarbonate and sodium acid phosphate; the former will make the water more alkaline, the latter will tend to increase the acidity. Such changes must always be made slowly, as fish are sensitive to sudden shifts in pH.

Most aquarists pass through a phase where pH is the all-important factor in their minds; sometimes it becomes an obsession. All success or failure in breeding is, in their opinion, entirely due to the pH value. They add strong acids or alkalis to the water in order to obtain the correct hydrogen ion concentration, only to find that by the next day the water has reverted to its original state. Again they readjust it, until finally the tank contains an excess of chemicals. As a result the water becomes unfit for breeding purposes.

Small quantities of acids or alkalis are sufficient to alter greatly the pH. Even the carbon dioxide in the air above the tank has an appreciable effect. Unless certain precautions are taken to buffer the solution it is difficult to maintain a definite pH value for any length of time. The majority of fishes adapt themselves to the prevailing conditions, and will breed. There are, however, a few problem species which definitely require a low pH value and very soft water before success can be achieved. Preparations are now available which mean that aquarists can create the pH conditions required by these fish, as indicated above, and changes to prevailing water conditions must be carried out gradually.

HARDNESS OF WATER

Hardness can be divided into two kinds, temporary or permanent, and is related to the amounts of certain dissolved salts which are present. The temporary is that which is removed by boiling, when substances such as calcium bicarbonate and magnesium bicarbonate are broken down. Permanent hardness is that which cannot be removed by boiling, and is chiefly due to calcium and magnesium sulphates and chlorides.

SOFTENING WATER

Temporary hardness can be removed by the following methods:
  (i) By boiling the water, since this process decomposes the bicarbonate present; carbon dioxide passes off as gas, and the monocarbonates are left suspended in an insoluble and inert form.
 (ii) By decomposing the bicarbonates with any alkali soluble in water, lime being generally used.
(iii) By passing the water through a porous mass of zeolite. This sodium alumino-silicate gives up its sodium in exchange for an equal amount of lime or magnesia in the water.
Permanent hardness can be removed from water by:
  (i) Distillation—*i.e.*, boiling the water and condensing the steam. This method is the only one for fully purifying water rich in soluble sodium or potassium salts, such as sea-water.
 (ii) By the addition of a soluble carbonate, such as sodium carbonate (soda). Any soluble calcium or magnesium salts present in the water are then precipitated.
(iii) In both instances only method (i) produces water that is suitable for fish-keeping, although these can be rather inconvenient for the average hobbyist and, in the case of distillation, water that is 'too pure' is produced.

Domestic water-softeners do not produce water which is suitable for fish-keeping, as water produced in this fashion often contains water that is too rich in sodium. Fortunately, a number of water-softening devices are now available that have been specially developed for aquarium use, and these should be available from good aquarium shops.

Peaty water

Generally speaking, tap-water is slightly alkaline and moderately hard. It is only in a few peaty districts that the water is inclined to be acid and very soft. For breeding the problem fishes, such as neons, glowlights and killifishes, the softness of the water is a more important factor than the pH. All of these fishes come from areas where the water has been found to be very soft, and a pH of 5·0 to 6·6. Such water is of a clear brownish colour, and is practically free from bacteria, which are harmful to fish eggs.

Experience has shown that rain-water passed through a peat filter or, better still, rain-water that has stood for some time in a container with a few inches of peat fibre or moss at the bottom, becomes brown in colour and often soft and acid. Such water is ideal for use in breeding the problem fishes.

Aquarists wishing to breed the more difficult species should keep at hand a supply of soft brown peaty water. To obtain this, proceed as follows. In a darkish place fill a spare aquarium or polythene bucket with clean rain-water, and throw into this peat (aquarium peat is best). The peat will float, so add sufficient to form a 2″ layer. In 10 to 20 days the peat will become water-logged and sink. Once it has all sunk the water will be clear and clean but tinted brown. In towns where clear rain-water is not available, boiled tap-water may be used. (See p.38.)

TESTING FOR HARDNESS

The simplest method of determining the hardness of your tap water involves seeing how easy it is to obtain a lather with soap; soap lathers easily in soft water, less easily in hard water. Also, kettles 'fur up' more quickly in hard-water areas.

Fortunately, test kits are also available from aquarium shops, and these easily and accurately measure water-hardness. As with pH test kits, hardness-measuring kits usually employ the addition of an indicator solution to a vial containing the water sample, but noting how many drops of indicator are required to bring about a specific colour change.

Water-hardness is usually expressed in 'parts per million of calcium carbonate' (ppm $CaCO_3$) or 'degrees of German hardness' (°dH). To convert °dH to ppm $CaCO_3$, simply multiply by 17·9. The old-fashioned system of measuring water hardness in parts per million of calcium oxide (ppm CaO) is rarely used nowadays.

The following table provides a comparison of the two types of water-hardness, and an indication of how they are normally referred to in aquarist circles.

°dH	ppm $CaCO_3$	Known as
0–3	0–50	Soft
3–6	50-100	Moderately soft
6–12	100–200	Slightly hard
12–18	200–300	Moderately hard
18–25	300–450	Hard
Above 25	Above 450	Very hard

NATURE OF THE WATER USED IN AN AQUARIUM

Earlier we pointed out that tap-water in many localities is quite suitable for most fishes. In some districts, however, the Water Boards chlorinate heavily, and this may cause the aquarist trouble. Generally speaking, the chlorine content can be reduced by drawing water from the tap and allowing it stand for several hours in the open air. Furthermore, new tap-water can be made ready for immediate aquarium use by adding one of the tap-water conditioners that are available from aquarium shops.

Distilled water

This is unnatural: it is too pure, and lacks the salts and minute organisms present in ordinary water that give it life. Distilled water can be used occasionally with advantage in a breeding tank, but under ordinary conditions the cost is not justified, and the water in any case would soon become contaminated in the tank.

Well water

Some aquarists are fortunate enough to have a well on the premises. If the water is free from sewage pollution it can be used in an aquarium. Well water usually contains a wealth of minerals, and is generally crystal clear but rather hard.

Rain-water

This is the most natural water. In country districts where the air is pure the rain-water will be practically neutral, but in industrial areas smoke and fumes are present in the atmosphere, and some of these will be absorbed, making the rain-water acid.

Rain-water is best collected in a wooden butt, an iron bath, or polythene bucket, but a galvanized container should be avoided. It will be found that the water is cleaner and purer if one waits at least a quarter of an hour after the start of a shower before starting collecting, as initially a considerable amount of dirt and dust from the air and on roofs is washed down. The pollutants can also be diluted by collecting the rain into a continuously overflowing butt.

Pond water

Water taken from most natural ponds is excellent, provided it is carefully filtered to eliminate harmful pests such as dangerous larvae and undesirable organisms.

It is surprising how a small change of any water, providing it is good, will stimulate the fishes in an aquarium. They appear to enjoy it as much as human beings enjoy a change of air. As will be shown later, it is often advantageous to mix a quantity of rain-water into a breeding tank, as this freshening up may excite and stimulate the fishes.

Green water

It was explained earlier that clear water will turn green from excessive light or lack of plants. From what has been said before, the cure is to cut down the light, or to increase the number of plants.

Brown water

This occurs naturally when the catchment area draining into the reservoirs is of a peaty nature. The same effect is produced if a peat filter is employed. Peaty water has a yellowish to brown tint, is clear, and is usually good; it impedes the multiplication of bacteria.

If, however, the clear water in an aquarium turns brown and cloudy it may be harmful. The cause is usually insufficient light, when the vegetable life starts to die and decay and bacteria begin to multiply. Over-feeding may be another cause, where once again the surplus food is encouraging millions of bacteria to breed. The cure for this type of brown water is to increase the plants, and to maintain their development by giving more light. Discourage bacteria by taking care not to over-feed the fishes. In addition it will be beneficial to give artificial aeration to dissipate undesirable gases in the water.

Cloudy water

The water in most aquaria when newly set up, although initially clear, may turn a cloudy grey after a few days. This is a natural process which takes place as the cycle of life adjusts itself. But when equilibrium is reached the water will begin to clear and should remain so, unless the aquarist interferes too much with the natural processes going on in the tank. Should cloudy conditions persist they are generally caused by over-crowding, excessive feeding, a large production of bacteria, or minute vegetable cells.

Cloudy water, therefore, may be the initial stage of either green water or brown water, as yet insufficiently developed to determine the ultimate colour. After a few days the reproduction of the organisms becomes so great that in the mass they colour the water. This will be brown if caused by bacteria, or green if by vegetable matter.

Home-made peat water

Since this book was first published so many aquarists from all over the world have written asking the authors for more details that we give our method. Obtain two old baths, sinks or water butts from a junk-yard. Scrub them clean, place one so that it catches all the rainwater from a down pipe — this will soon be permanently full. The other is filled with rainwater, but not allowed to overflow; into this throw five or six bucketfuls of broken-up peat, sold in compressed bales. Cover with glass and leave, but protect it from too much light to minimize algal growth, weighted-down polythene sheeting being ideal.

Eventually the peat will become waterlogged and sink. This may take two or three months. Once it has all sunk the water above will be soft, have a low pH, and be a clear red-brown colour. When required siphon off carefully into a clean enamel bucket, warm up to 80°F., by adding a little boiling water from a kettle and it is ready for use in a breeding tank. Immediately after drawing off any water top up the bath again with clean rainwater from the first bath. The supply can be kept going for two or three years without adding more peat. This is because a saturation-point is reached, but when such water is drawn off and replaced with rainwater saturation-point is raised, and draws again from the peat.

This is a natural process, and no attempts should be made to hurry the procedure. Never boil the peat in a muslin bag and use the strained water: this is so strong with humic acid it will quickly kill the breeding fish. Avoid using peat which has had plant fertilizers added to it.

Chapter Five

Miscellaneous Apparatus

Numerous pieces of equipment are available to aquarists; some are good, many are unnecessary, and the beginner is recommended to wait until he finds a certain item essential. The handyman may be able to construct something which will meet his own requirements. We find that some of the simplest apparatus is the most satisfactory.

Glass jars

The first and most useful articles are a selection of glass jars — *i.e.*, jam-jars, sweet jars, preserving jars. When a single fish is being examined closely ordinary jam-jars are needed; they are also useful for transferring fishes from one tank to another, particularly when temperatures are different and require time to equalize. For sorting fry a larger container, such as a sweet jar, is useful: a spawning can be netted into it, from which the larger specimens can be extracted. Lastly, the wide-necked jar with a screw-on lid serves as a good transporter for carrying fishes for short distances, say to or from a shop or show.

Nets

It is advisable for the aquarist to possess several different-shaped nets. They can be purchased in most aquarium shops, or even made at home.

For catching nets nylon mesh is recommended, as it lasts much longer than muslin, does not become slimy, or deteriorate so soon through becoming alternately wet and dry. A small round one that will fit inside a jam-jar is essential. The frame should be made of fine-gauge wire, as this is easily bendable and will accommodate any curve of arc. Two stout-framed, medium-sized nets approximately 6″ square are ideal for catching most fishes in the average aquarium; there should be a kink in the neck of the frame (see Fig. 5), so that it fits tightly against the front glass of the aquarium. It is important to remember that the bag should be made as deep as it is wide, as this facilitates catching.

Once a fish is caught it will make every endeavour to escape, and if the net is shallow it is extremely difficult to keep the fish confined in the small space available and bring it to the surface of the water. With a deep net the captive can be driven into the back of the bag and lifted out easily. Furthermore, once withdrawn from the tank it is simple enough to place one's hand underneath and fold the fingers round the captive, entirely enclosing it. Held in this position, one can turn the net inside out and drop the fish into a narrow-necked jar. With a shallow net the most one can do is to spread the hand over the top of the net and hope that the fish does

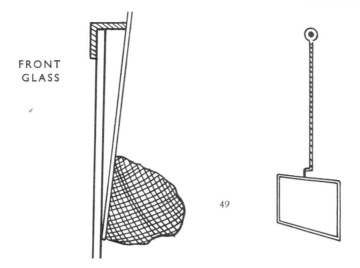

FRONT
GLASS

49

Fig. 5

not jump between one's fingers. There still remains the difficult operation of getting the fish into a jar.

Fine Nylon Net for Filtering

In addition to nets used for catching fishes, the authors have found that two other types of net are invaluable. Both are employed as strainers and have the bag made of fine nylon similar to that used for making shirts or blouses; the smaller net, approximately 3″ diameter, fits over the mouth of a large jam-jar, and is most useful for straining newly hatched brine shrimps.

The larger should be made in a rectangular shape approximately 8″ × 8″: it should have a minimum depth of 8″, and a handle about 10″ long. The frame must be constructed of heavy-gauge wire, which will need to be bent into shape by using a vice or a strong pair of pliers. Since the net will be called upon to hold a heavy weight of water, the frame must be robust enough to remain rigid. When siphoning mulm from a tank the net will be found an extremely useful article. Placed across the top of a bucket, the end of the siphon tube can be put inside the net, which will strain the water as it passes through. The aquarist may be surprised at its efficiency.

Siphon tube

This is an essential article for removing mulm from tanks, and for emptying an aquarium. Generally speaking, a piece of tubing about 6 feet long with an internal diameter of ¼-½″ is ideal. The tubing should be long enough to reach from the bottom of the tank over the top rim, down to the floor, and up to the aquarist's waist. This will ensure a rapid and powerful discharge. By pinching the tube the flow of the water can be controlled, or stopped immediately should a fish approach the danger zone too closely.

41

Some aquarists complain that sucking, in order to start the siphon working, invariably gives them a mouthful of water. This is because the siphon tube is too short. With a long tube the water rises over the rim of the tank and descends to the floor, often with a distinctive thud; but before it reaches the mouth the tube is pinched, and the end placed in a bucket. For those who prefer a more rigid end to the siphon it is only necessary to insert a length of strong Perspex or plastic tubing into one end of the rubber tube. 'Gravel washers' are also available from aquarium shops, which siphon out water whilst cleaning the gravel — without removing the gravel from the tank.

Bucket
At least one 2-gallon bucket used solely for the aquarist's purpose is essential. It is required when siphoning from the tank, or for sterilizing nets in boiling water.

It should never be used for household tasks. A polythene brewing bin is ideal.

Dip tube
A dip tube is useful for picking out of the aquarium one or two odd bits of food that remain uneaten. The small amount of water withdrawn would hardly justify the use of a siphon.

Any piece of glass tubing will act as a dip tube. Hold the tube vertically, and place a finger over the upper end to prevent the escape of air. The tube can now be introduced into the aquarium and located so that the open end is immediately over the particle to be extracted. This will be flushed into the tube as soon as the finger is withdrawn from the top end. To prevent the unwanted matter from re-entering the tank the finger is reinstated and the tube is raised sufficiently to allow another finger to seal the lower end, when the tube can be withdrawn.

A more elaborate type of dip tube is shown in (Fig. 6). It consists of a glass tube

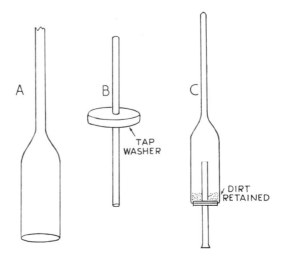

Fig. 6

A, with an enlarged end. Into this is inserted *B*. This is merely a short glass tube passing tightly through a tap washer which fits closely into the mouth of *A*. The method of use is the same as before, but due to the greater volume of the tube more water can be sucked up, and the particles which have been extracted are trapped in the pocket. Before the dip tube needs emptying it can be used to collect several separate particles in different zones of the tank. Cleaning is easy, as the tube can be dismantled.

 Fig. 7

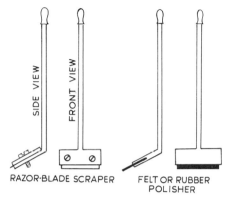

RAZOR-BLADE SCRAPER   FELT OR RUBBER POLISHER

Scrapers
A scraper (see Fig. 7) for removing algae from the walls of the aquarium is another cheap, yet useful, piece of equipment. Essentially a scraper is a long rod bent to an angle of 45 degrees at the bottom to which is attached a razor blade, a strip of rubber, or a piece of felt. When applied to the inside face of the tank and moved up and down the scraper either scrapes or polishes the glass. The razor-blade type usually has two holes in the fittng and two screws to secure the blade. The rubber and felt types are provided with a slot which firmly grips the material. Do not use sharp scrapers in plastic tanks, as they scratch them very easily. Magnetic algae scrapers are also available. These consist of two magnets, one of which is placed on the inside of one of the glass panes, while the other is placed in the same position on the outside of the pane. If the magnet on the outside of the aquarium is moved up and down the pane the magnet on the inside moves likewise, thus scraping off algae — all without getting the aquarist's hands wet!

Forceps or tongs
Forceps can hardly be regarded as being essential, although they have their uses at times. In a marine tank they are perhaps of more use than in the ordinary fresh-water aquarium. This is because relatively static animals such as anemones need to be fed by placing the food within reach of their tentacles. There are two types of forceps, one made of wood, the other of metal. The former can easily be made at home, and are probably the most satisfactory. The method of construction is as follows. Cut two pieces of three-ply or other flexible wood, 12″ long and ½″ wide at one end, tapering to ⅛″ wide at the other end (Fig. 8 overleaf). Next, make a small wooden block about 1″ long, ½″ square at one end, tapering slightly at the

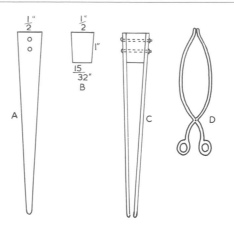

Fig. 8

other end, as shown at *B*. Now with two small bolts secure the three pieces together as shown at *C*. If properly constructed the pointed ends of the pincers should remain slightly apart; owing to springiness these can now be pinched together by a slight pressure, enabling small objects to be picked up and released at will.

The metal type illustrated at *D* are in the shape of scissors, and these and similar ones can be purchased at most aquarium shops. Metal forceps do not have the advantage of springing open of their own accord as do the wooden type referred to above. Plastic spring tongs are also available from aquarium shops.

Planting sticks

Planting sticks occasionally have their uses. For example, they serve when it is desired to plant a single stem in the centre of a bunch of similar stems; also the sticks are useful when planting in awkward positions, such as between two rocks where it is impossible to reach with the hand. Otherwise it is preferable to insert plants with the fingers, which are less likely to shear off or damage the roots.

A planting stick can be made out of a thin strip of wood or metal approximately 15″ long, ¼″ wide, and ⅛″ thick. At one end a V-shaped notch is cut out to guide the plant into position.

Plant-pots and trays

Some aquarists prefer to have a few special show plants in pots (Fig. 9). If used, the pots are best made of unglazed earthenware with a few small holes round the base to allow root growth to penetrate through, and so prevent cramping. Where possible the whole pot should be buried beneath the sand in the aquarium to hide its unnatural and unsightly appearance. The few advantages of using pots are:

(i) They can be removed from one position to another in the tank, or they may be transferred to another aquarium without seriously interrupting the plants' root growth.

(ii) A special medium such as loam or clay, which the plant may prefer, can be used in the lower part of the pot, the upper stratum being sand.

(iii) They reduce the adverse effects of undergravel filtration on plant growth.

Fig. 9

SPECIAL PLANT IN POT WHICH IS
BURIED OUT OF SIGHT UNDER THE SAND
(Note growth of roots through holes)

Feeding rings

Feeding rings (Fig. 10 overleaf) are not essential, although some aquarists advocate their use. Generally they are constructed of plastic or glass tubing in the form of a square or a circle. They float on the water and serve to limit the spread of dried food. Fishes get accustomed to these rings, and come readily to the appointed place at feeding time, though the larger species tend to get the greater share more easily than when the food is not confined to one area.

The aquarist who persistently indulges in the harmful practice of over-feeding his fishes with dried food may find a feeding ring to be an advantage. All particles of uneaten food fall directly below the ring, and so limit any blackening of the sand to one area. When, therefore, it is necessary to siphon out and cleanse the sand, only a relatively small amount needs to be dealt with.

Fig. 10B shows another type of feeding ring, sometimes used when feeding with white worm or *Tubifex*. The ring is usually made of plastic in the form of a well-perforated basin with a large rim. The basin floats with the perforations below

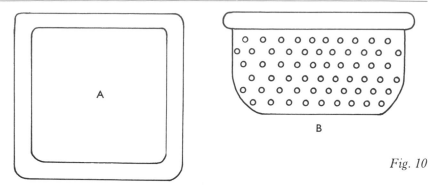

A

B

Fig. 10

the surface of the water. When a small mass of worms is dropped into it they break up and gradually wriggle through the holes, giving all the fishes an opportunity of getting a few worms each. Without the basket the worms tend to cling together in small masses, thereby giving the larger fishes the opportunity of grabbing whole mouthfuls at the expense of the smaller inhabitants of the aquarium.

Suction cups
A few cheap suction cups are worth stocking, as they have many uses. Applied to the inside of the tank, they may be used to anchor feeding rings, thermometers, heaters, thermostats, aerator and filter tubes. If it becomes necessary to partition off a section of the aquarium with a sheet of glass, suction cups serve to retain the glass division in position.

Thermometers
A good thermometer, preferably one that floats in a vertical position, is an essential item. It should be located in an unobtrusive position, but one in which it can be easily read. Mercury thermometers, though costing a little more than the alcohol type, are generally more accurate, and worth the extra money. Most are dual calibrated for Fahrenheit and Centigrade. When purchasing one of these instruments it is advisable to verify the accuracy by comparing the readings of several. Should some of these disagree, choose one which corresponds with the majority. Another type of thermometer possesses a circular dial about 1¼" diameter, and a pointer which moves like the hand of a clock round the scale. These unobtrusive instruments adhere by means of a suction cup to the glass of the aquarium. Liquid crystal thermometers which stick on to the outside of the aquarium glass are also very popular.

Plastic channelling
For the more advanced aquarist who raises fry from egg-laying fishes, a few feet of channelling is invaluable. This material enables a tank to be tightly partitioned so

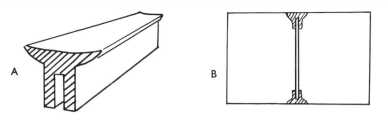

Fig. 11

that the babies cannot pass into the neighbouring compartment. Without channelling it is almost impossible to divide a tank so that fry can be segregated satisfactorily. Fig. 11A shows a section through a piece of channelling. It will be seen that there is a slot to receive the glass or Perspex, and the slightly concave outer face permits it to be pressed flat against the walls of the aquarium; it is the flexibility of the channelling that makes the tight joint. Fig. 11B illustrates a tank partitioned by a sheet of glass secured each side by channelling as seen from above. Ready-made perforated tank dividers are available from aquarium shops.

Nylon mops

These mops can be made easily at home, and are excellent for spawning many of the problem fishes, in otherwise bare tanks containing peaty water. The mops can be sterilized by boiling and used time and time again.

Skeins of pure nylon are cut into lengths roughly 10″ long. With one of the threads tie the strands in the middle, then fold over double, and tie again near the bend, to form bushy mops. See Fig. 12.

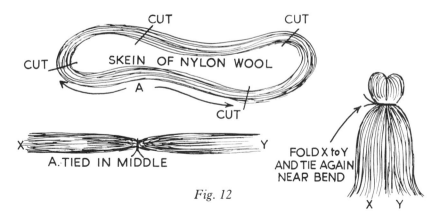

Fig. 12

Traps

Most beginners start with live-bearing fishes, and are immensely thrilled when the first batch of young is born. Their joy, however, does not last long, as most of the babies are gobbled up by other fishes. Even though the mother may be isolated by herself in a separate container before she has her young, she is not averse to eating them after they are born. This unpleasant characteristic also sets a problem for the commercial breeder, whose aim is to get the maximum number of fry from several females.

To prevent the females from satisfying their appetite at the expense of their young, traps are used. A trap is a device that can be suspended in a separate breeding tank, confining the mother but permitting the young to escape from her by swimming through small holes to safety. Most traps on the market are made of plastic, and are provided with holes or slots (see Fig. 13, *A* and *B*) in the base through which the fry pass. Usually these traps are too small to allow the female or females adequate freedom, and the holes or slots in the base of the trap provide insufficient exits for the babies. Fig. 13*A* shows a plastic trap with a single opening at the base, while *B* illustrates a plastic box with a row of holes running along the bottom of the ends into which are inserted glass or plastic bars.

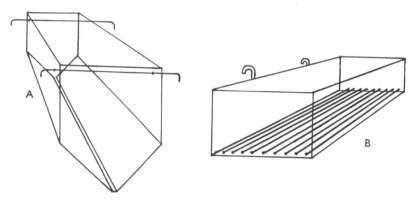

PLASTIC BREEDING TRAPS

Fig. 13

Another trap (*C*) can be made quite cheaply at home from fine stainless steel wire gauze with a mesh of approximately ⅛″. Cut one piece of this material 12″ square, and two pieces 5″×6″. Turn over all projecting ends to make smooth edges. Roll the large piece into a semicircle to form a long trough, and by means of wire attach the two ends as shown in photograph. All that is now required is to push two lengths of wire through the mesh at each end of the trough and bend over the extremities of this wire to fit the tank in which the trap is to operate. The trap will then be suspended with its top rim just above the surface of the water. Alternatively, in a very shallow tank the trap will stand on its two square ends which act as legs. In a trap of this size several females can be placed with safety; babies can escape with ease in any direction.

It may be thought that, since the babies are able to get out of the trap so easily, they will just as readily re-enter. Undoubtedly a few do this, but the majority realize by instinct that danger abounds and stay outside until they are strong enough to dart about and evade capture. At first the females may try to snap at the

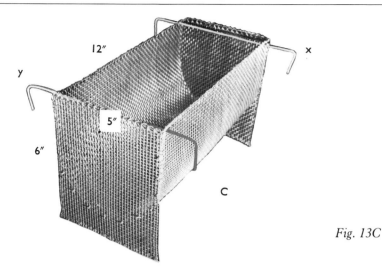

Fig. 13C

fry they see swimming outside the trap, but quickly realize that such attempts are futile. Later, if a few fry re-enter the trap the females still seem to consider them beyond reach, and do not molest them. By this time, however, the babies are strong enough to dart through the mesh should such a quick exit become necessary.

Commercial breeders will find that they are able to remove from the trap females that have given birth, and substitute others about to have young. It will be appreciated, therefore, that large traps may be in use for prolonged periods. Here is one final word of advice that applies to all traps: keep all plants, whether of the rooted or floating variety, *outside* the trap, since fry instinctively make for the nearest cover.

Diffusers, or Air-stones

To obtain the maximum effect from artificial aeration it is best to have a thick column of fine bubbles rising to the surface rather than a chain of large single ones. To create this effect diffusers are used.

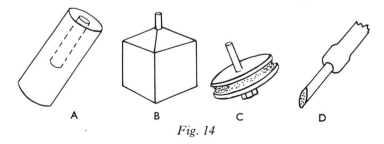

Fig. 14

Fig. 14 shows just four types of diffuser. *A* is made of porous stone and is shaped like a small log with a hole in one end into which is inserted a short length of air-line tube to receive the air from the pump. *B* shows a similar pumice-stone diffuser of a different shape, and one which is provided with a piece of tube cemented in. An old-fashioned metal-type diffuser is illustrated at *C*. It consists of two metal discs screwed together with a piece of felt sandwiched between. A short pipe rises from the centre of the upper disc. Air passes through the felt, and the size of bubbles can be adjusted by varying the pressure between the two metal discs.

Although these three diffusers are inexpensive, they all eventually become clogged. *A* and *B* can be baked in an oven to shrink the particles clogging the pores, while *C* can be fitted with a new piece of felt.

The authors have found that an inexpensive and satisfactory diffuser can be made out of a length of ordinary cane used for basket-work. 12 ft. will cost only a few pence. The cane is the correct diameter to fit the standard air-line tubing, and when cut in ¾" lengths will make nearly 200 satisfactory diffusers. To improve the action the end of the diffuser is cut obliquely as shown in Fig. 14*D*. After many months the short pieces of cane rot, but it is only a matter of seconds to cut them off with a razor blade and insert a replacement. A myriad of other types of air-stone are available from aquarium shops.

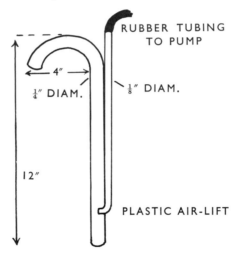

Fig. 15

Air-lift

This is a tube, usually of plastic, with a longish stem. The top curves over and ends in a spout, as shown in Fig. 15. About 2" from the bottom is inserted an air inlet in the form of a short length of tubing which is sealed into position. When the air-lift is stood vertically in the tank water enters the bottom of the stem and rises to the normal level. Air-line tubing connects the air inlet to the pump, and the rising bubbles lift the water sufficiently to discharge it from the spout.

Air-lifts are a method for aerating and circulating water in the aquarium, and are much used in the filters available from aquarium shops.

Air-line valves

Connecting valves, T-pieces, clamps, etc, are very useful for splitting the air supply from an air pump to serve more than one filter or air-stone — or more than one tank. They also permit fine control of filters and aeration.

Bottle brushes

Small to medium-sized bottle brushes are very useful for cleaning out filter tubes, siphon pipes, and the like. They should always be well rinsed after use, and allowed to dry.

Chapter Six

Fish-foods and Feeding

Fish, like human beings, if they are to remain in perfect health require a balanced diet. This must include proteins, carbohydrates, fats, minerals, and vitamins. Since some aquarists find these terms confusing, a brief explanation may be helpful.

Proteins

These are the body-building foods, and serve to replace worn-out tissues. Just as a stove consumes fuel, and ultimately will go out unless replenished, so is the body continually consuming itself and requiring replacements to make good the loss. Animal proteins are found in meat, liver, kidney, chicken, fish, eggs, and cheese. In addition, there are vegetable proteins in certain leguminous foods such as peas, beans, and lentils.

Carbohydrates

These are the energy-giving foods. Included under this heading are bread, biscuit meal, oatmeal, and other starchy foods. Sugar is a carbohydrate.

Fats

Fats and oils also help to produce energy; they also feed the nerves. Fats and oils are stored up as a reserve supply of food on which the body can draw in times of shortage. They are found in meat, milk, fish, cheese, and some vegetable foods.

Minerals

In most foods there are minerals — salts of calcium, phosphorus, iron, etc.; their chief functions are to develop bones and teeth, to ensure the healthy working of the nervous system, circulation, muscles, and certain glands.

Vitamins

These serve to promote health and prevent disease. They are present in animal fats and oils, in fresh fruit and vegetables, and in wheat germ.

Balanced diet

Since the body requires different kinds of food to fulfil different functions, it will be appreciated that a normal healthy diet must contain some items from each of the aforementioned groups. As far as aquarists are concerned, fish food may be classified under four main headings:

    (i) Dried foods.

    (ii) Fresh, tinned, or frozen foods.

    (iii) Cultured foods.

    (iv) Pond foods.

DRIED FOODS

There are many brands of dried and freeze-dried fish-food — flakes, tablets and pellets — on the market. A first-class product should contain a balance of the various kinds of food previously referred to. There are important advantages in dried food. Due to its high concentration, a little will last for a relatively long period. This food is readily obtainable, and most can be stored for a considerable time without deterioration.

Dried food acts as an excellent form of roughage, and the authors recommend that where fish are fed twice daily one of these meals should consist of a good dried food.

If, however, too much be given at a time it remains uneaten and sinks to the bottom. Here, due to its colour and fineness, it becomes invisible against the gravel, and is difficult to siphon away. The particles of food then work their way down through the gravel until they are out of reach to all fishes, even including the scavenging species which will dig below the surface for their meals. Once they sink too deep decomposition may set in, causing harmful bacteria, fungus, and so forth. If over-feeding continues the bacteria multiply rapidly; foul gases are generated, and the gravel turns black. The roots of plants near by soon become affected, and instead of being strong, healthy, and white, turn black, soggy, and rotten. The plants themselves begin to die, and cease their functions of absorbing mulm on which the roots normally feed.

A state of affairs has now arisen where bad gases from the decomposing matter and the carbon dioxide given off by the fishes begins to build up in the water. If this unhealthy process continues serious problems may result. Fish may appear swimming just below the surface at an angle of about 30 degrees, with their tails down and mouths up. They are not searching for more food but struggling to obtain the vital oxygen from the atmosphere.

From the foregoing it will be clear that over-feeding with any type of food is dangerous, but, generally speaking, it is more easily done with dried foods than with fresh ones. In either case the gravel will blacken; this will necessitate its removal and cleansing, and in addition there will be the trouble and expense of replacing the rotting plants.

A number of lifelike freeze-dried foods are now available which as a result of their careful preparation are more nutritious than ordinary dried foods. Being lifelike in appearance, they can be useful for weaning problem feeders on to dried food from live food.

Hormones and other additives
In recent years experiments have been carried out to produce dried foods containing hormones for special purposes such as increasing normal growth or retarding growth; sex stimulation to induce breeding, ovum-production, the attempted increase of the proportion of male or female births in a spawn, colour intensity, and mutation. The aquarist, however, should verify the claims of certain of the products offered before accepting them as being infallible. Moreover, he should have some knowledge of what he is doing, as irresponsible use of these foods may be dangerous.

FRESH, TINNED, OR FROZEN FOODS

No matter how good any dried food may be, fishes, like human beings, need a change.

Fresh foods can be either vegetable or animal. First, we will consider the vegetable. These give the fishes minerals and vitamins.

Algae
As previously explained, algae are a natural vegetable growth; they are present in most aquaria, as they grow in water through the action of light. Many species of fish enjoy algae, and will keep them cropped and under control provided excessive light does not produce them in exorbitant amounts. Where no algae are present the fishes will often require alternative vegetable matter. In the summer this may consist of finely shredded fresh lettuce-leaves or duckweed, and in the winter chopped cooked spinach or tinned spinach, sieved well. Practically any green vegetable matter can be given in small quantities, if finely chopped.

Animal foods
These include shrimp, prawn, crayfish, lobster, crab, white fishes, roe, lean meat, (particularly heart, liver, kidney), also cheese and hard-boiled yolk of egg. Many of these foods are to be found in every home. All are equally good whether fresh, tinned, or frozen, though the latter must be thawed out. The process of gamma-irradiation means that frozen foods, even if from aquatic sources, can be disease-free. Most good aquarium shops stock a range of irradiated frozen foods, which can be used to feed even the most delicate fishes.

Fish, meat, and offal require scraping or chopping, and may be served raw or cooked; most are easier to chop fine when cooked. Cod roe is highly nutritious yet cheap; it is best boiled for 20 minutes, and the outer skin peeled off. The remainder is broken into small pieces for large fishes, or if rubbed between the fingers it will sink as single eggs, and is ideal for fry and the smaller species.

Hard-boiled yolk of egg, squeezed through a piece of muslin and shaken under water, produces a cloud of minute particles perfect for newly hatched fry, but must be fed sparingly, or it will soon foul the water. Hard-boiled egg yolk pushed through a very fine sieve and served on the point of a knife does not disintegrate into a cloud, and may be given to most fishes.

Ordinary Cheddar cheese finely chopped or grated is also appreciated occasionally.

Most of the above foods are greedily taken, but should too much be given they will not decompose for 24 hours, and by that time very little remains. A few uneaten pieces may sometimes be seen developing a fungus growth, but these cannot sink into the sand, and are easily removed with a dip tube.

CULTURED FOODS

Having purchased an initial supply, the following foods may be cultured, and, with a minimum of trouble, provide a permanent form of nourishment.

Infusoria

This is a general term for various groups of minute organisms such as *Paramecium* which, under certain conditions, live and multiply in water. Infusoria are suitable for feeding to newly hatched fry. The spores of many infusoria are airborne, so the resulting organisms may be found in most water which has been standing exposed to the air. When the spores come in contact with water containing suitable feeding matter they grow and multiply; some merely by a process of division.

Infusoria may be found in ponds, butts, or even in a flower vase which has contained stems for several days. Unless, however, the source of supply is abundant it will be necessary to make a culture in order to obtain adequate quantities for raising a batch of fish fry. A limited culture may be developed by boiling chopped hay in water for about 20 minutes, and straining the liquid into jam-jars. These may be either infected with an initial supply of infusoria, or the jars may be exposed to the atmosphere until they become infected. Another method is to dry lettuce-leaves for a short period in an oven, and then crumble them, and sprinkle them into jam-jars containing water. Some people employ banana skins, potato peelings, or fresh lettuce-leaves. Since a good batch of fry is capable of consuming three 2-lb. jam-jars of infusoria per day, it will be appreciated that fresh cultures must be made in rotation every few days to replenish the supply.

Today it is possible to purchase various proprietary products which contain or produce infusoria, so those aquarists who do not desire to go to the trouble of culturing infusoria are able to obtain some by these modern methods.

For the commercial breeder requiring a permanent supply of infusoria perhaps the best and easiest method is to keep a large number of *Ampullaria* snails in a battery of bare tanks. Lettuce-leaves are fed to the snails daily. The more snails the thicker the infusoria produced. The snails should breed and replenish themselves, thereby ensuring a permanent source of infusoria. The snails live in water at a temperature of approximately 78°F., so when feeding infusoria to fry it is only necessary to take a jam-jar full of water from the culture tanks and empty it into the tank containing the fry. As the water-level in the snail tank drops it is replenished with clean, fresh water of the same temperature. The next day the second snail tank is used, and so on. By the time the last tank has been reached the first one is again thick with infusoria.

In addition to lettuce, *Ampullaria* snails will eat dandelion leaves, Savoy cabbage, and spinach. But the nature of the culture of infusoria obtained depends largely on the kind of food given to the snails, since it is their droppings that form the culture medium. The aquarist anxious to obtain a particular type of infusoria must experiment by giving the snails different kinds of food, and examining the resulting organisms under a microscope.

It is important to bear in mind that all cultures of infusoria poured into tanks of fry must be at aquarium temperature. If one of the jar methods is employed the infusoria will have to be warmed up; the jars of infusoria should be floated in the aquarium for some time before being tipped out. Better still is to culture infusoria at a temperature of 78°F. It not only multiplies quicker, but is warm enough to add direct to a breeding tank.

Brine shrimps (Artemia salina)

These small crustaceans make an excellent food for feeding to many of the larger fry. Unfortunately, they are expensive, and a little trouble is required to prepare them. The tiny brown eggs look like black pepper. Although they may have been dried for some years, it is remarkable to find that if they be placed in a brine solution of the right temperature they will hatch in 24 to 36 hours.

The method is as follows. Fill jars or other glass containers with, say, half a gallon of tap-water. Add to this 2½ tablespoons of ordinary block salt. The temperature should be maintained at 78°F. Once the salt has dissolved sprinkle in a level saltspoonful of the eggs, which will float on the surface. In approximately 30 hours nearly all the eggs should have hatched, and the small shrimps, bright pink in colour, will be hopping about near the bottom of the jar. Strong aeration increases the percentage of hatching. A thin siphon tube can now be inserted deep into the container, and the shrimps drawn off. These are strained through a nylon net placed over another jar; afterwards the water that has passed through is returned to the hatchery. When siphoning try to avoid sucking up unhatched eggs or egg-shells. The mass of newly hatched shrimps in the nylon net can be fed to the fry with the point of a penknife.

An alternative method, which some aquarists prefer, is as follows. A shallow rectangular dish is divided approximately in half by a thin wall of wood which fits tightly at the sides, but a space of about ⅛″ is allowed to remain between the lower edge of the wood and the bottom of the dish. The brine-shrimp eggs are placed in the rear half of the dish, which is now covered with a sheet of cardboard to keep it in semi-darkness. When the shrimps have hatched they make their way under the wooden division and reach the light end of the dish. From here they are siphoned off as before, and, if care is taken to ensure that the surface of the water is not allowed to drop below the wooden division, few if any egg-shells will pass into the front compartment. The salt water in the hatchery may be used a number of times before losing its strength or becoming foul. But as soon as the percentage of eggs hatching out falls the containers must be cleaned and refilled with clean salt water.

Newly hatched brine shrimp is an excellent food for the slightly larger fry, and can be fed as first food to fry of angel fish and other cichlids, as well as the larger barbs. The smaller fry require infusoria initially, but as soon as they are large enough to eat brine shrimp it should be given to them. It will soon be evident if the shrimps are being swallowed, as their pink colour will show through the distended stomach walls of the fry. Brine shrimp 'hatcheries' are also available from aquarium shops, and the percentage hatch of a batch of eggs can be improved by using marine salts, not rock salt.

Microworms

Working up the scale, we next come to microworms. This is the term applied by aquarists to the tiny nematode worms known commonly as 'eels' or 'eelworms'. These minute worms are whitish in colour, and may be cultured easily. They make an excellent food for very small fishes, particularly the species that grub about near the bottom of the aquarium, being ideal for baby fishes such as *Corydoras*, dwarf cichlids, etc. The tiny worms sink slowly to the bottom of the tank, and although during this descent some are eaten, by far the greater number reach the gravel. Since they do not swim, microworms are not ideal for the fry of angels and similar fishes, which normally feed in mid-water.

Culturing microworms. First acquire a few shallow dishes about 4″ in diameter and 1″ deep, preferably of a material with a rough surface. Into some of these containers place about one tablespoonful of cooked porridge, which has cooled, and been mixed with cold milk to a creamy consistency. Infect the centre of each container with about a saltspoonful of microworms; cover with a sheet of glass, and keep in the dark at a temperature of 70° to 75°F. If there is no dark place where the cultures may be housed cover them with a black cloth. Now the microworms begin to multiply, and in about a week to 10 days they will have become so numerous and overcrowded that they require more room. As a result the tiny worms swarm up the sides of the containers; this, however, they cannot do unless the surface is rough enough to grip. The worms are removed by wiping a finger round the sides of the dish; they may then be deposited into several tanks by momentarily inserting the finger into the water. Do not over-feed.

The culture will continue to increase and maintain itself in strength for about a week, after which it will deteriorate and the worms will decrease in number. Before this stage is reached more dishes must be brought into use. New porridge is placed in them and infected by taking a few worms from the old culture. As before, these will take a week to multiply and be thick enough to use. In order to maintain a continual supply it is necessary to employ three sets of culture in different stages of development. Starter cultures of microworms (and grindal worms and white worms) are available from aquarium shops.

Grindal worms

This is another white worm — named after Frau Grindal, who discovered them — considerably larger than the microworm, growing to a length of ⅛″ to ¼″. They make excellent food for all the smaller tropical fishes. Grindal worms are too fatty to be used exclusively, and, although eaten greedily at first, they may become monotonous after a time.

Grindal worm culture. Make a few small wooden boxes approximately 7" long by 5" wide by 1½" deep, fill with a well-moistened mixture of peat, soil, and leaf-mould, to within ¼" of the top. Place the culture in the centre of the boxes and feed by sprinkling over them a dessert-spoonful of dry baby-cereal food. Now cut a piece of glass, preferably with one corner nicked out, to fit inside the box. Keep the boxes dark, and stand in a *warm* place, approximately 75°F. After a few days the worms should have multiplied and consumed the food. Lift the glass, and with a razor blade collect the worms, afterwards re-feed the remainder and store as before. They will continue indefinitely, provided they are fed regularly, kept moist, and maintained at the correct temperature. Occasionally dig up the soil to keep it well aerated.

White worms
This excellent food is useful for all fishes. Being larger than grindal worms, yet always having young ones among them, they are taken by all fishes, large and small. They are particularly useful for feeding to those species of fish which will touch nothing but living food. This applies particularly to fishes such as *Mastacembelus* which have very small mouths, but are able to suck in these worms end on.

Similar to grindal worms, white worms are somewhat fatty, and should not be used exclusively. They are cultured in exactly the same way as grindal worms, except that they differ in not liking warmth, so should be kept at a temperature of 50°F to 60°F.

Earthworms
The common garden worm is, surprisingly, one of the finest foods for fishes. It is of great nutritive value, and seems to have almost everything in its favour. The great disadvantage is that the worms have to be cut up to a suitable size. Most fishes, even the marine species, are attracted by the earthworms, though they cannot normally come across them under natural conditions. The smaller pink worms up to 1" long are eaten whole by medium-sized fishes. Large fishes, like cichlids, will take worms up to 5" long and keep returning for more. But for the small tropicals, chopping or mincing is inevitable.

Since earthworms are such an excellent and appetizing food for fishes, and common enough throughout the world, it is surprising that they are not used more often. City dwellers and those living in flats who cannot dig up worms in the garden can usually purchase them from pet stores, or find them when on a trip in the country. They may even be cultured in an old sink filled with soil and leaf-mould, provided they are fed with household scraps such as vegetable peelings, stale bread, and so forth, and kept damp and cool.

When feeding fishes with worms collect them in a jam-jar, wash them free of mud, and place them on a board to be chopped finely with a very sharp razor blade. Since worms contain an appreciable amount of soil, the resulting mince is rather muddy and may cloud the tank if put in before cleansing. So scrape the mince from the board into a fine muslin net, hold under a running tap, and shake well. Now wash the board, and by reversing the net drop the clean mince on to the clean board; serve to the fishes on the point of the razor blade. The net will contain mud and slime, but if this is allowed to dry it will rub off easily, and the net be ready for further use. There is no finer food for putting body on to fishes than garden worms, and it cannot be equalled for getting breeding stock into prime condition before spawning.

Crushed snails

Sooner or later most aquarists find they have an unwanted culture of snails infesting their tanks, which has to be netted out and thrown away. Instead of discarding the snails, they can be crushed with the bottom of a jam-jar on a thick piece of glass and fed to the fishes, who will gobble them up except for the small bits of shell. When these become too numerous they can be siphoned off.

POND FOODS

The foods to be covered in the following pages are found in ponds and streams. Throughout most of the year supplies can be caught if the aquarist is prepared to go to a little trouble in making nets, and is lucky enough to discover a good hunting-place which is not over-fished by other enthusiastic aquarists. Too wide a publicizing of the merits of a pond will soon result in it being denuded. On the other hand, it is not always advisable to be too mean about sharing a pond with a few others, since a reasonable removal keeps the pond life from becoming over-crowded.

These live foods have purposely been considered last, for they are generally regarded to be of such importance that the other excellent foods referred to earlier in this chapter are often ignored.

Rotifers

These are minute animals, slightly larger than infusoria, and are generally found in ponds. The commoner rotifers include *Brachionus* and *Hydatina*. Under very favourable conditions they are so amassed that they will appear to colour the water. They are not easy to culture (although 'culture kits' are available from aquarium shops), so the aquarist is dependent mainly on finding and catching them. For this purpose a net of very fine material, such as nylon, is suitable. It should be about 6" in diameter at the mouth, 24" long, and tapering to a blunt point.

This type of net may be used in shallow water where most rotifers are to be found. To prevent larger organisms from entering the net, a piece of fine nylon gauze should be clipped over the mouth to act as a strainer. Rotifers carried home in jars can be strained through nylon, and served to the fishes on the point of a knife.

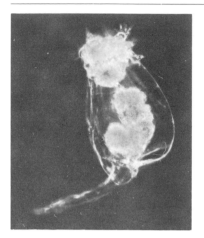

Daphnia

Rotifer

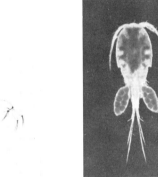

Glass worm

Cyclops

Blood worm

Gnat larva

Daphnia

There are many species of *Daphnia,* the commonest, probably, being *Daphnia pulex,* but for food purposes we need not differentiate between them. The colour of *Daphnia* in the mass varies in shades of grey to green and brown to red, according to the nature of their diet. They are usually found in shallow farm ponds, particularly those which are frequented by ducks, geese, cattle, or other livestock whose droppings create organic matter which encourages the life of animal and vegetable cellular organisms upon which the *Daphnia* feed. *Daphnia* may also be found at waterworks where large, shallow filter beds are exposed to sunlight and depend on the growth of algae to assist the filtration of the water; and, because of the abundance of algae, *Daphnia* soon appear and multiply rapidly. Similarly, the cleaner filter beds at sewage works frequently provide a good crop.

These little crustaceans, distantly related to crabs, are of a similar form, having a hard outer shell enclosing a soft interior which contains the nutriment; the shell acts merely as roughage, with little or no food value. For this reason *Daphnia* is not the perfect food which many aquarists believe it to be. Nevertheless, it is a natural live food, and its hopping motion in the water attracts the eye of a fish and gives it the urge to pursue its prey. Furthermore, fishes which are inclined to refuse food may be tempted to eat *Daphnia.* The *Daphnia* may be sifted through fine muslin nets; the smaller crustaceans passing through are good for young fry. Not only do these get exercise in pursuing their food, but since *Daphnia* are aquatic creatures, they will live in the tank and not die before all the fry have satisfied their hunger. City dwellers unable to catch their own *Daphnia* can usually purchase them from pet stores during the summer months, but the price is high for the relatively small amount obtained.

Catching Daphnia

Assuming that the aquarist has found a pond of the type already mentioned, although no *Daphnia* may be visible he is advised to investigate, since there may well be some near the bottom. The equipment required consists of a muslin net about 12″ deep, stitched to a frame roughly a 12″ in diameter. The shape of the bag thus formed should resemble a bowl rather than a pointed cone, since any *Daphnia* caught in the latter may be crushed as the net is drawn through the water, and most will be found to be dead on arrival home. The net is attached to a handle as long as can be wielded conveniently and, if it is to be carried in a car, it should be made in sections which can be connected together. The only other piece of equipment required is a can with a large surface area to allow plenty of oxygen to contact the water in which the *Daphnia* will be transported.

After having filled the can with pond water, all is ready to start operations. Reaching out as far as possible into the pond to avoid the shallows, insert the net sideways, and take care not to submerge it completely. Now start weaving the net in a figure of eight about a dozen times. Haul it in, and, provided one has not fished too deeply and *Daphnia* are present, it will contain no mud but a solid mass of *Daphnia,* either green or red in colour. Tip the contents into the can, where the *Daphnia* will hop about with their normal swimming motion. Catch only sufficient for the immediate needs, as most of that taken will not live longer than a day or two, after which it is unfit for food. To catch more *Daphnia* than necessary is a pure waste; it is far better to leave the remainder to breed naturally, and to return for further supplies as required.

Daphnia are most prolific in the late spring and early summer, when the increased daylight encourages the growth of algae. Although some *Daphnia* are to be found during the winter, the majority of the last batch of eggs laid by the females in the autumn remain dormant much longer than the normal hatching period, thus enabling them to weather the winter, when their food is short.

Attempts have been made to breed *Daphnia* in tubs and baths, and although a few can be produced, nothing like enough can be obtained artificially, and the attempts at culturing are certainly not worth the bother. A word of warning: in sweeping for *Daphnia* in a natural pond sooner or later some harmful creatures will be picked up with the catch. Some of these, including water tigers and dragonfly larvae, are referred to later. The larger enemies can be seen and removed, but the smaller pests such as *Hydra*, particularly when contacted, are inconspicuous, and therefore cannot be eliminated. For this reason it is advisable to make a rule that *Daphnia* is never fed to breeding fish which have been put into a breeding tank to spawn. If by mischance a crop of *Hydra* is introduced into the tank they will devour greedily any fry in their initial swimming stages. The wise breeder will also exclude *Daphnia* in tanks containing fry until the young fish are large enough not to fall prey to *Hydra*.

Dried Daphnia

Much of this is offered for sale, but a large proportion of the nutrient has been driven off in the drying process, leaving behind little other than dried shells or husks of practically no food value. But, as previously explained, when mixed as an ingredient of dried food such *Daphnia* supplies excellent roughage.

Cyclops

These little crustaceans get their name from the Greek giant Cyclops (since they have only one eye, which is situated in the centre of the forehead). They are found with *Daphnia*, as they live and feed under the same conditions. As a fish-food *Cyclops* are good; they are rather smaller than *Daphnia*, and are usually greyish-green in colour. The females can often be seen carrying two clusters of eggs near the end of the body, which increases their bulk and makes them look rather different creatures from the males. If anything, *Cyclops* appear to be more hardy than *Daphnia*, and in the colder months are often obtainable in larger quantities than the latter.

Though *Cyclops* make an excellent food for baby fishes of not less than ¼″ length, they must not be introduced into a breeding tank of egg-layers such as neons, cardinals, glowlights, etc. Any *Cyclops* that are not eaten by the breeding fishes can remain among the spawn, puncturing and devouring the eggs, or eating the fry as they hatch.

Where *Ampullaria* snails are kept solely for producing infusoria, care must be taken to keep this tank also free of *Cyclops;* the crustaceans will thrive and multiply along with the infusoria, making the latter dangerous for use as fry food, furthermore they will bore into the ampullarias' shells, damaging them so much that they lose their smooth glossy texture, and become pitted, rough, and dull, in extreme cases causing the death of some of the snails. Endeavour, therefore, to eliminate *Cyclops* by first washing thoroughly any vegetable matter which is fed to the ampullarias.

Tubifex worms

These are thin, dull reddish worms varying in length from ½" to 2", or even more. They are sometimes found in the filthiest of farm ponds, those which are virtually sumps of liquid manure draining from adjacent buildings. Large quantities of *Tubifex* live where sewage is discharged into a tidal estuary or river. The worms bury their heads in the sludge and leave their tails waving in the shallow water above. But at the slightest movement they contract their bodies and disappear from sight. To collect the worms it is necessary to haul in a quantity of sludge in a net or bucket. The substance is then washed through fine nylon or butter muslin until most of the dirt has been removed, leaving behind a mass of the worms. Most of the *Tubifex* sold in pet shops is sent by rail by individuals who undertake the cold and unpleasant task of collecting the worms.

Once the worms are purchased from a pet shop it is advisable first to wash them, and then to feed them to the fishes as soon as possible; any *Tubifex* remaining over should be put in a dish or trough, and placed under a tap where a slight trickle of water is allowed to flow over them continually. The receptacle will eventually overflow, so must be stood in a sink. In this running water the worms will live longer, but, having nothing to eat, may well die. The dead ones turn greyish in colour, and to eliminate them the mass should be stirred before feeding to the fishes, in order that the dead and decomposing worms may be washed away in the overflow.

From what has been said it will be appreciated that *Tubifex* live and eat in most unhygienic surroundings. For this reason the authors do not favour this form of fish food, and prefer *never to use it*. Not only can many forms of harmful bacteria be introduced into an aquarium when feeding the fishes on imperfectly cleansed *Tubifex*, but the worms themselves, having lived on filth, seem to bring out diseases in some fishes.

For some time there have been rumours that *Tubifex* worms may continue to live in the intestines of a fish, and bore their way through various organs, thus bringing about the death of the host. The authors have never been able to establish this as a fact, and consider that it is most improbable. Nevertheless, if *Tubifex* is fed to fishes, it can be chopped with a razor blade, as some of the worms are so long that they will entwine themselves in a fish's gills and cause discomfort, even death. If the aquarist decides to feed his pets with *Tubifex* it is advisable to do so sparingly, as they quickly sink to the bottom and bury their heads in the gravel. Although the tails oscillate in the water, the approach of a fish looking for a meal makes the

63

worms contract immediately and disappear into the gravel. It is true that such fishes as *Corydoras*, which rout in the top layers of the gravel, are able to extract a few of the worms; but when many worms are present a great number will die, decompose, and tend to foul the tank. Some *Tubifex* well established in a tank live on matter which has penetrated the gravel; they make a most unsightly spectacle of waving red fronds, impossible to dislodge unless the whole tank is dismantled and thoroughly cleansed before re-setting.

Glass worms

These transparent creatures — known also as 'phantom larvae' — include the larvae of the gnat *Chaoborus*, and measure about ¼" to ½" in length. They are found in natural ponds, and are caught in a net in the same manner as *Daphnia*. For fishes large enough to eat them, glass 'worms' make an excellent diet, and have the advantage that they survive for a considerable time in the aquarium. They are often found in small ponds overhung by trees and not necessarily frequented by domestic animals. It would appear that the larvae subsist on vegetable matter such as decaying leaves. One great advantage of this larva is that it can be caught in the winter months, even if one has to break the ice to reach it; and at this season *Daphnia* and *Cyclops* are almost impossible to obtain.

Glass worms are too large to be fed to small fry; in fact, the reverse is the case. Being equipped with a sharp hook on their heads, glass worms can ensnare very small fry and devour them. Bigger fishes enjoy the worms, and delight in the chase after their prey. From a motionless position in mid-water the worms, noticing the approach of a fish, coil themselves into a spring, then with a jerk they dart away an inch or two and finally come to rest, relying upon their immobility and transparency for protection.

Blood worms

These are the larvae of *Chironomus* midges, and are deep blood-red in colour, the body being formed of numerous segments. They are an excellent food, which is easily digested and beneficial to the system. It is highly desirable to serve this diet at least once a week to all fishes capable of devouring these rather thick 'worms'. Unfortunately, however, the worms are not available throughout the year, and even when obtainable are difficult to find in large quantities.

Blood worms are usually found in old water-butts and small pools containing decaying vegetable matter, algae, and rotting wood. Where the water is old but clear the worms are not dangerous or harmful.

Mosquito larvae

The mosquito lays its eggs on stagnant water. These develop into the larvae, which, although living in water, still depend upon air to breathe. The respiratory organs are situated at the tail end of the larvae, which must frequently wriggle their way to the surface of the water, and, while hanging head downward, extend their breathing tubes to the air. Equipped with large eyes, they are quick to see the slightest movement or passing shadow above the water. At the least disturbance the larvae will dive to the bottom and remain there until danger is past. They are provided with formidable pincers to catch their prey, and are able to grab newly hatched fry. For this reason the larvae must be fed only to fishes which are large enough to be immune from attack.

Mosquito larvae are seasonal, appearing in water-butts, old cans, or anywhere where there is stagnant water; a static pond may produce great numbers. To catch them a large, long-handled net is required. Make a stealthy approach, plunge the net into the water, and with a quick scooping action collect all those which have come up to breathe. The remainder will dive to the bottom, and there is nothing to do but to wait until they reappear to breathe, imagining that the danger has passed. Then another swift action with the net will trap more. During the waiting period the net must not be allowed to cause disturbing ripples by dripping into the water, and the catcher must stand still and not make the least movement likely to throw a shadow on the pool. An aquarist who falls a victim to mosquito bites has the double satisfaction of knowing that every mosquito larva swallowed by his fishes is not only benefiting his pets but indirectly himself, since it is one that will not develop and bite him.

Gnat larvae are very similar to those of the mosquito, but smaller. Some may be sifted through fine nylon mesh and fed to smaller fishes. Since both gnat and mosquito larvae breathe air, they do not quickly deoxygenate the water in the aquarium, so quite large quantities may be fed at one time. But there are limits, and it is well to remember that those not eaten by the fishes can hatch out and escape into the room.

Sandhoppers
Those aquarists living near the sea may find under boulders on the shore small crustaceans commonly known as sandhoppers. When discovered they leap about, but quite a number can be picked up and placed in a jar of sea-water. On arriving home these can be caught or strained through a net and fed to medium-sized fishes, who seem to enjoy the change. Sandhoppers, of course, make an excellent food for many of the marine coral fishes, who pounce on all they can see, the remainder living quite happily in the crevices of the coral until they venture out.

Other foods
There are numerous other creatures — mayfly grubs and so forth — which will serve as fish-food. It is quite impossible to list them all here, but if a source of supply is available to any aquarist it is advisable to try a small amount initially and see how the fishes react. Most natural foods will be found to be satisfactory, but care should be taken to avoid introducing dirt, harmful bacteria, or other fish enemies.

Chapter Seven

Snails

Most beginners think that snails are essential as scavengers, and purchase, at quite a high price, a few red ramshorns only to find that after a day or two these have been attacked by the fishes, who nip their antennae every time they are extended, finally killing them or forcing them to remain inside their shells until they starve to death. It is a remarkable fact that if one desires to keep snails they are frequently killed off, but when not wanted they usually multiply profusely and become a pest.

Hard and alkaline water is necessary for most snails, as they require certain minerals to maintain their shells in condition. In soft water containing little or no calcium the shells may become brittle and even disintegrate.

A few colourful snails in a community tank may be decorative, and they certainly will dispose of some uneaten food and some algae. They will not, however, eat fish excreta; on the contrary, they will add their own to that already in the tank. Snails are therefore of no great advantage in an aquarium where the fishes are not over-fed; in fact, a little extra food may have to be provided to enable the snails to live.

Should they survive they are likely to become too numerous, and to compete with the fishes for oxygen and food. Periodically, therefore, it will be essential to remove and dispose of most of the snail population. Another disadvantage is that any dead snails are unsightly and detrimental. Some not only eat algae, but devour plant leaves as well, puncturing them all over, and often biting right through the stems, which float to the surface of the water and rot.

The aquarist who wishes to breed fishes will find that most snails are a definite nuisance. Although a breeding tank is set up with washed sand, rinsed plants, and clean water, it is impossible to remove every tiny snail smaller than a pin's head. Worse still, a few eggs adhering to the underside of plant leaves hatch surprisingly quickly, and the young snails devour any fish eggs they can find.

In spite of what has been said above, there are a few species of snails which are a boon to the fish-breeder, notably *Limnaea stagnalis* and *Ampullaria.*

Ampullaria (or Pomacea) (apple snails)
To the fish-breeder this snail has great advantages. There are, however, at least four distinct species of *Ampullaria.* Three of these are ravenous plant-eaters, and should be kept out of planted aquaria. All are sometimes known as 'infusoria snails,' as when kept in unplanted tanks and fed on lettuce-leaves their droppings create ideal conditions for the production of infusoria, the first food for very small newly hatched fry. Water from the *Ampullaria* tank is poured into the one occupied by the free-swimming fry, but in doing so baby snails will also occasionally be

transferred. This will not matter if only *Ampullaria cuprina* are kept, but if any of the other three species be inadvertently introduced they will wreak havoc with the growing plants. It is therefore necessary for the aquarist to be able to identify the species.

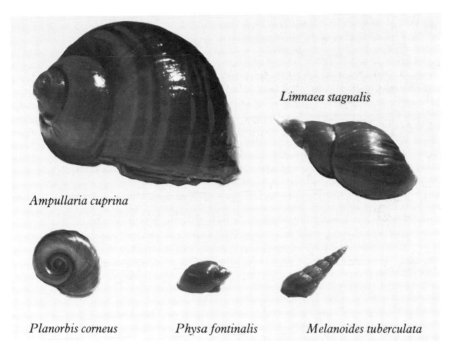

Limnaea stagnalis

Ampullaria cuprina

Planorbis corneus   Physa fontinalis   Melanoides tuberculata

A. canaliculata has a raised spiral coming to a point, and a deep groove is formed between the coils. *A. cuprina* has a raised spiral and a slight groove. *A. gigas* is the largest of all fresh-water snails. Its salient features are a low spiral which is not very pointed, and a deep groove. Finally, a low spiral with only a slight groove characterizes *A. paludosa*.

Ampullaria have four horns and are equipped with an extendable breathing tube which they stretch upward to the surface of the water, and with a pumping action breathe in sufficient air to last them for some time while submerged. These snails are not bisexual, so to breed them it is necessary to have a male and a female. It is possible to sex *Ampullaria* even when they are closed up, since the operculum (the trap-door with which they close the mouth of the shell) of the female is slightly concave, whereas that of the male is slightly convex. In breeding, the male (which is usually the smaller) climbs over the back of the female a little to the right of the head and inserts a long, thick muscular organ, whitish in colour, into the vent under her shell. During this act the snails are locked together, and should not be forcibly parted or injury may result.

When laying eggs the females climb up the walls of the aquarium and out of the water, where they hang motionless. The bright pink eggs emerge from under the shell and pass singly along a groove outside her body to become attached to the glass. A steady stream of eggs moves upward and sticks to the mass now forming on the walls of the tank, until the cluster resembles a large raspberry. This hatches in approximately three to four weeks, providing it does not fall into the water or become too dry. When sufficient snails are kept egg-laying is profuse, and without special care sufficient will hatch to keep the species going. Should an abundance be required for stocking or selling, the clumps of eggs should be carefully removed from the glass with a razor blade. They are then placed on a glass platform stood on two jam-jars in a small tank. This is then filled with water until it reaches the platform. The water is kept at 78°F., and to ensure the correct humidity the tank is covered by a sheet of glass.

On hatching, the baby snails make their way into the water and search for food, *A. cuprina* has an enormous appetite, and must be fed regularly with the leaves of lettuce, dandelion, or Savoy cabbage. *Ampullaria* will not stand foul conditions, so their home must be given a thorough clean-out, dead snails removed, and the tank refilled with clean water at least once a month.

Bulinus australianus (Australian red snail)
This snail, which comes from the Southern Hemisphere, has a pretty yellowish-red shell. The spiral twists in the opposite direction to that of the Physa snail. *B. australianus* is a prolific breeder; it is rather larger than *Physa*, but similar in shape.

Limnaea auricularia (paper shell)
Occasionally seen in aquaria, this rather pretty snail has short horns. The shell is yellowish, marked with dark blotches. *L. auricularia*, coming from Northern Europe, can withstand fairly low temperatures. It dislikes heat, so is not really suitable for use in tropical tanks.

Limnaea stagnalis (common pond snail)
This is found in most ponds, natural or artificial. The snails are greyish in colour, with sharp spiral cone shells about 1½″ long when full grown. They breed profusely, laying a mass of eggs encased in a glutinous jelly usually in the form of an elongated oval about 1″ in length. Development of the young snails can be observed. When first hatched they are slightly smaller than a pin's head; they are voracious and will eat animal or vegetable matter. They have the great advantage to the fish-breeder that they will devour *Hydra* with relish. It is unwise to bring the snails straight from a cool pond and place them direct into a tropical tank, but if warmed up gradually they will stand the change.

Should a breeding tank containing fry be found to have *Hydra* in it a dozen *L. stagnalis* will quickly clear the pests, and not harm the fry. The aquarist can watch the snails devouring *Hydra* attached to the front panel of the aquarium; they are sucked into the snail's mouth, whose scythe-like tongue slices the pest clean off the glass. The snails perform this feat much quicker and better than the generally recommended gouramis, which are not only more costly to obtain but have to be kept very hungry before they will oblige, sometimes inefficiently. Care, however, must be exercised to control the snails. They should be removed after clearing the *Hydra*, and kept in a spare jar until required again.

Marisa rotula (Colombian ramshorn)
This snail is rarely seen in British aquaria, but may be more popular in America. It has a smart flat-spiralled shell lined longitudinally with alternate stripes of dull yellow and brown. The antennae are long, and the foot is of a mauvish colour. *M. rotula* reaches a diameter of 1½". This snail has the drawback of nibbling plants.

Melanoides tuberculata (Malayan live-bearing snail)
These small live-bearing snails rarely exceed ¾" in length, and have long, sharp-coned shells. They have two advantages: in the first place, they scavenge deep into the sand, which is thereby kept loose. Secondly, they reach uneaten food inaccessible to other snails. During daylight these snails hide beneath the sand. At night, however, the aquarist may experience quite a shock to find hundreds of them swarming all over the walls of the tank. Because of their nocturnal habits they are difficult to eliminate. When over-abundant, probably the best method is to remove the sand, scald, and then sift, to remove the larger shells.

Physa fontinalis (American pond snail)
Common in ponds, these small snails rarely exceed ⅓" in length. They are nearly black in colour, extremely hardy, and have very tough shells which discourage fishes from eating them. They breed quickly, and soon become a pest, especially in breeding tanks. Once in an aquarium they are difficult to eradicate. They tend to cover the sand with unsightly black droppings. These snails are not to be recommended for the aquarium.

Planorbis and Helisoma (ramshorn snails)
The shells take the form of flat spirals, like the mainspring of a watch. They are generally black, but there is a pretty red variety. Ramshorns are the snails usually seen in tropical aquaria. Red ones may add a little colour to a community tank, but have virtually no other advantage. In breeding tanks they are a nuisance, as they consume fish eggs and eat much of the food fed to the fishes. The snails breed profusely throughout the year, laying eggs enclosed in small globules of yellow-tinted jelly.

Viviparus (Japanese live-bearing snail)
This gives birth to fully formed young snails, and does not lay eggs. The snail is quite a large one, and may be confused with *Ampullaria*, but the spiral of *Viviparus* is much more raised, and the shell is wider than it is high. This snail is not

hermaphrodite, so for breeding male and female are necessary. Sex may be distinguished, as the male has a shorter and a curved right antenna in comparison with the female. After mating the young hatch inside the mother's shell, and emerge about the size of small pearls. It does not like high temperatures, and is not altogether happy in a tropical tank. A great advantage is that it is not a plant-eater.

FRESHWATER MUSSELS AND CRUSTACEANS

Some aquarists occasionally keep freshwater mussels, crayfish and freshwater shrimps and prawns. Temperate species do not usually thrive in a tropical aquarium, as they need relatively cool and well-aerated water. Tropical or semi-tropical species can be kept in a tropical community aquarium, although large, active crayfish (for example) may pose a threat to slow-moving fishes.

Mussels are filter feeders and may need an occasional feed on a liquid invertebrate diet for marine shellfish, or a liquid fry food. Crustaceans like crayfish, prawns, etc. are excellent scavengers on plant and animal remains, although they should be offered a fish-food tablet or pellet from time to time.

The keeping of marine invertebrates is mentioned elsewhere in this book.

Chapter Eight

Some Aquarium Pests

The aquarist who catches his own live foods from ponds may occasionally come across a number of pests. A few of these are large enough to be seen easily, caught, and removed. Those which are practically invisible can be dealt with by other means. Below the commoner enemies are listed, their characteristics described, and methods of eliminating them explained.

Dytiscus marginalis (water tiger)
Both the beetle and its larvae are extremely dangerous; the former is large, and can be seen and removed. The larva varies in length from $\frac{1}{2}''$ to $2''$ or more; it is long, slender, and greenish-yellow in colour; the tail end is equipped with breathing apparatus; from the head project formidable pincers. It must surface occasionally, tail up, to breathe, but can remain submerged for longish periods, and then it is most dangerous. A voracious creature, it will pounce on anything it can grab and suck the victim's juices. Water tigers will attack small to medium-sized fishes, and once the prey is seized it is unlikely to escape. These enemies abound in most natural ponds, and are frequently collected with *Daphnia*. As a safeguard it is advisable to net some *Daphnia* from the can and tip them into an enamel basin containing clear water. The tigers can then be picked out before the *Daphnia* is fed to the fishes.

Hydra
So called after the mythological many-headed monster which, when decapitated, sprouted new heads. The pest is well named. When contracted it is as small as *Daphnia*, and is hardly visible. It attaches itself to plants, rocks, sand, or the sides of the aquarium. Nevertheless, *Hydra* can move about by bending over its trunk, extending and gripping with the tips of its tentacles, and then transferring its sucker foot to a new position, repeating the action for further progress. Stretching its trunk to a length of about $\frac{1}{4}''$, it unfurls numerous long tentacles which wave in all directions in search of prey. When magnified each tentacle resembles that of an octopus and bears rows of circular sucking discs equipped with stinging cells, with which the *Hydra* can grasp its victim, at the same time stinging and paralysing it. The tentacle is then drawn to the mouth and the food swallowed. Nevertheless, while this operation is taking place the other tentacles are actively searching for more prey. It is possible for a *Hydra* to ensnare several victims simultaneously.

The *Hydra* reproduces itself by budding from the stem; the process is similar to a side shoot branching from the trunk of a tree. If the creature is cut or broken into

71

pieces each of these will develop into a new *Hydra*. *Hydra* are harmless to fishes over ¼″ in length, but deadly to newly hatched fry of the egg-laying species of tropicals; *Hydra* in a breeding tank can clear a spawn of hundreds of fish in a few days. The pests are usually introduced with *Daphnia* or *Cyclops*; sometimes they come in attached to plants. For this reason breeding tanks should be set up with plants that have been thoroughly washed, and soaked in salt water. On no account should the fish put out to breed be fed on *Daphnia*.

When an aquarium becomes infested with *Hydra* they may be killed as follows:

(i) Add 1 teaspoonful of vinegar to every 2 gallons of water in the tank. The dose may be increased slightly if the treatment does not prove to be 100 per cent effective. A little vinegar will not harm most fishes.

(ii) Another good method is to introduce into the tank a number of *Lymnaea stagnalis* snails, which will soon devour the *Hydra*. If the snails are taken from a cold pond they must be warmed up slowly to aquarium temperature. The snails should not be used in a breeding tank until the spawn has hatched; though they will not harm the minute fry, they will devour fish eggs.

(iii) Perhaps the best method of all is to use a small battery. To do this take a 4-volt battery of the type used in a torch and two pieces of copper insulated wire. Bare both ends of both wires to expose about 2 inches of copper. The other two ends are connected one to each terminal of the battery. Place the bare ends of the wires in the water at the opposite ends of the tank. In about 4 hours the *Hydra* will be seen dropping to the bottom. This method seems to have no effect whatever on minute fry even as small as dwarf gouramis.

Leeches

In an aquarium these unpleasant creatures are more unsightly than dangerous. When contracted small ones are about twice the size of a pin's head, and attach themselves firmly to any object. By stretching their bodies, gripping with their jaws, and then drawing forward their hindquarters they can move about. Generally they are too slow to catch fishes, but if the tank becomes infested with leeches they can drop on to a victim and suck its blood. Leeches may be introduced inadvertently into the aquarium on plants, but this may be avoided by alternately dipping the plants in warm and then in cold water. After this treatment they should be left soaking for half an hour in a gallon of water to which has been added two level tablespoonfuls of salt.

When feeding *Daphnia* to the fishes, a few leeches may get into the tank, but they should be removed immediately.

Nepa cinerea (water scorpion)

This predatory bug may be recognized by its scorpion-like front legs and the pointed tail; this consists of two grooved rods which serve as breathing tubes. It abounds in most ponds, but if introduced into an aquarium can be seen, and should be removed.

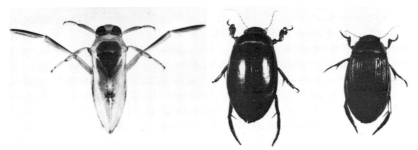

Water Boatman   Diving Beetles

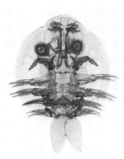  

Fish Louse   Water Tiger   Hydra
(see Chapter Nine)

Water Scorpion   Planarian Worm   Fresh-water Leech

Notonecta (water boatman)

This insect is often seen skimming over the surface of ponds, using its large rear legs as oars. It is approximately ½" long by ⅛" broad when full grown, so is large enough to be seen and removed. The water boatman is harmless to all but very small fishes, which it may seize in its front legs and attack with its beak. Large fishes will eat the bug.

Odonata (dragonfly larvae)

Like the dragonfly they will develop into, these thick, large-eyed larvae have enormous jaws. These are covered by a mask, which is in effect an enlarged lower lip. The larva is able to thrust its jaws forward, thereby extending its long pincers. From a motionless position it grasps the unwary prey. Dragonfly larvae usually live near the bottom of most ponds. The creatures are not so frequently caught as water tigers, as these are more active in the upper strata of water.

Planarian worms

Grey to brownish in colour, these flat worms are about ¼" long, and some have a diamond-shaped head. They may be seen on the plants and on the glass sides of the aquarium; often congregating just under the surface of the water. When a mass appear adhering to the glass they can be wiped off with a cloth. Planarian worms will eat spawn and very small fry, but seem to be harmless to bigger fishes. Treat as for leeches.

Plumatella

These bryozoans are small creatures rather like miniature *Hydra*, except that the trunk is much shorter and the tentacles are less numerous and more feathery. *Plumatella* increase by sending out runners or side shoots from the base of the trunk; if left alone they will form long brown threads in all directions. The creatures are not large enough to be of much danger, but they may be able to catch a few of the smallest fry. It is mostly the minute organisms in the water, such as infusorians, that are eaten by *Plumatella*, so probably their worst feature is to consume some of the food for the fry.

Utricularia (bladderwort)

The aquatic plant *Utricularia* takes the form of a mass of slender filaments bearing numerous small sacs. These bladders engulf minute forms of aquatic life, on which the plant feeds. Bladderwort is of a pretty shade of green, and is used for decorative purposes in some aquaria. It is harmless, except in breeding tanks, where it may engulf and digest some newly hatched fry of egg-laying fishes.

A small species of *Utricularia* is similar, but, the bladders being much smaller, the plant has long been considered safe for all except minute organisms. It is frequently used for spawning purposes, particularly for some of the pencil fishes which produce extremely small fry. There is no doubt that lesser bladderwort can and does engulf some of these baby fishes, but the majority escape.

Other pests

The undermentioned usually concern outdoor pools, but are referred to here in case some are introduced as additional pets to an indoor aquarium. Frogs, terrapins, and water snakes should not be kept with fishes. In the outdoor pool there is the added danger of fish-eating birds such as herons and kingfishers. Cats, otters, snakes and even alligators are enemies which will eat fishes.

Pesticides

Many of the enemies of fishes are obvious, but few aquarists realize the danger of modern pesticides. Various washes and sprays used on trees or indoor plants if allowed to contaminate the water in pond or aquarium can quickly prove fatal, as can some household sprays and chemicals. Read all instructions for use carefully.

Chapter Nine

Some Common Diseases

Fish can suffer from a huge range of infectious diseases, yet perhaps just a handful of these account for the majority of disease problems encountered by aquarists. Prompt diagnosis and effective treatment of these common ailments is well within the capabilities of most hobbyists—often using available, proprietary treatments. Many of the proprietary fish-disease treatments contain well-known chemicals like malachite green, methylene blue, acriflavine and formalin, and home-made equivalents can be concocted by the aquarist. However, home-made recipes bring with them the risk of miscalculation, which can have unfortunate consequences. Reliable shop-bought treatments are to be recommended. What is often forgotten, however, is that most diseases can actually be *prevented*, by a combination of *quarantine* of all new stock and *correct care* of the aquarium or pond.

A small aquarium, baby bath or paddling pool can be used as a quarantine (and when necessary, treatment) tank. This should be aerated (and preferably filtered), and heated if it is for tropical fish. Some form of refuge (e.g., flower pot, plastic plant) should be provided for timid fish, and all new fish so quarantined for at least two weeks. A preventative course of treatment with a white-spot remedy (in fresh-water) and a copper-based remedy (in sea-water) is also a good idea.

Furthermore, the importance of correct care in preventing many fish diseases should not be overlooked. Most of the organisms responsible for the common diseases of fish occur widely as environmental 'contaminants' or 'latent' infections in apparently healthy fish. If the fish are subjected to less than ideal pond or aquarium conditions, this will be sufficient to trigger off the disease organism(s), with the infection moving from a 'latent' to an 'active' condition. Outbreaks of a disease are therefore almost invariably an indication that something is wrong with the basic aquarium set-up, including overcrowding, incorrect diet, inadequate water changes, poor or fluctuating water conditions, and so on. Such factors must be identified and improved for long-term disease prevention.

White-spot and other skin parasites
The most ubiquitous of fish diseases is surely white-spot, as caused by the ciliate protozoan *Ichthyophthirius multifiliis* (and hence its other common name 'Ich'). The 'Ich' parasite lives on the skin, fins and gills of fish, but most fall away from the host to divide. On the aquarium floor many hundreds of daughter parasites, or 'swarmers', are produced, which then reinfect the same fish or other fish in the same aquarium. The life-cycle can turn over in 3 or 4 days at 75°F., and have rapidly built up to epizootic proportions in a well-stocked tropical aquarium (or in a coldwater aquarium or pond in the summer). Conversely, the parasite can lie

dormant on the host for weeks at temperatures below 50°F., suddenly causing a problem when temperatures increase. Since the white-spot parasite is situated under the skin of the host, it is only susceptible to treatment once it falls away to divide. Hence treatments must be added to the infected tank or pond rather than removing the fish to a separate treatment tank. Fortunately, there are a number of excellent white-spot treatments on the market.

In tropical marine tanks a similar parasite by the name *Cryptocaryon irritans* occurs, and causes similar problems. This is best treated with one of the available copper-based remedies, noting that such treatments cannot be used in the presence of invertebrates.

Heavy infestations with a range of tiny parasites such as *Chilodonella*, *Costia*, trichodinids, *Gyrodactylus* and *Dactylogyrus* irritate the skin of fish and clog their gills, causing a range of symptoms including rubbing against rocks, marks on the skin, and rapid gill movements. These parasites may occur with 'Ich' and are particularly common on newly imported fish or coldwater fish in the spring. Fortunately, with anti-white-spot remedies, or similar proprietary remedies, treatment is simple and effective.

Fish fungus

Fish fungus (as caused by fungi such as *Saprolegnia* and *Achlya*) is a very common disease, especially on fish that are in poor condition because of fighting, rough handling, recent spawning activity, and perhaps unsatisfactory tank conditions. Since the 'seeds' or spores which give rise to fungus are very common in water, fungus is a continual threat to fish. However, if spotted early enough it can be effectively treated by adding a proprietary remedy to the aquarium, and subsequently prevented by correct care. Mouth 'fungus' (which is actually caused by the bacterium *Flexibacter*) often occurs on newly imported fish and is best treated as described below for 'fin rot'.

Neon tetra disease

Loss of colour and appetite, and wasting, among neon tetras (as well as other characins, and perhaps some barbs and danios) may be the result of infestation by the tiny *Plistophora* parasite. This highly contagious but largely untreatable disease can cause severe problems in overcrowded, unhygienic tanks. Affected dying as well as dead fish must be removed, and special attention paid to improving general hygiene by increased siphoning out of debris and better filter maintenance. Few of the proprietary treatments seem very effective against this problem.

Dropsy

This ailment is sometimes concurrent with an ulcer disease problem, and sometimes occurs on its own. Fish may take on a swollen dropsical appearance. The condition is not always infectious, but affected fish are best isolated. Antibiotic therapy (under a vet) is a possibility, although not always successful. The condition need not be fatal, and the fish may recover on its own.

Hole-in-the-head disease
This is a common problem affecting cichlids and gouramis, but less often other fish. Symptoms include darkened coloration, loss of appetite, emaciation, pale stringy faeces—and pale shallow lesions in the head and sides of the fish. While a tiny parasite called *Hexamita* may be involved in the disease, unsatisfactory water conditions, inadequate tank care and poor diet are also important predisposing factors. Proprietary treatments are available too.

Fin rot
Fin rot is a common problem among newly imported fish, or fish which have been fighting or kept in unhygienic conditions. It is usually related to a localized bacterial infection, which can have serious consequences if not promptly treated. Acriflavine-based or phenoxethol-based proprietary treatments are recommended, although antibiotic treatment (with the help of a vet) is a possibility for stubborn cases. Of course, the problem is likely to recur if the underlying causes are not eliminated.

Hole-in-the-body disease or ulcer disease
This disease (which should not be confused with hole-in-the-head disease of cichlids, see above) is most common among coldwater fish and is usually the result of a bacterial infection. However, the bacterium that is responsible for the disease (often an aeromonad) is quite common, and may affect tropical fish. Like so many other fish diseases, it can only cause problems in already weakened hosts. Importation, rough handling, overcrowding and poor water conditions all result in stress, and provides predisposing factors for this disease: this suggests the long-term prevention of this problem. When an outbreak of hole-in-the-body disease occurs antibiotic-medicated flake food can be used, or antibiotics can be injected or added to the water of a treatment tank. Whichever method is chosen, veterinary assistance will be required. Because fish showing symptoms of this disease are actively shedding large numbers of bacteria into the water, isolation into a separate tank is recommended. Affected fish should be isolated and treated with a suitable proprietary remedy, although a local vet may be able to assist by prescribing suitable drugs.

Pop-eye
Fish may occasionally show symptoms of one or both eyes being noticeably swollen. This may be related to a number of possible causes, and although it is not usually a very infectious condition, affected fish are best isolated from the rest of the stock. There is no reliable treatment, and the swelling may disappear with time.

Fish lice
The fish louse (*Argulus*) is a small (quarter-inch) crustacean parasite which is

especially common on pond fish during the summer and early autumn, and is sometimes seen in aquaria. It has piercing mouthparts which intensely irritate the host and it feeds on the blood and tissue fluids of fish. The wounds made by *Argulus* may also become infected with bacteria and fungus.

Fortunately, this disease is easily treated using proprietary remedies. However, some fish (e.g., orfe, rudd and piranha) are rather sensitive to such chemicals, and they should be maintained in a separate tank for 7 to 10 days, while the infected tank (or pond) is treated.

Velvet disease

Velvet disease is caused by a number of different species of *Oodinium* parasites, and although it occurs in fresh-water, it is a particularly serious disease in marine tanks. It may occur as a skin and/or gill infestation, and at the temperatures in most tropical marine systems can have sudden and quite drastic effects. A copper-based treatment (perhaps used in conjunction with a short fresh-water dip) is the best remedy for an existing problem. As indicated above, copper cannot be used when invertebrates are present, and hence the value of quarantine and a prophylactic copper treatment to prevent the introduction of *Oodinium* (and *Cryptocaryon*) to mixed fish-invertebrate systems.

Where velvet disease occurs in fresh-water aquaria, proprietary velvet or white-spot remedies can be used.

Some Points to note when treating Fish

Calculate volume of any tanks carefully. Deduct 10 per cent from the apparent volume for gravel, etc. (if present).

Turn off filtration over activated carbon during treatment. Ensure adequate aeration.

Do not overcrowd fish during treatment. Do not treat fish in galvanized containers.

Always try a remedy out on one or two individuals before treating a whole batch of delicate or expensive fish.

Excessive amounts of organic matter will reduce the activity of most remedies.

Never mix remedies unless you know it is safe. A 50 to 75 per cent water change and filtration over activated carbon for 12 to 24 hours should remove most active ingredients.

Treat marine fish in a separate tank unless you know the remedy will not harm the biological filter and the invertebrates.

If you are in any doubt about the diagnosis and treatment of a disease of your fish, contact a local vet or fish health specialist.

If possible, use a reliable proprietary treatment rather than a home-made remedy, following the instructions for use carefully.

Chapter Ten

Plants for a Beautiful Aquarium

Plants are important in any permanent fresh-water aquarium where beauty and the well-being of the fishes is concerned. The different shades of green or red and the diverse forms of foliage not only add greatly to the attractiveness of the under-water scene, but create the conditions which are natural to the fishes. Plants afford refuge and shade, and often provide places for spawning. Besides all these advantages, plants absorb carbon dioxide, give off oxygen, and feed to a large extent on waste matter in the aquarium.

Plants vary greatly in their habit of growth; some remain short, others grow tall, bushy, or straight. A few float at the surface. All help the aquarist to decorate his tank. Below are listed most of the common species seen in the majority of aquaria. In addition, some rarer ones are described. Nevertheless, new plants are continually being introduced and it is impossible to cover every specimen suitable for an aquarium. In this chapter plants are considered in alphabetical order; their methods of growth and reproduction are described, and any special requirements stated.

Acorus gramineus var. intermedius　　　　　　*Acorus gramineus var. pusillus*

***Acorus gramineus* var. *intermedius*.** These little plants are not true aquatics, but marginals. They do not like high temperatures, but if acclimatized slowly will hold their own in a tropical tank. Growth is slow. This plant has stiff, sword-like leaves, ¼" wide at the base, which taper to a point, usually reaching a length of 6" to 7". The foliage grows from one point on a rhizome. This sends down thick, stout roots, and occasionally produces next to the parent a young plant which may be severed with a sharp knife and transplanted.

***Acorus gramineus* var. *pusillus*.** Similar to the foregoing, but the leaves are thinner and shorter, reaching a height of only 3". Propagation as for the above.

Anubias lanceolata   Aponogeton ulvaceus

***Anubias lanceolata*.** A favourite aquarium plant, it prefers soft water, and makes a good centre-piece in small tanks. The stout leaves, lanceolate in shape, are borne on stems which shoot from a root stock. foliage is darkish green, and attains a lenghth of 5"×¾". *A. lanceolata* is a slow grower. Propagation is from small offshoots which spring from the root stock.

***Aponogeton madagascariensis*.** The famous Madagascar lace plant, of which there may be several species varying in colour and size. It is called the lace plant because the leaves are merely a network of veins which run lengthwise and crosswise in a lattice formation. Since the plant requires very soft acid water for growing, and is difficult to propagate, it remains scarce, fetching a high price. Some other species of lace plants are not truly aquatic, and fare poorly in an

81

aquarium, usually dying after a few months. These, if planted in a half tub and rooted in 4″ of earth covered by a 2″ layer of sand, can grow to a height of 2 ft., sending their leaves well clear of the water. Some of these leaves will grow 18″ long by 4″ wide.

If the aquarist is fortunate enough to obtain one of the aquatic species it will, with care, live in the aquarium. Contrary to the old contention that the plant should be grown in semi-darkness, we find that it likes a fair amount of light. But the lattice-work of the leaves must not be allowed to become choked with algae, which will weave themselves in and out of the veins and be difficult to remove. Snails eat some algae, but may destroy the leaves; it is better to use fishes to consume the algae.

Though the leaves look most fragile, they are in reality tough and fibrous; under good conditions new ones appear every day or so, as long, thin filaments. These grow, widening as well as lengthening, and usually attain 10″ in length by 1½″ in width. When several leaves of this size are flourishing the plant is superb, and should be left alone: it abhors being moved. For this reason it may be preferable to plant the bulb in a shallow pot containing soil below and sand above. When flourishing the plant will flower, but propagation from seed is difficult. Occasionally the bulb will sprout a side-shoot, forming a baby plant. When this has attained a length of 3″ or 4″ it can be separated from the parent and grown on its own.

Aponogeton ulvaceus. Naturally a marginal plant, as the Latin name (*ulva*, sedge) implies, It will grow in an aquarium, where it develops into a show specimen. The plant does well in soft water of 12″ depth, and requires plenty of space and light in which to spread its large, graceful, pale green, almost transparent leaves. These grow from longish stalks, and attain 6″ in length by 1½″ in width; they have undulating edges, and the veining runs length-wise. The plant has a delicate texture, and the leaves are easily torn or damaged. The stems can be bruised and broken if handled roughly. (Illus. p. 81.)

Growing from a bulb, *A. ulvaceus* sends up aerial runners which flower; it also produces young plants at intervals along its length. Occasionally the bulb will spring a side-shoot which may be divided off when large enough. When grown in natural daylight *A. ulvaceus* dies down in the winter, but shoots out again in the spring. During the annual cycle three different leaf formations are developed.

Aponogeton undulatus. A showy plant, and a little stronger than *A. ulvaceus*. It prefers slightly acid water, but is not too sensitive about this. Probably it is the commonest of the aponogetons. Growing from a bulb, the long, thin leaves, carried on slender stalks, end in a fine point; they may reach a length of 10″, though they rarely exceed ¾″ in width. The edges are closely undulated, giving the appearance of a continuous ripple. The plant likes a depth of 12″ to 15″, but does not spread quite as widely as *A. ulvaceus*.

Aerial stems are sent upward prolifically, and these terminate in a spike of pale mauve flowers which rise above the water surface. The bloom may be trained through a corner of the cover glass and enclosed in an upturned jam-jar; it will then

Aponogeton undulatus

continue to grow in the moist, warm atmosphere inside the jar until the flower-head reaches as much as 4″ in length. The flowers produce pollen, and if this is distributed with a very soft brush seeds will develop. When these are about ⅛″ in diameter the aerial runner should be cut off and the whole piece suspended over a small tank containing gravel and water. The seeds ripen, burst, and release minute plants with tiny roots. Great care must be taken to anchor these into the gravel where they will grow. They should not be moved, neither must boisterous fishes be put in the tank, as they will bruise or uproot the seedlings. Well-grown ones in due course will produce bulbs.

Azolla caroliniana. Essentially this is a floating plant. Each small piece looks like an enlarged snowflake bearing minute leaves. These vary in colour from bright green to rusty red, depending on the amount of light received. Under suitable conditions the plant spreads rapidly; it will form a compact covering on the surface of the water, and provide excellent shade. If allowed to become too thick it may prevent the light from reaching plants below, and so cause them to suffer. Green water, if caused by excessive top light, can be effectively checked by *Azolla.* Unfortunately, it rarely makes a sufficient depth of growth to provide a spawning ground or a refuge for small fishes.

Bacopa amplexicaulis. This is different from most plants in its growth and appearance, but makes a pleasant change. It is a bright green, and the small, round leaves, orbicular in shape, are carried on short stalks ¼″ long from a central stem. The plant will grow to a height of 12″ or more, the top leaves pointing in an upward direction. Half-way down the stem the leaves spread horizontally, while lower down they tend to droop.

B. amplexicaulis is a slow grower. The stems may be cut in half and the upper part replanted. Under a good light this portion slowly roots itself. The original stem will sprout again below the cut. The plant is tall and narrow; it looks better if several stems are bunched together.

Bacopa caroliniana. Very similar to the aforementioned, but the leaves are slightly longer and more pointed. The plant is perhaps a little hardier, and is more apt to send out side-shoots.

Bacopa rotundifolia. As its name implies, this plant has round leaves. These grow from a central stem. *B. rotundifolia* is a larger-leafed *Bacopa*. The foliage is a bright green, and somewhat thick. Propagation is by cuttings.

Bacopa caroliniana   *Bacopa rotundifolia*

Cabomba aquatica. One of the finest of aquarium plants. This is one of several related species, all of which have the same form of growth. The leaves, like open fans, are supported on short stalks. These appear opposite each other from a central stem at intervals of 1¼". The next pair of leaves is set at right angles to those below. When in a situation to its liking *Cabomba* bears magnificent heads, sometimes measuring 1½" to 2" in diameter. If these grow towards the viewer they present rosettes of vivid green, not easily forgotten. The plant prefers slightly acid water and a good illumination. Under these conditions it remains bushy and colourful. In alkaline water and under too strong a light the growth of the stems is forced, and these tend to become pale and spindly.

Stems may grow several feet in length, trailing back and forth across the surface of the water. Long stalks may be cut, and look best if planted in bunches, where they soon root. The decapitated stems quickly shoot new heads. The plant is ideal for spawning egg-laying fishes.

Cabomba caroliniana. Similar to the foregoing, but the foliage is denser, the pairs of leaves appearing every ½″ up the stem, and the fronds of each fan are more tightly packed.

| Cabomba caroliniana | Cabomba aquatica | Ceratophyllum demersum |

Cabomba piauhyensis. A reddish species.

Ceratophyllum demersum (Hornwort). A common plant which abounds over most of Europe and North America, but there is also a tropical variety which comes from India. All varieties are rootless and bushy, consisting of long stems bearing side-branches. The leaves are short, thin spikes, sharp and harsh to the touch. The general colour is a darkish green. Under strong light this rootless plant is a profuse grower, spreading in all directions under the surface of the water. *C. demersum* is useful for spawning *Mastacembelus* species, who like to rest supported in the fronds, and deposit their eggs in the prickly thickets.

Ceratopteris pteroides (Floating fern). A useful floating plant. The leaves, ovate in shape, grow radially from a bunch of roots which hang submerged in the water. The leaves attain a length of 6″ and a breadth of 2″, and are carried on short stems which have a spongy core. In strong light numerous baby plants appear at the edges of the leaves. The young plants, when large enough, float off and grow independently. So prolific is the growth that the water surface soon becomes densely packed, and in the crush some of the leaves are forced out of the water. Unless thinned out, this plant will cut out all overhead light. It is an excellent plant for combating green water. Many of the bubble-nest-building fishes like to make their nests under the leaves.

Ceratopteris pteroides   *Pistia stratiotes*

Ceratopteris thalicroides (Broad-leafed Indian fern). An excellent aquarium plant, not particular as to water, though when fully mature it needs a large tank. It grows to a height of 15″ and spreads as much as 12″ in diameter. These dimensions need not deter the aquarist with a small aquarium, since young plants can be accommodated easily.

It is light green in colour, and looks a typical fern. It is composed of many stalks and numerous fronds. Near the base of each stalk the fronds appear as separate leaves, but higher up the stems these are joined together as one irregular-edged leaf. The somewhat hairy roots of the plant are comparatively small. The leaf stems are crisp externally but have a spongy interior; if bent they will kink and rot away, but are quickly replaced by new ones which appear with their tips curled up, but unfurl as they grow.

Ceratopteris thalicroides (two forms)

From the stems young plants are produced in great quantity, and they soon develop their own roots; if left undisturbed many will grow quite large while still attached to the parent. Others get knocked off and float to the surface, where they will form a dense mat. As soon as any of these are large enough to handle they may be rooted in the gravel. By this time the parent plant may have grown too big for the tank, and become very buoyant, so that the short, shallow roots can no longer anchor it down. It can now be removed without any trouble or disturbance to the gravel, and be replaced by one of the larger youngsters.

The Indian fern in its various stages of development has many uses. Being such a quick grower, it has no equal for clearing green water. Medium-sized plants, if bunched together and planted in a breeding tank, make a good spawning place for egg-layers. A handful of young ferns left floating are ideal for spawning those bubble-nest-building fishes which combine leaves and bubbles. A carpet of young ferns rooted in a breeding tank will hide the spawn of fishes like danios, who are liable to devour all the eggs they can find. Finally, young plants left floating at the surface make an excellent cover for baby live-bearers and provide good shade from strong light.

Cryptocoryne affinis.   First introduced into Britain by the authors just after the Second World War, the plant has proved to be the best *Cryptocoryne* to date. The dark green leaves, 6″ long by 1″ wide, are striped longitudinally, with veining of a paler shade. The under side is a vivid bright purple which shines like satin. Under subdued illumination the tints of the leaves are intensified. The under sides become so rich in colour that it is a pity these are mostly hidden from view. Under most conditions *C. affinis* is a prolific and rapid grower, sending out an array of runners in all directions. If left undisturbed they rapidly cover a large area of sand so thickly that a veritable forest may quickly spring up. The great mass of young

Cryptocoryne affinis

87

plants vie with each other for nourishment. In their struggle they become dwarfed, and their leaves spread horizontally in a dense mat about 2″ above the sand. If any of these struggling youngsters are moved and given greater space they will quickly attain mature size, indicating that no permanent harm has been done.

A single *C. affinis* will grow to a height of 12″ and a width of 8″, the long stems being robust enough to support the leaves at a graceful angle, without drooping. Individual mature plants create an excellent centrepiece for the aquarium, or a few specimens spaced along the rear of the tank make a delightful background. Smaller runners, if bunched in the foreground of the tank, will form a dense carpet. Few fishes molest this tough *Cryptocoryne*. Moreover, since it is a heavy feeder, its numerous roots break down quantities of mulm.

Cryptocoryne beckettii. The smallest *Cryptocoryne* at present used by aquarists. The leaves, lanceolate in shape, are a light green shade. The upper surface is smooth, and usually convex in form. Each leaf has a 1″ stem which grows from a root stock. Development is slow. After about a year the whole plant may be lifted and divided for propagation purposes. Occasionally small runners from the parent grow outward for an inch or two, and these may be cut off and transplanted.

The plant rarely exceeds 3″ in height, and then only under strong light, with the leaves growing in a nearly vertical direction. Under subdued illumination, which it prefers, the height may not exceed 1½″, and the leaves may fall into a more horizontal position. *C. beckettii* is used more for compactness than utility. It is suitable for growing in the front of the aquarium.

Cryptocoryne beckettii

Cryptocoryne bulosa

Cryptocoryne bulosa. At first glance it resembles *Aponogeton undulatus*. Springing from long stalks, the leaves have a length of 10″, and are ½″ wide, tapering to a point. They are of a bright green, and intensely crinkled. The stem continues right through the leaf to the tip, and the translucent foliage reflects the light as it strikes the shiny, crinkled surface. Growth is slow, but occasional runners spread over the sand. Each produces a new plant, which can be cut off and transplanted when 3″ high.

Cryptocoryne ciliata   *Cryptocoryne cordata*

Cryptocoryne ciliata.   This is the giant of the genus. When young its pale green pointed leaves resemble *Anubias lanceolata*. As it grows the stems lengthen to 9″ to 10″, and the large oval leaves may measure as much as 8″×3½″. These are a pale green, the veining being clearly visible. This is a superb plant.

Cryptocoryne cordata.   It grows to a height of 6″ or 7″ and bears numerous leaves, 4″ long by ¾″ wide; these are olive green on top and pink to rusty red underneath. The colour of the under side varies greatly according to the amount of light received. When this is subdued — which the plant prefers — the leaves are more luxuriant, and the under sides deeper in colour. Under powerful illumination the upper sides of the leaves tend to be more yellow, while the lower faces are pale. The foliage is tough, and those species of tropicals that devour plants rarely chew *C. cordata*. Like most of the genus, it is very slow-growing, but may be lifted after 12 months, when small subsidiary plants can be divided from the parent. Once established, quite a thicket can be grown, and will live for years.

Cryptocoryne griffithii.   This plant reaches a height of 12″. The long leaf-stems grow 6″ or 7″ high to bear large, glossy, dark green leaves, 3″ long by 1½″ wide, somewhat oval in shape, with a pointed tip. Here and there the under side of the leaf bears brownish-pink dots or blotches. The plant likes subdued light, and should not be disturbed once established.

Under ideal conditions it will flower, sending up a long, trumpet-shaped bloom terminating in a pennant-like tongue. Inside is a long cream-coloured spadix. The spathe is yellowish-green externally, the interior varying from pink to bright red. Once flowering begins a dozen or more blooms may follow each other during the season. The plant is a slow grower, but does send out three or four runners a year. These may be cut off and transplanted when about 3″ high. *C. griffithii* makes a decorative background or centre plant.

Cryptocoryne longicauda. Being somewhat like a bigger edition of *C. griffithii*, it bears large, deep green leaves, approximately 4″ long by 2″ wide, on long, rigid stems. Its erect habit of growth makes it ideal as a show-piece. Reproduction is by runners. Like most *Cryptocoryne*, it is not a rapid grower, but will last for several years.

Cryptocoryne nevillii. Pale green in colour, the leaves are long, narrow, and smooth. They grow on stalks about 2″ long. Growth is slow, and therefore its main use is decoration. Propagation is by runners.

Cryptocoryne willisii. The brownish-green leaves, 4″ long by ¼″ wide, have wavy edges, and the under sides show red veining. They grow from long, slender stalks which emanate from a root stock. Part of this often emerges from the gravel, and forms a kind of trunk from which side-buds, as well as roots, appear. Eventually this trunk grows several inches tall, making the plant appear to have pushed itself out of the gravel. The top part may be pinched off and, providing some of the aerial roots are attached, may be replanted. The lower half will sprout side-shoots. *C. willisii* is not a prolific grower, nor is it extremely robust. Nevertheless, it is decorative, and somewhat dainty.

Cryptocoryne willisii   Echinodorus cordifolius

Didiplis diandra. It comes from North America, particularly Texas and Missouri. It is very brittle and weak, and not such a good aquarium plant as *Naias microdon* which it strongly resembles.

Echinodorus bleheri (Broad-leafed Amazon sword plant). A beautiful, showy aquarium plant, which will make a magnificent centrepiece, but needs a fair amount of space. It has broader leaves than *E. intermedius* below, but is in all other respects similar.

Echinodorus cordifolius. Here is a beautiful member of the genus, but somewhat difficult to describe, as it has three types of foliage. When young the leaves are rather transparent; they are broad, but taper to a point. Later they develop even longer stalks with floating foliage; finally these stand above the water. In summer the plant is most attractive, but dies down during the winter months. Reproduction is by runners carrying young plants. *E. radicans* also sends up a stalk which bears white flowers. These if pollinated produce seeds, which may be planted to form new specimens.

Once established this plant should be left alone, as the somewhat tender leaves are easily bruised and damaged by buffeting. Snails ruin the plant by biting holes in its leaves. It is definitely a plant of beauty rather than utility.

Echinodorus intermedius (Amazon Sword Plant). Here is a magnificent aquarium plant, providing one has sufficient room to house it. When mature it will reach a height of 20″, and spread out to a diameter of 18″. It bears numerous pale green translucent leaves. Each leaf, growing from a 4″ stem, will reach a length of 14″ by 1¼″ width. They are usually carried loftily, and do not droop languidly. When rolled between thumb and forefinger the square-sided stems feel like a match-stick. Unfortunately, they are rather brittle, and if severely knocked or bent will kink, and afterwards rot away.

E. intermedius in perfect condition is a truly gorgeous sight, but so often it is marred by torn and broken leaves which tend to turn brown. Grown in soft water, under a good light, the plant throws up from the crown long, flat-sided runners,

Echinodorus intermedius

91

which grow upward and travel 12″ or more just below the surface of the water. At intervals along these runners there are joints, from which young plants appear complete with leaves and small roots; these may be cut off and transplanted when large enough. Because of the numerous large leaves, the Amazon sword plant is excellent for combating green water.

Echinodorus major.   A plant similar to *E. intermedius,* but with broader leaves which are undulated.

Echinodorus tenellus (chain sword).   This attractive plant resembles most of the swords, but does not grow so large, being happy in a depth of 10″ of water. Propagation is by runners, which grow from the crown and spread outward along the sand. A young plant appears, but long before it has grown to full size the same runner has travelled on and produced four or five more youngsters, each becoming progressively smaller as the extremity of the runner is reached. Leaving a portion of runner on either side, the plantlets may be cut and transplanted in exactly the same way as for *E. intermedius.*

Echinodorus tenellus

Egeria densa.   This plant, under the name of *Elodea densa,* is very common. The foliage is a darkish green, and forms dense whorls springing from a central system. Under a strong light it will grow as much as 1″ per day, becoming rather too long and straggly. Stems should be cut back and planted in bunches, when they root easily. Because of its rapid growth a mass of *E. densa* will often prevent the formation of algæ, and help to clear green water. (See illus. p.99.)

Eichhornia crassipes (Water hyacinth).   A showy floating plant, thought rather large for the average aquarium. The bright green, oval-shaped, spongy leaves rise above the surface from bulbous stems which give the necessary buoyancy. Under suitable conditions the plant bears a head of pale lavender flowers, somewhat like a small hyacinth — hence the common name. Beneath the surface of the water *E. crassipes* sends down a jungle of fine, hairy roots; these are useful for catching adhesive fish-eggs, and make an excellent hiding-place for newly hatched fry. Propagation is by floating runners.

Eleocharis acicularis (Hair-grass).   A dainty plant which is a delightful shade of green, and consists of hair-like stems growing to a height of 3″ to 4″. In good light hair-grass sends out numerous runners. Sometimes it divides half-way up the stems, where young plants are formed; these too will send runners downward to reach the sand.

When amassed in a breeding tank *Eleocharis* is excellent for protecting the spawn of non-adhesive egg-layers. The falling ova drop between the fronds out of reach of the parent fish. Similarly, a mass of hair-grass makes a perfect retreat for young fishes. Unfortunately, it is inclined to die away in winter, especially in fish houses with glass roofs where daylight provides the only illumination.

Eleocharis acicularis

Elodea canadensis.   Not truly a tropical plant, it is found in natural ponds throughout the temperate regions of North America and Europe. It adapts itself to tropical tanks, but the heat and light force growth so much that it becomes long, straggly, brittle, and tends to be a nuisance. If cut back and planted in bunches it serves for decoration, a hide-out for young fishes, and a good clearer of green water. Another use not generally known is that a large bunch tied loosely with raffia and floated into hard water seems to absorb some of the salts, thereby reducing a certain amount of the hardness.

Elodea canadensis

Fontinalis antipyretica.   This plant is not recommended for tropical tanks. Its tiny leaves grow from branching stems, which resemble some forms of coral. Being less bushy, it is not even useful for spawning fishes. The plant does not like warm water, and soon dies.

Hemianthus species

Hemianthus species. Very like, but not to be confused with, *Lysimachia* (creeping jenny) which rarely survives long as an under-water aquatic. These plants have small, oval-shaped, pale green leaves, which grow on short stalks carried on the main slender stem. Aerial roots are profuse, and if cuttings are made and placed together, the plant may be grown in dainty clusters.

Heteranthera zosterifolia. The plant is attractive because of its delicate form. The tall stems bear small, thin leaves which are pale green in colour; these are stalkless, and grow alternately right and left at ½″ intervals horizontally up the stem. *Heteranthera* can be made to look denser if several stems are planted together. It is hardly bushy or robust enough to be used as a spawning or refuge plant. Propagated easily from cuttings.

Heteranthera zosterifolia   *Hydrocotyle vulgaris*

Hydrocotyle vulgaris. A strange little plant, which unfortunately is not very robust. It is of such a distinctive appearance that it makes a pleasing change in the front of an aquarium. A creeping runner travels along the top of the gravel, anchoring itself here and there with short roots. Slender stems, about 1″ apart, grow vertically upward. Each of these bears a single round, flat leaf with an indented border. These circular leaves are pale green and dip slightly in the centre where they join the stalk. Propagation is by division.

Hygrophila corymbosa. This plant was introduced to Britain from Thailand in 1955. It is also known as *Nomaphila stricta*.

The plant has a central stem which is thick, strong, and rigid. The leaves, lanceolate in shape, are a beautiful glossy bright green, and attain a length of 5" by 1¼" wide; they grow in pairs opposite each other on short stalks. If the plant is left undisturbed it will grow right out of the water. The leaves then become a darker green with a coppery tinge. Small flowers, mauve in colour, resembling miniature antirrhinums, appear in the joints between stem and leaf stalks. If the plant be decapitated, and the top part pushed into the gravel, it soon produces a bunch of strong, hairy roots which anchor firmly. This continues to grow in a single column; but the decapitated portion will throw out numerous branches and form a thick tree-like growth, reaching a height of 18", and spreading out to a diameter of 10". This will make a magnificent centrepiece. It is a prolific grower, and so easily propagated that even a single leaf nipped off and pushed into the gravel will root and start a new plant. One drawback is that snails and some larger fishes seem to enjoy eating the leaves, and so destroy the plant.

Hygrophila polysperma   *Hygrophila corymbosa*

Hygrophila polysperma.   This plant was introduced to Britain in 1945, and soon many tanks were well stocked with it. Some months later the plant was imported from America, and from both stocks it has now become an established favourite in Britain.

H. polysperma is an excellent grower in neutral water, bearing many pairs of bright green leaves. These grow direct from a central stem, and have no stalks. Under good light the leaves attain a length of 3" by ¾" wide, and are lanceolate in shape. When illumination is poor the leaves are smaller. The stems grow quickly, and send out aerial roots. Cuttings root very easily, and if several stems are planted together in a bunch the effect is very pleasing. *H. polysperma* has the advantage of being shallow-rooted; this allows bushy clumps to be transplanted here and there with very little disturbance to the sand. Sufficient clumps will prevent green water. Short, thick bunches are good for use in breeding tanks. The plant is highly recommended for use in all tropical aquaria.

Lagarosiphon major

Lagarosiphon major. Somewhat similar to *Elodea*, but it has a harsher foliage which grows in tight whorls. Each leaf curls downward and inward so that its tip touches the leaf below.

Lemna species (Duckweed). Found on most ponds, this miniature-leaved bright green plant floats at the surface of the water in summer and bear minute submerged roots. In the autumn the plants sink to the bottom and remain inert until the following spring, when they start new growth. Duckweed is usually introduced into the aquarium with pond food, and rapidly spreads over the surface, becoming a pest and shutting off much of the overhead light, but most of the growth can be skimmed off with a net and thrown away, or better still, fed to larger barbs, who will obligingly eat every bit.

Limnophila sessiflora (Ambulia). It is a lovely pale green colour, and presents a feathery growth. The leaves radiate from a central stem, making circular fans, which get closer together as they near the top of the plant—this crowns each stalk with a beautiful bunched head. Ambulia requires a fair amount of light, and grows ideally in soft water of a depth of 12″. Rooting should take place in gravel which is free of lime. Looking best if planted in bunches of seven or eight strands, the stems splay outward gracefully, and are stiff enough not to droop in an untidy manner. When grown in quantity it is one of the better plants for counteracting green water.

97

Limnophila sessiflora

Aerial roots appear from long stems and sometimes anchor themselves in the gravel; from any piece thus layered a new plant will grow. Otherwise propagation is by cuttings. The decapitated stems will bring forth new heads.

Being feathery for catching eggs, and soft enough for the fishes to push in among the fronds, the plant is ideal for spawning many of the egg-laying fishes. If the stalks are crushed between the fingers the sap will be found to give off a pungent odour.

Ludwigia mulertii.   This South American species is the best of *Ludwigia*, all of which are really bog plants. Even when growing under congenial conditions in an aquarium, *Ludwigia* prefers to rise above the surface of the water, and may trail over the top rim of the tank, and cascade down the outside. It is an attractive plant, bearing shiny darkish green obovate leaves, the under sides of which are a beautiful pinkish-brown, sometimes being quite rosy. Unfortunately, the central stems are inclined to twist and droop, giving a straggly appearance when several stems are bunched. Moreover, it does not thrive everywhere. Sometimes the leaves rot and drop off, the plant finally succumbing altogether.

Propagation is by cuttings. In comparison with *Hygrophila polysperma* it is not such a good grower, is less robust, and does not hold itself in such a stately manner. There is a red form which, if its tints remain, adds colour to the aquarium; but usually when this plant is removed from its native home its leaves revert to green.

98

Ludwigia mulertii   *Egeria densa*

Marsilea quadrifolia (Australian four-leafed clover).   An aquatic plant that resembles field clover. The small, round leaves, dark green in colour, are carried on thin stems about 2″ high. When in alkaline water the plant spreads rapidly by sending out runners, frequently in a straight line. These give the appearance of a line of posts. Each stem is rooted at the bottom, and if the runners are severed here and there a section of five or six stems, still joined together, may be transplanted. If given too much light the plant stems become so long and straggly that they reach the water surface.

Marsilea quadrifolia

99

Microsorium pteropus (Java fern).   A very tolerant plant that will grow in most tropical aquaria. It grows in a creeping fashion over rocks and logs, with underwater fronds up to 10″ long. It will also grow in damp conditions above the water surface. It is best planted not by burying into the gravel, but by attaching it with loose thread to rocks or logs in the aquarium. Propagation is by division of adult plants or by transplanting tiny plantlets that form on older leaves.

Myriophyllum brasiliense.   The water milfoils supply the aquarist with many species of superb aquarium plants. They are perhaps the most widely used of all in breeding tanks, especially with the smaller egg-laying species. All have long stems from which a profusion of hair-like fronds grow radially. These fronds are in themselves divided, and each bears smaller fronds along its length. Some species attain a height of 2 ft. or more, and end in thick, clustered heads. Nearly all the milfoils are a bright green, but one or two kinds are a coppery red. *M. brasiliense* is typical of the genus, and may be readily identified because the heads at the top of each stem close up at dusk. Propagated from cuttings which quickly take root in the gravel.

Myriophyllum hippuroides.   A fine, dainty plant of bushy growth and pale green in colour. The branched fronds grow opposite each other from a central stem; they are rather widely spaced apart, giving a less heavy appearance than other species of *Myriophyllum*. Best planted in bunches, it does not seem to collect so much thread algæ or harbour such quantities of mulm as other members of this group. Propagation is by cuttings, and under good conditions growth is fairly rapid. *M. hippuroides* is an excellent spawning plant.

Myriophyllum verticillatum.   Being both useful and beautiful, this is the most popular feathery plant used in the aquarium. Up the entire length of the stem dark green fronds radiate thickly, and these terminate in a small, but showy, head. To look at its best several stems should be planted together, when the feathery mass appears to be branches of one bushy plant.

The fine fronds of this plant make it ideal as a spawning medium. Most egg-laying fishes delight in quivering side by side as they push their way through the silky texture of the foliage. The shining eggs deposited in a clump are easily seen, as the network of leaves supports masses of spawn.

Myriophyllum has two drawbacks. In the first place, many algae are apt to adhere or entwine themselves tenaciously round the fronds, and are difficult to remove without doing damage. Secondly, where an aquarium contains much mulm, this may be stirred up if an aerator is used. The sediment then settles and sticks to the foliage, clogging it with unsightly dirt. The green stems become brownish and, if not cleaned, the coating will cut off the light rays. The lack of illumination will make the plant brittle, so that it tends to disintegrate, and may even die.

There is a red variety, but unfortunately it often reverts to green when removed

*Myriophyllum
species*

*Myriophyllum
hippuroides*

*Myriophyllum
verticillatum*

from its natural habitat. If the foliage can be kept red it makes a beautiful contrast to other green plants in the aquarium. Like all the milfoils, propagation is by cuttings.

Najas species. Dainty pale green fronded plants with many side-shoots from the main stem. The spear-shaped leaves form cluster-like heads at the extremities of

Najas species

each branch. They prefer a good light, and will grow either planted or floating, being prolific in either case. Long stems cut in half and bunched together in the gravel form a bushy growth. This plant is very similar in shape to *Didiplis diandra*, but is not so brittle, and its leaves are perhaps paler and thinner.

Nitella gracilis.   It is a rapid grower, especially in alkaline water receiving good light. The pale green fronds sprout sparsely from the central stem, forming a very open network. The plant is somewhat harsh to the touch, and is brittle. Any pieces broken off grow independently without roots. For spawning purposes it can be left to develop a mass of growth at the surface of the water, or several strands can be anchored in the gravel to form a bush.

Nymphaea species

Nuphar and Nymphaea.   There are numerous cold-water *Nuphar* and tropical *Nymphaea* sold to aquarists as aquarium plants. Most of these are unsuitable for tropical aquaria, the former on account of their preference for cooler water, the latter because they require too much space. Nuphars can sometimes be acclimated and look decorative. From a stout rhizome pale green stems shoot out and bear heart-shaped leaves of a bright green. In good light growth is rapid. But this often results in the leaves climbing to the surface, only long stalks being seen through the front glass of the tank. Under poor light the leaves tend to rot round the edges, and are often attacked by a virus which punctures the foliage with many small holes; these enlarge as the perimeter rots away.

Occasionally side-shoots appear on the rhizome, which by now has grown long, stout roots. If the side-shoots are cut off and transplanted many will rot from their open wound. To prevent this trouble the severed shoots should be tied with a piece of string and suspended from the top of the tank. The leaves should remain under water, but the cut rhizome is kept exposed to the air. Oxidation takes place, the cut portion turning brown and becoming sealed. When hardened the cutting may be planted in the gravel.

Pistia stratiotes (Water lettuce).   Possibly the prettiest of the floating plants, appearing like a miniature velvety cabbage lettuce. The spongy, fluted leaves stand above the water, and are covered with fine, silky hairs. The plant produces numerous floating runners; these, under a good light and in a moisture-ladened atmosphere, multiply quickly. Beneath the surface bunches of hairy roots make an ideal spawning ground for fish such as *Aphyosemion australe*; the growth also creates a refuge for newly hatched fry. (See illus. p. 86.)

Riccia fluitans (Crystalwort).   The fronds of this rootless plant are a very bright green; they grow in all directions, and each section is shaped like the letter Y. Crystalwort must have plenty of light; then growth is so prolific that it forms a dense mat, sometimes 2″ or 3″ in depth, at the surface of the water.

Because of its rapid growth the plant is a good oxygenator, becoming literally filled with silver bubbles of this life-supporting gas. The mass of fronds can easily be broken up and transferred to other tanks.

Unfortunately, *Riccia* has two drawbacks. Firstly, it becomes so much entangled with bladderwort and thread algae that it is impossible entirely to remove these from the fronds. Secondly, without artificial illumination the foliage tends to die off in the winter, and is difficult to keep going from one year to another. For breeding purposes the plant is ideal for all egg-layers that spawn near the surface. Furthermore, bubble-nest-building fishes that use plants to bind their bubble nest together utilize crystalwort.

Sagittaria species (Dwarf sagittaria).   This diminutive plant grows numerous short, sword-like leaves, ⅛″ wide and up to 2″ in length. These shoot upward and outward from a crown. Given a fair amount of light, and placed with smaller fishes who will not continually uproot it, numerous runners are sent out, and soon create a miniature bright green lawn in the front of the aquarium. The runners often form a chain of plants; these can be severed and transplanted elsewhere, for they have surprisingly good roots in relation to their size. When this plant thoroughly carpets a breeding tank it makes an excellent refuge for non-adhesive fish eggs which the parents would otherwise devour.

Sagittaria subulata var. gracillima

Sagittaria subulata   *Sagittaria species (dwarf variety)*

Sagittaria subulata. Of all the *Sagittaria*, this is the most common, not only because it grows almost anywhere, but also on account of its average height, which suits most aquaria. The grassy leaves grow to a length of 8″ to 10″, and are about ¼″ wide. They are darkish green in colour, and are thick and tough. If they are closely examined, very thin grains will be seen running across the leaves. It will send out several runners which soon form a dense thicket. Few fishes attack its leaves, and therefore once established it will last a long time and multiply.

Sagittaria subulata var. gracillima. An attractive member of this hardy genus. The grassy, emerald green leaves are thickist in section, and narrow. The foliage, growing from a crown, is carried nearly vertically for two-thirds of its length, then curves outward in a graceful arc. The plant is an exceptionally good grower, under most conditions. Propagation is by runners, and is so prolific that a considerable mass of youngsters will soon develop. Cut runners transplant easily.

Sagittaria sagittifolia

Sagittaria sagittifolia (Giant sagittaria). This is the largest member of this excellent genus of aquarium plants. All are hardy enough to stand acid, neutral, or alkaline water, and grow in either good or poor light. Nature, it would seem, has supplied *Sagittaria* in stock sizes to suit all aquaria, large or small. Even in a single tank they provide the aquarist with beautiful greenery ranging from small in the front, medium in the middle, to tall at the back. This species has broad, thick leaves which splay gracefully upward and outward. Propagation is by runners.

Salvinia species. Floating plants which grow in short lengths, each of which consists of a stem with a row of small leaves on either side. A large species, *S. natans*, has bigger and thicker leaves. The foliage is hairy and varies in colour from medium green to brownish-red. There are short roots. Development is rapid under strong light, and soon the surface of the water is carpeted. Such growth helps to combat green water; otherwise the plant is of little use.

Samolus floribundus (Green water rose). Quite an attractive pale green plant, though more like a young lettuce than a rose. When growth is short the top view resembles a rosette. The leaves sprout from a crown and gradually broaden up their length to a round end. It prefers a medium light and not too high a temperature; even so, it develops slowly. Reproduction is from young plants which grow up through the centre of the rosette. These should be carefully separated and replanted.

Samolus floribundus

Saururus cernuus (Lizard's tail). This attractive plant does well in tropical tanks with a medium light. Stems bearing single leaves rise from the root stock. These may be divided and replanted.

Saururus cernuus

Synnema triflorum (Water wisteria). Also known as *Hygrophila difformis*, this plant is popular. Pale green leaves on short stalks grow from a central stem. The foliage at first is oval in shape, with a slightly serrated edge. However, as it ages the leaves split into fronds, not unlike those of *Ceratopteris thalicroides*, but carried horizontally. The full development of the plant is not yet known by the authors; very probably it will flower above water. Propagation at present is mainly by cuttings, or the aerial roots on the stem often layer the plant naturally.

Synnema triflorum

Vallisneria gigantea. All members of the genus are grassy-leaved plants growing from a crown. Beginners sometimes confuse *Vallisneria* and *Sagittaria*. The leaves of Vallisneria are not so thick in section. They are more ribbon-like, have a more delicate appearance, and are more translucent. If they are examined closely, faint grains are seen running longitudinally through the foliage. Each leaf has a wide central band which is edged on either side by a narrower one.

V. gigantea, as the name implies, is the giant of the family, and is rather too large for the home aquarium. It bears leaves 1¼" wide by 5 or 6 feet in length, and makes an effective background in huge tanks such as those seen in public aquaria. The plant does not like great heat.

Vallisneria spiralis. Well deserves its reputation of being one of the best aquarium plants. The tall, narrow, pale green leaves, ¼" in width, reach a length of 18" to 36", and will trail over the surface of the water if the depth is insufficient. *V. spiralis* likes plenty of light, when it sends out numerous shallow-rooted runners. These soon make a perfect background of graceful growth. Propagation may also be from seeds, the female sending up long, thread-like, spiral flower stems. It is from these that the plant derives its name.

107

Vallisneria tortifolia.   Although fairly common, this is one of the most beautiful grass-like plants. From a crown a cluster of broad ribbon-like leaves of a brilliant green grow to a height of 12″. These are gracefully twisted to form a spiral growth. Contrary to general belief, the plant does not like excessively strong light. Under these conditions the foliage grows pale and spindly, eventually becoming so weak that it fades away altogether. Under medium illumination the leaves remain a deep green and will be ½″ wide, the three longitudinal veining bands becoming very pronounced.

Propagation is by runners; these often extend into a chain of plants. *V. tortifolia* is somewhat crisp, and the leaves will crack across if bent too sharply. It is often alleged that *Vallisneria* and *Sagittaria* are allergic to each other and will not grow in the same tank. The authors, however, are not convinced that this is true, for clumps of both of these plants do well together in some tanks, yet not in others. It would seem that conditions are the governing factor. *Sagittaria* will thrive in a weak light or a strong light, whereas *Vallisneria* abhors extremes in either direction.

Vallisneria tortifolia   *Vallisneria spiralis*

Chapter Eleven

Fishes in General

Fish have been in existence for more than 300 million years — much longer than many other kinds of animal, including Man. During this long evolutionary history different species of fish have developed to live in most of the watery habitats of the world. The result is that there are over 20,000 species of fish alive in the world today, and new ones are still being described by scientists.

Although living fishes can be divided into three broad groupings — the jawless fish or Agnatha, the cartilaginous fish or Chondricthyes, and the bony fish or Osteichthyes — it is species from the latter grouping, bony fishes, that are most often kept by aquarists. This is an amazingly diverse group of fishes, with very varied feeding, breeding and behavioural characteristics. Some of these features will be touched upon here as well as elsewhere in this book, although anyone wishing to pursue the details of ichthyology further should consult the scientific texts in the Reading List.

External covering
Externally most fishes are covered with fine skin, scales, or bony plates. These scales and plates overlap rather like tiles on a roof, the anterior covering the posterior, and forming a complete shield which also presents a streamlined surface to the water. The scales are covered with a protective mucus.

The fins
Usually there are seven fins. Three of these are single (dorsal, anal, and caudal); the remaining four are in two pairs (one pair of pectorals and one pair of ventrals). Some species have the dorsal split into two separate parts, while others possess a small adipose fin situated on the back between the dorsal and the caudal (Fig. 16 overleaf). A few fishes have dorsal, caudal, and ventral fins united into one continuous median fin. The various fins and their functions will now be briefly considered.

The dorsal fin stands up on the fish's back, and may be in one piece or divided into two separate parts. When divided the front portion is called the anterior dorsal, the rear section the posterior dorsal. The front rays, whether single or double, are usually hard and spiny; those in the rear are soft. The dorsal fin or fins act as a stabilizer, and keep the fish upright when cutting through the water.

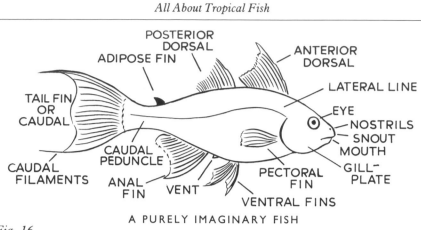

A PURELY IMAGINARY FISH

Fig. 16

The pectoral fins are to be found on each side of the body, behind and just below the gills. The pectorals correspond to human arms, or the forelegs of an animal. In a few species these fins are used as legs, enabling the fish to crawl forward in an irregular manner. The pectorals are used mainly for balance and in swimming upward and downward. These movements are performed by inclining the angle of the leading and trailing edges. This means that when moving forward the water pressure bears against the pectorals, as does the wind against the wings of a bird or an aeroplane, giving lift or dive as required. When paddling the fish moves the pectoral fins forward by flattening them horizontally, like feathering an oar. They are brought back vertically, thereby reacting at a maximum against the water. Moreover, to minimize resistance, these fins are somewhat compressed on the forward stroke, but they are expanded to obtain a greater effect when moving backward.

Another use of the pectorals is seen when a stationary fish desires to turn. The fins are again employed like oars. By moving one forward and the other backward, the fish can pivot on its own axis. Lastly, the pectorals are used as a brake when the fish is slowing down and stopping. This action corresponds to holding a paddle rigidly below the water surface when halting a canoe.

Beneath the fish project the second pair of fins, known as the pelvic or ventral fins. These correspond to the hind-legs of an animal, and some species of fishes use the ventral to cling to and move along flat surfaces. Generally, however, they act as stabilizers, performing a similar function to the anti-roll devices now fitted to each side of the hull of many ships. If one ventral fin is cut off, a fish is unable to swim in an upright position, and may roll over and even turn upside down. A few species use the ventrals as a form of basket for the temporary carrying of eggs.

Behind the ventrals is the anal fin. This acts as a keel to keep the fish in an upright position, and helps to steer it straight when gliding ahead. The forward rays are often hard and spiny, the remainder being soft. In the live-bearing species the anal fin of males undergoes a change. Originally it is fan-shaped like that of a female, but in males at puberty the front rays get thicker and form a pencil-like appendage known as the gonopodium. Normally this is carried with the tip pointing backward, but can be moved at will either sideways or forward. When breeding the gonopodium is pointed forward and the tip inserted into the vent of the female. Spermatozoa are injected, and the ova are fertilized inside the female's body. This subject is dealt with more fully in Chapter 12, on fish-breeding.

Finally, we come to the caudal or tail fin. This is the principal means of locomotion, and acts as a rudder for turning. Beautifully streamlined, the caudal is a perfect instrument for under-water propulsion.

Propulsion

Man's nearest approach to a fish's caudal fin is a propeller, which, though effective, is nothing like so efficient. The rotating blades of the propeller create a pressure which drives the ship forward. Nevertheless, a resistance is set up in front of the propeller which lowers efficiency. Moreover, the spinning blades cause the water to move backward in a spiral. This means that the propeller is pushing on water spiralling in the same direction as the blades; but the push would be greater if the water were turning in the opposite direction. If one stirs water in a bucket at first a resistance will be felt, but as the water gains speed the back pressure falls to practically nil. Now reverse the motion, and the resistance will be found to be very great. The tail fin of a fish operates on this principle. It is continually pushing against the water moving in the opposite direction to the movement of the fin (Fig. 17).

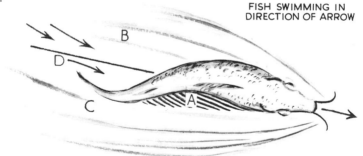

FISH SWIMMING IN DIRECTION OF ARROW

CAUDAL PEDUNCLE OF BODY MOVING FORWARD MEETS LITTLE RESISTANCE BECAUSE OF SLIPSTREAM (A). POWERFUL STROKE OF TAIL FROM B TO C DRIVES FISH FORWARD. AFTERWARDS WATER AT D TENDS TO RUSH IN, GIVING ADDED IMPETUS.

Fig. 17

It may be thought that in swinging from side to side the tail must also encounter a back pressure, but this is not the case, as will be seen in Fig. 17. The slight curve made by the fish's body shown in the shaded portion permits most of the slipstream of the water to pass by when the tail is curved as shown, and no back pressure is encountered. Furthermore, when in this position the rays of the fin are closed, making it narrower. At the same time the upper or lower edge is inclined so that the fin may cut with a minimum resistance through the water. And what is more, the forward movement of the fish would cause a vacuum to form behind it, were it not for the water rushing in to fill the void. This water flowing in behind the fish actually provides a forward impetus.

Now the tail is about to begin the powerful backward stroke. First, the inclined fin is straightened, and the rays are spread out to make as large a surface as possible. It is then thrust backward against the incoming water. This action produces the maximum force to propel the fish forward. At the same time the curve of the body is straightened, and the fish speeds like an arrow with negligible resistance. This process is repeated as the tail moves from side to side.

So great is the impetus of this action that one stroke of the tail can not only propel the fish many times its own length, but frequently enables it to leave the water and to travel many yards through the air. The so-called flying fish does not use its pectoral fins as air-beating wings. They are merely employed to prolong the glide.

Eyes

The eyes are generally large, and so placed that the fish is able to see in all directions. Fishes have no eyelids, and vision is acute. Hence, to avoid startling nervous fish, it is a good idea to turn the room lights on before the tank lights, and to turn off the tank lights before the room lights. This prevents the fish being plunged into sudden darkness or bright light. Some of the mud skippers have eyes perched on the top of their heads. In *Anableps*, the four-eyed fish, the retina is of double formation, so that the lower pair has an all-round under-water view, while the top pair covers aerial vision. A few species which have lived in subterranean streams where there is no light have no eyes, as these organs would be useless.

Nostrils

Between the eyes and the mouth are situated the nostrils. These enable the fish to smell within a limited range — sharks and piranhas soon gather on the scent of blood — and, like human beings, the nasal organs help to provide the sense of taste, which accounts for some particles of food being eaten, while others are rejected.

Mouth

Most fish have large mouths, often equipped with sharp teeth for gripping and biting, though mastication of food is usually performed by bony plates in the throat. Some species have sucker lips to enable them to cling to leaves, or rocks, and browse on algal growth. Besides eating, the mouth is used to draw in water, which is passed through the gills.

Gills

These highly complicated organs, equipped internally with fine capillary tubes, extract the oxygen from the water and pass it into the blood-stream. Some fishes possess a labyrinth organ situated above and behind the roof of the mouth. The species which are endowed with this organ rise to the surface of the water, take a mouthful of air from the atmosphere, and store a certain amount of oxygen in the labyrinth.

A few species are equipped to take a mouthful of air from above the surface of the water, which is then passed through the intestines or into a primitive 'lung'. These, being lined with many capillaries, are able to extract the oxygen. The gills are covered by the operculum or gill-plate, for protection.

Vent

Behind the ventral fins is the anus, through which waste products are discharged. In some species immediately behind the anus is the cloaca, or terminus of the urinary and genital ducts.

Lateral line

Running along each side of the fish is the lateral line. This may be seen on most fishes, and looks as though it had been scratched with a pin. The lateral line is not always straight from gill-plate to caudal peduncle. In some species it takes an upward curve behind the gills, descending again to finish straight through the caudal peduncle. In other species the line will take a downward arc behind the gills.

The lateral line consists of canals which contain sense organs developed in the epidermis. These pick up sound waves travelling through the water and, it is thought, enable fishes to recognize their own species by the frequency of the waves received. Different wave lengths may give warnings of enemies. In some cases vibrations are also passed to the swim-bladder, which acts as an auxiliary hearing organ.

Since fish are sensitive to vibrations in this fashion, it is vital that no-one is allowed to bang on the side of an aquarium.

Colour

There are special pigment-containing cells, called chromatophores, in a fish's skin. These cells are capable of expansion and contraction. This is shown very diagrammatically in Fig. 18 overleaf. If several chromatophores in close proximity begin to expand colour spreads. Suppose all the chromatophores in this part are red; then a red patch will develop. But where the cells are differently coloured a mixture or blending produces another hue. Similarly, when the cells contract a red patch on the fish may shrink into a few brown spots or bars.

Light acting on the visual organs often brings about an expansion or contraction of the colour cells, thus enabling a fish to match its surroundings. Emotions transmitted through the nervous system also affect the colour cells, accounting for brilliant hues at courting time. Fear usually results in a shrinkage of the cells, and a

CELL CONTAINING
PIGMENT CONTRACTED   EXPANDING

FULLY
EXPANDED

Fig. 18   CHROMATOPHORE, GREATLY ENLARGED

corresponding loss of colour. Finally, age and health affect the chromatophores, and are responsible for brilliance, or lack of it.

Another factor of importance regarding coloration is that fishes possess a peculiar reflective tissue. This tissue contains iridocytes formed of guanin, a product of waste excretion. It is deposited in granules in the skin and muscles. Iridocytes are opaque, and highly reflective. Light striking the tissue is reflected back and split up into prismatic colours. This accounts for the brilliant iridescence displayed by most fishes.

Although both chromatophores and iridocytes are present in fishes, where the chromatophores are plentiful the iridocytes are scarce, and vice versa. Chromatophores are abundant on the head, back and upper sides of most fishes. It is here that pigmented coloration is seen. But on the lower sides and belly, chromatophores are scanty and iridocytes abound. Here there is little pigment; what one sees is reflected light split into one or more of the colours of the spectrum. Thus the silvery belly of a fish may shine pink when viewed from one position, yet look pale blue if seen from a different angle.

Internal organs
Internally fishes have a nervous system and the usual organs, such as heart, liver, kidneys, intestines, but to go fully into all these is beyond the scope of this book. A brief reference, however, will be made to the swim-bladder and ova.

Swim-bladder
The function of the swim-bladder is to render the fish, bulk for bulk, of the same weight as the water it displaces. This enables equilibrium to be reached, so that the fish floats without effort at different levels. On rising or sinking it is subjected to an increase or decrease of hydrostatic pressure, bringing about an expansion or contraction of the volume of gas in the swim-bladder. To counteract this, gas is either absorbed from the swim-bladder, or more gas is secreted into it, via the bloodstream. Also in some fish there is a connection between the alimentary tract and the swim-bladder, enabling the volume contained therein to be altered by the fish at the water surface.

Ova

There are two types of fish eggs — pelagic, which float, and demersal, which are larger and heavier, and always tend to sink. The outer membrane may be viscid and adhesive, in which case these eggs stick to rocks or plants, and do not always fall to the bottom. The eggs of some fishes are equipped at one end with several fibres, so that when deposited they stick and hang. When fanned by the parents they wave up and down like seaweed swaying in the tide.

Each ovum has a minute nucleus surrounded by a small mass of protoplasm and a large quantity of yolk, the whole being enveloped in protective membranes. Near the nucleus the egg membranes are perforated by a small aperture. This is so minute that only a single spermatozoon can enter at a time.

When spawning the female discharges her eggs, and the male ejects thousands of spermatozoa into the surrounding water. The majority of these die, since only one is necessary to fertilize each egg. Nevertheless, thousands of spermatozoa are necessary to ensure that one shall find its way through the minute opening of the ovum.

When the head of the sperm penetrates the nucleus the egg is fertilized and undergoes a change; the cells divide and development is initiated. The embryo in the egg lives on the yolk. After emerging, nourishment is provided by the remaining yolk contained in a sac attached to the fry. When this is fully absorbed the baby fish is strong enough to go in search of food. In some fish (e.g. livebearers) fertilization is, of course, internal.

Chapter Twelve

Fish-breeding

The keen aquarist will wish not only to keep fishes but also to breed them. The breeding habits of fish can be considered under a number of broad headings, including:

Livebearers which produce live, fully formed young.

Egg-layers which scatter non-adhesive eggs.

Egg-layers which drop or attach adhesive eggs.

Egg-layers which protect their eggs in a 'bubble nest'.

Egg-layers which carefully deposit and tend their eggs and young fry.

Egg-layers which brood their eggs and young fry in their mouth, eventually releasing free-swimming fry.

Within this chapter the breeding habits of fish will be dealt with in general terms, although specific information can be found in the chapters which follow. Most of this information is based on the personal experience of the authors or their colleagues, although in a few instances breeding suggestions are made on the basis of observations on similar or closely related fishes.

LIVEBEARERS

Since most beginners in the tropical fish hobby start with livebearers, these will be dealt with first. The species are distinguished from the egg-layers in that at the onset of maturity the anal fin of the male livebearer becomes thickened and usually rod-like, the organ being called a gonopodium. When mating the tip is inserted into the vent of the female; spermatozoa are injected, and the eggs fertilized.

The female has the normal-shaped anal fin. Slightly forward of this, inside her body, appears a dark area known as the gravid spot. It is, in fact, equivalent to the womb, but, unlike mammals, the egg of most livebearers is not attached to the mother's body and fed by her direct. Each egg contains an embryo, and is well furnished with nutritive elements on which it feeds during development.

As the eggs incubate the eyes of the fry are sometimes visible through the thin walls of the gravid spot. To accommodate the developing eggs the mother's body expands, becoming deeper and broader. A few days before delivery she develops a bulge below the gills, her outline becoming fairly square in this region, while the gravid spot has enlarged its area. When the young are perfectly formed they lie in a semicircular position and are delivered, usually tail first, one at a time over a period of hours. On birth the fry fall a few inches through the water, but quickly straighten out and, if strong enough, make for cover among the plants. If these are not near by the fry sink to the bottom and take refuge in the sand, mulm, or whatever other cover there may be. They lie motionless for a short time while gathering strength.

The majority of livebearers are born about ¼″ long, and all their fins are formed in the normal shape. The are not only much larger than the newly hatched young of egg-layers, but are also capable of swimming and looking for food and protection. Most newly born live-bearers are large enough not to require infusorians as first food. In a few hours after birth they will take brine shrimp and sifted *Daphnia*.

Mating

The males are persistent drivers, so mating occurs frequently. Where a few livebearers of the same species are kept breeding is inevitable. Any male will serve any female of the same (or even related) species, so that the parents do not pair off. Neither is there a prolonged courtship; the males merely seize any opportunity afforded them, though the females rarely, if ever, make advances.

For the benefit of beginners who are anxious to know whether their specimens are breeding the answer, nine times out of ten, is 'yes'. If any particular male is observed, sooner or later he will be seen darting around a female, his fins spread and quivering. Then, advancing from behind, he will momentarily bring his gonopodium to a forward or sideways position and insert it into the vent of the female. Often the resulting thrust tips her slightly off balance, so that her tail end is tilted upward.

Gestation

The period of gestation depends considerably on temperature, and on the species concerned. Moreover, since mating occurs so often, it is difficult to give the exact number of days from fertilization to birth. Generally speaking, it is about 30 to 35 days at a temperature of 76°F. Experience will be the best guide as to the probable date of birth, but the size of the female and the squareness of her body under the chin give some indication.

Delivery

From the foregoing it will be seen that there is no reliable indication of imminent delivery, so the beginner is advised to remove the female to a separate breeding tank long before she is expected to give birth. It is only necessary to transfer her, the male having completed his function some time before. Furthermore, it is dangerous to handle or disturb a female on the point of delivery. Such a move can cause premature birth, and the young may be born with part of the yolk sac on which they feed not fully absorbed. This frequently causes the death of the fry. Although giving premature birth does not appear to harm the female, the natural cycle has been curtailed, and this can do her no good.

Size of brood
From 8 to 30 or 40 fry may be expected from a young female; medium-sized ones may produce 50 to 100; large fishes can bear from 100 to 250.

Cannibalism
Most fishes large enough to eat others often attempt to do so. This applies equally to the mother, as she is not averse to devouring her brood. In a thickly planted breeding tank a lone female may not be able to find and eat all her own young; some will escape among the plants. To save most of her brood she should be put into a large trap so designed that the fry can easily escape.

Later broods
Many female livebearers may produce three or four, sometimes five, consecutive broods from the original mating, since the female can store sperm in her body. Each family is delivered after a lapse of the normal gestation period.

Selective breeding
If the aquarist desires to produce young live-bearers from a particular male and female he should select a young female while she is still in the virgin state, and isolate her until large enough to mate with the chosen male. As a result she will produce several consecutive broods from this one mating. Had the female been previously mated she might bear a number of families as a result of being served once by a male. Although after her first delivery she may be placed alone with a special male, there is no certainty that her next brood will be from this partner; they could be a second family from the original mating. A female may be allowed to produce her succession of broods; then, if after an interval of at least another month she has delivered no more young, it would be safe to serve her by a selected male.

Cross-mating
Many beginners are under the impression that if they keep in a community a pair of red platys, a pair of blue platys, and a pair of tuxedo platys, each male will mate with his own coloured female. But this, of course, is not the case. Any male of a species will serve any female of the same species, irrespective of colour. Thus if the breeder wishes to produce pure red platys none of his female reds must ever be allowed to come in contact with any other coloured males.

Hybrids
It is possible to produce hybrids intentionally or by accident. Usually the male and female of two different species are brought together, having never seen one of their own kind before. Nevertheless, mating does not always take place, and even though it may occur, young are not necessarily produced. Moreover, often these

hybrids are sterile like mules. It is, however, possible to produce new coloured platys by applying Mendel's laws of inheritance. But to go into genetics here would take up too much space, and those aquarists keen on this subject will find books devoted to it. Here we must point out that it is quite impossible to cross a livebearer with an egg-layer. Often a strange fish appears in an aquarium and the owner is convinced that it is such a cross. But, of course, it must be that the newcomer has hatched from an egg which has been introduced into the tank on a plant or in a net.

Trapping

To save as many young as possible the expectant female should be transferred in a jam-jar and placed into a trap in a separate breeding tank. This tank should be moderately shallow, and well planted. To allow the female ample room for free movement the trap should be capacious—say 8″ long by 4″ wide. It should be suspended so that the depth of water inside is about 4″. The advantage in keeping the water shallow is twofold. Firstly, the hydrostatic pressure is low; secondly, the young have to fall only a few inches to reach safety. Where floating plants are also used these should be placed outside the trap, as the fry tend to hide in the foliage. If this is inside their refuge is insecure.

Removal of female

After giving birth to her brood the female will be quite slim, and the gravid spot considerably shrunken. She may now be removed from the breeding tank, and returned to her normal quarters. She will most likely be hungry, and is sure to be pestered by the males. For these reasons if a spare aquarium is available she will appreciate a short resting period. Unless it is desired to house another female about to deliver young, the trap may also be taken out. It is important to remember that the breeding tank has a limited capacity. If overcrowded with young fishes they will not grow rapidly; on the contrary, too many may result in considerable losses.

Feeding young livebearers

As these fishes are fairly large at birth, feeding is no problem. They will take fine powdered dried foods, liquid fry foods, brine shrimp, *Cyclops*, and sifted *Daphnia*. Only small amounts should be fed. Feeding little and often is better than a large meal once a day. The fry have small stomachs, and cannot hold much. On the other hand, because of their limited capacity the amount eaten does not last long, and replenishment is frequently necessary. A tiny pinch of dried food, as much as will go on the end of a match-stick, should be fed three times a day or, alternatively, a teaspoonful of sifted *Daphnia* or *Cyclops* twice daily, since these crustaceans hop about in the water where they can easily be seen and caught by the fry. Furthermore, most will be devoured, and the risk of fouling the tank is minimized. To sift *Daphnia* they are netted from the can in a fine muslin net, which is then suspended in the fry tank for a few minutes. Only the finest *Daphnia* will pass through the mesh; the bigger ones remaining in the net can be fed to larger fishes in another aquarium.

Growth of fry

Given normal healthy conditions and correct feeding, the fry should double their length in a month. By then there will be signs of sex development in some cases. When line breeding to bring out a certain characteristic the sexes should be segregated as soon as possible in order that, say, a virgin daughter may later be mated back to her father. Likewise, the choicest son can be crossed back to his mother.

The baby fishes may be returned to the community tank only when they are large enough not to be eaten by the bigger occupants. This may mean sorting the babies into two sizes, the smaller ones being put back in the breeding tank. It is often surprising to find that may of the smaller fry, suspected of being runts, now put on rapid growth. This is because they have more room and are able to receive their full share of the food which was previously grabbed by their larger brothers and sisters.

Sexing and sex changing

It is often thought that once young fishes begin to mature they cease to grow. This is not necessarily so. Nevertheless, those which are the last to develop the gonopodium often become the biggest. The aquarist should give adequate food and space in order to promote early growth.

Some cases are on record of females which, after bearing young, have developed into males, although they are likely to be sterile rather than reproductively active.

EGG-LAYERS

We now come to the numerous species of tropical fishes which are oviparous, or egg-layers. Not all behave in the same manner: some scatter non-adhesive eggs and, save for eating as many as possible, take no more interest in them. Others drop semi-adhesive eggs. Several build bubble-nests, and generally the males tend the eggs and ward off enemies. Certain species carefully place and fan their eggs, male and female guarding the young. Finally, there are those which lay eggs and after fertilization take them up and incubate them in their mouths.

Because the newly hatched fry of many of the egg-laying fishes are so minute, and need special care and microscopic food, many beginners—and for that matter more experienced aquarists—are reluctant to try their hand at breeding them. It is well-nigh impossible to go wrong with livebearers. No aquarist, except those who line breed, feels that he has achieved much until he has raised some of the beautiful egg-laying species. Once having done so, however, his confidence is raised, and he is spurred on to tackle the more difficult ones.

The authors feel that many aquarists are deterred from becoming breeders by the fear of failure resulting from lack of knowledge. They imagine that such a venture is bound to be beyond their capabilities. But every expert had to make a start, and this comforting thought should help to encourage those who aspire to become skilled breeders. Unlike the pioneers who had nothing to guide them, the breeder of today can reconstruct the conditions which have proved successful in the past, and thereby follow the path already partially cleared in front of him.

It is the object of this book not only to describe the various species for recognition, but also to assist those aquarists who would like to breed the fishes of their choice. Nearly all breeding methods described in the following pages are from the authors' first-hand experience, and have proved successful. It is hoped that the information given will be helpful, and enable the reader to achieve his objectives.

Many of the egg-layers are easy to breed. Providing they are mature enough, in superb condition, and given a clean and properly planted tank, they will usually spawn within 24 hours. Some species require special soft water with a low pH value before they can be induced to spawn. Even so, these conditions can be created. A few fishes respond with artificial aids such as flower-pots, pieces of slate, etc. These are readily obtainable, and are inexpensive.

Since the newly hatched fry are so small, microscopic live food has to be provided, and to be plentiful by the time the fry hatch out. It must, therefore, be started well in advance. And it is the provision of this food which deters many aquarists from breeding egg-layers. Producing microscopic food, however, is not as difficult as may be imagined. If the instructions given in this book are followed the problem can be surmounted.

With oviparous fishes it is preferable to house males and females in separate tanks. This segregation allows the females to become full of roe. Where males are present they may drive the females, who may frequently scatter a few eggs, thereby remaining slim. Such eggs, of course, have no chance of hatching, since they are immediately eaten by the other fishes in the tank. When a chosen pair are deliberately placed in a breeding tank the male, not having seen a female for some time, is all the more excited and anxious to start the courtship.

It is essential to have a separate breeding tank for each species. There are, however, occasions when two males and three females of one species may be placed together in a breeding tank and a greater number of fertilized eggs obtained. Other details are mentioned either under the family concerned or the individual species.

Spawning the egg-scatterers or egg-droppers (particularly barbs and characins)
It is impossible to give one formula for spawning all the various species of egg-scatterers. Some spawn in floating plants, others in rooted thickets, some species spawn over a period of days while others complete the act in a matter of hours. There are eggs which hatch in 24 hours, while others take several days, and some even weeks or months. Beginners are advised to start with the easier fishes first. Many barbs and characins spawn easily and hatch quickly, particularly *Barbus conchonius*, *Barbus nigrofasciatus*, and various *Hyphessobrycon* tetras, so with these in mind we give a typical example to show the procedure likely to prove successful.

For most barbs and characins a breeding tank approximately 24″ long by 8″ wide by 8″ high should be set up as follows. On the bottom is placed a 1″ layer of well-washed fine sand or gravel. Now the tank should be filled with clean water (two-thirds rain, one-third tap) giving a pH of approximately 6·8 and a hardness of

100 p.p.m. Temperature 78°-80°F. Numerous short, well-washed plants should be inserted in the sand. Near each end there should be a clump of *Myriophyllum*, *Ambulia*, or *Cabomba* standing higher than the rest of the foliage. This arrangement allows free swimming space in the middle section of the aquarium.

Assuming that the sexes have been kept in separate tanks, a deep-bodied female should be selected. Besides being deep, her belly when seen from the front should resemble a broad letter U, not a V. The best-coloured male should be chosen as mate, and the two placed in the breeding tank in the afternoon about an hour before sunset. This gives them time to become acquainted with each other and settle down in their new surroundings before darkness falls. With the dawn the pair should no longer feel strange, and as the light increases the male will start to court his mate.

His colour heightens, and with fully spread fins he shows off his beauty, which the female rarely ignores. He will butt her with his nose and generally excite her. She will respond by intensifying her colour, extending her fins, and nudging and nosing him. Now and again she may coyly swim away but the male, as intended, will follow closely in order not to lose her. When she is completely worked up she may even chase after the male. Excitement grows until the pair, cavorting in the clear space in the centre of the tank, work their way towards one of the bushy clumps of plants at either end. Now, side by side, the couple tremble together, the female expelling a few eggs, and the male discharging his sperm. The eggs, oval in form as they leave her body, absorb the sperm-laden water and swell to a spherical shape. Thus fertilized, they fall among the feathery fronds of the plants.

The breeding pair continue to spawn until the female has expelled all her eggs, which may take an hour or two, or sometimes more. She is then very thin, and the male likewise considerably leaner. The excitement being over, their attention turns to food, and both parents may start looking for eggs to eat. If the aquarist is present, he should remove both fish and place male and female separately to recuperate from their exertions. After a good feed and a rest, the male may be returned to the original male tank and the female to her former quarters.

If the aquarist has not been up early enough to witness the spawning, he should at least be about before all the eggs are eaten. His first move is to approach the tank stealthily and see how the couple are behaving. If spawning, they should be left alone and inspected again later. On the other hand, should the fish not be spasmodically trembling together the female should be scrutinized, and should she appear much slimmer the two fish should be removed forthwith. Afterwards, with a magnifying glass, some eggs may be observed among the plant fronds. If about 50 eggs are visible the spawn is likely to be three times this figure, as many more eggs will have dropped out of sight among the plants, while others have nestled between the grains of sand and are hidden from view.

Many beginners ask what fish eggs look like, and no doubt it helps when one knows what one is looking for. Eggs are about the size of a pin's head, and the colour is that of clear plastic. They should not be confused with air bubbles, which, though of the same size, shine like silver. On close examination each circular egg will be seen to have a smaller nucleus inside, though this is not always central. Some eggs may turn opaque white. These may be infertile and eventually become covered with fungus; ignore them, they will not affect the rest. The remainder start to develop, usually within 12 hours, when the eyes of the embryo may be seen. Later, the unhatched fry may be observed making an occasional jerky turn inside the egg.

The following morning, 24 hours after spawning has occurred, minute babies may be found hanging from the under sides of plant leaves or on the walls of the aquarium. These fry with black eyes appear like splinters of clear glass, and can sometimes only be seen as the light shines through their bodies. Each is hanging perpendicularly with the head uppermost. They remain in this position for nearly 24 hours, occasionally shifting a fraction of an inch. During this time they feed on the egg-sac on their bellies. After absorbing the nourishment provided, the fry have gained a little strength. They drop through the water and struggle upward again, to hang beneath the foliage. In a short while some may be seen darting here and there and coming to rest under a horizontal plant leaf. At this stage they are extremely difficult to see, and many a brood has been lost as the aquarist, believing that all have died and disappeared, clears out the tank. Actually the fry are merely taking cover, for in the wild state many would be gobbled up if they carelessly flaunted themselves in mid-water.

Once free-swimming, the babies need food, and since they are too frightened and too weak to go far in search of it, infusorians must be plentiful enough to come to them. If *Ampullaria* snails are not permanently kept cultures of infusorians should have been started several days previously, and by now be thick. Two 2-lb jam-jars will be required daily, one in the morning, the other in the afternoon. Most beginners starve their fry, and lose large numbers.

Through pouring in two jam-jars of infusoria daily, naturally the water level in the tank rises until it is necessary to siphon some off. To prevent fry being sucked up the tube a fine nylon bag should be used as a strainer. This should be placed in the tank, and the siphon end held inside the bag. By spreading the fingers the bag is kept away from the siphon.

After a week the babies will have grown big enough to take newly hatched brine shrimp, so this should be available when required. About 10 days later microworms may be given, and when the young fish have reached a length of ¼" sifted *Daphnia*, *Cyclops*, and fine dried food should be served.

So far we have assumed that the selected pair have spawned quickly and the eggs hatched, but this is not always the case. If spawning has not occurred within 3 days it is generally useless to keep the male and female together longer. Usually the disappointed male becomes bad-tempered and bites, buffets, or injures the female. The aquarist should be on the look-out for this during the three days, and the fish separated before harm is done. Should the female still be fat and full of roe, another male may be tried. But generally it pays to change both fish for another pair. Breeders that do not spawn on the first morning may require food; this, however, must not be allowed to contaminate the sand or the water. *Daphnia* or other pond foods should not be fed, as these may also introduce into the tank *Hydra* which will devour most of the fry that hatch later. It is far better to feed a few small pieces of shrimp or prawn, which cannot cause trouble. Any uneaten particles are easily removed. The tank must be clean and free of snails before further breeding attempts are made. Should all the eggs turn white and fungus, the reason is most probably bacteria. Try again with cleaner water. Rarely are the parents sterile, though repeated failures may prove this to be the case.

Danios

All are prolific breeders, but avid egg-eaters. For spawning a suitable-sized tank would be the standard 24"×8"×8". The bottom should be covered with clean, coarse gravel, and very thickly planted with the feathery-type plants and young Indian ferns. It should be filled with water of a pH value of 7·0 to a depth of 3" or 4". Like all other egg-laying fishes, breeding-sized males should be kept in a separate tank from females. In the late afternoon the deepest- and roundest-bellied female is selected and placed in the tank with a suitable male. The pair rarely fail to spawn next morning, but unless the aquarist is up early the parents will eat many eggs. If the female looks slimmer both fish should be removed at once. The eggs, no larger than a pin-head, are difficult to see, since they are non-adhesive, and drop through the plants into the crevices of the gravel. At a temperature of 78°F. they take 3 or 4 days, or even longer, to hatch, and many a good spawning has been thrown out by beginners who are usually informed that the hatching period is 24 hours. Failing to see any young, they clear the tank or put out another pair. Either the eggs are discarded or the new fish devour the young as they hatch.

After hatching the fry may be seen hanging from plant leaves or on the glass sides of the aquarium. They are so small that they require infusoria as first food. Growth, however, is rapid, and soon larger nourishment can be given. The babies should reach 1" in length in about 8 weeks.

Protecting the eggs

Some aquarists favour the use of traps in unplanted tanks. The traps permit the eggs to fall through slots or openings which are small enough to prevent the passage of the parents. These traps take various forms. Some are merely clean pebbles or glass marbles in layers at the bottom of the tank. But occasionally one of the spawning fish manages to wriggle down and get stuck, so perhaps a fine wire or nylon mesh, ⅛", cut to fit the tank, is better. The trap is lowered on to two pieces of slate, one at each end of the aquarium, so that it is raised about 1" off the bottom. Care must be taken to ensure that the parents cannot squeeze down between ill-fitting sides. Another advantage of mesh is that some plant-stalks can be inserted through the gauze and stand upright. This arrangement makes the fish feel more at home than in a bare tank. Some aquarists construct a large trap, having a base of glass or plastic bars, the whole being immersed in the breeding tank. But very often with these methods a high proportion of the eggs fungus and fail to hatch. In view of this, perhaps a clean, well-planted tank is the best in the end.

Egg-laying tooth carps, killifish and their kin

In the majority of cases the breeding tank need not be large, our standard

24″×8″×8″ being quite suitable for most species. This should be filled with dark brown peaty water, with a pH between 6·0 and 6·6, and a hardness of only 50-75 p.p.m. In addition, a teaspoonful of salt should be added to every 2½ gallons of water used.

The bottom of the tank should be covered with a thin layer of crumbled waterlogged peat, and a good thick mat of lesser bladderwort or *Riccia* should float on the surface of the water. Alternatively, the tank may be filled to a depth of 1″ with lime-free sand, and then filled with old soft rain-water, planted with a few grassy plants such as *Sagittaria*, *Vallisneria*, *Cryptocoryne*, and one or two bunches of *Ambulia* or *Cabomba*. Given these conditions, most species show themselves to be prolific spawners, and details of their precise spawning habits can be found in the relevant chapter later in the book. The young when hatched are large compared with most egg-layers, the greater number being able to take brine shrimp and sifted *Daphnia* straight away. They enjoy live foods, but most can be trained to take dried food, which after a time they accept with relish. The fry grow fairly rapidly. When they are half-grown the peaty water in which they are living may gradually be made less acid, and the pH increased, until they are happily conditioned to the average water found in most aquarists' tanks. Any sudden change from acid to alkaline conditions or vice versa will result in a folding of the fins, lack of appetite, lethargy, and, unless corrected, may soon end in death.

Corydoras catfish
Most of the genus are not difficult to breed provided they are large enough, in good condition, and given the correct requirements. In the past a mistaken idea has been circulated, and as a result it is now believed that to spawn these fishes the bottom of their tank should contain a good layer of mulm. This is quite wrong. Mulm with minute particles of food in it contains bacteria, and since the eggs take 5 or 6 days to hatch they are open to attack during the whole of this time. Should bacteria or infusorians puncture the shell of the egg, water will enter and it will fungus. When this fact was pointed out the adherents of the mulm theory then maintained that the mulm hid the youngsters and saved them from being devoured. But since the parents do not eat, fan, or look after their eggs, there is no point in leaving them in the tank after spawning.

Many aquarists are unable to distinguish sex differences in these fishes. Generally speaking, females are slightly larger than males, and their bellies are rounder below. In some cases the dorsal fin of the male is considerably more pointed than the female's. The best check, however, is to put the fish into a glass jar and look down on them from above. Males will be found to be torpedo-shaped; that is to say, from behind the gills they taper evenly to the tail. A female, however, is more diamond-shaped; in other words, she widens behind the gill-plates, and only tapers off again about half-way along her length (see Fig. 19 overleaf). Once sexed, breeding fish should be kept apart, males in one tank, females in another. They should be well fed on chopped earthworm. As the mating urge approaches many species begin to take on a slightly rosy hue from the belly to the anal fin.

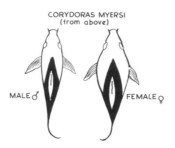

CORYDORAS MYERSI
(from above)

MALE ♂   FEMALE ♀

Fig. 19

For breeding a tank 24″×12″×12″ should be set up. It should have a 1″ layer of well-washed sand, and be filled with fresh tap-water, pH 7·2-7·4, hardness 150-180 p.p.m., temperature 70-72°F. In the tank should be planted a few *Cryptocoryne* and one or two broad-leafed *Sagittaria*. When all is ready a pair of fish may be introduced just before dusk. A good couple will start spawning next morning, and may continue to do so for several hours. Should they not mate after 2 or 3 days, another pair should be tried.

When spawning the male seems over the female's back and head, and the pair continue to keep in close proximity. After a while the male seems in front of the female, hovering just above her face. She rises slightly, puts her mouth to his vent, and receives some sperms. She then swims away, examining plant leaves or the walls of the aquarium to find a suitable spot to place her eggs. During this time she clasps her ventral fins together and expels four or five eggs into the pocket formed by her fins. Once satisfied with a depositing place, she spits out the sperms and, opening her ventral fins, sticks the adhesive eggs on to the plants among the sperms. She may even do this on the under sides of thin leaves. While performing this act her swim-bladder keeps her poised upside down in the water, so the leaf does not have to bend with her weight as might be expected. She then returns to the sand, and the male immediately starts to court her again. More sperm is taken in her mouth, more eggs are deposited, until some 300-400 are literally plastered on most of the leaves and in patches on the glass sides of the tank.

Once the pair separate and move about the aquarium singly spawning is over, and the couple should be removed. Even though the aquarist has taken pains to provide complete cleanliness, a few bacteria and infusorians infect the tank over the ensuing days. It is advisable, therefore, to eliminate the unwanted organisms, perhaps by adding about five drops of 5 per cent. aqueous solution of methylene blue.

In 2 or 3 days numerous eggs will have turned white, but the aquarist should not despair, for in another 50-70 hours many of the eggs, difficult to see because they have not turned white, will hatch. Very probably 100 or more fry will develop, though possibly only one-tenth of these are initially visible. Newly hatched brine shrimp and microworms should now be fed to the babies, sparingly at first, and more generously when additional fry are seen. The young fish grow rapidly, and should reach ½″ in length in 6 weeks.

Bubble-nest-builders

Many of the anabantoids, like gouramis and fighting fish, are bubble-nest builders. Nest-building is achieved as follows. The male goes to the surface of the water and takes in a mouthful of air. Breaking this into tiny bubbles, he coats each with saliva, and spits them out. They float to the surface, but, due to their filmy covering, do not burst immediately. The process is repeated continually, until in a few hours the nest may measure several inches in diameter, and be mounded up in the centre to a height of ½" or more. Some species construct the nest solely of bubbles; others reinforce the structure with bits of plant. A forceful male may even build such a nest in a community tank. He will monopolize one top corner, and all other fishes will be driven away from this area. Once he starts to build he will only break off to visit his mate for further excitement and encouragement.

Eventually, when the nest is complete, the male entices his mate underneath the canopy of bubbles. Here, after some show and courtship, she will prod him in the flanks with her nose. The male then curves his body towards her and envelops her from slightly below. This is called the nuptial embrace. His curved position causes him to roll over on his side, while the female, gripped in his embrace, is tilted upside down. His grip tightens, and with quivering fins he squeezes her until she releases several eggs. At the same time he exudes his sperm so that the spawn is fertilized. In a few seconds the male relaxes his grip, and slowly the female drops away from his embrace. As she does so she rights herself from her upside-down position, and the eggs lodged between her fins start to sink slowly. Either the males alone, or more often both fish together, swim down and gather every falling egg in their mouths. These are surrounded with bubbles of air coated with saliva, and spat out beneath the nest, where they float. After a little more display the male and female re-embrace and spawning continues. Usually some 250-300 eggs are finally placed in the nursery; the male then takes charge. His first act is to drive away any fish he thinks may eat the spawn. More often than not his mate is the first to be attacked. Having cleared his domain, he continues to keep his nest in repair; as fast as any dilapidation takes place he makes good the damage with fresh bubbles.

In 24-30 hours the young hatch. Bursting their way out of the imprisoning bubbles, they tend to sink; but the ever-attentive male picks them up in his mouth and blows them back beneath the nest, where they hang in masses tail downward. If, as is presumed, all this has taken place in a community tank it is now time for the aquarist to intervene. For once these tiny fry are free-swimming they will spread all over the tank. It is quite impossible for the male to guard all the hatch at once. This means that they will be eaten by the other inhabitants of the aquarium. Taking a wide-mouthed jar, the aquarist should press the base below the surface of the water. Tilting the mouth towards the nest, the jar should be pressed slowly down until the nest and all the hanging bunches of young are drawn into the jar. Very few fry will be lost at this stage. The contents are then emptied into a breeding tank containing water which is chemically similar and of the same temperature as that in the aquarium.

In a further 48 hours the fry will be free-swimming, and must be fed copiously with fine infusorians. An occasional feed of hard-boiled yolk of egg squeezed through a piece of fine muslin is advisable. In yet another 10 days brine shrimp may be added to the diet. Later on, when the fry are ½" long, *Cyclops* and sifted *Daphnia* may be given. The babies feed in mid-water, and food like microworms will be snapped up as they sink; but once the worms reach the bottom of the tank they are mostly ignored. Such foods are not strongly recommended.

The above procedure applies when a pair of bubble-nest-builders spawns unexpectedly in a community tank. The method is not the best under ordinary circumstances. It is preferable to select pairs and put them into a breeding tank. This should be about 24"×12"×10". An inch of fine sand is placed on the bottom before filling with water, which should have a pH of 6·8-7·2, and a hardness of 100-150 p.p.m. Clumps of foliage are planted here and there so that the female may take refuge.

Where the male is aggressive it is a wise plan to place a female bulging with roe in a large glass jar and float this in one corner of the breeding tank, the male being allowed the freedom of the aquarium. A few floating plants may be needed in the construction of his nest, so these should be supplied. He is able to see his mate, and the sight of her excites him and prompts him to build a nest, but during this time he is unable to damage his partner. Only when the nest is complete should she be lifted with a net out of her jar and placed in the tank. In all probability the ardent male may be too impetuous, and unless the female responds immediately he is apt to feel frustrated and bad-tempered. If this occurs he will attack her and tear her fins. The pair should be given time to adjust themselves, when all may be well. But should the female be insufficiently worked up she is likely to be damaged. In such a case after an hour or two her fins will be torn, and she will be too scared to spawn. She should therefore be caught and returned to the safety of her jar. A further attempt may be made the next day, or the one after.

Once spawning has taken place the white eggs may be seen among the silvery bubbles, and the female will have been driven well away from the nest. She should now be placed in the jar and returned to her usual tank. Some males will raise and protect their fry until they are beyond the need of parental care; but it is often safer to remove the male when the babies have just become free-swimming. Feeding should be carried out as detailed above.

CICHLIDS

Cichlids are not difficult to breed, but the procedure differs slightly where large, medium, and dwarf species are concerned. Below is given a general description covering these groups. Where individual species differ from the general, details will be found under the fishes concerned. For the aquarist's convenience we will divide the family into three groups. These are:

    (i) Large cichlids.
    (ii) Medium cichlids.
    (iii) Dwarf cichlids.

Large Cichlids
The above-mentioned grow much too big for the average aquarist, and only

specialists with large tanks can house them satisfactorily to maturity. These giants live 5-8 years or more; they will not usually tolerate plants, tearing them out by the roots. This means that their tank is unlikely to remain clear unless filters are kept in constant operation. In place of plants they should be given large rocks, round which they may dodge when attacked. Alternatively, beneath the ends of the rocks they like to dig depressions in the sand, where they lie when resting. Finally, it is usually on some flat surface of these boulders that they place their spawn when breeding.

Even a large tank 6' × 2' × 2' will hold only six or seven of the biggest cichlids. Should a pair decide to spawn they may insist on having the aquarium entirely to themselves, inflicting such damage on the other occupants that the aquarist is forced to find an alternative home for these.

Mating

Quite a number of cichlids refuse to accept a mate chosen for them by their owner. If not allowed to pair naturally they may kill the partner offered. Natural selection usually means keeping 4 or 5 of the same species, so that choice is available. This is not only initially costly, but all the fish have to be kept to maturity, and then the unwanted ones discarded. Mating can sometimes be arranged by placing a pair of fish in a tank divided by a sheet of glass, allowing them to see each other, and yet do no harm. In a few days, when the pair have become familiar, the glass partition is removed, but the aquarist must watch and intervene should they prove incompatible. In this case the male will chase the female, biting her sides and ripping her fins till she cowers in some corner. If the pair are not separated she is likely to be killed. On the other hand, the couple may show off to each other, and then, gripping lips, tug and wrestle together. Providing the female does not flee, all may be well.

Spawning

Now the pair select a spawning-site, usually on some flat rock. This they clean with their mouths, and both male and female show protruding tubes just in front of the anal fin. In females this tube, called the ovipositor, is thicker and blunter-ended than is the male's counterpart. Having cleaned the rock thoroughly, spawning takes place. The female deposits eggs one after another in rows. On completing a line she moves away, and her mate comes in and fertilizes them. The process continues until some 300-1500 or more eggs are laid. Both parents now take turns to fan the spawn, which hatches some days later. Once the fry are wriggling a depression is dug in the sand, and the babies are transferred one by one to the new site, having been thoroughly washed in the parent's mouth while in transit. When the fry are free-swimming it is a wonderful sight to see how the parents guard them. As dusk approaches the cloud of youngsters is gathered in a tight cluster for greater protection. When these are ½″ long the parents may be removed and the fry reared on their own.

129

Medium Cichlids

With regard to the medium-sized cichlids, most of these will live in a large community tank with other big species. They will usually not tear out plants until urged to spawn. But as this occurs quite frequently, uprooting vegetation and digging pits in the gravel becomes a nuisance.

Mating and Breeding

Mating is similar to the large cichlids just described, though spawning often occurs in flower-pots, or on rocks. Generally it is advisable to remove the males after spawning, as occasionally they become aggressive, and may kill their mates. Alternatively, the rock or flower-pot on which the eggs are deposited may be removed to a bare tank and the eggs hatched separately. Aeration must be provided, and a few drops of 5 per cent. methylene blue added to the water to prevent fungus.

Dwarf Cichlids

Lastly we come to the dwarf cichlids. These are the most colourful, will live happily with other small to medium-sized fishes, will enjoy any food, and breed easily. Unfortunately, some rarely live longer than 2 years. Mating is not so difficult, most males accepting any female offered, providing she is full of roe. Spawning nearly always occurs in flower-pots. Having laid their eggs, both parents may be removed, but aeration must be employed to circulate the water normally provided by the fanning action of the adults. Five to seven drops of 5 per cent. aqueous solution of methylene blue should be added to every 2 gallons of water to kill bacteria. This method not only permits the eggs to hatch, but means that the pair can be spawned again in a short period. In our experience we find quite a number of species which, instead of spawning conveniently inside the pot, tunnel away the sand beneath and spawn on its under side. Here the eggs are out of sight

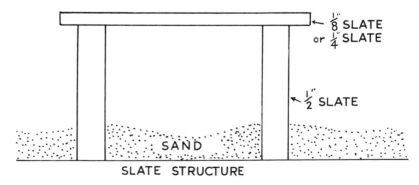

SLATE STRUCTURE

NOTE: UPRIGHT WALLS BEDDED THROUGH SAND AND STANDING ON BOTTOM OF TANK

Fig. 20

unless the pot is lifted and examined daily; but such a disturbance is likely to deter the pair from breeding.

In order to surmount this difficulty the authors use a simple slate structure. This consists of two walls, roughly 3″ square, cut from ½″ slate. A roof about 6″ long by 3″ wide is made from a piece of ¼″ slate. The two end walls are placed on edge near the centre of the planted breeding tank about 5″ apart. These must be bedded down through the sand until they stand firmly in an upright position on the bottom of the tank. The roof is then laid on top of the two walls (Fig. 20). The breeders are unable to dig underneath any part of this structure, and wherever their eggs are deposited the spawn is visible.

Spawning usually occurs on the inside face of one of the walls. Now the parents are removed, also the roof and blank wall. The wall coated with eggs is next turned to face the viewer, and an aerator tube placed under it so that the bubbles rise ½″ in front of the eggs. Five to seven drops of methylene blue are now added to the water. In a few days the eggs hatch and the young may be seen wriggling. Two or three days later the fry drop to the sand, and in a further 48 hours some begin to hop about. Do not feed until the whole batch leaves the sand and swims like a cloud of midges through the water. At this stage the fry are large enough to take brine shrimp and microworms. The methylene blue in the water will by now have faded, and the babies should be fed twice daily.

Chapter Thirteen

Live-bearing Fishes

FAMILY EXOCOETIDAE

These quaint fishes (which include the half-beaks), of which there are many species, all come from the Far East. They have tubular bodies and a long, protruding lower jaw. The upper jaw is pointed, but usually extends only about half the length of the lower. The jaws are rigid, but can be broken and snapped off when fighting, or if the fish hits a solid object head on when travelling at speed. Careless handling may also damage this magnificent feature. Many of the species come from coastal areas; some inhabit brackish water, others live in fresh.

These fishes have been used by natives for fighting, wagers being placed on the outcome. Two males will often spar and interlock their jaws, writhing and twisting in an endeavour to throw the opponent off balance, tire him out, or even break his jaws. Frequently no damage is done, as the loser quits the ring before the knock-out blow. The fish below are not generally aggressive, though they will snap up and swallow young fry. Females when giving birth are very cannibalistic. They should therefore be trapped or placed in thickly planted aquaria containing feathery foliage, as well as a good layer of floating plants such as *Riccia*.

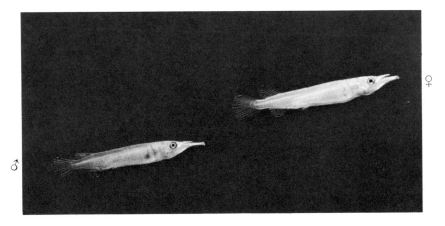

Dermogenys pusillus – Half-beak

India, Burma, Thailand, Indonesia   ♂ 2½"   ♀ 3"   Community
DIET: Mosquito larvae, Daphnia, White worms, Floating dried food
SWIMS: Upper half of tank

This is the most commonly imported species, and is slightly smaller and chubbier than most. In comparison with other members of the family the lower jaw is shorter; often it is carried at a slightly drooping angle.

The addition of one teaspoonful of salt per gallon of water seems to be appreciated.

The body is a silver-grey, the sides being paler and the belly nearly white, though prismatic light produces tints of blue or green. Such colouring may serve as camouflage, because the species prefers to lie immediately below the water surface.

At first glance the males and females look alike, but the anal fin on the male is split. The forward portion is slightly thickened, and serves as a gonopodium, though the rear part of this fin is rounded. Males have a bright red patch in the lower front part of the dorsal fin, a red streak in the lower jaw, and black tips to the ventral fins.

Breeding. *Tank: 24"×8"×8". pH: 7·2-7·4. Hardness: 150-180 p.p.m. Temperature: 78°F. Produces live young. Method: trap female. Young: 20-50. Freeswimming: at birth. Food 1st week: brine shrimp, Cyclops. 2nd week: sifted Daphnia, fine dried food.*

The females are very inclined to eat their young, so the mothers should be trapped in shallow water near the surface. Otherwise, a female may give birth and immediately turn round and snap up the baby before it has fallen an inch. Young are delivered over a period of days.

Hemirhamphus pogonognathus – Slim half-beak

India, Burma, Thailand, Indonesia   ♂ 2¹/₂"   ♀ 3¹/₂"   Community
DIET: Small live food, dried food   SWIMS: Upper half of tank

This half-beak, in comparison with the last-mentioned, has a longer and straighter lower jaw, the tip of which ends in a flattened nodule. The body is longer and slimmer and has more colour.

There is a silvery blue sheen on the sides with three bluish dashes between the gill-plates and the anal fin. The dorsal, caudal, and ventral fins have their edges tinted with reddish-orange, which varies in intensity according to the mood of the fish and the background against which it is seen.

The males are generally smaller and slimmer than the females. Sex can be ascertained from the shape of the anal fin.

Except when scared, the fish prefers to lie just under the surface of the water, making quick darts for any tasty morsel which catches its eye.

Breeding. Tank: 24"×8"×8". pH: 7·0-7·2. Hardness: 120-160 p.p.m. Temperature: 78°F. Produces live young. Method: trap female. Young: 20-50. Freeswimming: at birth. Food 1st week: brine shrimp, Cyclops. 2nd week: sifted Daphnia, fine dried food.

Females of this species are not so inclined to eat their own young; these are delivered over a period of days.

FAMILY POECILIIDAE

The majority of this family of live-bearing tooth carps come from the south of North America, Mexico, the West Indies, Venezuela, Colombia, Guyana, Ecuador, and Brazil. The family is very adaptable to aquarium life. The majority are hardy, of medium size, easily bred, and will eat most foods. Furthermore, these fishes do not require excessive space or heat; generally they are not aggressive.

Gambusia affinis – Mosquito fish

Virginia, Florida ♂ *1½"* ♀ *2¼" Non-community* DIET: *All foods*
SWIMS: *Mid-water*

Due to its unpleasant habit of nipping the fins of other fishes this fish has lost its chances of remaining popular. It likes live food, especially mosquito larvae, and for this reason the fish have been exported to malaria-infested countries to eat the larvæ of the pest. When live food is absent *Gambusia* attacks small fishes, and has the effrontery to nip some species larger than itself.

The body colour is mainly grey, dusted with black spots and blotches. A few specimens are so thickly marked that they are almost black. These, being the more highly prized, are sometimes sold as a distinct species, *Gambusia holbrookii*, although they are really just a sub-species. A few almost black males are found in nature; it is from these that most of the best stocks are bred.

The male is considerably smaller than the female.

Breeding. Tank: 24"×8"×8". pH: 7·0-7·2. Hardness: 150-180 p.p.m. Tempera-

ture: 78°F. Produces live young. Method: trap female. Young: 20-50. Free-swimming: at birth. Food 1st week: brine shrimp, grindal worms. 2nd week: sifted Daphnia, dried food.

More young escape being eaten if the female is trapped and removed after delivering her brood.

Girardinus falcatus – Yellow belly

Cuba   ♂ *1½"*   ♀ *2"*   *Community*   DIET: *All foods*   SWIMS: *Upper half of tank*

A pleasant, peaceful little fish which will withstand most conditions, and is ideal in a community tank.

The overall colour is pale gold set off by an intensely bright blue iris to the eye.

Males are considerably smaller than females, but make up for loss of stature by possessing great stamina. They constantly court the females, which develop a large gravid spot when pregnant.

Breeding. *Tank: 24"×8"×8". pH: 7·0-7·2. Hardness: 120-180 p.p.m. Temperature: 78°F. Produces live young. Method: trap female. Young: 20-50. Free-swimming: at birth. Food 1st week: infusoria, brine shrimp. 2nd week: microworms, dried food.*

Girardinus metallicus – Girardinus

West Indies   ♂ *1½"*   ♀ *2½"*   *Community*   DIET: *All foods*
SWIMS: *Upper half of tank*

Although this fish is quite attractive, and is peaceful and hardy, it does not seem to be universally popular, and is not often stocked by dealers in Britain. The gonopodium is long and bent over slightly at the tip.

Both sexes have a metallic sheen, hence the name. The sides are covered with short light-coloured bars; greenish dots mark the gill-plates. At the base of the posterior end of the dorsal fin there is a black spot.

The gonopodium of the male determines sex.

Breeding. *Tank: 24"×8"×8". pH: 7·0-7·2. Hardness: 120-180 p.p.m. Temperature: 78°F. Produces live young. Method: trap female. Young: 20-40. Free-swimming: at birth. Food 1st week: infusoria and brine shrimp. 2nd week: dried food, microworms.*

135

Heterandria formosa – Mosquito fish

Virginia to Florida ♂ *¾"* ♀ *1¼"* *Community* DIET: *All foods*
SWIMS: *All depths*

The smallest of the live-bearers, these little fish should be kept on their own or with other small species. They are lively, active, and attractive. Unfortunately, however, they are too small for the average community tank. Here the larger inhabitants bully and buffet them, forcing them to take refuge in plant thickets or dark corners of the tank where they are not seen and their lively disposition is lost. The species will withstand a temperature range of from 60° to 90°F. if gradual.

The general colour is olive to brown on the top half, the belly being white. A dark brown line runs from the tip of the nose to the base of the tail. Above this, thin vertical black bars cross the body. The one subdued splash of colour is a red spot above a black one in the dorsal fin.

Males show long gonopodiums in comparison to their size.

Breeding. *Tank: 24"×8"×8", or smaller. pH: 7·0-7·4. Hardness: 120-150 p.p.m. Temperature: 76°F. Produces live young. Method: young delivered over a period. Young: 10-25. Free-swimming: at birth. Food 1st week: infusoria, brine shrimp. 2nd week: microworms, fine dried food.*

Females deliver live young over a period of days. If the tank is well planted, and contains a layer of *Riccia* at the surface, the population will increase rapidly, as only hungry parents will eat their fry.

136

Phàllichthys amates – Merry widow

Guatemala, Honduras ♂ *1½"* ♀ *2" Community* DIET: *All foods*
SWIMS: Upper half of tank

A lively fish, hardy, and ideally suited to community life. The male has a striking dorsal fin which he carries upright and well spread at all times. This fin has an outer border of white immediately below which runs a black crescent. A smaller and less colourful crescent appears in the middle of the fin.

The body colour is an olive-grey becoming more golden on the under side. There is, however, on the flanks a bluish-green sheen which is intensified on the gill plates and below the mouth. Numerous faint black bars appear on the sides of the male.

In relation to his size, the gonopodium is long. Females are larger than males.

Breeding. *Tank: 24"×8"×8". pH: 7·0-7.2. Hardness: 120-150 p.p.m. Temperature: 78°F. Produces live young. Method: well-planted tank or trap. Young: 10-30. Free-swimming: at birth. Food 1st week: infusoria, brine shrimp. 2nd week: microworms, dried food*

The species is a prolific breeder. If kept well fed they are not inclined to eat their young.

♀  ♂

Poecilia hybrid – Black molly

Southern U.S.A. to Venezuela ♂ *3"* ♀*3½"* *Community* DIET: *All foods*
SWIMS: *All depths*

The familiar black molly has been produced by selective breeding from *Poecilia sphenops* and (perhaps) *P. formosa.* The wild forms are green, though they may show some speckling.

Breeding of black mollies should produce jet-black young which retain their colour, and should not become speckled as they grow. The best of these have completely black eyes, but some others still have a ligher-coloured iris. Other varieties occur too.

When feathery plants such as *Myriophyllum* become coated with algæ the best method of cleansing is to put the bunch into a tank containing mollies. These fish will eat every scrap of algæ, and yet not damage the fine fronds of the plant.

Sex is determined by the gonopodium of the male.

Breeding. *Tank: 24"×8"×8". pH: 7·4. Hardness: 150-180 p.p.m. Temperature: 80°F. Produces live young. Method: large, well-planted tank. Young: 30-70. Free-swimming: at birth. Food 1st week: brine shrimp and Cyclops. 2nd week: fine dried food, sifted Daphnia.*

For further details see *P. latipinna.*

Poecilia latipinna – Sailfin molly

SE States of USA ♂ *3½″* ♀ *3½″ Community* DIET: *All foods.*
SWIMS: *Mid-water*

The main feature of this fish is the magnificent dorsal fin seen on good specimens. The dorsal fin on a good male will extend from the back of the neck to the beginning of the caudal peduncle, and will stand 1¼″ high in front to ¾″ at the rear.

The colour is hard to describe, though the general appearance is metallic green splashed liberally with yellow. Here and there on the body blue highlights show up, but they are more prominent in the upper and lower portions of the tail. A few half-bars, more like blotches, appear on the lower sides of the fish. Several fine brownish stripes of a rather zig-zag pattern traverse the body horizontally from gill-plate to caudal peduncle.

Males are generally slightly larger than females, and when courting put on a magnificent display, expanding the caudal and dorsal fins until it would seem that they must split. At this time male colours are at their height, and shine like burnished metal. Usually the best and biggest males are those which grow to a good size before developing their gonopodium.

Mollies are constant feeders, and it is advisable to provide small but frequent meals. Dried food is readily taken, particularly that which floats. Since the lower lip protrudes slightly beyond the upper one, the mouth opens towards the water surface. The fish like to swim with their lips at surface level and suck in quantities of floating dried food. They also enjoy a vegetable diet, and are constantly nibbling at algæ growing on the plants and walls of the aquarium. Plant food is a real need to them, and must be available at all times. Mollies come from warm, alkaline water, and do better in aquaria where the pH is 7·2 to 7·6 and the temperature 78°–82°F. A small quantity of salt in the water is beneficial.

Breeding. *Tank: 30″×15″×15″. pH: 7·4. Hardness: 150-180 p.p.m. Temperature: 80°F. Produces live young. Method: large, well-planted tank. Young: 30-70. Free-swimming: at birth. Food 1st week: brine shrimp and Cyclops. 2nd week: fine dried food, sifted Daphnia.*

Breeding habits are similar to other live-bearers, but once gravid the females resent handling or any change from one tank to another. Where possible the male should be removed. If the females have to be transferred it must be done very early in the gestation period. Otherwise premature birth may occur. As a result she may waste away, and not return to her former condition.

♂

♀

Poecilia melanogaster – Black-bellied limia

Jamaica   ♂ 1¾"   ♀ 2"   Community
DIET: All foods   SWIMS: All depths

Many experienced aquarists do not know this fish. Somehow it has been overlooked; because it is not often asked for, few dealers stock it. Yet when seen under good lighting it is one of the prettiest live-bearers. It has a lively disposition, and is suitable for most community tanks, provided these are not stocked with large fishes which may be bullies.

Bright blue is a colour not common among fresh-water tropicals. This fish, however, is generously spangled with shining scales of rich royal blue on an olive background. The females, though not quite as bright as the males, are none the less attractive, and the large gravid spot is also tinted with dark blue. Males in perfect condition are beautiful. The blue spangles are set off by yellow crescents in the dorsal and tail fins, the outer edge of each being bordered with black. The base of the dorsal in both sexes is blue-black, and four or five short vertical black bars cross the hind portion of the body.

Breeding. *Tank: 24"×8"×8". pH: 7·0-7·4. Hardness: 120-180 p.p.m. Temperature: 75°F. Produces live young. Method: trap female. Young: 10-25. Free-swimming: at birth. Food 1st week: infusoria, brine shrimp. 2nd week: microworms, fine dried food.*

Males are persistent courters, and sometimes show tremendous pace when chasing females. Nevertheless, the species is not prolific, broods being small. Several females may be trapped together.

Poecilia nigrofasciata – Hump-backed limia

West Indies.   ♂ 2″   ♀ 2¼″   Community   DIET: All foods   SWIMS: All depths

Here is another very popular fish. It is robust, hardy, and not aggressive and is somewhat chunkier than the foregoing. With age the males develop a splendid dorsal fin on an arched back. This feature accounts for their popular name, though they are also known as striped limias.

The overall body colour is old gold striped with many thin black bars. The fins of the female are tinged with yellow. The dorsal of the male is black-laced with a yellow crescent across the middle, and his tail is black-edged.

Breeding.   *Tank: 24″×8″×8″.   pH: 7·0-7·2.   Hardness: 120-150 p.p.m.   Temperature: 78°F.   Produces live young.   Method: trap female.   Young: 10-25.   Free-*

swimming: at birth.   Food 1st week: infusoria and brine shrimp. 2nd week: microworms, dried food.

Females produce small broods, and are very inclined to eat their own young, so it is advisable to use a trap. If this is large enough several females can be placed in it together. It has been observed that deep-bodied females which look likely to give immediate birth are in reality far from this state. Only when they become square in profile under the chin are they about to deliver young.

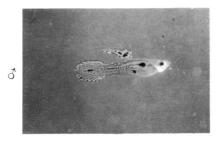

Green-lace guppy

Scarf-tail guppy

Veil-tail guppy

Sword-tail guppy

Poecilia reticulata – Guppy

Venezuela, Guyana   ♂ 1¼"   ♀ 1¾"   Community   DIET: All foods   SWIMS: All depths

The attractive guppies are known throughout the world by nearly everyone, whether aquarists or not. They have become so commonplace and inexpensive that they are not generally treated with the respect due to such magnificent fish. Were they rare, and their cost ten times as great, they would be highly prized, for no two males are identical in colour and markings. Even the ordinary guppy is a lively, colourful, hardy little fish, and is generally the first species kept by beginners.

In spite of unsuitable treatment due to inexperience, the guppy not only survives but reproduces regularly. Later, when the aquarist has acquired some skill, he begins to ignore the beauty of this fish, and treats him mainly as a guinea-pig. For example, when ascertaining if certain water is suitable for fishes, often guppies are thrown in for observation. They have been subjected to various conditions such as excessively high or low temperatures, and extremes of acidity and alkalinity.

Again, guppies are used for tests of endurance when there is a lack of oxygen. Frequently the fish are purposely infected with diseases so that new drugs may be tried out on them. More often than not these happy little fish withstand all these experiments, and yet when returned to normal conditions will produce lively youngsters none the worse for the ill-treatment of the parents.

It is practically impossible to state accurately the colour or pattern of the present-day guppy: all are beautiful. Several types are shown in our colour plates. A few specialists devote much time to line breeding various types. Among these there are recognized sword-tail, double swords, lyre-tails, scarf-tails, veil-tails, laced guppies, red, green, gold, chain, bird's-eye, and numerous others. Not only do some breeders produce new types, but achieve great success in establishing definite colour patterns and markings. Such super guppies still demand a high price, and rightly so. The breeder's knowledge and patience have to be devoted over many generations. The majority of fish produced have to be thrown out, and only a select few retained to advance a step further towards the aim in view. But, once established, the buyer with no further trouble can reproduce many of the particular type, before non-selective breeding causes the strain to revert.

The males, though smaller, are the more colourful, and constantly show off to the stately females. The latter are generally grey, though some have been developed with colour in the tail fin. Many breeders are devoting their time to producing an all-coloured female, but as yet this has not been achieved.

Breeding. *Tank: 24"×8"×8". pH: 6·8-7·4. Hardness: 100-180 p.p.m. Temperature: 78°F. Produces live young. Method: thickly planted tank or traps. Young: 20-70. Free-swimming: at birth. Food 1st week: infusoria and brine shrimp. 2nd week: microworms, dried food.*

Guppies are prolific breeders, and the young grow rapidly; as many as four generations may be raised in a year. This gives specialist breeders the opportunity of selecting suitable specimens for producing new strains.

Poecilia velifera – Sail-fin molly

Yucatan, Mexico ♂ 4½" ♀ 4½" Community DIET: All foods SWIMS: Mid-water

Known as the sail-fin molly, this is the king of live-bearers. It is the largest of the mollies, and has a dorsal fin which is unrivalled by any other fish of the same size. This enormous fin may be as high as 1½", and has 17 to 18 rays, whereas *P. latipinna* usually has 14 or 15.

The colour of the two species is similar. *P. velifera* reproduces young with large dorsal fins. *P. latipinna* sometimes fails to pass on this feature to its offspring. Most of the finest specimens come from stock raised in outdoor pools. It is doubtful whether specimens reared in tanks will ever attain the size and finnage of the outdoor fish.

Females lack the huge sail-fin.

Breeding. *Tank: 30"×15"×15". pH: 7·4. Hardness: 150-180 p.p.m. Temperature: 80°F. Produces live young. Method: large, well-planted tank. Young: 20-50. Free-swimming: at birth. Food 1st week: brine shrimp and Cyclops. 2nd week: dried food, sifted Daphnia.*

Details as for *P. latipinna.*

144

Poecilia vittata – Spotted limia

West Indies ♂ *1³⁄₄"* ♀ *1³⁄₄" Community* DIET: *All foods* SWIMS: *All depths*

In shape this limia is somewhat like *P. melanogaster,* though deeper-bodied, but not so chunky as *P. nigrofasciata.* Both sexes have diffused gold in the dorsal and tail, and these are overspotted with black. Males have larger fins and more spots, whereas females have a pale bluish-silver belly devoid of spots. The flanks in certain lights show the brilliant blue so prominent in *P. melanogaster.*

The females do not seem over-prolific, and are quite adept at eating their own newly born young.

Breeding. *As for P. nigrofasciata.*

145

Gold swordtail

Green swordtails

Albino swordtail

Red swordtail

Xiphophorus helleri – *Swordtail*

Mexico   ♂ 4½″   ♀ 3½″   Community   DIET: All foods   SWIMS: All depths

All the swordtails are hardy, prolific, inexpensive fish, and many books recommend them as an essential species to most beginners. The authors hold the opposite view, because the average beginner rarely starts off with a large tank, and swordtails grow big. Many of them turn spiteful, and a rogue male frequently becomes a downright bully, constantly chasing and worrying his smaller companions. Realizing that most of the fishes in his community tank are unhappy, the beginner is apt to feel that this is due to his mismangement. Often gaining the impression that tropicals are too difficult to keep, he may give up in despair and dispose of his tank. Had he removed the swordtails the serenity of the aquarium would have been restored quickly, and possibly the aquarist would have become a life-member of the fold.

Nevertheless, swordtails when kept in large aquaria with biggish fishes are attractive and colourful. The most striking feature is the magnificent sword-like extension formed by the lower rays of the caudal fin in the males. This sword is purely for adornment, and is never used as a weapon; indeed, it is far too flexible even to penetrate a piece of tissue paper.

Through line breeding the common green sword has now been developed into several distinct colour varieties. These include red, red-eyed red, albino, black, berlin, gold, red-wag, etc. Our colour plate shows four examples. Each will breed true to type if not crossed with any other. *Xiphophorus helleri* are so common and well known, and bred in so many colour varieties, that a full description of each will not be given.

Excluding the length of the sword, males and females are approximately the same size.

Like the mollies, the mouth of the swordtail is inclined upward, and is well equipped for taking in floating dried food, which it seems to enjoy. Even so, these fish have no objection to scavenging head downward on the bottom of the tank. Between feeding-times swordtails are constantly pecking algæ from the plants and the sides of the aquarium.

When not eating, males are either chasing other fishes or courting a female of their own species. While paying homage to his lady the male shows to the greatest advantage. Adorning himself in his best colours, and with fins stretched to full extent, he darts around her. Often during these antics the male will shoot backward two or three times his own length. This feat must be performed with the pectoral fins, though no doubt his sword helps him to cut through the water when in reverse.

Breeding. Tank: 30"×15"×15". pH: 7·0-7·4. Hardness: 120-180 p.p.m. Temperature: 78°F. Produces live young. Method: well-planted tank or trap. Young: 20-200. Free-swimming: at birth. Food 1st week: brine shrimp, fine dried food. 2nd week: Cyclops, microworms.

Swordtails are prolific. A large female may produce a brood of 250 at one time. The young are born about ¼″ long. They are robust and easy to rear. In order to obtain large specimens it is necessary to give plenty of food, warmth, and space, so that the fish can grow as much as possible before the males develop a gonopodium, and later the start of the swordtail.

Yellow wagtail platy

Red platy

Blue platy

Variatus

Xiphophorus maculatus and Xiphophorus variatus – Platy

S. Mexico   ♂ 2"   ♀ 2½"   *Community*   DIET: *All foods*   SWIMS: *All depths*

These two species are very popular, and do not show the same aggressive traits as *X. helleri*. *X. maculatus* has 9 or 10 rays in its dorsal fin, while *X. variatus* has 11 or 12. Typical markings for *X. variatus* are shown in the picture; a number of tank-bred varieties of platy exist.

These include red, gold, blue, black, tuxedo, berlin, variegated, red-wag, yellow-wag, sunset, bleeding heart, festival, moons, etc. Still more varieties are being established. In view of the diversity of colour, no attempt will be made to describe any particular fish. Our plate shows four varieties. All have been developed by line breeding. In each variety both sexes are similarly coloured, though males are frequently a little brighter and often slightly smaller.

Platys have a cheerful disposition and are not shy. They sport their gay colours at all depths, and frequent the unplanted front portion of the aquarium. They enjoy nibbling at algae, and spend much time bumping their lips on the side of the tank in their efforts to dislodge this vegetable food.

Breeding. *Tank: 24"×8"×8". pH: 7·0-7·2. Hardness: 100-150 p.p.m. Temperature: 78°F. Produces live young. Method: well-planted tank or trap. Young: 10-75. Free-swimming: at birth. Food 1st week: infusoria, brine shrimp. 2nd week: fine dried food, microworms.*

All platys are prolific breeders, bearing about 10 to 75 young at each brood. These remain unmolested in the majority of cases, but an occasional female has cannibalistic tendencies. The young are hardy, and grow quickly, thereby lending themselves for line breeding.

Chapter Fourteen

Barbs, Danios and their Relatives

FAMILY CYPRINIDAE

This is one of the largest of all fish families in the world. It inhabits most of Europe, Asia, Africa, and North America. The fishes vary in size from a few inches to several feet; the larger ones are used for food in many lands. But it is the smaller species that are of interest to aquarists. Most of the carps have barbels, small appendages which hang from the lower lips like miniature whiskers. They do not have teeth, but grind their food with bony plates in the throat. One method of identification is that they do not possess an adipose fin.

BARBUS

Certain aquarium inhabitants gain temporary favour, only to lose it again shortly after. The barbs, however, have always been popular, and will remain so. This is because they are highly coloured, generally peaceful, not shy, keep their fins well spread, breed readily, and are very adaptable to aquarium life. The majority have large, shiny scales which often give the appearance of enclosing the body in a fine network. Moreover, they come in two sizes; the smaller ones averaging 2″ in length are happy in moderate-sized tanks; the large fish of 3″ upward are best in bigger homes.

Barbs like warmth and plenty of light. They are happy at temperatures from 75° to 85°F., and prefer slightly acid water with a pH value of 6·8. Space and oxygen are important considerations. Barbs will not stand crowding, so if ample surface area is not available they must have artificial aeration. Never should more than two barbs be carried a long distance in a jam-jar: they will most likely suffocate. After an exertion, such as breeding, it is important to make sure that the exhausted parents are given plenty of space and oxygen, or death may result.

Breeding. The spawn of most barbs hatches in 24 hours. With species of 2″ and upward the fry, as soon as free-swimming, are large enough to be fed brine shrimp as first food. The newly hatched babies of species under 2″ should be fed with infusoria. For further information see Chapter 12.

♀   ♂

Barbus aurulius – *Filament barb*

S.E. India ♂ 6" ♀ 6"   *Community, with larger fishes*   DIET: *All foods*
SWIMS: Mid-water

One of the larger barbs, and too boisterous to be kept with smaller fishes, though it is peaceful enough with medium-sized species. The markings are clearly shown in our plate above, but our specimens were young, and the maximum colour and length of finnage have not reached full development. When this occurs the male is more brightly coloured, his fins are redder, and his dorsal is considerably longer than the female's; the rays in this fin then curve backward. The beginnings of this can be seen in our photograph.

Breedng. *Tank: 24"×12"×12". pH: 6·4-6·8. Hardness: 50-80 p.p.m. Temperature: 80°F. Spawns: in plant thickets. Method: standard for barbs. Eggs: 100-200. Hatch: in 48 hours. Fry hang on: 3 days. Free-swimming: 6th day. Food 1st week: infusoria, brine shrimp. 2nd week: brine shrimp, microworms.*

Not difficult to induce to spawn, but the tank should be thickly planted to prevent egg-eating. Remove parents immediately after spawning. Fry grow rapidly, and should be 1" long in 9 weeks.

Barbus bimaculatus – Two-spot barb

Sri Lanka   ♂ 2¼″   ♀ 2¾″   Community
DIET: All foods   SWIMS: Lower half of tank

This attractive little barb has quickly gained popularity. In shape it is long and slender. It is of lively disposition, but a little shy. It spends most of its time swimming around the base of plants and scavenging in the sand.

A broad pink band traverses the sides from nose to tail. Above this is another of bright green. The back is olive, the belly silvery. Two small but intense black spots are prominent, one at the base of the dorsal fin, the other at the root of the tail.

The pink band on males is more pronounced, and they are slimmer than females.

Breeding.   *Tank: 24″×8″×8″.   pH: 6·8.   Hardness: 80-100 p.p.m.   Temperature: 80°F.   Spawns: in plant thickets.   Method: standard for barbs.   Eggs: 75-120.   Hatch: in 48 hours.   Fry hang on: 1 day.   Free-swimming: 4th day.   Food 1st week: infusoria. 2nd week: brine shrimp, microworms.*

The pair behave like other barbs, but remain near the bottom of the tank. Eggs are usually deposited in the lower fronds of plant clumps.

Barbus binotatus – Spotted barb

Malaya, Thailand ♂ *4"* ♀ *5" Community, with larger fishes*
DIET: *All foods* SWIMS: *Lower half of tank*

Though not aggressive, this is one of the larger barbs, and is inclined to buffet smaller fishes out of the way.

The main colour is silver-grey, a dark blotch appearing on the back just below the first rays of the dorsal fin. Another elongated spot lies horizontally in the caudal peduncle. The eyes are golden brown.

Any food, particularly duckweed, is eaten.

Females are larger and deeper-bellied than males.

Breeding. *Tank: 30"×15"×15". pH: 6·8. Hardness: 80-100 p.p.m. Temperature: 80°F. Spawns: in plant thickets. Method: standard for barbs. Eggs: 200– 500. Hatch: in 48 hours. Fry hang on: 2 days. Free-swimming: 5th day. Food 1st week: brine shrimp. 2nd week: fine dried food, microworms.*

The parents are inclined to eat their eggs, and should be removed immediately spawning ceases. The young have numerous spots in the rear portion of the body, mostly along the lateral line. These spots fade with growth.

Barbus conchonius – *Rosy barb*

India   ♂ 3"   ♀ 3¼"   Community   DIET: All foods   SWIMS: All depths

Probably the commonest of all the barbs kept in aquaria. The male when in colour is truly gorgeous. Below the lateral line of the body is a rich red; above it is bright green. The dorsal, anal, and ventral fins become solid black in fine specimens, though poorer ones are often only edged with black. There is a black diamond in the rear portion of the body in both sexes. The female is a golden olive colour and her fins lack the black of the male, who is often slightly smaller.

First indications of sex in young fish is that the males develop a black area in the dorsal fin. Strange as it may seem, males show their best colours when kept together. Now and then they perform a circular dance. Head to tail, they gyrate round and round until the viewer becomes giddy from watching them. During this spin the fins are fully extended, and their colouring is superb. When placed with a female in a breeding tank spawning will take place; but the male rarely adorns himself in the colours produced when two males perform their strange dance.

Breeding.   Tank: 24"×8"×8"   pH: 6·8.   Hardness: 120-150 p.p.m.   Temperature: 80°F.   Spawns: in plant thickets.   Method: standard for barbs.   Eggs: 200-250.   Hatch: in 24 hours.   Fry hang on: 1 day.   Free-swimming: 3rd day.   Food 1st week: brine shrimp. 2nd week: microworms, fine dried food.

This barb is one of the easiest to breed, and is specially recommended to beginners.

♀

♂

Barbus cumingi – Cuming's barb

Sri Lanka ♂ *2″* ♀ *2″* *Community* DIET: *All foods* SWIMS: *Lower half of tank*

One of the smaller barbs ideally suited to life in a community tank. It is peaceful, colourful, and breedable, thus making it one of the most popular species in the family. When in slightly acid water the fins are carried in an erect manner and are always well spread, giving the impression that the fish is healthy, vigorous, and happy.

As will be seen from our plate, the male is more colourful, and slimmer. In good specimens the female's dorsal is orange-yellow with black markings. Many poor males are seen which have clear fins. Sexing is not easy until the fish are nearly breeding size.

Breeding. *Tank: 24″×8″×8″. pH: 6·8. Hardness: 120-150 p.p.m. Temperature: 80°F. Spawns: in plant thickets. Method: standard for barbs. Eggs: 100-150. Hatch: in 24 hours. Fry hang on: 1 day. Free-swimming: 3rd day. Food 1st week: infusoria. 2nd week: brine shrimp.*

Barbus dorsalis – Long-snouted barb

Sri Lanka   ♂ 3½"   ♀ 4"   Community, with large fishes
DIET: All foods   SWIMS: Lower half of tank

Although not one of the brilliant barbs, and little known, this fish is quite attractive.

The edges of the scales are darkish, giving the body the appearance of being covered by fine network. The back and sides are brownish; the belly is silver. The outstanding mark is an elongated spot in the base of the dorsal fin. The fins of the male are reddish-brown, while those of the female are brown. The mouth is set lower than in most barbs; the lips are alternately extended and contracted as the fish grubs about on the sand. When scavenging it swims with the head tilted downward.

Breeding. *Similar to B. everetti.*

156

♀

♂

Barbus everetti – *Clown barb*

Malaya, Borneo   ♂ *4½"*   ♀ *5½"*   *Community, with large fishes*
DIET: All foods   SWIMS: Lower half of tank

This is another of the larger barbs, and is extremely colourful. Growth is rapid, and soon a large tank is rquired. If the fish remained smaller it would be more popular. When many are kept together they have the bad habit of chewing the more tender plants. This means that their home becomes bereft of all but cryptocorynes. These, being slow-growing plants, are unable to consume all the mulm formed; neither can they compete with algæ. As a result the water turns green and, unless continually siphoned off, the bottom of the tank is covered with mulm. Clown barbs are rather timid; when frightened their quick movements and large size soon stir up the sediment, causing the tank to become so clouded that the fish are rarely seen.

Our colour plate shows a breeding pair.

Sexing is difficult until the fish are mature. Then the male is slimmer than the female, and the red in his fins is more intense. When not frightened the fish will swim in the upper portion of the tank. They are not aggressive, but on account of their bulk should be kept with species of a similar size. Like other large barbs, they are wonderful dustbins for unwanted duckweed, which they devour with relish.

Breeding. *Tank: 30"×15"×15". pH: 6·6-6·8. Hardness: 50-80 p.p.m. Temperature: 80°F. Spawns: in plant thickets. Method: standard for barbs. Eggs: 2000-3000. Hatch: in 48 hours. Fry hang on: 2 days. Free-swimming: 5th day. Food 1st week: infusoria. 2nd week: brine shrimp, microworms.*

If the female is really fat, and the pair have previously been kept apart, spawning may start in 15 minutes, so it is advisable to put these fish out to breed in the early afternoon. The male drives the female vigorously. He pushes his flank close to hers, the pair press together, then with a flick of their tails they shoot apart. Tiny eggs are expelled and fertilized. Little of the spawn remains on the plants. Being non-adhesive, it falls through the foliage and nestles out of view between the grains of sand. In about 2 hours the spawning is over. It is important to remove both fish as soon as they start picking up mouthfuls of sand from which they sift and swallow the eggs. If the parents are removed at once the fry, which hatch in 36 to 48 hours, may number as many as 2000. But if the adults are left in for as little as an hour after spawning they may consume nearly every egg, and only 20 or so fry may hatch. For such large fish the babies are minute.

♀ ♂

Barbus fasciatus – Striped barb

Borneo, Sumatra, Malaya   ♂ 4″   ♀ 4½″   *Community*
DIET: All foods   SWIMS: Mid-water

A not so common or colourful species. Nevertheless, this barb has a peaceful disposition, and an attractiveness all of its own. The nose is more pointed than in most barbs, and, what is more, the bars run horizontally. These are composed of lines of black dots. The main colour of the body is silver.

Females are deeper-bodied, and have fins slightly smaller than the males. They will spawn when 2″ long.

Breeding. *Tank: 24″×8″×8″. pH: 6·6-6·8. Hardness: 100-120 p.p.m. Temperature: 80°F. Spawns: in plant thickets. Method: standard for barbs. Eggs: 100-200. Hatch: in 24 hours. Fry hang on: 1 day. Free-swimming: 3rd day. Food 1st week: infusoria. 2nd week: brine shrimp, microworms.*

Barbus filamentosus – Filament barb

Sri Lanka ♂ *5"* ♀ *4½"* *Community, with larger fishes*
DIET: *All foods* SWIMS: *Mid-water*

When very young the fry have little colour, although they bear black spots. But when three months old they become most attractive. The belly and sides are silver; the back is golden. A black bar passes from the nape of the neck forward through the eye. A large vertical black blob or bar shows in the middle of the body, and a large black spot of diamond shape appears in the forward portion of the caudal peduncle. It is, however, the fins that add the striking colours, the dorsal being solid red at the base and faintly black above. The tips of the forward rays are greyish-white. The tail fin has an intense red splash followed by a black one in the upper and lower lobes. On reaching maturity the bars and coloured blotches fade out completely, but the large spot in the caudal peduncle remains permanent. In males the dorsal fin retains the greyish-white tip and the rays extend into long filaments.

The fish is streamlined and a swift swimmer. When being caught it will speed through the water, leap from the surface, and travel several yards before landing. The species is excellent for clearing unwanted duckweed.

Females do not grow the long filaments in the dorsal fin.

Breeding. Tank: 30"×15"×15". pH: 6·8. Hardness: 100-120 p.p.m. Temperature: 80°F. Spawns: in plant thickets. Method: Standard for barbs. Eggs: 800-1200. Hatch: in 48 hours. Fry hang on: 2 days. Free-swimming: 5th day. Food 1st week: infusoria. 2nd week: brine shrimps, microworms.

The breeding tank should be filled with rain-water and be thickly planted. The following morning the pair will spawn in the normal manner of barbs. Immediately afterwards they should be removed. The fry grow quickly, and soon will eat sifted *Daphnia* and dried food.

159

♀

♂

Barbus gelius – *Miniature barb*

India ♂ *1¼"* ♀ *1½"* *Community* DIET: *All foods* SWIMS: *Lower half of tank*

This is one of the smallest barbs kept in aquaria. Owing to the diminutive size, and lack of bright colours, it misses the popularity it deserves, for it is a game little fish, and is quite prepared to look after itself, even with companions twice its size. This does not mean that it is in the least aggressive, but merely that it will not be pushed into the background. It likes to be in the forefront of the aquarium, and to have its share of the food. When driven off it repeatedly returns until finally the aggressors, becoming tired of chasing away such a determined little fish, allow it to remain unmolested.

The upper sides and back of the body are bright gold, the belly silver-white. The shades are deeper in the males, and the rear portion of the body from below the dorsal fin to caudal peduncle is a rich red gold.

The female is slightly larger, and her belly is deeper and rounder. She lacks the deep red gold possessed by the male.

Breeding. *Tank: 24"×8"×8". pH: 6·8. Hardness: 100-120 p.p.m. Temperature: 80°F. Spawns: in plant thickets. Method: standard for barbs. Eggs: 50– 100. Hatch: in 24 hours. Fry hang on: 1 day. Free-swimming: 3rd day. Food 1st week: infusoria. 2nd week: brine shrimp, microworms.*

For spawning pure rain-water is best. The tank must be thickly planted, since the parents are liable to eat the eggs, which are large relative to the size of the fish. When a little spawn is seen among the plants the parents should be removed; if this is done in time 70 to 100 fry may be expected to hatch out.

Barbus hexazona – Six-zoned barb

Sumatra, Malaya   ♂ 2″   ♀ 2¼″   Community
DIET: All foods   SWIMS: Mid-water

This is one of the prettiest barbs, but somewhat rare in Britain and America. Although prolific in Malaya, the species travels badly. Once settled in an aquarium and cured of *Ichthyophthirius*, to which it is very subject, the fish live happily. The species is somewhat shy, and often remains hidden among the plants at the back of the tank.

Breeding.   *The species is difficult to induce to spawn, and rather prone to eating its eggs.*

Barbus lateristriga – *Spanner barb*

Malaya, Sumatra, Borneo, Thailand   ♂ 5½″   ♀ 6″   Community, with larger fishes
DIET: All foods   SWIMS: Lower half of tank

This is one of the largest barbs kept by aquarists. Due to its size, and lack of bright colours, it is not among the most popular. In Britain it is called the spanner barb; in America the 'T' barb.

The main colour of the body is silver-grey, the forward portion being crossed by two vertical bars, while the rear bears a long horizontal line. Though distinct in the young, these bars fade with age, and become less clear-cut.

The fish normally cruises slowly around, but when attempts are made to catch it can show a surprising turn of speed.

In adult specimens the female is rounder and deeper-bellied.

Breeding. *Tank: 30″×15″×15″.   pH: 6·6-6·8.   Hardness: 50-80 p.p.m.   Temperature: 80°F.   Spawns: in plant thickets.   Method: standard for barbs.   Eggs: 800-1200.   Hatch: in 48 hours.   Fry hang on: 2 days.   Free-swimming: 5th day.   Food 1st week: infusoria. 2nd week: brine shrimp, microworms.*

The breeding habits are similar to those of the clown barb.

Barbus lineomaculatus – Spotted barb

Zaire ♂ 1¾" ♀ 2" Community
DIET: All foods SWIMS: Lower half of tank

Similar in size and shape to *B. bimaculatus,* this newly imported barb is interesting, though not highly coloured.

The back is olive, the sides greyish-brown, the belly white. From gill-plate to tail a single line of dots, spaced equally apart, give the fish its name. It is somewhat shy, and spends most of its time grubbing about the surface of the sand, under low leaves.

Breeding. *Tank: 24"×8"×8". pH: 6·6-6·8. Hardness: 80-100 p.p.m. Temperature: 82°F. Spawns: in plant thickets. Method: standard for barbs. Eggs: 70-100. Hatch: in 48 hours. Fry hang on: 1 day. Free-swimming: 4th day. Food 1st week: infusoria. 2nd week: brine shrimp, microworms.*

The breeding habits closely resemble those of *B. bimaculatus.*

Barbus melanamphyx – Ember barb

India   ♂ 4½"   ♀ 4"   Community, with medium-sized fishes
DIET: All foods   SWIMS: Lower half of tank

This somewhat elongated barb is peaceful enough, but, because of its size, should not be kept with the smallest fishes. Male and female are so different in colour and markings that a novice could be excused for thinking they were two different species.

Females have a cream-coloured body, and a centre vertical bar over the top half of the back. The male's body is mostly covered by a deep red flush. His dorsal and anal fins are black. He lacks the centre vertical bar, but has instead a fairly extensive horizontal black patch, and a black bar running from the head over the back to the first rays of the dorsal fin. The barbels are moderately long.

The fish busies itself in scavenging about the sand. Sexing is easy from the coloration, and often males are bigger than females.

Breeding. *Tank: 24"×8"×8", or larger. pH: 6·0-6·8. Hardness: 20-50 p.p.m. Temperature: 80°F. Spawns: in plant thickets. Method: standard for barbs. Eggs: 100-200. Hatch: in 48 hours. Fry hang on: 2 days. Free-swimming: 5th day. Food 1st week: infusoria, brine shrimp. 2nd week: microworms.*

The species is not one of the easiest barbs to spawn. As they are inveterate egg-eaters, the tank must be very thickly planted so that the parents do not find too many eggs too quickly. The adults must be removed from the breeding tank immediately after spawning if one hopes to raise a good number of fry.

Barbus nigrofasciatus – Black ruby barb

Sri Lanka ♂ *2½"* ♀*2¾"* *Community*
DIET: *All foods* SWIMS: *Mid-water*

With the possible exception of *B. conchonius* this barb is the commonest seen in aquaria. No wonder, as it is one of the most beautiful, and easy to breed and feed; also it is hardy, peaceful, and of ideal size.

The female is silvery. Four broad black bands cross the body vertically, the centre one sometimes being so wide that it becomes a broad blotch. Her dorsal, ventral, and anal fins are black on the inner portions, but the edges are clear. The male, out of colour, is similar to the female, except that his dorsal, ventral, and anal fins are solid black right to the edges. But when in full colour he is hardly recognizable as the same fish. Now the whole rear portion of his body and all his fins turn jet-black, the bars disappearing. His front half, however, turns a complete strawberry red, and, with fins spread to splitting point, he literally sparkles like some exotic gem. Males more frequently don their party dress if kept together and apart from females. On occasions the males perform the spiral dance described under *B. conchonius*. At such times their coloration is at its best, and few exotic fish can surpass them.

Breeding. *Tank: 24"×8"×8". pH: 6·8. Hardness: 120-150 p.p.m. Temperature: 80°F. Spawns: in plant thickets. Method: standard for barbs. Eggs: 100-150. Hatch: in 24 hours. Fry hang on: 1 day. Free-swimming: 3rd day. Food 1st week: infusoria, brine shrimp. 2nd week: fine dried food, microworms.*

One of the easiest egg-layers to breed. If a good pair which have been kept apart are placed in a breeding tank in the late afternoon, they rarely fail to spawn the following morning. For breeding two-thirds rain-water and one-third tap-water is best. Though not difficult to rear, the fry grow rather slowly, and often stick when about ½" long, suddenly shooting ahead again. They can be sexed when quite young, since the dorsal fin of the males is black throughout, whereas this fin in young females is not black on the outer edge.

Barbus oligolepis – *Chequer barb*

Sumatra ♂ *1½"* ♀ *1¾" Community*
DIET: All foods SWIMS: Lower half of tank

Here we have one of the most colourful of the smaller barbs. Hardy and peaceful, it is an excellent fish for beginners, though somewhat shy until well at home. It derives its popular name from the colouring of the central scales, which produce a chequer pattern from gill-plate to tail.

The males have bright orange fins, all of which are edged with a thin black border. The colour is more intense when in breeding condition. The female's fins are yellow, and the black border is absent save on the dorsal. Her back is golden, whereas the male's is more orange.

The species always carry their fins erect. Should these drop the fish is unhappy or suffering from some disease.

Breeding. *Tank: 24"×8"×8". pH: 6·8. Hardness: 120-150 p.p.m. Temperature: 80°F. Spawns: in plant thickets. Method: standard for barbs. Eggs: 75-100. Hatch: in 24 hours. Fry hang on: 1 day. Free-swimming: 3rd day. Food 1st week: infusoria. 2nd week: brine shrimp, microworms.*

Spawning usually occurs in or around the lower stems of bunched plants, and consequently the eggs are more difficult to see. The parents are very inclined to eat these. If the female is obviously slimmer and pecking about the sand, both parents should be removed.

167

♀

♂

Barbus 'schuberti' – Golden barb

Origin uncertain ♂ 2½" ♀ 3" Community
DIET: All foods SWIMS: Lower half of tank

As a complete contrast, this medium-sized barb is a bright golden-yellow, and said by some to be a colour variety of *B. semifasciolatus*. All the fins except the pectorals are brick red. Males are slightly smaller than females, and can be identified immediately by a row of black spots which run horizontally from the gill-plate to the caudal peduncle. Females are deeper-bodied; they lack the row of black dots, though they have a few odd spots here and there on the upper portion of the back.

Breeding. Tank: 24"×8"×8". pH: 6·6-6·8. Hardness: 80-120 p.p.m. Temperature: 80°F. Spawns: in plant thickets. Method: standard for barbs. Eggs: 150-200. Hatch: in 24 hours. Fry hang on: 1 day. Free-swimming: 3rd day. Food 1st week: infusoria. 2nd week: brine shrimp, microworms.

Pure rain-water is required. Sometimes the fish are difficult to induce to spawn, mainly because the males are not in condition. At breeding-time he develops a red coloration which stretches from the belly to the anal fin, and it is useless to attempt spawning until this adornment is apparent.

Barbus schwanenfeldi – *Tinfoil barb*

Thailand ♂ *6″* ♀ *6″* *Community, only with large fishes*
DIET: All foods *SWIMS: Mid-water*

This barb was introduced into Britain by the authors in 1955 through the aid of a pilot in Pan-American Airways who described the fish, which he saw in Bangkok. The species travelled well. Owing to the minute scales, which resemble burnished silver, it was immediately nicknamed the tinfoil barb by the wife of one of the authors. This title has since become established. Unfortunately, the specimens have grown so large that the fish is unlikely to be very popular except in public aquaria.

The outline of the body is diamond-shaped, and, unlike most barbs, which are rounded in section, this one is flat with compressed sides like the angel fish. All the fins are large, and its streamlining makes the fish a fast mover. It prefers to swim in shoals. The species is excellent at clearing duckweed. When this is not available the fish is inclined to devour the more tender plants.

In young specimens the outer edges of the ventrals, the anal, and the tail fin are red. But when maturity is reached these fins become red throughout. The pectorals are pale yellow. The dorsal is dark grey on the outer portion and orange on the inner. The upper and lower edges of the tail are also dark grey. The top half of the eye is orange.

Breeding. *So far the authors' specimens show no indication of sex. It is thought that, although 6″ long, they are still too small to breed.*

Barbus semifasciolatus – Half-banded barb

S. China ♂ *3"* ♀ *3½"* *Community*
DIET: All foods *SWIMS: Lower half of tank*

Here is another of the larger barbs which has lost popularity mainly because of its size and lack of gaudy coloration.

Generally the body is greenish-gold slashed with numerous thin black bars which are irregular in length. The fins are pale orange. Recently imported specimens from Singapore may restore the species to favour, since the body colour is much more intense, and all the fins are broadly bordered with rusty red, making quite a showy fish. The same effect has been produced when ordinary dull tank-bred specimens were fed with colour-mutation hormone foods.

Males are slimmer than females, and the latter are rather the larger.

Breeding. Tank: 24"×8"×8". pH: 6·8-7·0. Hardness: 120-150 p.p.m. Temperature: 80°F. Spawns: in plant thickets. Method: standard for barbs. Eggs: 150-200. Hatch: in 24 hours. Fry hang on: 1 day. Free-swimming: 3rd day. Food 1st week: infusoria. 2nd week: brine shrimp, microworms.

The species is one of the easiest to breed, though they are very prone to eating their eggs. A good deep female should be chosen; but this should be done only when one of the males shows reddish colouring on the lower part of the body similar to that described under *Barbus 'schuberti.'*

170

Barbus stoliczkanus

India, Sri Lanka ♂ 2¼" ♀ 2½" Community
DIET: All foods SWIMS: Mid-water

There is some doubt as to the true identification of this species. Certain authorities consider it to be *Barbus ticto*. It is a colourful, peaceful fish, and does well in aquaria. It has a sprightly bearing and keeps its fins well spread.

The dorsal fin of the male bears a black crescent near its base. This is surmounted by an intense red arc, which is set off with a thin black border on the outer edge.

All the fins of the female are pale yellow, and she is deeper in the belly.

Breeding. *Tank: 24"×8"×8". pH: 6·8-7·0. Hardness: 100-120 p.p.m. Temperature: 80:F. Spawns: in plant thickets. Method: standard for barbs. Eggs: 150-200. Hatch: in 24 hours. Fry hang on: 1 day. Free-swimming: 3rd day. Food 1st week: infusoria, brine shrimp. 2nd week: fine dried food, microworms.*

The species is easy to spawn and raise.

171

♀

♂

Barbus tetrazona – Tiger or Sumatran barb

Sumatra, Borneo, Thailand ♂ 2″ ♀ 2¼″ *Community*
DIET: *All foods* SWIMS: *Mid-water*

Probably the most striking and colourful of all the barbs, but it has one serious drawback: some males become aggressive. In bad cases these bullies will not only make life intolerable for other barbs but, having killed them off, will even set about adult angel fish. By constantly pecking the fins and body they will turn a show fish into a ragged, unhappy listless specimen which, unless protected, will give up the ghost. Luckily, not all tiger barbs are so bad. The bullies should be eliminated, and breeding confined to the more docile members so that the vicious trait is less likely to be perpetuated. The fish has a lively disposition, and always keeps its fins erect and well spread. When resting the body is often inclined nose downward.

Four broad black bands, evenly spaced, cross the fish vertically. In some lights these bands reflect a deep bottle green. The pectoral and ventral fins are bright red. The dorsal is red beyond the black bar. The anal fin is bordered with red, and intense red streaks appear in the upper and lower lobes of the tail.

In males all the red markings are more intense, and when in breeding condition they have a red snout. The female is larger than the male, and much deeper in the belly.

Breeding. *Tank: 24″×8″×8″. pH: 6·8. Hardness: 80-120 p.p.m. Temperature: 80°F. Spawns: in plant thickets. Method: standard for barbs. Eggs: 150-200. Hatch: in 24 hours. Fry hang on: 1 day. Free-swimming: 3rd day. Food 1st week: brine shrimp. 2nd week: microworms.*

The species breeds readily in pure rain-water. Parents should be removed immediately after spawning to prevent egg-eating. They should then be rested separately, and given space, or aeration, or death may occasionally occur from exhaustion.

Barbus tetrazona partipentazona – Banded barb

Malaya, Thailand ♂ *1¾"* ♀ *2" Community*
DIET: All foods SWIMS: Mid-water

This attractive little fish was popular before the Second World War, and is a sub-species of the tiger or Sumatran barb, *B. tetrazona tetrazona*.

The silverish body is divided by five vertical bars, though all of these do not cross the fish completely. The first bar travels from the nape of the neck forward through the eye; the second, often incomplete, runs from in front of the dorsal across the belly; the third bar passes through the middle portion of the dorsal fin and just into the upper part of the back; the fourth bar crosses from well behind the dorsal to the ventral fin; the final bar is at the caudal peduncle. There is a bright red streak in the dorsal fin. Faint red also appears in the ventrals and upper and lower edges of the tail.

Male and female are similar, though the red in the males is brighter.

Breeding. *Tank: 24"×8"×8". pH: 6·8. Hardness: 100-120 p.p.m. Temperature: 80°F. Spawns: in plant thickets. Method: standard for barbs. Eggs: 100-150. Hatch: in 24 hours. Fry hang on: 1 day. Free swimming: 3rd day. Food 1st week: infusoria. 2nd week: brine shrimp, microworms.*

The fish is as easy to breed as *B. nigrofasciatus*.

Barbus ticto – Two-spot barb

Sri Lanka   ♂ 2"   ♀ 2"   Community
DIET: All foods   SWIMS: Lower half of tank

As will be seen from the plate, this barb is somewhat similar to *B. stoliczkanus,* and it is not surprising that they are so often confused.

The males in their native habitat are said to be bright red, but in aquaria they often only show a diffused pinkish red band along the sides and the fins are clear. The shoulder spot is small, and in the caudal peduncle there is a black dot immediately followed by a black dash. The females are rather drab.

Breeding. *Tank: 24"×8"×8".   pH: 6·8.   Hardness: 80-120 p.p.m.   Temperature: 80°F.   Spawns: in plant thickets.   Method: standard for barbs.   Eggs: 100-150.   Hatch: in 24 hours.   Fry hang on: 1 day.   Free-swimming: 3rd day.   Food 1st week: infusoria. 2nd week: brine shrimp, microworms.*

174

Barbus titteya – Cherry barb

Sri Lanka ♂ *2"* ♀ *2¼" Community*
DIET: All foods SWIMS: Lower half of tank

One of the smaller barbs which is attractive, peaceful, and popular. It is hardy, easy to keep and fairly long-lived.

When not in breeding garb male and female are somewhat similar. Both have a pale brown body and an intense dark brown line which runs from tip of snout to base of tail. Above this is a pale golden stripe. The fins of the female are nearly clear, while those of the male have a brownish tint which is intensified on the edges. When he shows off, however, he is beautiful. The whole body becomes a reddish mahogany, the centre line disappearing altogether, and a bluish tinge adorns the back in some lights. At such times the male spreads all his fins, which look like little round fans stretched to splitting-point. These become deep mahogany veering to copper. This is well illustrated in our colour plate.

Two males often perform the circular dance described under *B. conchonius*, and then show their finest array.

Breeding. *Tank: 24"×8"×8". pH: 6·6-6·8. Hardness: 50-100 p.p.m. Temperature: 80°F. Spawns: in plant thickets. Method: standard for barbs. Eggs: 100-150. Hatch: in 24 hours. Fry hang on: 1 day. Free-swimming: 3rd day. Food 1st week: infusoria. 2nd week: brine shrimp.*

The species is not difficult to breed in rain-water. But the parents are avid egg-eaters. As soon as they cease spawning and start to search for eggs they should be removed.

175

Barbus vittatus – *Banded barb*

India, Sri Lanka   ♂ *1¾"*   ♀ *2"*   *Community*
DIET: All foods   *SWIMS: Lower half of tank*

Perhaps the hardiest of all the barbs, this little fellow makes up in longevity what he lacks in brilliance. Once settled down in an aquarium he is likely to be a friend for many years, eight or nine being by no means unusual.

The body-colour is silverish below, shading from olive green on the sides to brownish on the back. An arching green line is sometimes seen in the upper flanks, starting just behind the gill-plate and ending at the base of the tail. The fins are pale yellow. In the lower half of the dorsal there is an oblique dark stripe; this surmounts a triangle of orange which may be seen in the bottom front rays.

Adorning the sides are a few dark spots; a larger one appears in the caudal peduncle, and another just above the vent.

The male is slightly smaller than the female; his orange triangle is somewhat deeper in colour.

Breeding.   *Tank: 24"×8"×8".   pH: 6·8-7·0.   Hardness: 120-150 p.p.m.   Temperature: 80°F.   Spawns: in plant thickets.   Method: standard for barbs.   Eggs: 100-120.   Hatch: in 24 hours.   Fry hang on: 1 day.   Free-swimming: 3rd day.   Food 1st week: infusoria. 2nd week: brine shrimp.*

Breeding is not difficult. Water conditions need not be exact. A good pair will spawn for six or seven years, long after many other barbs have lived, loved, and died.

Balanteocheilus melanopterus – Bala or silver shark

Thailand ♂ 5″ ♀ 5″ Community, with larger fishes
DIET: All foods SWIMS: Mid-water

Here is an attractive species belonging to the genus *Balanteocheilus*, which also comes under the family Cyprinidæ. The fish is slim and streamlined; it has large, graceful fins which at all times it keeps well spread and erect. This gives it a pleasing appearance, and an air of well-being. It is a fast swimmer, extremely active, and if frightened will sometimes leap several feet out of the water. *B. melanopterus* is not aggressive, but should be kept with species of similar size. It lives happily in an aquarium with a pH of 7·4.

The body is silver all over. The fins are orange-yellow, and are vividly set off, since each is surrounded by a black border nearly ⅛″ thick.

Breeding. *Little information available.*

Barilius christyi – *Gold-lipped mackerel*

Belgian Congo ♂ *4½"* ♀ *5" Community, with larger fishes*
DIET: All foods SWIMS: Upper half of tank

Still belonging to the family Cyprinidæ, one species of the genus *Barilius* is shown.

The body is long and slim; the mouth is large. Since it is an extremely fast swimmer it should not be placed with small fishes, but with species of its own size. Then it is not aggressive.

The body colour is silver, the black is bluish-green, the flanks are barred with numerous thin, blue-black, vertical stripes. The lips are a shining gold. The fish prefers neutral water, pH 7·0, and though liking plenty of live food may be taught to take the dried product.

Breeding: *Few details are available.*

DANIOS

Again belonging to the same family Cyprinidae are the following minnow-like fishes which come from India, Sri Lanka, Indonesia, and Thailand. The larger species are placed in the genus *Danio,* the smaller members being *Brachydanio* (from the Greek *brachys,* meaning short). All are swift, streamlined fishes which scatter non-adhesive eggs in shallow water among plant thickets. They do well in ordinary aquarium conditions, preferring neutral water. They delight in swimming in shoals in the upper part of the tank, and usually are not scary.

They will take any food of suitable size, dried, fresh, or live.

Brachydanio albolineatus – Pearl danio

Sumatra, Burma, Thailand ♂ *2″* ♀ *2¼″ Community*
DIET: All foods SWIMS: Upper half of tank

This is the pearl danio, though there seem to be two types. They are hardy, not timid, and peaceful. One, the gold danio, has a yellowish tone over the body, and in our view is not so attractive as the mother-of-pearl variety, which has a pinky-bluish hue. In both types there is a translucent sheen of various colours depending on the angle of the reflected light. *B. albolineatus* grows slightly larger than the other two species in the plate. Like all danios, they are fast swimmers, and prefer to move in shoals.

Males are considerably slimmer and slightly shorter than females. A shoal of pearl danios in good daylight, particularly against a background of dark plants, is extremely beautiful.

Breeding. *Tank: 24″×8″×8″. pH: 7·0-7·2. Hardness: 100-150 p.p.m. Temperature: 78°F. Spawns: in plant thickets. Method: standard for danios. Eggs: 200-300. Hatch: in 4 days. Fry hang on: 2 days. Free-swimming: 7th day. Food 1st week: infusoria. 2nd week: infusoria, brine shrimp.*

Easy to breed, following standard for danios.

Brachydanio frankei – Leopard danio

Thailand ♂ 1¼″ ♀ 1½″ Community
DIET: All foods SWIMS: Upper half of tank

Slightly smaller than the other three *Brachydanio*, it is peaceful, lively, and easy to breed.

Males have a silvery body with a golden sheen well flecked all over with minute navy blue spots. The females are slightly bigger and deeper-bodied, and although they have a golden sheen this is not quite so strong as that of the male.

Breeding. *Tank: 24″×8″×8″. pH: 6·8-7.2. Hardness: 60-100 p.p.m. Temperature: 78°F. Spawns: in plant thickets, or may be trapped in unplanted tank. Method: standard for Danios. Eggs: 150-250. Hatch: in 4 days. Fry hang on: 2 days. Free-swimming: 7th day. Food 1st week: infusoria. 2nd week: infusoria, brine shrimp.*

180

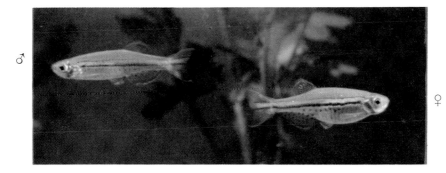

Brachydanio nigrofasciatus – Spotted danio

Burma, India ♂ 1¼" ♀ 1½" Community
DIET: All foods SWIMS: Upper half of tank

Males are considerably slimmer than females, and, with the exception that it is more difficult to induce spawning, all the points previously mentioned under danios apply here.

Brachydanio rerio – Zebra danio

India ♂ 1½" ♀ 1¾" Community
DIET: All foods SWIMS: Upper half of tank

One of the most popular of all aquarium fishes. It is adaptable, peaceful, active, easily fed, and breeds prolifically. The fish is usually recommended to those making their first attempts at spawning the egg-layers. This advice, however, is not endorsed by the authors, as the eggs take several days to hatch, and the fry are so small that they require infusoria.

The first impression of this fish would seem to denote a colour pattern of blue

181

and silver stripes running horizontally from the gill-plate to the end of the tail. But on closer examination it will be found that the males are really blue and gold.

Breeding fish are very often trapped in shallow water to prevent the spawn from being eaten.

♀

♂

Danio devario

Northern India ♂ *3½"* ♀ *3½"* *Community, with medium-sized fishes*
DIET: *All foods* SWIMS: *Mid-water*

Rather less common than the Giant Danio, this species is slightly smaller and deeper-bodied. Behind the gill plate there are three vertical yellow bars, but the rest of the body is traversed by alternate pale blue and yellow horizontal bands. The fins are rusty red. The female's are deeper and thicker laterally than the male's. In all other respects it is similar to *D. malabaricus.*

The fish are not difficult to spawn, but unless the tank is well planted they are apt to become frightened and dash themselves against the side glasses. A well-planted tank avoids this, and saves more eggs from being eaten.

For further details see *D. malabaricus.*

Danio malabaricus – *Giant danio*

India ♂ 4" ♀ 4¼" Community, with larger fishes
DIET: All foods SWIMS: Upper half of tank

This is the largest of the danios, and for many years an old favourite with those aquarists having big tanks. It is an active, showy fish, fairly peaceful, and hardy.

It is a very fast swimmer, and quite difficult to catch, sometimes leaping from the water to avoid the net.

Males are much slimmer than females, and the fins are brighter red.

Breeding. *Tank: 24"×8"×8". pH: 7·0-7·2. Hardness: 100-180 p.p.m. Temperature: 80°F. Spawns: in thickets. Method: standard for danios. Eggs: 200-300. Hatch: in 3 days. Fry hang on: 2 days. Free-swimming: 6th day. Food 1st week: infusoria. 2nd week: brine shrimp, microworms.*

Caecobarbus geertsi – *Blind barb*

Equatorial W. Africa   ♂ 3″   ♀ 3¼″   *Community*
DIET: All foods   SWIMS: *Mid-water*

Here we have one of the blind fishes, of which there are several. Though without eyes, it rarely bumps into any object or plant. Using its lateral line, the nervous system sends a message to the brain, and so permits evasive action to be taken. In shape *C. geertsi* is long and slender, with a rather pointed head.

Like many other blind species which live in permanent darkness, colour (which helps other fishes to camouflage themselves) has slowly been lost. The Blind Barb is a pale cream all over, the fins being almost clear. The gill-plates are transparent, and the pink membranes beneath show through.

Females are deeper-bodied, and slightly larger, than males.

Breeding. *Few details are available.*

ESOMUS

These are small, slim fishes recognizable by very long, slender barbels, which curve back from the mouth and reach to the middle of the belly. They have large, wing-like pectoral fins.

Esomus danricus – Flying barb

India, Sri Lanka   ♂ 1¾"   ♀ 2"   Community
DIET: All foods   SWIMS: Upper half of tank

The popular name is misleading, for the fish does not belong to the genus *Barbus*. The nickname refers to the large pectoral fins and the long barbels emanating from the mouth.

The fish like light and warmth; they spend their time gliding about just below the surface of the water.

Extending from the gills to the tail is a black line bordered above by another of gold. The fins are clear.

Males are slightly smaller and slimmer than females, though even she is of a long, slender shape.

Breeding. *Tank: 24"×8"×8".   pH: 6·6-6·8.   Hardness: 80-120 p.p.m.   Temperature: 80°F.   Spawns: in plant thickets.   Method: similar to danios.   Eggs: 100-150.   Hatch: in 48 hours.   Fry hang on: 2 days.   Free-swimming: 5th day.   Food 1st week: infusoria. 2nd week: infusoria, brine shrimp.*

The species is not difficult to spawn. The male drives the female towards clumps of plants and bumps her gently to excite her. Pale yellow eggs are scattered among the foliage. Once past the hanging-on stage, the fry stay near the bottom of the tank, but when able to swim strongly and have more confidence they take to the clearer water above the plants.

Esomus malayensis

Malaya ♂ *1¾"* ♀ *2"* *Community*
DIET: *All foods* SWIMS: *Upper half of tank*

This species, as the name implies, comes from Malaya. The fish has the same long barbels and wing-like pectoral fins as *E. danricus*, but is slightly deeper in the body.

The overall colour is a golden-hued mother-of-pearl with bluish high-lights in the region of the back. It lacks the strong horizontal stripe, but has a dark spot at the base of the tail.

In all other respects the remarks concerning *E. danricus* apply here.

Breeding. *Tank: 24"×8"×8". pH: 6·6-6·8. Hardness: 80-120 p.p.m. Temperature: 80°F. Spawns: in plant thickets. Method: similar to danios. Eggs: 100-150. Hatch: in 48 hours. Fry hang on: 2 days. Free-swimming: 5th day. Food 1st week: infusoria. 2nd week: infusoria, brine shrimp.*

Breeds as *E. danricus*.

Epalzeorhynchus kallopterus – Flying fox

Sumatra, Borneo, Thailand ♂ *4½"* ♀ *4½"* *Community, with medium-sized fishes*
DIET: *All foods* SWIMS: *Lower half of tank*

Another somewhat 'shark-like' fish, at least in looks. It is a long-bodied fish, a swift swimmer and a fairly good scavenger. At times it will nibble algae from leaves.

The colour is black and silver, and most striking. The top of the back is black; a thin silver line runs from above the eye across the body to the top half of the caudal peduncle. Beneath this a broad black band runs from the tip of the nose and passes through the eye. It traverses the whole length of the body and ends in the fork of the tail. Below this band from mouth to tail the fish is silver. The outer portions of the dorsal, ventral, and anal fins carry black blotches, but the tips are silver-white.

Females are slightly deeper-bodied than males, but have the same colour and markings.

Breeding. *Few details available.*

Epalzeorhynchus siamensis – Siamese flying fox

Thailand ♂ 5½″ ♀ 5½″ Community, with larger fishes
DIET: All foods SWIMS: Lower half of tank

The mouth is prehensile. From the corners a pair of drooping barbels hang, and two shortish ones protrude forward from the upper lip. Like the genus *Labeo*, the circular-shaped lips are used as suckers for cleaning algae from leaves, and for extracting particles of food from sandy or muddy river beds.

The overall body colour is golden, the fins being rather more orange. The dorsal and caudal fins are large, and the first rays in these are tinged with red. A pronounced black line runs from the lips to the fork of the tail. *E. siamensis* grows large, but is quite peaceful, though occasionally it makes a playful dart at other fishes without doing harm.

Male and female are the same size, though her fins are paler in colour and her belly is rather deeper and rounder.

Breeding. *Few details available.*

LABEOS

Within the last few years some interesting fishes belonging to the family Cyprinidae have been imported from Thailand. We shall first deal with the genus *Labeo*.

The genus *Labeo* comes from India, Burma, Thailand, Cambodia, Laos, and Indonesia. These fishes have long, cylindrical bodies with large fins. The head is somewhat pointed, the snout bearing pairs of barbels. The mouth is round and appears to have lips, hence the name *Labeo*. These fishes do well in aquaria in slightly alkaline water, eating most foods, but also partaking of algae, which they browse off leaves and rocks. Often they turn upside down in their efforts to reach this vegetable matter growing in nearly inaccessible places. As a result of their overall appearance, they are often referred to as 'sharks', although they share little else in common with these marine predators.

♀

♂

Labeo bicolor – Red-tailed black shark

Thailand ♂ 4½″ ♀ 4½″ Community, with larger fishes
DIET: All foods and algæ SWIMS: Lower half of tank

First introduced into Britain by the authors in 1953, the fish caused quite a sensation. Similarly, the first exports sent to America a few months later also created a stir. Though nicknamed a shark, this attractive fish is not shark-like in habits. The popular name refers to the graceful lines and the large, triangular dorsal fin which, as in some sharks, is tipped with white. The body and fins are a velvety jet-black; the tail is bright red. Two pairs of short barbels protrude from the upper lips.

Male and female are similar, though the red in her tail is less intense, and the enamel white tip in her dorsal is slightly more pronounced. Her body is also fuller.

Happiest in alkaline water with a pH value of 7.4, the fish is not shy, and performs delightful antics in the front part of the aquarium, often coming to rest on the sand. On occasion it will roll over on to its side for a more comfortable rest. This habit sometimes gives the owner a fright, for generally this attitude in other species foreshadows death. But not so here. After a few moments the fish swims off gaily. The lips protrude and form a sucker mouth with which to clean algæ off plant leaves and the glass sides of the tank. To reach this delicacy on the under sides of leaves the fish often turns upside down. The snout is rounded and equipped with short barbels; these act as feelers to assist when scavenging along the bottom in search of food. Occasionally *L. bicolor* makes a dart at its companions and chases them a short distance, but this is more a playful habit, and rarely if ever is any harm done.

Breeding. *Only rarely.*

Labeo erythrurus – Red-finned shark

Thailand ♂ *4½″* ♀ *4½″* *Community, with larger fishes*
DIET: All foods and algæ *SWIMS: Lower half of tank*

Though not black, this is another attractive member of the family. It is slightly different in shape from the one previously mentioned species. The head is more pointed, and the mouth is not situated so far underneath.

The red-finned shark has large, beautiful fins and a streamlined body. It is a fast swimmer, and occasionally, without vicious intention, makes playful darts at other fishes. Like the rest of the family, *L. erythrurus* is found in alkaline water with a pH value of 7·4.

The general body colour is bluish-grey. All the fins are bright red. A dark line runs from the snout through the eye to the edge of the gill-plate, and a dark spot adorns the base of the tail. Male and female are similar, though she is slightly deeper-bellied.

189

The fish is not shy, and will take any food, being particularly fond of chopped shrimp. Vegetable matter is enjoyed, and plant leaves continually searched for algae.

Breeding.   *Few details available.*

Laubuca laubuca – *Winged danio or glass barb*

Sri Lanka   ♂ 3"   ♀ 3¼"   Community
DIET: All foods   SWIMS: Upper half of tank

This attractive fish (also known as *Chela laubuca*) has rather beautiful fins, particularly the pectorals and ventrals. The former are large and wing-like, the latter long and pointed, the front rays being elongated with a graceful backward curve. The species is not so active as the giant danio. It swims more slowly, and rests here and there for long spells.

The body colour is mother-of-pearl with a beautiful sheen. A faint stripe made up alternately of pale blue and gold runs from the pectoral fins to the caudal peduncle. Immediately above the end of this stripe is a brilliant golden splash. The fins are yellow with a tinge of orange in the forward portion of the ventrals.

The female is larger and deeper-bodied than the male, but her colouring is the same.

Breeding.   *Similar to Brachydanio albolineatus.*

Morulius (Labeo) chrysophekadion – Black shark

Indonesia, Thailand   ♂ 10"   ♀ 10"   Community, with larger fishes
DIET: All foods and algae   SWIMS: Lower half of tank

This was the first *Labeo* to be imported from the Far East, and was received many years ago. Once fabulously expensive and highly prized, it is no longer in such demand, having been superseded by *L. bicolor*.

The scales of *M. chrysophekadion* are clearly visible, each containing a pinkish spot in the middle which becomes more apparent in specimens of 6" and upward. The fish is large, slightly aggressive, and not a jet velvety black; these are the main factors which account for it taking second place to its red-tailed cousin.

There appear to be two distinct species that are termed 'black shark'. One, with a name derived from the Greek word *chrysos*, meaning gold, is said to develop a golden tail with age. This has not been observed by the authors, who presumably possess the other species. Their specimens, received at 3" in length, have grown to 10", but they still retain a black tail which shows no sign of changing colour.

The fish is somewhat shy, and frequents the back of the tank, lying on the sand behind the plants. It does not behave in the attractive manner of *L. bicolor*, which seems to enjoy showing itself off in the foreground of the aquarium.

Although *M. chrysophekadion* eats algae, it rarely crops this vegetable food from the leaves of plants, seeming to prefer scraped algae that has settled on the floor of the tank. The fish is a bottom feeder, and its two pairs of barbels no doubt assist it in feeling for food. Large specimens develop an extra bunch of barbels below the chin, giving the appearance of a distinct beard.

Breeding. *Few details available.*

191

RASBORAS

Still under the family Cyprinidae, we come to the rasboras. Dealing first with the genus *Rasbora*, there are many species. The fishes differ so greatly in appearance and size that it is hard to believe that all belong to the same genus. The majority are long and slender, but a few are short and deep-bodied. Most of the larger ones are rather dull, but the smaller species are colourful, and firm favourites.

Rasboras do well in aquaria, particularly if the water is soft and slightly acid, with a pH of 6·6.

Unfortunately, the larger and less popular rasboras are easier to breed than their smaller cousins, which are in greater demand. Since the methods of spawning differ, breeding habits will be given under the various species.

Rasbora borapetensis – *Red-tailed rasbora*

Thailand ♂ *1½"* ♀ *1¾"* *Community*
DIET: All foods *SWIMS: Mid-water*

This is one of the smaller rasboras of elongated shape, and has only recently been imported. Though not brilliant, the fish is colourful. The body is a golden grey. A black stripe bordered above by gold runs from the gill-plate to the base of the tail. The dorsal, ventral, and anal fins are tinged with red.

The female is longer than the male; her belly is rounder and deeper.

Breeding. *Very prolific, although the parents are notorious egg-eaters. Dense planting in the breeding tank will help prevent this.*

Rasbora daniconius – *Slender rasbora*

India, Sri Lanka   ♂ *3¹/₂"*   ♀ *4"*   *Community, with larger fishes*
DIET: All foods   SWIMS: *Mid-water*

Here is a medium to large *Rasbora* of the typical elongated shape.

The body is silver. Running from the gill-plate to the caudal peduncle is a thin black line bordered on each side by one of gold. The back is overcast with olive brown. the fins are slightly tinted yellow.

The female usually grows a little larger than her mate, and is fuller in the belly.

Breeding. *Tank: 30"×15"×15".   pH: 6·8-7·0.   Hardness: 100-120 p.p.m.   Temperature: 80°F.   Spawns: just above sand.   Eggs: 300-500.   Hatch: in 3 days.   Fry hang on: 2 days.   Free-swimming: 6th day.   Food 1st week: brine shrimp. 2nd week: fine dried food, microworms.*

For breeding the tank should be filled with rain-water, and thickly planted with feathery clumps. The fish chase each other swiftly; when they come into contact eggs are discharged; these are fertilized among the plants. On other occasions the fish will wriggle side by side just above the sand, with their noses in a corner of the aquarium. Large eggs are expelled and fertilized. The parents set up such a current in the water that the spawn is carried across the tank, and builds up in a mound against the glass at the opposite end. After spawning parents should be removed before they can devour their eggs.

Rasbora dorsiocellata – Eye-spot rasbora

Sumatra, Malaya ♂ *1½"* ♀ *1¾"* *Community*
DIET: All foods *SWIMS: Mid-water*

This little *Rasbora* is hardy, peaceful, and active.

Though lacking in bright colours, it makes up for loss of brilliance by other prominent features. A green highlight adorns the lower half of the eye, and slants across the body, ending just in front of the anal fin. Another highlight of gold appears horizontally in the caudal peduncle. A large black spot in the dorsal fin contrasts with a white splash immediately below.

Male and female are alike, except that she grows larger; when she is mature her belly is much rounder and deeper.

Breeding. *Tank: 24"×8"×8". pH: 5·4-6·0. Hardness: 5-20 p.p.m. Temperature: 80°F. Spawns: in plant thickets or nylon mops. Method: standard for egg-droppers. Eggs: 50-100. Hatch: in 48 hours. Fry hang on: 2 days. Free-swimming: 5th day. Food 1st week: infusoria. 2nd week: infusoria, brine shrimp.*

The fish will spawn among plants in brown peaty water which is extremely soft and has a very low pH. But the authors get better results by using nylon mops placed in a bare tank containing only 4" of water.

194

Rasbora einthoveni – Brilliant rasbora

Malaya, Sumatra ♂ 3½" ♀ 3¾" Community, with larger fishes
DIET: All foods SWIMS: Mid-water

The species illustrated here, being long-bodied and slender, is typical of some of the larger rasboras.

They prefer slightly acid water, and when settled down swim idly in the middle of the aquarium. But they can show a surprising turn of speed when attempts are made to catch them.

Like many species of the family, *R. einthoveni* is not brilliantly coloured, neither are the fins outstanding. The general colour of the body is a greyish-olive. A black line runs from the tip of the lower lip through the eye right through to the base of the tail. The line is not quite straight, but dips slightly in the middle. The fins are tinged with pale yellow, which is more rust-coloured in the male, who also in some lights carries a mauvish sheen here and there on the back.

The female is a little larger and deeper-bellied than the male.

Breeding. *Tank: 30"×15"×15". pH: 6·8. Hardness: 80-120 p.p.m. Temperature: 80°F. Spawns: in plant thickets. Method: standard for egg-droppers. Eggs: 500-600. Hatch: in 3 days. Fry hang on: 2 days. Free-swimming: 6th day. Food 1st week: brine shrimp. 2nd week: Cyclops, microworms.*

The tank should be thickly planted and the adults should be removed when spawning is completed. Some of the eggs turn white, presumably because unfertilized, but from the enormous quantity laid sufficient hatch to produce several hundred fry.

195

Rasbora elegans – Elegant rasbora

Malaya, Sumatra ♂ *4"* ♀ *4½"* *Community, with larger fishes*
DIET: All foods SWIMS: Upper half of tank

This is one of the largest of the rasboras kept in aquaria. The name is rather misleading, as the fish is not particularly elegant. Though not aggressive, when mature *R. elegans* should be kept with larger fishes.

The overall body colour is a silver-grey. A black rectangle adorns the centre of each side, and a dark spot lies at the base of the tail. These blotches lose their crispness as the fish grows. Above the anal fin there is an oblique black line.

The female exceeds the male in length, and her belly is deeper.

Breeding. *Tank: 30"×15"×15". pH: 6·6. Hardness: 100-120 p.p.m. Temperature: 80°F. Spawns: in plant thickets. Method: standard for egg-droppers. Eggs: 500-600. Hatch: in 2 days. Fry hang on: 2 days. Free-swimming: 5th day. Food 1st week: brine shrimp. 2nd week: Cyclops, microworms.*

In spite of being prolific in their natural habitat, the fish do not spawn readily in captivity. Large specimens occasionally tremble together in plant thickets and discharge numerous clear eggs. The parents should be removed after spawning, as they are inclined to eat the eggs.

Rasbora heteromorpha – Harlequin

Malaya, Sumatra ♂ *1¾"* ♀ *1¾"* *Community*
DIET: All foods *SWIMS: Upper half of tank*

This little beauty differs so greatly in shape from the elongated members of the group that the inexperienced aquarist may be excused in thinking that *R. heteromorpha* belongs to another genus. Since the advent of air travel harlequins are imported in thousands, 500 travelling quite comfortably in a plastic bag a foot in diameter, containing 1½ gallons of water, and blown up with pure oxygen. Few die, but in spite of the constant demand the source of supply is not depleted. They literally swarm in numerous pools in Malaya.

Our colour plate shows the fish in their normal hues, but at breeding-time these are intensified, and there is more suffused pink over the body.

Male and female are the same size, but the sexes are easily distinguished. Males are much redder in the dorsal and tail fins, also in the caudal peduncle region. The female is more golden, and when full of roe her belly is deeper than that of her mate. It is surprising that so many aquarists are under the impression that the fish are unsexable. Many people consider that the corner of the black triangle nearest the belly is more pointed and extends farther forward in males. This does occur sometimes, but is an unreliable guide to distinguish sex. The males are always redder; in our plate they will be seen as the leading fish, the one above in the third plate, and the last one in the shoal.

When seen in a well-planted tank, containing peaty acid water, the fish are at their best, and present a beautiful and impressive sight.

Breeding. *Tank: 24"×8"×8". pH: 5·0-6·4. Hardness: 10-50 p.p.m. Temperature: 80°F. Spawns: adhesive eggs. Method: eggs deposited under plant leaves. Eggs:*

197

50-70. Hatch: in 24 hours. Fry hang on: 1 day. Free-swimming: 3rd day. Food 1st week: infusoria. 2nd week: brine shrimp.

Breeding is not easy, but possible, given the right conditions. The tank should be filled with rain-water that has stood on peat for a week or two. The water should be a deep brown, and very soft. The tank should be planted with cryptocorynes. A well-coloured male and the roundest, fattest female should be selected. In a day or two the male will make short darts at his mate and, with fins well spread, show himself off. Soon she responds to his attentions. After a time she will swim to a leaf and turn upside down under it. The male follows, and curves himself against her. They tremble together, while the eggs are laid and fertilized under the leaf, to which they adhere. This behavour is repeated at short intervals for an hour or two, after which the parents should be removed, otherwise they may eat any eggs they can find.

Harlequins are sometimes bred communally, using two males and four females. But should only one pair start spawning the remaining fish are apt to devour the eggs. Occasionally the authors have witnessed a couple of the fish, not in an upside-down position, trembling together in a thicket of fine-leaved plants. Later eggs have been observed caught in the foliage. It would seem, therefore, that the upside-down spawning position is not always used.

Rasbora hengeli

Malaya, Sumatra   ♂ 1¼″   ♀ 1¼″   Community
DIET: All foods   SWIMS: Upper half of tank

This species is similar to the foregoing, except that it is slimmer, more elongated, and the black triangle is not nearly so deep. There is a more rosy glow over the body.

Breeding. *As for R. heteromorpha.*

♀

♂

Rasbora kalochroma – *Clown rasbora*

Malaya   ♂ 3"   ♀ 3"   Community
DIET: All foods   SWIMS: Mid-water

As will be seen from the photograph, this is an attractive *Rasbora*. It is peaceful, and, because of its long, slender shape, is a fast swimmer. The fish seems happy in captivity.

The body is suffused with red. A blue-black spot appears on the flanks a little behind the gill-plates. A larger block of the same colour adorns the forward portion of the caudal peduncle. The fins are red, but the ventrals and anal fin of the male are tipped with black.

Breeding.   *Few details available on captive breeding.*

Rasbora maculata – *Spotted rasbora*

Malaya   ♂ ⅞"   ♀ 1"   Community, with small fishes
DIET: All foods   SWIMS: Mid-water

Until recently the smallest of all rasboras, this pretty little fish is imported in hundreds. But frequently it fails to survive the journey.

The overall colour is reddish mahogany, and a large black spot adorns the forward part of the body. The dorsal fin is red; the forward rays are tipped top and bottom with black spots. A further small spot is found at the base of the tail, and another on the upper portion of the anal fin. In males there is a spot on the body above the anal fin, but females show two spots here. These features enable the sexes to be distinguished when quite young. At maturity, however, the male is a richer red and generally more colourful than his mate; she is somewhat rounder in the region of the belly.

Breeding. *Tank: 10"×5"×5".   pH: 5·4-6·0.   Hardness: 5-20 p.p.m.   Temperature: 80°F.   Spawns: in plant thickets or nylon mops.   Method: male locks female in caudal grip.   Eggs: 50-100.   Hatch: in 48 hours.   Fry hang on: 2 days.   Free-swimming: 5th day.   Food 1st week: infusoria. 2nd week: infusoria, brine shrimp.*

The species may be spawned in a very small tank containing soft brown peaty water, and planted with one or two clumps of *Myriophyllum*. But recently the authors have found it less trouble to place a pair in a glass jar, roughly 8" long by 5" wide, filled with very soft brown peaty water to a depth of 4". In this place two nylon mops which have been sterilized in boiling water. The male soon starts driving the female, and, coming side by side, he presses her into the foliage or mops, though sometimes this action takes place above the plants or mops. Then,

200

quivering together, the male locks the hinder portion of his body—*i.e.*, his tail and most of the caudal peduncle area—over and round the same part of the female. Immediately eggs are discharged and fertilized, dropping into the plants or mops. The procedure is repeated for an hour or more, after which the parents should be removed. The small, slightly amber eggs are not easy to see. Neither are the tiny fry until free-swimming. They grow quickly, and are ¼" long in 3 weeks.

Rasbora pauciperforata – Glowlight rasbora

Malaya, Sumatra ♂ 2½" ♀ 2¾" Community
DIET: All foods SWIMS: Mid-water

This smallish rasbora when kept under ideal conditions rivals the neon tetras for brilliance. It is peaceful, quite hardy, and likes to swim in shoals, though frequently remaining motionless in one spot. If kept in a community tank it must only be housed with small fishes. To see *R. pauciperforata* at its best a few should be placed in a special aquarium containing soft brown peaty water. The tank should be thickly planted with cryptocorynes against a dark background, the whole lit from above with the light rays projected backward.

The brownish body is adorned by a fiery red stripe, edged below by one of black, and above by a thin one of gold. So brilliant is the red line that it literally seems to draw the eyes of the observer.

Sexing can only be told by the fuller belly of the mature female.

Breeding. *Tank: 24"×8"×8". pH: 6·0-6·0. Hardness: 70-90 p.p.m. Temperature: 76°F. Spawns: in plant thickets. Method: male and female tremble side by side. Eggs: 200-300. Hatch: in 48 hours. Fry hang on: 3 days. Free-swimming: 6th day. Food 1st week: infusoria. 2nd week: brine shrimp.*

The following method has proved successful in the past. A small tank with a bottom layer of peat was filled with rain-water. Unplanted *Cryptocoryne* roots and cuttings were placed so thickly in the aquarium that there was no swimming space left. It was then allowed to stand for 3 to 4 weeks. After this period fish were introduced on the off-chance of spawning: they started doing so the next day. Male and female could be seen trembling together, though no eggs were observed. The parents were removed in the evening. A week later fry were seen swimming. 250 youngsters were raised. The parents were stated to be three years old.

Rasbora trilineata – Scissor-tail rasbora

Malaya, Sumatra, Borneo, Thailand ♂ *3″* ♀ *3″* *Community*
DIET: *All foods* SWIMS: *Mid-water*

A firm favourite, this semi-transparent fish is light and dainty. In the wild it is said to grow to 8″ or 9″, but the aquarium specimens rarely reach more than a third of this length.

From the gill-plate to the base of the tail there runs a thin black line; the forward portion of this is sometimes less distinct than the rear half, which has a thin greenish-gold upper border. Another thin black line appears just above the anal fin. The back is a golden-green. All the fins are golden. But the tail is different; in fact, it is the most striking feature. The upper and lower lobes each contain an oblique black patch. This is bordered on either side by a yellow one which is fainter on the outside. As the fish swims the tail opens and closes, and the markings draw attention to the scissor-like action—hence the popular name.

Females are a little longer and deeper-bodied than males.

Breeding. *Tank:* *24″ × 8″ × 8″. Hardness: 30-80 p.p.m. Temperature: 80°F. Spawns: in plant thickets. Method: standard for barbs. Eggs: 1000-1500. Hatch: in 36 hours. Fry hang on: 2 days. Free-swimming: 4th day. Food 1st week: infusoria. 2nd week: brine shrimp, microworms.*

The species will spawn when only 2″ long. The tank should be filled with rain-water, and in the middle contain short plants, small Indian ferns serving well. At each end a clump of feathery foliage is provided. The fish should spawn the following morning, after which the parents should be removed.

There is a colour variety of this fish. It is called the golden scissor-tail, as the caudal fin is more yellow.

Rasbora urophthalma – Miniature rasbora

Malaya   ♂ ¾"   ♀ ¾"   *Community, with small fishes*
DIET: All foods   SWIMS: Mid-water

Like most fishes from this area, it prefers brown peaty water. It is so small that it vies with *R. maculata* for the distinction of being the smallest species of the genus.

When kept under these conditions this otherwise drab little fish assumes a quiet coloration. The back is reddish-brown, the belly bluish-silver. A blue-black line, edged above with gold, runs the length of the sides from gill-plate to tail, and ends in a spot of the same colour; hence the name *urophthalma* (literally, 'tail-eye').

Females are rounder and deeper-bellied than males.

Breeding. *Tank: 12"×8"×8". pH: 5·6-6·4. Hardness: 25-75 p.p.m. Temperature: 80°F. Spawns: in plant thickets. Method: standard for barbs. Eggs: 50-70. Hatch: in 48 hours. Fry hang on: 2 days. Free-swimming: 5th day. Food 1st week: infusoria. 2nd week: infusoria, brine shrimp.*

The following method proved successful for the authors. The tank was filled with soft brown peaty water, the bottom being covered with a half-inch layer of sieved peat that had become waterlogged. Two young Indian ferns with their roots held down by a small piece of slate were used as spawning plants. The male began to follow the female and drive her gently. The pair came together in the plant fronds, trembled side by side, and minute eggs were seen falling. The parents were removed, and young were observed hanging on 48 hours later.

203

Rasbora vaterifloris – Fire rasbora

Ceylon   ♂ 1¼"   ♀ 1½"   Community
DIET: All foods   SWIMS: Upper half of tank

This fish first appeared in Britain in 1955. In size and shape it resembles *R. heteromorpha*, but *R. vaterifloris* is more translucent and delicate-looking. The dorsal and anal fins are slightly longer, more pointed, and have a graceful backward curve.

This is no black triangle on the sides of this fish. The back is bluish-grey, the sides silvery. The whole body is overcast with reddish amber, being richer in the caudal region. All the fins are reddish amber, except the tail, which carries this colour only in the lower lobe, the upper one being clear.

In comparison with the male, the female is slightly deeper in the body. She is a little smaller and paler, being more amber in hue.

Breeding.   *Relatively difficult. Soft acid water at around 25°C is needed. The eggs are laid amongst vegetation. Since the parents are avid egg-eaters, they must be removed. The eggs hatch after 36-48 hours; the fry will feed on infusoria and brine shrimp.*

Tanichthys albonubes – *White cloud mountain minnow*

China   ♂ 1¹/₄″   ♀ 1¹/₂″   Community
DIET: All foods   SWIMS: Upper half of tank

One of the most attractive aquarium fishes, these little beauties will live happily in indoor tanks in cool rooms without any additional heat. Nevertheless, they are more lively and colourful if kept between 75° and 80°F., at which temperature they will breed. The fish are happiest swimming in shoals.

Adults are easy to sex, males being brighter. The females are slightly larger and deeper in the belly; this depth extends as far back as the anal fin. In males the chest may be deep but he tapers off just behind the ventrals. Unfortunately, the glowing green line loses its lustre with age, becoming a creamy green.

Breeding. *Tank: 25″×8″×8″. pH: 7·0-7·4. Hardness: 100-150 p.p.m. Temperature: 78°F. Spawns: in plant thickets. Method: similar to danios. Eggs: 100-150. Hatch: in 48 hours. Fry hang on: 1 day. Free-swimming: 4th day. Food 1st week: infusoria. 2nd week: brine shrimp, microworms.*

One of the easiest species to breed, but the tank should be thickly planted to prevent the parents eating their eggs.

Commercial breeders often favour spawning these fish communally. This is best done using a thickly planted large shallow tank or an old sink, the surface of the water being covered with a 1″ thick layer of *Riccia*. Then with an enamel soup-ladle the *Riccia* is pressed down each morning, and the tiny fry scooped up and transferred to small tanks.

Chapter Fifteen

Characins and their Relatives

SUB-ORDER CHARACOIDEI

A large group of fishes coming from most of South America, Panama, parts of Mexico, and Texas; also from Central, East, and West Africa. It includes the tetras, headstanders, pencil fishes and piranhas, which are divided between a number of families within the sub-order Characoidei. Although belonging to the same order as the carps and catfishes, characins, as they are popularly called, possess teeth and an adipose fin; the whole family does not have both these features, but at least one of them is possessed by all members. The fishes vary greatly in size and shape, the smaller ones being generally peaceful and attractive, but some of the larger specimens, particularly the notorious piranha, are very savage, and use their razor-like teeth to slash and devour anything meaty which happens to cross their path.

A few of the medium-sized species are apt to tear and chew up the more tender plants in the aquarium, and occasionally use their teeth to fray the tails of small fishes. Nevertheless, the small species are not only peaceful and good community fishes, but they provide the aquarist with some of the most beautiful inhabitants of the tank. Moreover, they are easily cared for and fed; dried food and any small live food will be taken.

Some are extremely easy to breed; others are difficult. The majority drop semi-adhesive eggs. The standard 24"×8"×8" tank is usually adequate, and procedure follows that laid down for spawning egg-droppers. The breeding of these species which are exceptions to the rule is described under the individual fish.

Alestopetersius caudalis

Zaire ♂ *2½"* ♀ *3"* *Community*
DIET: Live food, may be trained to take dried food *SWIMS: Mid-water*

It is slender in shape, the flanks are somewhat compressed, and, like so many of the West African fishes, the eye is large in comparison with the overall size.

Above the lateral line the body is pale blue, turning to golden along the centre line, and the belly is silver-white. Gold and blue highlights reflect from the scales as the angle of light catches them. The fins are rich yellow-gold, and in males the dorsal is large, with trailing points on the first few rays. These are edged with grey-black. The anal fin is long and pointed, and the tail has a central extension forming a point projecting between the upper and lower lobes. This spike is blue-black in colour. The fins of the female are similar, but she lacks the long points.

Breeding. *Tank: 30″×15″×15″. pH: 5·6-5·8. Hardness: 20-50 p.p.m. Temperature: 78°F. Spawns: in plant thickets. Method: standard for egg-droppers. Eggs: 50-100. Hatch: in 48 hours. Fry hang on: 2 days. Free-swimming: 5th day. Food 1st week: infusoria, yolk of egg. 2nd week: brine shrimp, microworms.*

These fish are difficult to induce to spawn, but will do so on occasions, using soft peaty water in which has been placed a large mat of bladderwort anchored down here and there with well-washed pebbles or pieces of clean slate. Spawning was not observed, but eggs were seen among the plant threads, which hatched in 48-60 hours.

Anostomus anostomus – Striped headstander

Guyana ♂ 5″ ♀ 5″ Community, with larger fishes
DIET: All foods SWIMS: Lower half of tank

An odd fish with a long, cylindrical body, a flattened, pointed head, and large eyes. It moves about slowly with the head inclined downward, but at the slightest disturbance it can speed through the water rapidly.

The body is divided by longitudinal stripes of blue-black and gold. A deep patch of blood-red adorns the forward portion of the dorsal fin, and appears again spreading from the caudal peduncle through the forepart of the tail. The other fins are clear.

The male is slimmer than the female, and his colours are a little more intense.

Breeding. *Few details available.*

Aphyocharax rubripinnis – Bloodfin

Argentina ♂ *1½"* ♀ *1¾" Community*
DIET: All foods SWIMS: Upper half of tank

This little fish has long been an aquarium favourite. It has a lively disposition, keeps its fins well spread, is extremely hardy, and easy to breed.

The streamlined body is a silvery grey-blue. The dorsal, ventrals, anal, and forward portion of the tail fins are bright blood-red, the edges of these fins being clear. The ventrals and anal are tipped with white.

Femaies are a little larger than males, and when full of roe are much deeper-bodied. Males caught in a fine net sometimes get hooked by a minute spine on the tip of the anal fin. But sexing by this method is unreliable, since this tiny hook does not always catch in the net.

Breeding. *Tank: 24"×8"×8". pH: 7·0-7·2. Hardness: 120-150 p.p.m. Temperature: 78°F. Spawns: in top weed; fish leaps out of water. Method: standard for egg-droppers. Eggs: 100-150. Hatch: in 48 hours. Fry hang on: 1 day. Free-swimming: 4th day. Food 1st week: infusoria. 2nd week: infusoria, brine shrimp.*

For breeding the tank should be filled with fresh tap-water, and very thickly planted with short Indian ferns or other wide-spreading leafy plants. Breeding takes place in the early morning under good light, the pair chasing each other, and finally leaping from the water. Their bodies come into contact above the surface, when numerous eggs are discharged and fertilized. These sink to the bottom and remain hidden among the low foliage. If some *Riccia* is floating near the surface the

208

fish will sometimes wriggle into it and spawn without leaping from the water, some of the eggs remaining among the green threads. Immediately spawning has finished the pair should be removed, as they are likely to eat every egg they can find. Though bloodfins are easy to spawn, the young are so small that they may be difficult to raise. Some breeders use egg-laying traps. Alternatively several pairs may be spawned by the method referred to in Chapter 12.

Astyanax mexicanus – Blind cave fish

Mexico   ♂ 2³/₄″   ♀ 3″   Community
DIET: All foods   SWIMS: Mid-water

Here we have a most interesting characin, which is naturally blind. This feature is by no means unique, as there are several species of blind fishes in the world. The majority of aquarists on seeing *A. mexicanus* for the first time are reluctant to buy it, having the mistaken impression that to keep such a creature is unkind and somewhat repulsive. The authors have no hesitation in saying that it is one of their favourites, and those aquarists who have been persuaded to overcome their prejudice have become equally ardent enthusiasts.

Thousands of years ago these fish were carried by currents into underground caves where little or no light existed; and because sight was of no use in this subterranean home Nature in the course of time ceased to provide these useless organs.

The fish is a brilliant shining silver, the fins being creamy. In large females the first rays of the anal and ventral fins are pink.

A. mexicanus swims at all depths; even in thickly planted tanks it rarely bumps into the foliage. The fish are equipped with extremely sensitive organs which warn them of obstacles in their path. It is amazing to see how they change direction to avoid plants, rocks, other fishes, and the sides of the tank.

Their blindness is no handicap, for the instant the aquarium cover is raised these docile fish become active and acute; they are first on the food, be this live or dried. Should anything edible be given during the hours of darkness 'blind caves' have a distinct advantage over all fishes with sight. As scavengers *A. mexicanus* are equally as good as the generally recommended catfishes, but whereas the latter after satisfying themselves frequently disappear among the foliage at the back, remaining hidden until the next meal, blind caves disport themselves at all times in full view in the forefront of the aquarium.

Sexing is easy, as females are much rounder and deeper-bellied than the males.

Breeding. Tank: 30"×15"×15". pH: 6·8-7·2. Hardness: 120-180 p.p.m. Temperature: 78°F. Spawns: in clear water above plants. Method: scatters semi-adhesive eggs. Eggs: 500-750. Hatch: in 24 hours. Fry hang on: 2 days. Free-swimming: 4th day. Food 1st week: infusoria. 2nd week: brine shrimp, sifted Cyclops.

Large fish breed easily. The tank should be filled with 4/5ths tap-water and 1/5th rain-water. The bottom should be covered with short plants, but two or three clumps of *Myriophyllum* should be provided. A good male and a very plump female should be placed in the tank shortly before dusk; they will spawn next morning. The pair swim about in the clear water above the plants. Periodically they approach one another head on and, with bodies touching, rapidly revolve round each other. Then, with a slap of their tails, they break apart, and scores of tiny eggs may be seen falling through the water. The process is repeated for about two hours. Occasionally, though not generally, a pair will swim side by side, pressing their bodies in close contact, and again with a slap of their tails they will break apart, showering fertilized eggs into the water. At the end of the spawn the female is so thin that she looks like a male, while he, slimmer to start with, is now so reduced that his lower sides cave in. Moreover, his anal and ventral fins may become streaked with blood, as though the strain had caused internal bleeding. Both parents should now be removed and placed apart, where they can receive peace and good food. In a few days the blood-streaks fade, and the fish return to normal weight. Most of the tiny eggs fall to the sand, disappearing from view; a few get lodged in the clumps of *Myriophyllum,* and can be seen.

Next day the tiny fry will be noticed hanging from plants and on the glass walls of the aquarium. Once the babies are large enough to eat brine shrimp it should be given. However, this should be fed alternately with other foods, since the saline diet used exclusively for more than 21 days kills the fish. It will be noticed that the fry have eyes, though it would appear that they are sightless, as movements of the hands in front of the tank are unnoticed. After several weeks scale grows over the eyes, which appear to degenerate, leaving a hollow socket in their place.

Carnegiella strigata – *Marbled hatchet*

Guyana   ♂ 1½" ♀ 1¾" Community
DIET: All foods   SWIMS: Upper half of tank

The hatchet fishes, as they are popularly called, are extremely deep-bodied, and their side view resembles an axe-head. They have large, wing-shaped, pectoral fins which are used for skimming about beneath the water surface, also for carrying the fish through the air, into which it leaps when pursued. The span of the pectorals enables the fish to glide for considerable distances; during these flights the deep body serves as a keel to keep an upright position. To prevent these fishes from leaping out of the aquarium a cover glass is essential.

Hatchets are extremely peaceful, but they should be kept on their own or with other small species. Larger fishes are apt to bully them, and shorten their aquarium life.

C. strigata is probably the prettiest of the hatchets, and is a most desirable fish in the small aquarium. Unfortunately, it is shy, and tends to hide in the top back corners until confidence is gained. In the right environment it lives well. It is not cheap.

The body is silvery. Dark wavy brown to black bars run diagonally across the flanks, giving a marbled appearance. Gold and green patches are reflected about the head, and behind the pectoral fins.

Breeding. *Few details are available.*

211

Charax gibbosus – Glass characin

Amazon, Guyana ♂ 3½″ ♀ 3¾″ *Community, with larger fishes*
DIET: All foods SWIMS: Mid-water

Here we have an attractive, rather transparent fish that is peaceful enough with other species of roughly the same size. Though most of the organs are enclosed in a silvery sac, the swim-bladder can be clearly seen. The position of the head and back suggests deformity, but this appearance is quite natural.

The body is covered with minute silvery scales. One large black spot appears on the side; another, somewhat elongated, is at the base of the tail. Just in front of the forward spot there is a bright splash of green-gold. Also, running along the lateral line, is a thin green-gold stripe, which is reflected in certain lights. As the fish turns away a green-gold hue on the lower portion of the swim-bladder shines through the transparent scales.

The male is slightly smaller and slimmer than the female. When she is full of roe, though laterally compressed, she is thicker in section than the male in the abdominal region.

The fish swim in mid-water, often stopping motionless for periods with their heads tilted downward. They occasionally make a playful dart at each other, but no harm is done.

Breeding. *Tank: 24″×8″×8″. pH: 7·0. Hardness: 100-150 p.p.m. Temperature: 80°F. Spawns: in plant thickets. Method: standard for egg-droppers. Eggs: 150-200. Hatch: in 24 hours. Fry hang on: 1 day. Free-swimming: 3rd day. Food 1st week: infusoria. 2nd week: infusoria, brine shrimp.*

Adults breed easily in well-planted tanks filled chiefly with tap-water plus a little rain-water. After spawning parents should be transferred to another tank. Some fry race ahead of others; these should be removed, or they will devour the smaller ones.

♀

♂

Chilodus punctatus – *Spotted headstander*

North-eastern S. America   ♂ 3"   ♀ 3"   Community
DIET: All foods   SWIMS: Mid-water

This is an attractive characin which spends most of its time with its head inclined downward at an angle of about 60 degrees from the horizontal. When not swimming or hovering in this position it is usually pecking small particles of food from the sand, with the body almost vertical. This habit makes it a good scavenger. It seems peaceful with other fishes, but makes short darts at its own brothers and sisters.

The body has a slight greenish sheen, but is covered with horizontal rows of brown spots. A brown line runs from the tip of the pointed snout through the eye to the edge of the gill-plate, and behind this there is a large brown spot. All the fins are clear except the dorsal, which has a dark brown front ray and a large brown patch in the upper foremost portion, the rest of this fin being sprinkled with brown dots.

Females are plumper than males.

Breeding. *Tank: 24"×12"×12".   pH: 6·6.   Hardness: 50-80 p.p.m.   Temperature: 80°F.   Spawns: in nylon mops.   Method: standard for egg-droppers.   Eggs: 150-200.   Hatch: in 3 days.   Fry hang on: 2 days.   Free-swimming: 6th day.   Food 1st week: infusoria.   2nd week: infusoria, brine shrimp.*

The species is not easy to induce to spawn, but the pale brown eggs can be seen in the nylon mops. After this both parents should be removed.

213

♀

♂

Copeina guttata – Spotted tetra

Guyana, Brazil   ♂ 4″   ♀ 3⅜″   Community, with larger fishes
DIET: All foods   SWIMS: Mid-water

A colourful, peaceful fish, but due to its size it is suitable for large tanks.

The back and sides are pale blue, the belly white. All the fins are pale yellow, bordered by cherry red. The dorsal, however, is lemon-coloured with an oblique black blotch in the forward central portion. This marking is less pronounced in the male, but he has rows of bright red spots along his sides, and his caudal fin has more red in it. He is also slimmer than the female.

Breeding. *Tank: 24″×8″×8″.   pH: 7·0-7.2.   Hardness: 100-150 p.p.m.   Temperature: 80°F.   Spawns: on flat surface.   Method: adhesive eggs fanned by male.   Eggs: 150-250.   Hatch: in 48 hours.   Free-swimming: 3rd day.   Food 1st week: infusoria. 2nd week: infusoria, brine shrimp.*

Breeding is simple. The tank should be filled with equal quantities of rain- and tap-water, and be moderately well-planted. In the centre of a clear space should be left, and a flat stone or saucer should be placed on the sand. After courtship the male and female quiver side by side and deposit about 200 fertilized eggs, which adhere to the saucer or stone. Afterwards the male drives the female away, and she should be removed. He now spends all his time fanning the spawn with his pectoral fins to circulate the water round the eggs.

214

♂

♀

Copella (Copeina) arnoldi – *Splashing tetra*

Northern S. America ♂ *2¼″* ♀ *2″ Community*
DIET: *All foods* SWIMS: *Mid-water*

Though not brilliant in colour, this delightful aquarium fish is by no means drab. The finnage on good males is magnificent. The female's fins are shorter, and there is no white spot in the base of her dorsal.

Breeding. *Tank: 24″×8″×8″. pH: 6.8-7.0. Hardness: 100-150 p.p.m. Temperature: 80°F. Spawns: above water surface. Method: adhesive eggs stuck to cover glass. Eggs: 50-100. Hatch: in 4 days. Fry wriggling: 1 day. Fry fall into water, becoming free-swimming: 6th day. Food 1st week: infusoria. 2nd week: infusoria, brine shrimp.*

This peaceful species has a unique method of breeding. It lays eggs above the surface of the water, which should be about 1″ to 1½″ below the cover glass. The tank should be moderately thickly stocked with assorted plants, merely to provide peaceful surroundings and afford a possible refuge for the female. A good pair is introduced, and a day later the male, coming alongside, presses his flank against the female and coaxes her to the surface. Suddenly the pair will leap from the water, and with quite a resounding smack hit and cling to the under side of the cover glass. Their damp bodies, having displaced some of the surrounding air, adhere momentarily to the flat surface. Eggs are laid and fertilized on the under surface of the glass; then the pair fall back into the water. The process is repeated several times. The male then drives the female away, and she is best removed. He

215

takes full charge from now on. Periodically he may be seen going to the surface beneath the eggs, then with a vigorous stroke of his tail he will splash up water to keep them moist. Between these damping bouts the male moves away from the eggs, as though not wishing to advertise their presence.

From above the eggs can be seen in little globules of water, and development can be watched. They must not be allowed to fall into the tank before the babies are strong enough to swim. Whenever the cover glass is raised for feeding, or for any other purpose, it must be held dead level. Otherwise the globules of water run down the slope and carry the eggs with them; these may prematurely drop into the tank, or even fall on the floor. When it is necessary to rest the cover glass on anything it is best to place it over two jam-jars so that the eggs on its under surface are not squashed. After a few days the fry can be seen moving in the globules still adhering to the under side of the cover glass. It is now time to remove the male. Later the fry in their struggles cause the globules to drop into the water, when the babies are liberated in the tank to swim freely about.

Occasionally a male is too vigorous when splashing the eggs, and the globules of water become too large and drop into the tank, carrying the developing eggs with them. These the male proceeds to devour. Should this happen, on the next occasion the fish are spawned both parents should be removed, and an air-line with a stone diffuser at its end should be placed in the water below the eggs. The minute rising air bubbles cause a tiny spray of water to be thrown upward; this proves to be sufficient to keep the eggs damp until they hatch.

Corynopoma riisei – *Swordtail characin*

Northern S. America   ♂ 2¾″   ♀ 2½″   *Community*
DIET: *All foods*   SWIMS: *Upper half of tank*

This peaceful characin derives its scientific name from the long filament which grows from the gill-plate of the male, and normally lies flat along the sides of the body. Due to the extended rays in the lower lobe of the male's caudal fin, the popular name is swordtail characin.

The body is creamy-coloured with no bright markings, but it is the fins of the male that strike the eye. When fully grown he has, relative to his size, large dorsal, anal, and caudal fins. The dorsal is somewhat kite-shaped, being broader at the top than at the base. The anal is wide, deep, and well-rounded, spreading from the vent to the caudal. His tail has several long rays in the lower lobe; these extend beyond the upper one.

The fins of the female are not spectacular.

Breeding.   *Tank: 24″×8″×8″.   pH: 6·8-7·2.   Hardness: 100-150 p.p.m.   Temperature: 78°F.   Spawns: male and female 1″ apart.   Method: eggs deposited on leaf.   Eggs: 100-200.   Hatch: in 24 hours.   Fry hang on: 1 day.   Free-swimming: 3rd day.   Food 1st week: infusoria. 2nd week: infusoria, brine shrimp.*

216

The species breed readily. The tank should be moderately planted. The male soon starts courting by spreading his fins to full extent and joyfully disporting himself in front of his mate. The pair do not come close together, but swim side by side about 1¼″ apart. The male then curves his anal fin towards the female. It is thought that this action directs spermatozoa towards her, for a few seconds later she may be seen depositing eggs on plant leaves. The process is repeated until up to 100 eggs are laid, when the male should be taken out of the tank. The female often transfers the eggs from one leaf to another with her mouth. It is just as well to remove her when the fry are free-swimming.

Some breeders believe that the male ejects spermatozoa into the spoon-like disc at the end of the gill filament and proffers it to the female. It is thought that she takes the sperm into her mouth, spitting it out on to the leaf which she has selected for laying her eggs. She certainly appears to mouth the leaves before depositing her ova. This theory would explain the need for the gill extension possessed by the male.

Though somewhat rarer, there is a golden variety of this fish.

Ctenobrycon spilurus – Silver tetra

Guyana ♂ *3½"* ♀ *3½"* *Community, with larger fishes*
DIET: *All foods* SWIMS: *Mid-water*

One of the larger characins, this fish has compressed sides, so that viewed head on it appears less bulky than seen in profile. It has lost much of its popularity, for it is inclined to nip the fins of other fishes. Worse still, it is an inveterate plant-eater, and will quickly ruin a beautifully planted tank. Furthermore, the fish is inclined to remain stationary, head inclined downward, in one of the back corners, refusing to display itself in an attractive manner.

The body is void of bright colours, being silvery all over, with one dark spot in the shoulder region and another at the base of the tail.

The male is slightly smaller than the female. When mature she shows a pinkish tint in the rear portion of the anal fin.

Breeding. *Tank: 30"×15"×15". pH: 7·0-7·4. Hardness: 100-150 p.p.m. Temperature: 78°F. Spawns: in plant thickets. Method: standard for egg-droppers. Eggs: 200-300. Hatch: in 48 hours. Fry hang on: 1 day. Free-swimming: 4th day. Food 1st week: infusoria. 2nd week: brine shrimp, sifted Cyclops.*

The species is easy to breed. The tank should be thickly planted at each end with bushy clumps. Spawning takes place in the morning, the pair trembling side by side in the thickets. After spawning the parents should be removed.

Ephippicarax orbicularis – Salmon discus characin

W. Africa ♂ *2½"* ♀ *2¾"* *Community, with larger fishes*
DIET: *All foods* SWIMS: *Mid-water*

This is in every way far superior to *C. spilurus*. Salmon discus are a better shape, and the fins are more attractive. The fish are not fin-nippers or destroyers of plants. Moreover, they delight in swimming backward and forward across the front of the aquarium, always displaying themselves to view. Though generally hardy, *E. orbicularis* are susceptible to shock. A sudden fright or, when in transit, a bad bump, will cause them to roll over; some recover, but others die.

The body is covered with small, shining silver scales. The gracefully backward-curved dorsal and anal fins are longish and pointed. The first rays in each are black, but are more pronounced in the anal. When in perfect condition both these fins are bordered with a thin black edge.

The female is slightly larger and deeper-chested than the male. When viewed from the front the lower portion of her body is U-shaped, whereas the male is sharper, and more resembles the letter V.

218

♀   ♂

Breeding. *Tank: 24"×8"×8". pH: 7·0. Hardness: 100-150 p.p.m. Temperature: 80°F. Spawns: in plant thickets. Method: standard for egg-droppers. Eggs: 150-200. Hatch: in 24 hours. Fry hang on: 1 day. Free-swimming: 3rd day. Food 1st week: infusoria. 2nd week: infusoria, brine shrimp.*

Breeding is not difficult. The tank should be filled half with rain-water and half with tap-water. The pair usually spawn the following morning, after which they should be removed. Eggs may be seen among the plants, but in any case the female is now so slim that it is difficult to distinguish her from the male. The young grow quickly, and reach ½" in diameter in 4-5 weeks. Fry should be occasionally sorted, as the bigger ones are liable to eat their smaller brethren.

♂

♀

Gasteropelecus levis – Silver hatchet

Colombia, Venezuela ♂ *2¼″* ♀ *2½″* *Community*
DIET: All foods SWIMS: Upper half of tank

It is the largest of the hatchets so far imported, and is moderately hardy provided it is given good conditions. Because of its size it does well with medium-sized fishes in a community tank. Like other hatchets, it can be trained to take dried food.

The body is a glistening silver; the back is olive. A dark blue stripe bordered above and below by silver runs from the pectoral fins to the base of the tail.

Males are usually a little smaller than females, but sexing is difficult.

Breeding. *So far as is known, G. levis has not been bred in captivity.*

Gymnocorymbus ternetzi – Black widow

Paraguay ♂ 1¾" ♀ 2¼" Community
DIET: All foods SWIMS: Mid-water

A firm favourite of long standing, this attractive fish is at its best when young, and if seen in a shoal against a green background. Under these conditions it resembles a black butterfly. When in health it always carries its fins erect, and is sprightly in its movements.

The fore-part of the body of a young fish is silvery, with two black bars running vertically across. The dorsal, large anal, and hind portion of the body is jet black. With age the fish becomes less sprightly, and the intense black fades to a dark grey. When stimulated the black reappears.

Many aquarists find it difficult to sex half-grown specimens. But if the eye is trained to observe only the body of the fish, and to disregard completely the fins, it will be noticed that the males are more elongated, whereas females are deeper in comparison with their length. When filled with roe females are so bulged that sex is obvious.

Breeding. *Tank: 24"×8"×8". pH: 6·8-7·0. Hardness: 100-150 p.p.m. Temperature: 78°F. Spawns: in plant thickets. Method: standard for egg-droppers. Eggs: 150-200. Hatch: in 24 hours. Fry hang on: 1 day. Free-swimming: 3rd day. Food 1st week: infusoria. 2nd week: infusoria, brine shrimp.*

Black widows are one of the easiest characins to breed. The tank should be thickly planted. If a really fat female and a good male are placed together before dusk they should spawn the next morning. The parents should then be removed.

221

Hasemania marginata – Silver tetra

Brazil ♂ 1¼″ ♀ 1½″ Community
DIET: All foods SWIMS: Mid-water

Now known as *Hemigrammus nanus*, this is an attractive little characin; it is sprightly, not shy, peaceful, and when mature is moderately colourful.

The body and fins of the male are old gold; vivid white tips stand out on the dorsal, ventral, and caudal lobes. A black wedge runs through the caudal peduncle and ends in the fork of the tail; this is adorned above and below by gold patches in the front part of the caudal fin. Females lack the golden hue, and consequently the white tips to the fins are less conspicuous.

Breeding. *Tank: 24″×8″×8″. pH: 6·6-6·8. Hardness: 80-120 p.p.m. Temperature: 78°F. Spawns: in plant thickets. Method: standard for egg-droppers. Eggs: 70-120. Hatch: in 24 hours. Fry hang on: 1 day. Free-swimming: 3rd day. Food 1st week: infusoria. 2nd week: infusoria, brine shrimp.*

222

Hemigrammus armstrongi – Gilded tetra

Northern S. America ♂ *1½"* ♀ *1¾"* *Community*
DIET: All foods *SWIMS: Upper haf of tank*

The body is a shining gold, the back being more brilliant than the lower flanks, and in the males there is often a bronzy sheen. There is a black blotch in the centre of the caudal peduncle which stretches into the shorter rays of the caudal fin. The fins of the male are longer and more pointed, and these have a bronzy coloration, the tip of the dorsal and anal being white.

Unfortunately, few of the home-bred fish produce the glisten of wild specimens, being more transparent and lacking the burnished golden sparkle. There is a faint glimmer of a golden line from eye to caudal peduncle.

Breeding. *Tank: 24"×8"×8". pH: 6·8-7·0. Hardness: 80-140 p.p.m. Temperature: 78°F. Spawns: in plant thickets. Method: standard for egg-droppers. Eggs: 100-150. Hatch: in 24 hours. Fry hang on: 1 day. Free-swimming: 3rd day. Food 1st week: infusoria. 2nd week: infusoria, brine shrimp.*

Quite an easy species to breed—but do not expect the young raised in an aquarium to obtain the glistening gold colouring of their wild parents.

223

Hemigrammus caudovittatus – Red-tailed tetra

Argentina, Uruguay ♂ *3″* ♀ *3½″* *Community, with large fishes*
DIET: All foods SWIMS: Mid-water

This is quite a showy fish of pleasing appearance, although its habits are rather unpleasant. It nibbles most of the aquarium plants, but does not seem to fancy the cryptocorynes. When *H. caudovittatus* reaches maturity it should be kept in a large tank with other fishes of similar size, as it is liable to chase little ones and nip their tails.

Both sexes are similarly coloured, but the males are slightly brighter.

Females are larger and deeper-bellied.

Breeding. *Tank: 24″×8″×8″. pH: 6·8-7·0. Hardness: 100-150 p.p.m. Temperature: 78°F. Spawns: in plant thickets. Method: standard for egg-droppers. Eggs: 150-250. Hatch: in 24 hours. Fry hang on: 1 day. Free-swimming: 3rd day. Food 1st week: infusoria. 2nd week: infusoria, brine shrimp.*

One of the easiest characins to breed. A large pair placed in a well-planted tank at dusk rarely fail to spawn next morning. Parents should be removed immediately afterwards.

Hemigrammus hyanuary – *Costello tetra*

Brazil ♂ 1½" ♀ 1½" Community
DIET: All foods SWIMS: Mid-water

Slightly elongated in shape, this silver fish has a faint gold line from eye to caudal peduncle. In some lights, and amongst younger specimens, this line shines a silvery-green. There is a diamond-shaped black splodge in the caudal peduncle, surrounded by a whitish area, which turns to brilliant gold on the upper side between tail fin and adipose fin. Dorsal, adipose, and all other fins are darkish, though the dorsal is tipped with white, and the front rays and tip of the anal fin are intense white.

Females are deeper-bodied than males, though sexing is not easy when the females lack roe.

Breeding. *Tank: 24"×8"×8". pH: 6·0-6·4. Hardness: 6-12 p.p.m. Temperature: 78°F. Spawns: in nylon mops in bare tanks. Method: standard for egg-droppers. Eggs: 80-120. Hatch: in 48 hours. Fry hang on: 1 day. Free-swimming: 4th day. Food 1st week: infusoria. 2nd week: infusoria, brine shrimp.*

225

Hemigrammus ocellifer – Beacon fish tetra

Guyana, Amazon ♂ *2"* ♀ *2¹/₄"* *Community*
DIET: All foods SWIMS: Mid-water

The beacon, or head-and-tail-light fish, derives is popular name from the splash of gold seen in the top half of the eye and the upper portion of the caudal peduncle. Both these splashes are bordered by red below. The fish are best seen in shoals lit from above against a dark background. When kept singly, or in pairs with other species, the head-and-tail-light effect, though still there, is less obvious.

The species is one of the most susceptible to *Ichthyophthirius* (white spot), and in a community tank is usually the first to show an outbreak of the disease. When purchased from a pet stores these fish should without exception be quarantined in an empty tank for a full ten days, and during this period the water should be tinted with methylene blue or a similar prophylactic.

Males are slimmer than females. Sex can be determined before maturity, since on close examination of the anal fin males show a faint, milky-white bar. This runs across three-quarters of the forward rays of this fin, a little lower than half-way down.

Breeding. *Tank: 24"×8"×8". pH: 6·8-7·0. Hardness: 80-120 p.p.m. Temperature: 78°F. Spawns: in plant thickets. Method: standard for egg-droppers. Eggs: 150-200. Hatch: in 24 hours. Fry hang on: 1 day. Free-swimming: 3rd day. Food 1st week: infusoria. 2nd week: infusoria, brine shrimp.*

Mature fish spawn readily. The procedure mentioned under *H. caudovittatus* applies here.

Hemigrammus pulcher – Black wedge tetra

Ecuador, Colombia ♂ 1½" ♀ 1¾" Community
DIET: All foods SWIMS: Mid-water

This chubby little tetra is peaceful and attractive. It should be kept with small fishes, as it is not an active swimmer, preferring to take life quietly and sedately.

Females are deeper-bellied and thicker than males.

Breeding. *Tank: 24"×8"×8". pH: 6·6-6·8. Hardness: 80-100 p.p.m. Temperature: 80°F. Spawns: in plant thickets. Method: standard for egg-droppers. Eggs: 100-150. Hatch: in 24 hours. Fry hang on: 1 day. Free-swimming: 3rd day. Food 1st week: infusoria. 2nd week: infusoria, brine shrimp.*

The species is not easily induced to spawn, but when a good pair do breed they should afterwards be segregated, and not be put back with the others. This facilitates selecting the same breeding pair for subsequent spawns. Such a couple can usually be relied on to produce many broods. Once the babies are free-swimming, they stay near the sand tucked under the lower leaves of plant clumps, making them very difficult to see. Feeding should be continued for at least a fortnight before abandoning hope. By then the young should be visible.

227

Hemigrammus rhodostomus – Red-nosed tetra

Brazil   ♂ 1¾"   ♀ 2"   Community
DIET: All foods   SWIMS: Mid-water

A long, slender characin, which is peaceful, hardy, and attractive.

The body is silver with a slight tinge of gold. On the flanks there is a thin black line which gradually widens until it reaches the base of the tail. It then narrows again, stretching across the tail, ending in a point. A black bar adorns the upper and lower lobes of the caudal fin. But the most striking feature is the bright red forehead and nose, which gives the fish its popular name.

Males are slimmer, smaller, and slightly brighter than females.

Breeding. *Tank: 24"×8"×8". pH: 6·8. Hardness: 50-80 p.p.m. Temperature: 80°F. Spawns: in plant thickets. Method: standard for egg-droppers. Eggs: 150-200. Hatch: in 24 hours. Fry hang on: 1 day. Free-swimming: 3rd day. Food 1st week: infusoria. 2nd week: infusoria, brine shrimp.*

Not easily induced to spawn.

Hemigrammus unilineatus – *Feather-fin tetra*

Northern S. America   ♂ *2"*   ♀ *2½"*   *Community*
DIET: All foods   SWIMS: Mid-water

A pleasing, though not strikingly beautiful, fish of peaceful habits. It resembles *Pristella riddlei*, but is not so colourful. One point in its favour is that it is long-lived.

The body is silver, the back olive. A black blotch appears in the upper portion of the dorsal fin; this is tipped with yellowish-white. The leading edge of the anal fin is yellow, and immediately behind this the second and third rays are black. The tail is rusty red.

Males are slimmer than females. When she is full of roe her bulging sides make sexing obvious.

Breeding. *Tank: 24"×8"×8". pH: 7·0-7·2. Hardness: 100-150 p.p.m. Temperature: 78°F. Spawns: in plant thickets. Method: standard for egg-droppers. Eggs: 200-250. Hatch: in 24 hours. Fry hang on: 1 day. Free-swimming: 3rd day. Food 1st week: infusoria. 2nd week: infusoria, brine shrimp.*

An easy-to-breed, prolific species. A pair put out overnight should spawn next morning. The parents should then be removed.

Hemiodopsis semitaeniatus

Northern S. America ♂ 5" ♀ 5" *Community, with medium-sized fishes*
DIET: *All foods* SWIMS: *Mid-water*

This is a graceful fish, the slightly compressed tubular body tapering at each end, denoting speed.

It is difficult to catch in the aquarium, and can shoot out of the water like a missile. Never leave it in an uncovered aquarium or, worse still, in an open-necked jar. It will leap out almost as soon as it is put in.

The scales are small, and the body has an overall silvery sheen which reflects, according to the angle of the light, gold or pale blue. The most notable feature is a circular black spot on the flanks midway between dorsal and adipose fin, and starting a little way behind is a black line which runs through the caudal peduncle and then drops through the centre of the lower lobe of the large forked caudal fin. This oblique bar is exaggerated by a contrasting white streak in the lower part of the tail.

The fish is peaceful and easily fed. Females appear to be rounder and deeper in the belly region.

Hyphessobrycon bifasciatus – Brass tetra

S.E. Brazil ♂ 2½" ♀ 2¾" Community, with larger fishes
DIET: All foods SWIMS: Mid-water

It is generally yellowish-silver, but from time to time wild specimens are imported which glow with a brassy gold to bronze colour—hence the popular name. Even these colourful importations fail to produce young of the same hue; this disappointment has no doubt contributed to the fish's fall from esteem.

Males are usually more colourful than females, but she is deeper-bodied. In large specimens the anal fin of the male is wider, and he may develop longer points on his ventrals.

Breeding. *Tank: 30"×15"×15". pH: 6·8-7·0. Hardness: 100-120 p.p.m. Temperature: 80°F. Spawns: in plant thickets. Method: standard for egg-droppers. Eggs: 200-300. Hatch: in 24 hours. Fry hang on: 1 day. Free-swimming: 3rd day. Food 1st week: infusoria. 2nd week: infusoria, brine shrimp.*

The fish are quite easy to spawn, following standard procedure. The parents should be removed immediately afterwards.

231

♀

♂

Hyphessobrycon callistus – Jewel tetra

Guyana, Brazil ♂ *1¼"* ♀ *1½"* *Community*
DIET: All foods SWIMS: Lower half of tank

H. callistus are chunky, of good disposition, and carry their fins well spread.

Deep red overcasts the sides. A round spot appears on the shoulder. The dorsal fin is black, tipped with white. The anal and ventrals are red, both being tipped with white at the lower points. A thin black line borders the rear edge of the anal fin; the hindermost tip of this is black. The caudal fin is red.

The male is slimmer than the female, and his colouring is more intense.

Breeding. *Tank: 24"×8"×8". pH: 6·6. Hardness: 50-80 p.p.m. Temperature: 78°F. Spawns: in plant thickets. Method: standard for egg-droppers. Eggs: 100-150. Hatch: in 24 hours. Fry hang on: 1 day. Free-swimming: 3rd day. Food 1st week: infusoria. 2nd week: infusoria, brine shrimp.*

Though some pairs do not spawn readily, others oblige frequently. Once a good couple has been discovered they should be kept where they can be recognized easily, and so used for further breeding.

232

Hyphessobrycon erythrostigma (also known as H. rubrastigma) –
Bleeding heart tetra

Northern S. America   ♂ 2"   ♀ 1¾"   Community
DIET: All foods   SWIMS: Lower half of tank

These fish were once quite rare in Britain. At first glance they look like *H. rosaceus*. They are similar in shape, and come from the same area, but the coloration is different, and the fins longer, and grander.

It prefers soft brown peaty water and, when in good condition, with fins spread, the stature and colour are magnificent. In hard water the colour fades, and the black edge to the anal fin vanishes.

Breeding.   *Tank: 30"×15"×15".   pH: 6·0-6·8.   Hardness: 50-80 p.p.m.   Temperature: 80°F.   Spawns: above plant thickets.   Method: the pair tremble side by side, dropping eggs.   Eggs: 100-150.   Hatch: in 48 hours.   Fry hang on: 2 days.   Free-swimming: 5th day.   Food 1st week: infusoria. 2nd week: infusoria, brine shrimp.*

Spawning follows the pattern of *H. rosaceus* (p.241).

♂   ♀

Hyphessobrycon erythrozonus – *Glowlight tetra*

Guyana   ♂ 1½"   ♀ 1¾"   Community
DIET: All foods   SWIMS: Lower half of tank

It is sometimes unbelievable how different fishes can appear when seen in ideal surroundings, as against being huddled together in a corner of a bare tank, frightened and unhappy. Here we have a case in point. The glowlight can be a drab, colourless fish, or a fiery, startling beauty that glows brilliantly. Seen in soft peaty water in a beautifully planted aquarium, having a dark background and lit from above, a shoal of these little gems is a sight not easily forgotten. This fish is only at its best when on its own or with other small fishes.

The body is translucent; a vivid red stripe runs across the flanks from eye to base of tail. The dorsal has red in the forward part. The other fins are clear, except for white tips.

When young, males may sometimes be identified, as in the anal fin they have the characin hook; this often gets caught up in a fine net. In adult specimens sex is obvious, the females being larger and much deeper-bellied.

Breeding. *Tank: 24"×8"×8".   pH: 6·0-6·6.   Hardness: 10-20 p.p.m.   Temperature: 78°F.   Spawns: in nylon mops.   Method: males and females lock fins and roll over.   Eggs: 150-250.   Hatch: in 24 hours.   Fry hang on: 1 day.   Free-swimming: 3rd day.   Food 1st week: infusoria, yolk of egg. 2nd week: infusoria, brine shrimp.*

Once considered to be a difficult species to breed, it now presents no problem whatsoever. A bare tank should be thoroughly cleaned, and contain soft brown peaty water with a hardness reading not higher than 20 p.p.m. In it are placed two or three nylon mops which have been sterilized by boiling. A large pair is selected, the female bulging with roe. They are placed in the tank in the late afternoon. Next day, after some love play which takes the form of short darts at each other, male and female come side by side, and lock fins. Then, trembling in close contact, they roll over in or against the nylon mops. Eggs are laid and fertilized, many falling to the bottom of the tank. The parents are removed after spawning is completed. When free-swimming the fry may be given a few feeds with yolk of hard-boiled egg. A tiny portion of this is dropped into the corner of a fine muslin net. This is then dipped into the tank, squeezed with the fingers, and shaken. As a result a cloud of egg yolk disperses into the water. Care must be taken not to overdo this food, as if much remains uneaten it will quickly foul the water. The fry will take fine infusoria, and a week later brine shrimp. After this the young are easy to raise, and grow quickly.

Hyphessobrycon flammeus – *Flame tetra*

Rio de Janeiro ♂ *1½"* ♀ *1¾" Community*
DIET: All foods SWIMS: Lower half of tank

A firm favourite with most aquarists, this colourful little fish has enjoyed great popularity in the United States. It is somewhat short and dumpy, is very lively, keeps its fins well spread, but is inclined to be shy until it gets used to its home.

Our colour plate shows that the male has redder fins than the female, and the edges of his ventrals and anal are bordered with black.

In a shoal the redder males are easily noticed. Colour, however, is not the only indication of sex; females when full of roe are much deeper and wider in the belly.

Breeding. *Tank: 24"×8"×8". pH: 6·8-7·2. Hardness: 100-120 p.p.m. Temperature: 80°F. Spawns: in plant thickets. Method: standard for egg-droppers. Eggs:*

235

150-200.   Hatch: in 24 hours.   Fry hang on: 1 day.   Free-swimming: 3rd day.   Food 1st week: infusoria. 2nd week: infusoria, brine shrimp.

So simple is this fish to breed that we recommend it to beginners who are spawning egg-layers for the first time.

Hyphessobrycon griemi

Brazil   ♂ 1″   ♀ 1¼″   Community
DIET: All foods   SWIMS: Lower half of tank

H. griemi resembles *H. flammeus* very closely. The main difference seems to be a darker second bar somewhat more crescent-shaped across the centre of the body, with a strong highlight of gold just in front of this. The outer edges of the dorsal, ventrals, and anal fin have a clear milky white tip and edge. This species does not seem to grow as large as *H. flammeus,* but in all other respects the two species are very similar.

Breeding.   *Exactly the same as for H. flammeus.*

236

Hyphessobrycon herbertaxelrodi – Black neon tetra

Brazil   ♂ 1½"   ♀ 1⅜"   Community
DIET: All foods   SWIMS: Mid-water

Why this fish should have been nicknamed the black neon is odd. It is much more like *H. heterorhabdus* (p.238) in shape and habit, though not so susceptible to white spot.

It is peaceful, attractive, and easy to breed. There is a thin gold line, in some lights pale silver-green, running from eye to tail, and below this a much broader dark band emanating from a darker spot behind the gill plate. The top of the eye is bright red, the back is olive, and belly silver. Fins clear, except for a faint milky tip to the dorsal.

Sexing is easy, as females are not only larger than males, but deeper-bodied.

Breeding. *Tank: 24"×8"×8".   pH: 6·0-6·6.   Hardness: 10-20 p.p.m.   Temperature: 78°F.   Spawns: in nylon mops, or feathery plant thickets.   Method: standard for egg-droppers.   Eggs: 100-150.   Hatch: in 48 hours.   Fry hang on: 2 days.   Free-swimming: 5th day.   Food 1st week: infusoria. 2nd week: infusoria, brine shrimp.*

Hyphessobrycon heterorhabdus – Belgian flag tetra

Northern S. America ♂ *1½"* ♀ *1¾"* *Community*
DIET: All foods *SWIMS: Mid-water*

This is another beautiful fish, but it only shows its best colours when happy and in good condition in a well-planted tank containing soft, slightly acid water.

The male is slimmer and slightly smaller than the female.

Breeding. *Tank: 24"×8"×8". pH: 6·0-6·6. Hardness: 10-20 p.p.m. Temperature: 78°F. Spawns: in nylon mops. Method: standard for egg-droppers. Eggs: 100-150. Hatch: in 48 hours. Fry hang on: 1 day. Free-swimming: 4th day. Food 1st week: infusoria, yolk of egg. 2nd week: infusoria, brine shrimp.*

♀

♂

Hyphessobrycon pulchripinnis – Lemon tetra

Amazon Basin ♂ 1³/₄″ ♀ 1³/₄″ Community
DIET: *All foods* SWIMS: *Mid-water*

This is another charming little tetra, peaceful, pretty, and of average size. It carries its fins jauntily, and likes to swim in the front of the aquarium.

The body is overcast with pale yellow; the upper half of the eye is bright crimson; but it is the yellow streak bordered by black in both the dorsal and anal fins that catches the eye.

The female is much deeper in the belly than the male, and he has slightly brighter colours.

Breeding. *Tank: 24″×8″×8″. pH: 6·6. Hardness: 20-50 p.p.m. Temperature: 80°F. Spawns: in nylon mops. Method: standard for egg-droppers. Eggs: 100-150. Hatch: in 24 hours. Fry hang on: 1 day. Free-swimming: 3rd day. Food 1st week: infusoria. 2nd week: infusoria, brine shrimp.*

The species is not difficult to breed, although individual fish sometimes will not spawn. Once a good pair has been bred they should be segregated from the others, so that they will not be muddled when selecting them again. If the fish do not breed within 3 days it is a waste of time to keep them in the breeding tank. Another pair should be selected, and the originals conditioned further. The parents are not avid egg-eaters, but nevertheless should be removed in case of cannibalism.

Hyphessobrycon roberti – *Roberti tetra*

S. America ♂ *1¾″* ♀ *1¾″* *Community*
DIET: All foods SWIMS: Lower half of tank

Somewhat similar to *H. rosaceus*, but the body is slightly more pink. The main difference lies in the finnage: in *H. rosaceus* the male's dorsal has a large black portion tipped with white, and in the female the white has a narrow top border of red; but in *H. roberti* the dorsal has more of a black bar crossing the rays at a tangent, and is bordered above and below by white bars, the upper one being tinged pink on the outer edge.

The male's dorsal and anal fins are longer and more pointed than those of the female, and she is deeper and plumper than he.

For further particulars of breeding see *H. rosaceus* opposite.

Hyphessobrycon rosaceus – Rosy tetra

Guyana, Brazil   ♂ 1¾"   ♀ 1½"   Community
DIET: All foods   SWIMS: Mid-water

One of the showiest of the characins, it is not always seen at its best. It prefers soft, peaty water, and should be kept on its own or with other small fishes requiring the same conditions. When in the correct environment the fish displays its finest colours, and spreads its fins to full extent. In community tanks it often carries the fins rather limply, and folded.

Sexing presents no difficulty, since the dorsal and anal fins of the male are much longer, and pointed. Moreover, the upper tip of the female's dorsal fin shows a fine edging of red.

Breeding. *Tank: 30"×15"×15". pH: 6·4-6·6. Hardness: 55-85 p.p.m. Temperature: 80°F. Spawns: in clear water above plants. Method: drops eggs into thickets. Eggs: 50-100. Hatch: in 48 hours. Fry hang on: 1 day. Free-swimming: 4th day. Food 1st week: infusoria. 2nd week: infusoria, brine shrimp.*

Conditions must be ideal before the species can be induced to spawn. Although the fish are not large, they will not spawn in a small tank. This must be filled with very soft peaty water to a depth of 10", and planted with short plants rising to no more than 4" above the sand. Two feathery clumps should be placed one at each end of the tank, and these should not exceed 6" in height. With fins spread to splitting point, the males make playful darts at the females, and resemble delta-winged aeroplanes in their dives and upward sweeps. The pair will come side by side, and swimming in the clear water above the plants, tremble together, dropping fertilized eggs into the foliage below.

After spawning, the adults should be removed.

241

Hyphessobrycon scholzei – *Black-line tetra*

Lower Amazon ♂ *2¼″* ♀ *2½″ Community*
DIET: All foods SWIMS: Mid-water

A popular fish, not by reason of its bright colours, but because it is extremely hardy, and one of the easiest of the egg-layers to breed. *H. scholzei* has a wide temperature range, and is not particular as to exact conditions. It should be kept with medium-sized species, as it may occasionally take sly nips at small fishes' fins.

The body is silvery, the back olive, the eye jet-black. A striking black line runs the length of the sides, ending in a large black spot at the centre of the tail fin. The first rays of the ventrals and anal fin are white.

The female is much deeper-bodied than the male. He sometimes shows a darkish area in the centre of the dorsal, particularly when young.

Breeding. Tank: 24″×8″×8″. pH: 7·0. Hardness: 100-180 p.p.m. Temperature: 78°F. Spawn: in plant thickets. Method: standard for egg-droppers. Eggs: 100-250. Hatch: in 24 hours. Fry hang on: 1 day. Free-swimming: 3rd day. Food 1st week: infusoria. 2nd week: brine shrimp, microworms.

Black-line tetras are extremely easy and prolific spawners, and are strongly recommended to any beginner attempting to breed egg-layers for the first time. If the procedure detailed in Chapter 12 is followed it is almost certain spawning will take place next morning. The eggs, the size of a pin-head, are very adhesive, and can be seen in great profusion sticking to most of the plant leaves. Another advantage to the beginner is that these eggs are robust, and hatch in 24 hours.

♀

♂

Hyphessobrycon serpae – *Serpae tetra*

Brazil, Guyana   ♂ 1¹/₂"   ♀ 1¹/₂"   Community
DIET: All foods   SWIMS: Lower half of tank

H. callistus and *H. serpae* are very similar in appearance, but the latter is a blacker red over the body, and has a dark vertical stripe on the shoulder; whereas *H. callistus* has a redder body colour and only a round spot on the shoulder. In all other respects the two are the same.

Mature females are wider and deeper-bellied than males.

Breeding.   *Tank: 24"×8"×8".   pH: 6·8.   Hardness: 60-100 p.p.m.   Temperature: 78°F.   Spawns: in plant thickets.   Method: standard for egg-droppers.   Eggs: 80-120.   Hatch: in 24 hours.   Fry hang on: 1 day.   Free-swimming: 3rd day.   Food 1st week: infusoria. 2nd week: infusoria, brine shrimp.*

243

Leporinus fasciatus – Striped leporinus

Northern S. America   ♂ 6"   ♀ 8"   Community, with larger fishes
DIET: All foods   SWIMS: Mid-water

This fish is elongated in shape, and has a sharp-pointed nose.

When young the general body colour is orange, and five black bars cross the sides vertically. As the body lengthens with age the bars split, one forming two, until the fish has ten altogether. The body colour fades to an ivory yellow. The small adipose fin is black and white, and the anal fin has two bands of black running across it.

The fish has a habit of remaining stationary in mid-water with its head dipped at an angle of 30 degrees below horizontal.

Breeding.   *There appear to be no records of this fish having been bred in captivity.*

♂

♀

Leporinus friderici – Spotted leporinus

Northern S. America ♂ 6" ♀ 8" Community, with larger fishes
DIET: All foods SWIMS: Mid-water

This fish is similar in shape to its cousin *L. fasciatus,* and swims with the head tilted down. It will take any food, and is peaceful when not too large.

The body is olive green, but in strong light thin stripes of a brilliant gold appear horizontally from head to tail. The back is marked with numerous short bars that reach to the lateral line, and the sides are adorned with numerous large, round black spots.

When mature the pectorals, ventrals, and anal fins of males develop a reddish tint, and both sexes appear more blotched.

Breeding. *Few details available.*

Leporinus striatus – Lined leporinus

Northern S. America ♂ *6"* ♀ *7"* *Community, with larger fishes*
DIET: All foods SWIMS: *Lower half of tank*

This fish, like other *Leporinus*, grows too large for the average aquarist. Among bigger fishes, it seems to do well, minding its own business, but refusing to be intimidated.

As will be seen from the photograph, the stripes or lines in this species run horizontally.

Breeding. *Few details available, although the caudal fin of the male fish has a larger upper lobe when compared to the lower lobe.*

♂

♀

Megalamphodus megalopterus – *Phantom tetra*

Amazon   ♂ 1¼"   ♀ 1¼"   Community
DIET: *All foods*   SWIMS: *Lower half of tank*

A smart, attractive, peaceful fish, which usually keeps its fins well spread, giving it an appearance of well-being and perkiness. The body has a faint rosy hue. Behind the gill-plate is a prominent black mark, which is wider at the top than the bottom, making it rather wedge-shaped. This shoulder adornment is enhanced by a greenish-gold border fore and aft. The dorsal and caudal fins are solid jet-black, the ventral and adipose fins are deep red, and the anal fin red darkening to black at its tip and along the lower edge.

Males are slimmer than females, and the dorsal is longer, more pointed, and curves gracefully backward.

Breeding. *Tank: 24"×8"×8", or smaller. pH: 6·0-6·2. Hardness: 5-10 p.p.m.   Temperature: 80°F.   Spawns: in nylon mop in bare tank.   Method: standard for egg-droppers. Eggs: 70-100. Hatch: in 24 hours. Fry hang on: 1 day. Free-swimming: 3rd day.   Food 1st week: infusoria. 2nd week: infusoria, brine shrimp.*

247

♀

♀

♀

♂

Megalamphodus sweglesi – *Red phantom tetra*

Amazon   ♂ *1½"*   ♀ *1½"*   *Community*
DIET: All foods   SWIMS: Lower half of tank

The body is much redder than *M. megalopterus*. There is a round black spot behind the gill-plate, approximately one-third of the distance along the fish's body. The dorsal has a black band across it, bordered above and below by creamy-white. The other fins are red, and the upper rim of the eye is also red. The fish is peaceful and very attractive.

Breeding.   *Similar to M. megalopterus.*

248

Metynnis schreitmulleri – Silver dollar

Amazon   ♂ *4"*   ♀ *4¼"*   *Non-community*
DIET: *All foods*   SWIMS: *Mid-water*

There are several species of *Metynnis:* all are disc-shaped, with laterally compressed sides. This is not a species for the average aquarist on account of its bulk and plant-eating habits, but it should be kept with bigger fishes in medium-sized aquaria. Even so, it may nibble the tenderer plants.

The body is silver, the fins are grey. A warm yellow tint appears on the edge of the anal fin. The dorsal is carried upright, and is adorned with several black specks. In its smaller sizes the fish seems peaceful.

Breeding.   *Up to 2,000 eggs are laid, with this species seeming to prefer neutral and not too soft water. At 27-28°C the eggs hatch after about 3 days and can be reared on tiny brine shrimp.*

Micralestes (Phenacogrammus) interruptus – Congo tetra

Zaire   ♂ 3"   ♀ 3"   Community
DIET: Live food, may be trained to take dried food
SWIMS: Upper half of tank

The fish is peaceful, active, and displays itself well if given a good-sized aquarium in which it can swim freely.

The upper portion of the back is mauvish, and the belly silvery. Along the lateral line is a broad, pale greenish band without defined edges. This band intensifies or fades according to the angle at which the light strikes across the sides of the fish. The fins are mauvish-blue edged with blue-grey, the dorsal is long and pointed, and the tail fin of the male has a jagged point. The female has the same colouring, but her dorsal is not so long and pointed, and she lacks the protruding point in the caudal fin.

Breeding.   Tank: 30"×15"×15".   pH: 5·6-5·8.   Hardness: 20-50 p.p.m.   Temperature: 78°F.   Spawns: in plant thickets.   Method: standard for egg-droppers.   Eggs: 50-100.   Hatch: in 48 hours.   Fry hang on: 2 days.   Free-swimming: 5th day.   Food 1st week: infusoria, yolk of egg. 2nd week: brine shrimp, microworms.

♂

♀

Mimagoniates microlepis – Blue tetra

Brazil, Argentina, Paraguay ♂ *1¾"* ♀ *1¾"* *Community*
DIET: All foods SWIMS: Upper half of tank

Not a brilliantly coloured fish, the back being olive and the belly silver; a broad blue band runs along the flanks from the centre to the caudal peduncle. The fins are bluish-silver; the dorsal is set well back. Males have longer, more pointed dorsal and anal fins, and the lower lobe of their caudal fin is considerably broader than the upper lobe. The species is lively and inclined to swim in shoals, males often sparring harmlessly with other males.

Breeding. *The authors have not bred this fish, but understand that the males make dashes at the females, and as their bodies come into contact inject sperms into the female cloaca. The sperms then pass into the oviduct. Thus the female is able later to lay fertilized eggs. After mating she may then be placed in a tank on her own, and will eventually lay her eggs, generally attaching them to the undersides of plant leaves. The young should hatch in 24-36 hours after the eggs are laid.*

Mimagoniates barberi is a very similar species, but the general colour is brown and not blue. Both species seem very prone to *Ichthyophthirius*.

251

♂

♀

Moenkhausia pittieri – Diamond tetra

Venezuela   ♂ 2½"   ♀ 2¼"   Community
DIET: All foods   SWIMS: Mid-water

Though not always available, this is a very desirable fish for those with medium to large community tanks. It is peaceful, and, although not brilliantly coloured, has striking fins which it displays well.

The body is silver-grey with an iridescent pale blue on the lower sides, and small green spots reflect here and there as the light catches them. The upper half of the eye is bright red. But it is the fins which mark this fish out among others: the dorsal and anal are long, wide, and gracefully pointed, being more exaggerated in the male. The female may be told from her fuller and deeper belly, and her shorter fins.

Breeding. *Tank: 30"×15"×15".   pH: 6·8-7·0.   Hardness: 80-120 p.p.m.   Temperature: 78°F.   Spawns: in plant thickets.   Method: standard for egg-droppers.   Eggs: 100-200.   Hatch: in 48 hours.   Fry hang on: 2 days.   Free-swimming: 5th day.   Food 1st week: infusoria, brine shrimp. 2nd week: microworms, fine dried food.*

The species is not one of the easiest to breed, but when spawning does take place many eggs are laid and fertilized in thickets of fine-leaved plants. The eggs are semi-adhesive, and may be seen clearly. The parents should be removed immediately after spawning.

Moenkhausia sanctafilomennae – Red-eyed tetra

N.E. South America   ♂ 3½"   ♀ 4"   Community, with larger fishes
DIET: All foods   SWIMS: Mid-water

This fish is not brilliantly coloured, and grows rather too large for the average community tank. When fully adult it may bully and kill smaller species.

The body is grey, with large scales; as each of these is edged with black, there is a network pattern over the fish. The upper half of the eye is brilliant red, and a large black spot appears at the root of the tail, and above this, behind the adipose fin, is a gleaming gold patch. The fins are grey, the first ray of the anal being creamy white. When the fish are young the contrast of eye, sides, and tail spot is clear-cut and pleasing, but this tends to fade with age.

Both male and female are deep-bodied, but she is considerably rounder in section.

Breeding. *Tank: 24"×8"×8".   pH: 6·8-7·4.   Hardness: 100-150 p.p.m.   Temperature: 78-80°F.   Spawns: in plant thickets.   Method: standard for egg-droppers. Eggs: 200-400.   Hatch: in 48 hours.   Fry hang on: 2 days.   Free-swimming: 5th day.   Food 1st week: infusoria and brine shrimp. 2nd week: microworms, fine dried food.*

The species breeds fairly readily even when 1½" long, scattering very tiny eggs among bunches of plants, after much chasing. They will spawn for a period of 1½-2 hours, the eggs being seen among the foliage, after which the parents should be removed.

253

♀

♂

Nannaethiops unitaeniatus – One-lined characin

Central Africa   ♂ 2"   ♀ 2½"   Community
DIET: All foods   SWIMS: Mid-water

By no means brilliant, this fish is none the less attractive, in a modest way. It is peaceful and quiet, and makes few demands.

The back is dark, but on closer examination proves to be made up of rows of small dark dots; the lower flanks and belly are silver-white. A dividing line of intense black runs through the eye along the sides, and ends just in the caudal fin; this is set off by another line of bright gold immediately above, giving the top half of the eye a golden lid. All fins are clear.

Males are slimmer and smaller than females.

Breeding.   *Tank: 24"×8"×8".   pH: 6·8-7·0.   Hardness: 100-150 p.p.m.   Temperature: 78°F.   Spawns: in plant thickets.   Method: standard for egg-droppers.   Eggs: 100-150.   Hatch: in 48 hours.   Fry hang on: 1 day.   Free-swimming: 4th day.   Food 1st week: infusoria. 2nd week: infusoria, brine shrimp.*

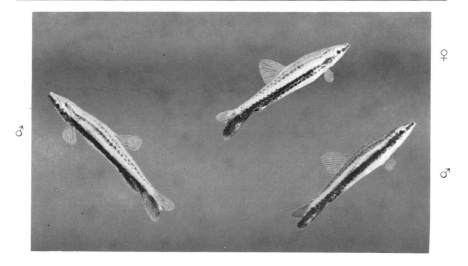

Nannobrycon eques – Black-tailed pencil fish

Guyana, Amazon ♂ *2″* ♀ *2″ Community*
DIET: *All foods* SWIMS: *Upper half of tank*

These are attractive, slender fish with slim, cylindrical bodies and tapering noses. They are harmless but rather shy, and should only be kept with small non-aggressive fishes. *P. eques* has a habit of sitting still in mid-water with its tail end curved downward at an angle of 20-30 degrees below horizontal, but when disturbed swims or darts off on a level keel.

The body is golden-brown, and a dark stripe runs from the tip of the snout through the eye to the lower lobe of the tail, where it spreads into a black patch. The black band is bordered above by a thin line of gold. The upper lobe of the tail is colourless, and tends to become unnoticed, and this helps to give the impression that the tail end of the fish curves downward. In males the anal fin has a dark red spot in its upper portion.

Breeding. *Tank: 24″×8″×8″. pH: 6·6-6·8. Hardness: 80-100 p.p.m. Temperature: 80°F. Spawns: on plant leaves. Method: male fans deposited eggs. Eggs: 50-75. Hatch: in 48 hours. Fry hang on: 1 day. Free-swimming: 4th day. Food 1st week: infusoria. 2nd week: infusoria, brine shrimp.*

Given the right conditions these fish are not difficult to spawn. They prefer soft water, and lay their eggs on the fine curving leaves of *Sagittaria subulata*. They do not seem to be prolific, but guard their eggs and occasionally fan them with their pectoral fins; but if the adults are removed the eggs hatch just as well without such attention.

Nannobrycon unifasciatus – Red-tailed pencil fish

Amazon, Guyana   ♂ 2″   ♀ 2″   Community
DIET: All foods   SWIMS: Upper half of tank

Even more slender in shape than *N. eques.*

A prominent band of black runs from the tip of the nose to the lower lobe of the tail. Below this are three crescents, red, white, and black, making a striking splash of colour. In all other respects the fish resembles *N. eques.*

Breeding.   *Tank: 24″×8″×8″.   pH: 6·8-7·0.   Hardness: 80-100 p.p.m.   Temperature: 80°F.   Spawns: on plant leaves.   Method: deposits adhesive eggs.   Eggs: 30-70. Hatch: in 48 hours.   Fry hang on: 1 day.   Free-swimming: 4th day.   Food 1st week: infusoria.   Food 2nd week: infusoria, brine shrimp.*

Nannostomus beckfordi – One-lined pencil fish

Amazon Basin, Guyana ♂ *1¾"* ♀ *1¾" Community*
DIET: All foods SWIMS: Mid-water

Here we have quite a common, but very attractive, aquarium fish. The body is elongated, and tapers at both ends, the nose being particularly pointed. Although shy at first, if kept with smaller species it will soon learn to be unafraid, and come forward to receive its share of food.

Sexing is not difficult, as the male's red ventral fins are tipped with silver blue. The belly of the female is considerably deeper.

At night, when the aquarium is dark, these fish change colour so completely that they are hard to recognize at once. Then the body bears large dark-brown patches in rectangular blocks along the sides.

Breeding. Tank: 24"×8"×8", or smaller. pH: 6·2-6·6. Hardness: 50-80 p.p.m. Temperature: 76-78°F. Spawns: in floating plants or peat. Method: eggs deposited over a period of 2 to 4 days. Eggs: 100-200. Hatch: in 48 hours. Fry hang on: 2 days. Free-swimming: 5th day. Food 1st week: infusoria and yolk of egg. 2nd week: brine shrimp, microworms.

The fish are easy to spawn, requiring only a small tank filled with soft brown peaty water. A little water-logged peat sprinkled over the bottom of the tank will hide any eggs that fall. On the surface place a good-sized patch of bladderwort. If a good pair, consisting of a colourful male and a deep-bodied female, are placed in the tank, probably in a few hours the male will start driving his mate. Both fish tremble side by side in the floating weed, and eggs are deposited freely. If well fed the parents need not be removed, and spawning will continue over several days.

Nannostomus espei – Barred pencil fish

Guyana, Amazon ♂ *1½"* ♀ *1¾"* *Community*

DIET: *All foods* SWIMS: *All depths*

This is a pencil fish of distinction, for the markings on the flanks are vertical. It is quiet and peaceful, though a little shy.

From the pointed snout a faint line of gold runs above the eye along the sides to the caudal peduncle. A short black line passes from the lips through the centre of the eye across the gill-plate. The body is slashed in the lower half by five short, thick blue-black bars which slant slightly forward at their base. Occasionally pinkish highlights appear in the abdominal region. The fins are clear.

Females are slightly shorter and thicker than males.

Breeding. *Tank: 24"×8"×8". pH: 6·2-6·6. Hardness: 5-10 p.p.m. Temperature: 78°F. Spawns: under plant leaves. Method: similar to Nannostomus. Eggs: 50-75. Hatch: in 2 days. Fry hang on: 2 days. Free-swimming: 5th day. Food 1st week: infusoria. 2nd week: infusoria, brine shrimp.*

The breeding tank should contain very soft brown peaty water, and have a layer of peat on the bottom. A cutting of *Hygrophila corymbosa* is anchored to a small piece of thick slate buried in the peat, so that the plant stands upright in the water. The surface is covered with *Riccia*.

The male, after courting the female, presses her sideward and upward under a leaf, and the two tremble in this position for nearly ten times as long as most fishes employing this interlocking method.

Eventually they break apart, and then eggs may be seen falling into the peat. The process is repeated on and off for a day or two, after which the parents should be removed. The eggs remain hidden in the peat, but on hatching the young fry take refuge in the floating *Riccia*.

Nannostomus marginatus – Dwarf pencil fish

Northern S. America ♂ *1"* ♀ *1¼"* *Community*
DIET: All foods SWIMS: All depths

This is the smallest of the *Nannostomus* known so far, and makes an ideal fish for those aquarists with smaller tanks. It is extremely peaceful, most attractive, lively, not shy once it has settled down, and will take any food. In comparison with *N. anomalus*, the body is shorter, and altogether stubbier.

The female is deeper-bellied than the male.

Breeding. *Tank: 24"×8"×8", or smaller. pH: 6·4-6·8. Hardness: 50-80 p.p.m. Temperature: 78-80°F. Spawns: in floating plants. Method: similar to N. anomalus. Eggs: 50-75. Hatch: in 48 hours. Fry hang on: 2 days. Free-swimming: 5th day. Food 1st week: infusoria. 2nd week: infusoria, brine shrimp.*

Eggs are deposited in *Riccia* or lesser bladderwort. The fry must be fed with very fine infusoria at first, as their mouths are particularly small. When they are about ½" long the tail fin of the babies is round at its outer edge, but the pointed lobes develop later.

Nannostomus trifasciatus – *Three-banded pencil fish*

Northern S. America   ♂ 1½"   ♀ 1½"   Community
DIET: All foods   SWIMS: All depths

Possibly the prettiest of the four *Nannostomus* shown in this book. It is a beautiful little fish, and highly recommended to those who keep small aquaria.

The back is olive, the belly silver. A dark band runs from the tip of the lower lip through the eye of the base of the caudal peduncle. Above this is a broad gold band, and in males this band is further beautified by a line of well-spaced red dots, giving the impression of an ermine robe. The golden band on females lacks the red spots. The dorsal, ventrals, anal, and tail fin are adorned with largish red blotches, the outer edges of all these fins being clear.

Breeding. *Tank: 24"×8"×8", or smaller.   pH: 6·6-6·8.   Hardness: 60-80 p.p.m. Temperature: 78-80°F.   Spawns: in plant thickets, Riccia, etc.   Method: similar to N. anomalus.   Eggs: 30-70.   Hatch: in 48 hours.   Fry hang on: 2 days.   Free-swimming: 5th day.   Food 1st week: infusoria, yolk of egg. 2nd week: infusoria, brine shrimp.*

The fish are not prolific breeders in captivity, but can be induced to spawn, slightly acid water being preferred. The fry are somewhat prone to dropsy, and on occasions the authors have lost a whole batch from this disease when about six weeks old.

Nematobrycon palmeri – *Emperor tetra*

Western Colombia   ♂ *1¾"*   ♀ *1½"*   *Community*
DIET: All foods   *SWIMS: Mid-water*

Not a brilliant tetra, but one that has a subdued, yet nevertheless attractive coloration. It is peaceful and quiet in habit, often floating gently around in a slightly head-down posture.

It is not only the tasteful colouring that will appeal to most aquarists, but the splendid finnage of the males. The male dorsal is a mellow yellow-brown, the front ray being almost black, and the extremity of the fin is long, pointed, and curves gracefully backward; it is usually held high in a proud arc. His tail is superb: the upper and lower edges are black and elongated. The centre of the fin is yellow, and carries a black central spike forming a trident. His anal fin is yellow with a black line near the outer edge, but finally bordered with bright yellow.

The rim of his eye is a brilliant electric blue-green. A broad blue-black band passes from the snout below the eye right through to the caudal peduncle. Above the latter half of this is a blue line, and above this a thin red line. The body is a suffused olive-yellow, but reflected light throws beautiful sheens of blue and purple.

Both fish have a protruding lower lip. The female has smaller fins, and the centre prong in her tail barely protrudes beyond the junction of the lobes. She appears slightly more golden, and the rim of her eye is bright gold.

Breeding. *Tank: 24"×8"×8". pH: 6·4-6·8. Hardness: 20-50 p.p.m. Temperature: 80°F. Spawns: in plant thickets. Method: standard for egg-droppers. Eggs: 50-100. Hatch: in 48 hours. Fry hang on: 1 day. Free-swimming: 4th day. Food 1st week: infusoria. 2nd week: brine shrimp.*

Quite an easy characin to breed, providing the water is fairly soft. The semi-adhesive small eggs are usually seen in the lower portion of plant thickets. Parents should be removed after spawning. The fry grow rapidly, and will breed at 5 months.

Neolebias ansorgi – African bloodfin tetra

Zaire, W. Africa   ♂ 1½"   ♀ 1¾"   Community
DIET: All foods   SWIMS: Lower half of tank

Quite a pleasing little fish of subdued colour and quiet nature—in fact, somewhat shy, staying in the background beneath the horizontal leaves of cryptocorynes.

When in soft peaty water the overall colour is rich mahogany, and green spangles appear as highlights on the sides. The fins are a rusty red, and a broad dark green band runs horizontally from gill-plate to caudal peduncle. This band deepens and fades according to the fish's whim.

Females are deeper-bodied and less brightly coloured.

Breeding. *Tank: 24"×8"×8". pH: 6·4. Hardness: 2-15 p.p.m. Temperature: 78-80°F. Spawns: in plant thickets, Riccia, etc. Method: similar to Nannostomus. Eggs: 100-150. Hatch: in 48 hours. Fry hang on: 2 days. Free-swimming: 5th day. Food 1st week: infusoria. 2nd week: brine shrimp, microworms.*

The breeding tank should contain dark brown peaty water, which is very soft, a layer of peat on the bottom, and a good layer of lesser bladder-wort floating on the water surface. Leave the pair for 2 or 3 days, and then remove them. Fry may not be observed for a week, but feeding should be continued, nevertheless.

The small fry grow slowly.

Paracheirodon axelrodi – Cardinal tetra

Peruvian Amazon ♂ *1⅛"* ♀ *1¼" Community*
DIET: *All foods* SWIMS: *Lower half of tank*

Paracheirodon axelrodi is named after Herbert R. Axelrod, the well-known author of aquarium magazines and books in the United States.

This beautiful fish resembles very closely the neon tetra, but in shape it seems a little longer and slimmer.

Though the colours are similar to the neon, the brilliant blue-green stripe and the deep red area below are not identical. The beginning of the blue stripe on the cardinal covers the whole eye, whereas in neons it adorns only the upper portion. In the cardinal the blue stripe is straighter, and fades out behind and below the adipose fin, whereas in neons it has a definite upward bend in the latter half, and ends on the back just in front of this fin. The red area in the cardinal covers most of the lower flanks and belly as well as the caudal peduncle, while in neons the red area is confined to a broad streak covering only the centre part of the flanks and caudal peduncle. A close study of the colour plates of the two species will show the main differences.

Sexing is difficult, except in adult fish. Then the female is obviously rounder and deeper.

Breeding. *This species requires the similar conditions described under P. innesi (neon tetras)—peaty water, pH 5·6-6·6. Hardness: 0-10 p.p.m. They spawn on nylon mops, but are not such ready spawners, though once they have spawned nearly every egg hatches.*

♀

♂

♂

Paracheirodon innesi – Neon tetra

Peru, Western Brazil ♂ *1⅛"* ♀ *1¼"* *Community*
DIET: *All foods* SWIMS: *Lower half of tank*

This is regarded by many aquarists as the gem of the tropical world. The neon tetra was named after William T. Innes, the celebrated author and well-known publisher of many aquarium books and periodicals; and it is fitting that such a universally sought-after fish should bear the name of a man who did so much to advance the hobby all over the world.

Neons are small, peaceful, extremely perky, and really beautiful fish. Once settled down they are not shy, and, although not aggressive, have the courage to stand up for themselves if the occasion arises.

Females are larger than males. It has been noticed by the authors that when the males are young the upper edge of the red splash starts on the back beneath the front rays of the adipose fin. With females the red begins farther back, just below the posterior rays of this fin. When they are mature the larger, bulging, deep-bodied females are unmistakable.

Breeding.   *Tank: 24"×8"×8".   pH: 5·6-6·6.   Hardness: 0-10 p.p.m.   Temperature: 78°F.   Spawns: in nylon mops.   Method: standard for egg-droppers.   Eggs: 80-150.   Hatch: in 24 hours.   Fry hang on: 2 days.   Free-swimming: 4th day.   Food 1st week: infusoria, yolk of egg.   2nd week: infusoria, brine shrimp.*

Neons are often considered to be problem fish to breed, and regarding the methods used various rumours are constantly circulated. Most of these purport to come second- or third-hand from German aquarists, and all these methods are most complicated. Some state that the breeding tank must be sterilized with chemicals and then filled with distilled water in which oak-leaves and bark are soaked for a fortnight. Later sterilized plants are introduced, and a pair of fish transferred into the breeding tank with the aid of a dip tube. After all this, if they do not spawn within two days the whole process has to be repeated. Such conditions are not provided in nature. The rumours do not explain how distilled water put into a tank remains free of bacteria for more than a few hours, or how to catch the parents in dip tubes.

In spite of the above, the authors have proved that success can be achieved quite simply. What is more, healthy fish will breed every ten days from the age of 12 weeks upward, provided that the correct conditions are created. These are: (i) perfectly healthy, medium-sized adult fish, free from *Plistophora* (neon disease); (ii) a clean, bare tank; (iii) very soft brown peaty water with a hardness not exceeding 10 p.p.m., which is practically bacteria-free.

The peaty water is prepared in advance; in fact, the wise aquarist will always keep a tank full at hand. It is best to start with rain-water into which is put several handfuls of peat. When all this has sunk to the bottom the water will be brown, practically free from bacteria, and the hardness will be between 0 and 10 p.p.m. The pH should be adjusted to come within the range of 5·6 and 6·6, though this need not be exact. The authors have frequently bred neons successfully in water anywhere within the pH range 5·0 to 6·8, but never where the hardness has exceeded 10 p.p.m.

It is only necessary to cleanse the breeding tank thoroughly and dry out with a clean cloth. The peat-water is now poured in to a depth of 4", and a couple of nylon mops which have been sterilized in boiling water are put in as spawn-receivers. The temperature should be adjusted to 76-78°F., and the tank placed where it will receive only subdued daylight. A female bulging with roe and a good male are put in the tank before dusk. They will probably spawn during the middle of the next morning for two hours. After this the parents should be removed with a net which has been dipped into boiling water. The tank is then covered with paper to exclude strong light.

Neon eggs are not easy to see among the nylon mops, but if a glass-bottomed tank is used many eggs lying on the floor of the tank are clearly visible through the base-glass. Quite a few turn opaque white in a few hours—these must be infertile, for many others remain clear and hatch, thus proving that the water is satisfactory, and not the cause of the trouble.

Provided the conditions are correct, the eggs will hatch in 24 hours, and a few minute fry may be seen hanging from the mops and on the glass walls of the aquarium. If none are visible do not be disappointed, as they are so small and transparent that they are easily overlooked. In a further 36-48 hours a few fry may be seen lying on the glass bottom of the tank or hanging on the side walls. Probably only the eyes (appearing as two black specks) will be noticed. When the paper covering is lifted one or two fry may be seen to dart to the sides, corners, and base of the tank, where they remain motionless. If close watch is kept on the bottom inch of water a few will be observed swimming short distances. They should be fed very carefully with the yolk of hard-boiled egg or fine infusoria. They will take brine shrimp in a few days. The fry show no colour until they are between 3 and 4 weeks old. At this stage the blue line appears on the sides and the eyes. The young, judging by the depth of body, are sexable in 10 weeks, and, as previously stated, will breed when 3 months old.

Since publication of this book the authors have bred and raised many thousands of neons and many hundreds of cardinals; and have heard from several other aquarists who, following our procedure exactly, obtain consistent and regular success.

Indeed, the authors are of the opinion that neons are easier to breed than zebra danios. Darkening the tank is not now considered necessary; in fact, in a bright light at 80°F. neons have often hatched in 5 hours.

The most important factor is the softness of the water, and absence of calcium and magnesium salts. This is not surprising. In their native habitat neons and cardinals are found only in very soft water. They have existed under these conditions for longer than man has been on earth.

True, the fish themselves are rugged enough to withstand gradual increases in hardness, and live; but the sperms and eggs, which were safe within their bodies, when expelled suddenly into water containing salts to which they are unaccustomed and ill-equipped have no natural protection, and succumb.

One theory is borne out by the relation of hatching to hardness: above 10 p.p.m. nil; 8 p.p.m. 20-25 eggs develop, though some fry die soon after; at 6 p.p.m. 70-75 get through; below 4 p.p.m. 80-100 should survive; and below 2 p.p.m. 120-180 healthy fry can be expected.

There is little doubt that the humic acid must contribute to the successful breeding and raising of neons and cardinals, for pure distilled water does not seem satisfactory. Neither do the chemical water-softeners, depending upon exchange resins, which replace the calcium and magnesium with equally unnatural alternatives such as sodium.

The breeders should be segregated, males in one tank and females in another, and the water in these tanks need not be very soft. When a pair is put into a breeding tank containing soft peaty water the sudden change will not upset them; on the contrary, they seem stimulated.

On returning the pair to the stock tank make certain that each sex is replaced in the correct tank. One male placed in with the females will spawn them all, over a few days. However, one female placed with several males is often able to fill with roe, because of the jealousy of the males. Should one male approach her he is often deflected from his purpose by the intervention of another male, who spars with him and diverts his attention.

266

Poecilobrycon harrisoni – Harrison's pencil fish

Northern S. America   ♂ 2″   ♀ 2″   Community
DIET: All foods   SWIMS: Lower half of tank

The fish strongly resembles *Nannobrycon eques,* but swims on an even keel.

The back is olive down to a thin dark line which runs from above the eye to below the adipose fin. A broader dark line runs from the tip of the snout through the eye and as far as the fork of the tail. Here it spreads out and covers the upper portion of the lower lobe of this fin. Between these two dark lines is a band of bright gold. The tips of the lips are also gold. Other fins are clear.

The females are slightly deeper-bodied than the males.

Breeding. *Tank: 24″×8″×8″.   pH: 6·6-6·8.   Hardness: 80-100 p.p.m.   Temperature: 80°F.   Spawns: on plant leaves.   Method: male fans deposited eggs.   Eggs: 50-75.   Hatch: in 48 hours.   Fry hang on: 1 day.   Free-swimming: 4th day.   Food 1st week: infusoria. 2nd week: infusoria, brine shrimp.*

Pristella riddlei – X-ray tetra

Venezuela, Guyana   ♂ 1½"   ♀ 2"   Community
DIET: All foods   SWIMS: Mid-water

Here we have a very popular, sprightly little characin. It swims in a rather jerky fashion, allowing its tail to drop slowly, and then with a flick of its fins the tail is raised again, only to drop slowly once more. When in a shoal the fish swim rapidly back and forth. It is peaceful, keeps its fins well spread, and is very active, but inclined to be shy, and stay in the background.

The popular name, X-ray fish, is only partly appropriate, for, although the swim-bladder can be seen, the stomach and intestines are quite opaque. The hinder portion of the body is only partly transparent.

Males are slimmer and smaller than females, and their colours are more pronounced. The tiny hook on his anal fin often gets caught in a fine mesh net.

There is a golden variety of this fish.

Breeding. *Tank: 24"×8"×8".   pH: 6·8-7·2.   Hardness: 80-120 p.p.m.   Temperature: 78-80°F.   Spawns: in plant thickets.   Method: standard for egg-droppers.   Eggs: 70-150.   Hatch: in 24 hours.   Fry hang on: 1 day.   Free-swimming: 3rd day.   Food 1st week: infusoria. 2nd week: infusoria, brine shrimp.*

The fish is one of the easiest characins to breed. The tank is set up according to the standard described in Chapter 12 and placed where it will receive plenty of light. Fish put out before dusk will spawn next morning, providing it is a bright, sunny day, or the tank is well-lit artificially. After spawning both parents should be removed. Once free-swimming, the fry hide under plant leaves, and are extremely difficult to see. It is not until they are about two weeks old that they take to open water and are noticeable. No doubt many a spawn has been thrown away during this period, the breeder imagining that the fry have perished. Once on to microworms and dried food the young grow rapidly, and start to colour in six weeks.

♀

♂

Roeboides guatemalensis – Guatemala glass characin

Guatemala, Central America   ♂ 3½″   ♀ 3¾″   Community, with larger fishes
DIET: All foods   SWIMS: Lower half of tank

Somewhat similar to *Charax gibbosus*, but slightly less deep-bodied. It swims and rests in a head-down position. The rather humpbacked body is covered with minute silvery scales, and on occasions shows a black spot, with a greenish-gold highlight immediately behind it and a diamond-shaped black blotch in the caudal peduncle. There are two white spots beyond this blotch, the upper one being more prominent than the lower. In some lights the fish has a greenish-gold sheen, but as it turns reflected light may show pale blue. The fins are pinkish, and a red lobe appears in each segment of the caudal fin. In males there is a distinct cream marking on the upper edge of the dorsal fin.

Breeding.   *As for Charax gibbosus, p.212.*

269

Semiprochilodus taeniurus – Silver prochilodus

Amazon, S. America   ♂ 5"   ♀ 5"   Community, with larger fishes
DIET: All foods   SWIMS: Mid-water

Belonging to the family *Curimatidae*, these fish grow to large sizes in nature, but under normal aquaria conditions attain a length of 5"-6", and are peaceful.

The most striking feature is the large barred dorsal and caudal fins. The anal fin is also barred. The centre bar and one immediately above it continue into the laterally compressed body for about half the length of the fish, but in some cases the line is not continuous, but broken into a row of dots. The general body colour is greenish-yellow, and the tiny scales are tipped with black, which give the fish the appearance of being striped with numerous thin longitudinal lines. The mouth can be distended, and the thick lips enable the fish to eat vegetable matter and algae from plants and rocks.

Though the fish swims lazily around, it is capable of high speeds when necessary. The large caudal fin and sharpened snout make the fish an excellent jumper: the tank should always be covered to prevent them leaping to their death. If they are captured and placed in a jar keep a hand or net firmly over the top, as the fish is more than likely to jump out in a few seconds.

S. taeniurus will take most foods, and soon learns to eat floating dried food from the water surface. There it will remain for longish periods sucking in the food like a vacuum cleaner. It likes and needs algae or other chopped vegetable matter.

Males appear slimmer than females, but the authors have not yet bred this species.

Serrasalmus species – Piranha

Amazon, Guyana   ♂ 8″   ♀ 10″   Non-Community
DIET: Animal protein   SWIMS: Mid-water

The red-bellied piranha (*S. natteri*) is one of the frequently kept and renowned piranhas, all of which are rather ugly, bulldog-faced fishes, whose mouths are equipped with formidable razor-sharp teeth which they have no hesitation in using on anything, large or small. Piranhas infest many tributaries of the Amazon, and stories are told of humans being literally stripped to the bone in a few minutes when attacked by large shoals of these predators. It is therefore not a fish for the average aquarist, but one for those who like something out of the ordinary, and which will always make a showpiece on account of its savage reputation.

The body colour is brownish-siver, flecked with dark patches. The fins are grey-brown with black borders, the eye large, and the incurving vicious teeth are clearly seen.

Sexing is uncertain, as they have been only rarely bred in captivity. Attempts at mating usually result in one being killed by the other. The species requires a high protein diet, taking meat, liver, fish, or any other flesh. They will seize and devour any fish, gulping small ones whole, and slashing out large pieces from others even larger than themselves.

Thayeria sanctaemariae – *Penguin tetra*

Amazon Basin   ♂ 2½"   ♀ 2¾"   Community
DIET: All foods   SWIMS: Mid-water

This is not a gaudy-coloured fish, but its contrasts of black and silver make it most noticeable in any tank. Generally its habits are good, but occasionally a large specimen will make darts at smaller fishes and rip their tails. Just after the Second World War the authors imported the first specimens into England, and Mrs Muir, late secretary of the Edinburgh Aquarists Society, remarked that they had a resemblance to penguins. Though somewhat far-fetched, the simile was accepted was accepted throughout the British Isles, and this popular name has now spread overseas.

This is one of the fishes that sits in the water, slowly dropping its tail; when it has reached an angle of 45 degrees it flicks its fins and brings the tail up to nearly horizontal, before allowing it to drop slowly again. When frightened it can swim with amazing speed, often leaping out of the water.

The back is olive, the lower sides and belly silver. A broad black band traverses the body from the gill-plate down into the lower lobe of the tail.

When adult, females are deeper-bodied and much thicker in the abdominal region than males.

Breeding. *Tank: 24"×8"×8". pH: 6·6-7·2. Hardness: 100-150 p.p.m. Temperature: 78-80°F. Spawns: in plant thickets. Method: standard for egg-droppers. Eggs: 100-150. Hatch: in 48 hours. Fry hang on: 1 day. Free-swimming: 4th day. Food 1st week: infusoria. 2nd week: infusoria, brine shrimp.*

The fish are not easily induced to spawn. Once a pair has bred they should be kept apart from others, so that they can be identified again. The spawning tank is set up to the standard pattern for egg-layers (Chapter 12), and a pair of fish introduced. The male may start chasing the female the next day or the day after, and when sufficiently excited she will retaliate by chasing him. Finally the pair quiver together in bushy plants and drop adhesive eggs among the foliage. The parents are then removed. The embryo of each egg is jet black, and consequently they show up quite clearly. Infusoria should be poured into the tank twice daily after the eggs have hatched. This should be done even if after a day or so no youngsters can be seen. The fry are adept at hiding themselves, and the slightest movement in front of their tank sends them into cover immediately. However, a slow, stealthy approach often reveals several dozen fry motionless in the water, but on approaching closer they vanish as if by magic. Thus it is advisable to keep feeding for a week or two. At the end of this time the fry will be ⅛″ long, and unable to hide so easily. They now begin to realize that danger is not inevitable, and gradually they acquire more courage.

A similar species, *T. obliqua*, is also available on occasion.

Chapter Sixteen

Egg-laying tooth-carps (Killifish)

FAMILY CYPRINODONTIDAE

These fish are found throughout the southern states of the USA, through Panama, over most of north-eastern and central South America, and much of Africa, Iran, India, Indonesia, and Indo-China. They are, in fact, related to the live-bearing tooth carps covered in Chapter 13, and often called egg-laying tooth carps, killifishes, or top-minnows.

Most are elongated and cylindrical in shape and, as the name implies, have teeth. Although many species come from the equatorial belt, frequently near the coast, they live in well-shaded pools and do not like excessively high temperatures or bright light. They do best between 72° and 76°F. The majority are small, and are rather particular as to water conditions. They are extremely colourful and prefer acid peaty water for spawning, to which has been added a small amount of salt. Given the right conditions, the majority are not difficult to breed, but in most cases the eggs take from 14 days to several weeks before they hatch. Since the parents spawn over quite a long period, they will still be laying eggs while the first day's spawn is hatching; and as time goes on some of the fry will have grown large enough to devour their newly hatched brethren. Therefore it is advisable to have periodic sortings to keep the babies in age groups, and thus circumvent cannibalism.

Aphyosemion australe – Lyre-tail killifish

Equatorial Africa ♂ 2¼″ ♀ 2″ *Community*
DIET: All foods SWIMS: Lower half of tank

One of the most beautiful of the lovely aphyosemions. It is particular about changes in water conditions, preferring very soft brown peaty water. Any change to harder conditions and increase of pH must be done gradually. The species is peaceful, and will take any food. Oxygen requirements are low, and they will therefore stand considerable crowding, 20 or more living quite happily in a tank 24″×8″×8″.

The fish often rests in the water with the back curved in a slight crescent, tail down, the pectoral fins oscillating forward and backward as though treading water; but at the slightest movement it will dart a few inches and resume its practically motionless position, with wary eyes seeking the source of danger. When kept under ideal conditions it soon loses all nervousness, and then, with fins spread to splitting point, displays its gorgeous beauty.

Sexing is easy, for the male has all the colour and splendour of finnage.

Breeding. *Tank: 24"×8"×8". pH: 6·2-6·8. Hardness: 20-50 p.p.m. Temperature: 74-76°F. One teaspoonful of salt to every 2½ gal. water. Spawns: in floating plants. Method: standard for Aphyosemion. Eggs: 200-300. Hatch: in 12-14 days. Free-swimming: 13th day. Food 1st week: brine shrimp. 2nd week: sifted Daphnia, microworms.*

A small tank, even an all-glass jar, is sufficient space to spawn one pair. In a slightly larger tank it is possible to use 2 males and 4 or 5 females together. The water should be old, acid, and brown with peat, and placed where it will receive subdued light. Some peat which has sunk to the bottom of the tank will hide any eggs that fall or are deposited low down. A good layer of lesser bladderwort or *Riccia* an inch thick should float on the surface of the water.

Males are continuous drivers, and chase the females into either the floating plants or the waterlogged peat that has settled on the bottom. Interlocking fins, the pair tremble side by side and deposit single eggs, the process being repeated many times a day. The parents if well-fed do not eat many eggs, but should be removed on the 12th day, as the first eggs laid will soon be hatching. The same parents may be placed in another breeding tank where spawning is likely to continue. The eggs are large, about the size of a pin's head, and are hard and robust. Alternatively, nylon mops tied to bottle corks will act as spawn-receivers, and once every two days these are lifted out. Taking a few strands at a time, run thumb and forefinger lightly down them. The eggs may be seen or felt, and these are dropped into a small plastic sandwich box, filled with the same water and kept at the same temperature. As soon as the first eggs in the sandwich box begin to hatch, start a second box. This avoids over-crowding, and prevents the older fry eating their newly hatched brethren.

Aphyosemion arnoldi

W. Africa ♂ *1¼"* ♀ *1⅛" Community*
DIET: All foods SWIMS: Lower half of tank

Probably the smallest member of the family, but equally attractive. Males have a rusty red hue over bluish flanks. Females paler and well speckled with brown flecks, all her fins being rounded. Several pairs may be bred at once in the same tank.

Breeding. *Tank: 24"×8"×8", or smaller. pH: 6·4-6·6. Hardness: 20-50 p.p.m. Temperature: 72-74°F. Base of tank covered with ½" layer of waterlogged peat. Spawns: in peat at bottom of tank. Method: buries eggs over a period. Eggs: 80-100. Hatch: in 5 weeks. Food 1st week: brine shrimp, sifted Daphnia. 2nd week: microworms.*

Aphyosemion bivittatum – Red lyre-tail

Tropical W. Africa   ♂ 2"   ♀ 1¾"   Community
DIET: All foods   SWIMS: Mid-water to upper half of tank

This beautiful fish has longer fins than the foregoing, though the colour is more sombre. It is extremely peaceful, and should be kept only with its own kind or other small fishes. It prefers very soft acid water, and likes plenty of small live food, though it will take dried food as well. Like other *Aphyosemion*, it has a habit of hovering in the water, making short darts.

Once again sex is told by colour and finnage.

Breeding. *Tank: 24"×8"×8".   pH: 6·2-6·8.   Hardness: 20-50 p.p.m.   Temperature: 74-76°F. One teaspoonful of salt to every 2½ gal. water. Spawns: in floating plants. Method: standard for Aphyosemion. Eggs: 200-300. Hatch: in 12-14 days. Free-swimming: 13th-15th day.   Food 1st week: brine shrimp. 2nd week: sifted Daphnia, microworms.*

One or more pairs may be spawned together, the procedure following identically that of *A. australe.*

♀

♂

Aphyosemion calliurum

W. Africa   ♂ 2"   ♀ 2"   Community
DIET: All foods   SWIMS: Centre of tank

There are two colour varieties: bright red and yellow, as shown here (often known as *A. calliurum ahli*), and blue-green. Both can be obtained from a single pair of fish. The females are similar, having a pinkish mauve tint, and barely spotted. Now called *A. nigerianum*.

Breeding.   *As for A. australe.*

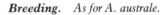

♀

♂

Aphyosemion cognatum – Spotted lyre-tail

Tropical W. Africa   ♂ 2¼"   ♀ 2"   Community
DIET: All foods   SWIMS: Lower half of tank

A pretty fish, similar in size and shape to *A. australe*, but the points on the tail are usually shorter, and not quite so lyre-shaped.

The gill-plate and forward portion of the body are adorned with blue, but the fish is so well sprinkled with rows of red dots that its overall colour takes on a reddish mahogany. The pectoral fins are orange; the dorsal and anal are maroon-striped and have a maroon edge; the caudal has the same maroon border, but the upper and lower edges are bluish-white.

The female is liberally sprinkled with red dots, which spread all over her body and into her rounded dorsal, anal, and caudal fins.

Breeding. *Tank: 24″×8″×8″. pH: 6·2-6·8. Hardness: 20-50 p.p.m. Temperature: 74-76°F. One teaspoonful of salt to every 2½ gal. water. Spawns: in floating plants or peat. Method: see A. australe. Eggs: 70-150. Hatch: in 12 days. Free-swimming: 13th day. Food 1st week: infusoria. 2nd week: infusoria, brine shrimp.*

The recommended procedure for breeding this species follows exactly that described under *A. australe.*

Aphyosemion gardneri – Steel-blue killi

W. Africa ♂ *2¼″* ♀ *1¾″ Community*
DIET: *All foods* SWIMS: *Lower half of tank*

Another beautiful *Aphyosemion* which has a lyre tail. The body is a pale shade of blue crossed by numerous wavy bars of mahogany, turning to deep red, particularly over the gill-plates. The fins are mottled with red spots; they shade from pale yellow to blue. A dark maroon line runs from the base of the caudal peduncle through the tail, dividing off the lower lobe.

Sexing is easy, as the fins of the female are rounded, and she is not so gaudy.

Breeding. *Tank: 24″×8″×8″. pH: 6·4-6·8. Hardness: 20-50 p.p.m. Temperature: 74-76°F. One teaspoonful of salt to every 2½ gal. water. Spawns: in floating plants or* *peat. Method: standard for Aphyosemion. Eggs: 70-150. Hatch: in 12 days. Free-swimming: 13th day. Food 1st week: infusoria. 2nd week: infusoria, brine shrimp.*

Breeding procedure follows that described under *A. australe.*

Aphyosemion shoutedeni – Golden lyre-tail

W. Africa   ♂ 2"   ♀ 1¾"   Community
DIET: All foods   SWIMS: Lower half of tank

Another attractive *Aphyosemion*, with a greenish-yellow tinge over most of the body, particularly in the hinder-quarters, the forward part being more bluish-green. Like most *Aphyosemion*, the body is sprinkled with red dots, and these form themselves into oblique lines on the gill-plates. The fins of *A. shoutedeni* are yellowish-green, the dorsal and caudal being edged with maroon.

The female lacks the pointed fins, but bears the same colours, rather less pronounced.

Breeding. *Tank: 24"×8"×8". pH: 6·2-6·8. Hardness: 20-50 p.p.m. Temperature: 74-76°F. One teaspoonful of salt to every 2½ gal. water. Spawns: in floating plants or peat. Method: standard for Aphyosemion. Eggs: 70-150. Hatch: in 12 days. Free-swimming: 13th day. Food 1st week: infusoria. 2nd week: infusoria, brine shrimp.*

This fish is a prolific breeder, and the procedure given under *A. australe* applies here.

Aphyosemion sjoestedti – Blue-throated aphyosemion

Tropical W. Africa   ♂ 3"   ♀ 2¾"   Community, when young
DIET: All foods   SWIMS: Middle to lower half of tank

This is another gorgeous *Aphyosemion*, but without the typical lyretail. It grows rather larger than most *Aphyosemion*, has a bigger mouth, and rather bulbous gill-plates. In its larger sizes it is apt to swallow small fishes, but is peaceful enough with medium-sized species.

The female is less brightly coloured. All her fins have rounded edges, and are clear except for a few red dots.

***Breeding.** Tank: 24"×8"×8". pH: 6·4-6·8. Hardness: 20-50 p.p.m. Temperature: 76°F. One teaspoonful of salt to every 2½ gal. water. Spawns: around base of plant thickets. Method: deposits eggs over a period. Eggs: 50-150. Hatch: in 3-5 months. Food 1st week: brine shrimp, microworms. 2nd week: sifted Daphnia, Cyclops.*

A. sjoestedti spawns readily, but the eggs take from 3 to 5 months to hatch. The tank should be filled to a depth of 6" with old acid water, brown in colour, and a 1" layer of lime-free sand placed in the bottom. Into this plant bunches of *Myriophyllum, Ambulia,* or *Cabomba*. Some floating plants will serve as a refuge for the female, as the males are rather aggressive drivers. After much chasing the pair come together at the base of the clumps of plants and, trembling, with fins locked, deposit their eggs in the foliage just above the sand. Spawning continues over several days. The large eggs are easily seen, and these should be lifted with the aid of a pipette or piece of glass tubing and then placed in shallow petri jars. If not well fed the parents will eat their eggs, so removal of the eggs daily prevents such cannibalism. The shallow petri jars should be floated in a small, bare tank at a temperature of 74°F. As the eggs lie in only ¼" of water, they can be examined daily. Any which fungus should be removed, but this should not occur if the water is soft enough, and deeply tinted by peat. In some cases the merest suspicion of methylene blue or similar fungal treatment in the petri jars helps to prevent eggs from fungusing.

After 7 or 8 weeks the embryo can be seen forming inside the egg, the eye showing first. A few more weeks and the young fish may be observed in a curved position moving jerkily now and then inside the shell. Even so, hatching does not occur for a week or two more, but eventually the young fry emerge, and are moderately large. They may now be tipped into a tank containing very shallow peaty water, and fed on brine shrimp, microworms, and sifted *Daphnia*. They grow rapidly, and need sorting for size, as the larger readily eat the smaller.

Nothobranchius guentheri

E. Africa   ♂ *2"*   ♀ *1¼"*   *Community*
DIET: *All foods*   SWIMS: *Mid-water*

The genus *Nothobranchius* includes some of the loveliest fishes ever to be seen in aquaria. They are not common, and are a little aggressive, particularly with males of their own kind.

They are annual fishes, in so much as they perish when their habitat dries out, but eggs buried in the mud remain dormant until the next rainy season, when they hatch. The fry must grow quickly to reach maturity and breed before they in turn perish with the dry season.

Breeding. *Tank: 24"×8"×8".   pH: 6·4-6·6.   Hardness: 20-30 p.p.m.   Temperature: 76-78°F.   Spawns: in waterlogged peat at base of tank.   Method: several pairs bury eggs in peat over a period of 10 days.   Remove breeders, siphon off water and allow peat to dry out slowly.   In 3 to 4 months, fill tank with warmed rainwater.*

Quite a few species have been successfully raised as above. *N. guentheri*, though beautiful, is not nearly so gorgeous as *N. rachovi*.

Nothobranchius rachovi

E. Africa   ♂ 2"   ♀ 1¼"   Community
DIET: *All foods*   SWIMS: *Mid-water*

In our opinion certainly the most beautiful of the *Nothobranchius*. It is a treasure worth keeping in a separate tank containing soft brown peaty water; though the females are drab, having a deep creamy-coloured body with a few red spots, and small colourless fins. But nature has certainly painted the males with a brilliance and splash of colour rarely equalled in the animal world.

The male has a glistening turquoise blue on the flanks streaked with deep red, orange, yellow and purple. His dorsal and anal fins are moderately large, and are turquoise blue crossed by curving bands of deep red, the edges of these fins having a deep purple-brown border. His ventral fins are deep red; and the pectorals blue, turning to gold at the extremities. His caudal fin is kept well spread; it is turquoise blue blotched with red, followed by a purple crescent, with beyond this a deep red crescent, and the outer edge is purple-black. The eye is golden, with a blue-green iris.

Males are aggressive towards each other, and drive the females constantly. Watch out for torn fins and battered females.

For breeding follow the procedure for *N. guentheri*. The authors, wishing to observe more of the spawning, placed a pair of *N. rachovi* in a small plastic sandwich box containing an inch or two of pale peaty water. It was observed that the male pinned the female down as he pressed against her, and then locked his dorsal fin over and around her back, thus helping to keep close contact. Both fish quivered for a second or two and then broke apart, but no eggs were laid by the female. It was noticed that eggs only appeared after both fish quivered together, then remained motionless for perhaps two seconds, quivering a second time before they broke apart. It is assumed that during the motionless period the male squeezes the female tightly to help her to expel one or two eggs. Spawning may continue for an hour.

The eggs left in this sandwich box began to develop, and in 4 to 6 weeks hatched out; but most of the fry were unable to swim properly, falling back to the bottom of the container as though exhausted by their activities. Some grew on to over ½" in length and were showing signs of sexing, but were never as healthy or robust as when the eggs were partly dried out for 3 months in damp peat. Perhaps running this species a close second for coloration is *N. orthonotus*, in which the body and fins are a rich burgundy red, the flanks being sprinkled with blue-green flecks.

THE PANCHAX 'GROUP'

This 'group' comprises of the genera *Aplocheilus*, *Epiplatys*, and *Pachypanchax*. They are all from Africa, India, Sri Lanka, and Indonesia. The body is long and tubular, the jaw large and pointed. They will swallow smaller fishes, and although many are safe in community tanks, because the majority like slightly acid water they are better on their own. Most are excellent jumpers, and it is well to see that their tank is securely covered.

Most of the fishes belonging to this group are extremely colourful, and nearly all swim just under the surface of the water. On the top of the head is a light marking which, though not an eye, is extremely sensitive to light and shade. Any shadow thrown by a moving hand causes the fish to dive for safety. When catching these fishes a net should be held immediately below them, and if this is raised gently they are ensnared before realizing what is happening.

Aplocheilus blockii – *Dwarf panchax*

India, Sri Lanka   ♂ 1¾"   ♀ 1½"   Community
DIET: All foods   SWIMS: Upper half of tank

A delightful little fish, and the smallest of the panchax group. It is also known as *Panchax parvus*.

The overall colour is green, the back being darker, but the sides are lit by shining scales of yellowish-green, further adorned by brilliant red dots. The gill-plates are semi-transparent, and the pink-coloured gills show through. The dorsal and anal fins of the male are long and pointed, greenish-yellow in colour, and are edged with orange-red. The tail is diamond-shaped, and, like the other fins, is sprinkled with red dots.

The female is similarly coloured, but her fins are smaller and more rounded. An oblique dark bar crosses the lower portion of her dorsal.

Breeding. *Tank: 24"×8"×8", or smaller. pH: 6·8. Hardness: 80-120 p.p.m. Temperature: 76-78°F. Spawns: in floating plants. Method: deposits eggs over a period of days. Eggs: 50-120. Hatch: in 12-14 days. Food 1st week: infusoria, brine shrimp. 2nd week: brine shrimp, microworms.*

The species is easy to breed and raise. The breeding tank need not be large: one 24"×8"×8" will hold 2 males and 3 or 4 females. It should be planted with one or two clumps of *Ambulia,* and here and there a small Indian fern. The top should be covered with a good mat of lesser bladderwort or a ½" layer of *Riccia.* The males constantly drive the females into the floating plants, then, taking a position alongside her and slightly below, he presses her upward against the plants until she is lying practically on her side. One egg is then deposited and fertilized. The process is constantly repeated for several days, after which the parents should be removed. The clear eggs hatch in 10-12 days.

Aplocheilus dayi

Sri Lanka   ♂ 3¼"   ♀ 3"   Community, with medium-sized fishes
DIET: All foods   SWIMS: Upper half of tank

One of the most beautiful of the panchax group, and rather similar to *A. lineatus.*
Although the fish is a good size, and has a large mouth, the authors have found that
it is inclined to be bullied by other panchax even slightly smaller than itself. Our
own specimens were then moved to a tank of small fishes, and have behaved
themselves and not molested them.

   Male and female are very similar in colour, but she is deeper-bellied, and has a
black dot at the rear end of the base of the dorsal fin.

Breeding. *Tank: 24"×8"×8".   pH: 6·6-6·8.   Hardness: 80-120 p.p.m.   Temperature:
78°F.   Spawns: in surface plants.   Method: standard for panchax group.   Eggs:
50-150.   Hatch: in 10-12 days.   Food 1st week: brine shrimp. 2nd week: brine shrimp,
sifted Daphnia.*

286

♀

♂

Aplocheilus lineatus – *Sparkling panchax*

India   ♂ 4"   ♀ 4"   Community, with larger fishes
DIET: All foods   SWIMS: Just below surface

This is one of the most beautiful of the panchax, also one of the largest. When adult it is not safe with smaller fishes. The mouth is large, and capable of swallowing a full-grown male guppy with ease.

All panchax have a light spot on the top of the head, but it is much more pronounced on *A. lineatus*. It is, in fact, a rudimentary eye, and although the organ now lacks sight, it still retains enough sensitivity to distinguish light and shade and pass a warning to the brain. A hand placed over the tank will soon show that the fish notices the cutting off of the light rays, and it will dart into cover.

The fins of the female are not so long and pointed, and she shows a dark spot in the lower portion of her dorsal. Her body is frequently more barred in the hind portion.

Breeding. *Tank: 24"×8"×8".* *pH: 6·6-6·8.* *Hardness: 80-120 p.p.m.* *Temperature: 78°F.* *Spawns: in floating plants.* *Method: standard for panchax group.* *Eggs: 100-150.* *Hatch: in 10-12 days.* *Food 1st week: brine shrimp. 2nd week: Cyclops, sifted Daphnia.*

The species is a prolific breeder, and if one male is placed with two or three females they will spawn over several days. If well fed they will not eat their eggs, but after 5 or 6 days, when the females are slim, remove all adults. Hatching over a period, the earlier fry are large enough to swallow their smaller brethren, so sorting is recommended.

♀

♂

Aplocheilus panchax – Blue panchax

India, Burma, Malaya, Thailand   ♂ 3"   ♀ 3"   Community, when young
DIET: All foods   SWIMS: Just below the surface

This is a typical panchax, with a long, cylindrical body, flattened head, and tapering mouth. It is not as highly coloured as others of the group, but is none the less attractive. The species is peaceful if kept among medium-sized fishes, but, as in most panchax, the mouth is large, enabling them to gulp in small fishes, provided these can be swallowed whole. They do not go in for biting or tearing fins.

The female as shown is similarly coloured, but bears an orange splash above the black mark in the dorsal. She lacks the blue border to her tail, but has a suspicion of red in the upper and lower edges. She has a tiny black dot at the extreme upper end of the caudal peduncle.

Breeding. Tank: 24"×8"×8". pH: 6·6-6·8. Hardness: 80-120 p.p.m. Temperature: 78°F. Spawns: in floating plants. Method: standard for panchax group. Eggs: 100-150. Hatch: in 10-12 days. Food 1st week: brine shrimp. 2nd week: Cyclops, sifted Daphnia.

Epiplatys dageti – Orange-throated panchax

W. Africa   ♂ 2"   ♀ 1¾"   Community
DIET: All foods   SWIMS: Upper half of tank

A medium-sized panchax of good behaviour, and in good condition one of the prettiest. It is not aggressive or dangerous.

The female does not have the sword-like extension to the lower portion of the tail, all her fins being more rounded.

Breeding. *Tank: 24"×8"×8".   pH: 6·6-6·8.   Hardness: 80-120 p.p.m.   Temperature: 78°F.   Spawns: in floating plants.   Method: standard for panchax group.   Eggs: 100-150.   Hatch: in 10-12 days.   Food 1st week: brine shrimp. 2nd week: Cyclops, sifted Daphnia.*

The species is a prolific breeder, and in the above-sized tank it is possible to breed 2 males and 3 or 4 females together. Spawning proceeds over several days, after which the parents should be removed.

Epiplatys fasciolatus – Barred panchax

Tropical W. Africa   ♂ 3½"   ♀ 3"   Community
DIET: All foods   SWIMS: Upper half of tank

This medium-sized species is safe with all but small fishes, and although not brilliantly coloured, the male is readily identified by the bright elongated yellow crescent in the oval tail, all fins being yellow and bordered by black. The upper half of the body is olive, but covered with horizontal rows of small red dots. The belly and caudal peduncle are patterned by short, dark, vertical bars. The female is mostly greenish-grey, her fins being almost clear, but the vertical bars on her flanks are more pronounced.

Breeding: *Tank: 24"×8"×8".   pH: 6·6-6·8.   Hardness: 80-120 p.p.m.   Temperature: 78°F.   Spawns: in floating plants.   Method: standard for panchax group.   Eggs: 70-100.   Hatch: in 10-12 days.   Food 1st week: brine shrimp. 2nd week: Cyclops, sifted Daphnia.*

The species spawns readily, but is not so prolific as others of the genus.

Epiplatys macrostigma – Spotted panchax

Tropical W. Africa   ♂ 2¼"   ♀ 2"   Community
DIET: All foods   SWIMS: Upper half of tank

Another pretty little panchax, although not as vividly coloured as most; neither is it as common. Like the rest of the family, it prefers old, acid water.

The body is bluish-green on the lower sides, shading to olive-brown towards the back. Numerous deep maroon dots sprinkle the sides and spread into the dorsal, anal, and caudal fins, these fins being bluish-green in colour.

The female does not have such a large anal fin, but this and her ventrals are tipped with bluish-green. She is also deeper-bodied.

Breeding. Tank: 24"×8"×8". pH: 6·6-6·8. Hardness: 80-120 p.p.m. Temperature: 78°F. Spawns: in floating plants. Method: standard for panchax group. Eggs: 50-100. Hatch: in 10-12 days. Food 1st week: brine shrimp. 2nd week: Cyclops, sifted Daphnia.

It breeds like most of the other members of the group, but does not seem so prolific.

Epiplatys sexfasciatus – *Green panchax*

Tropical W. Africa ♂ 3¼″ ♀ 3¼″ Community, with medium-sized fishes
DIET: All foods SWIMS: Upper half of tank

This is one of the larger panchax, and none too safe with smaller fishes. It lacks the brilliant colouring of *Aplocheilus lineatus*, which it resembles in size and shape.

The general body colour is dull green, shading to olive on the back. The sides are adorned with numerous dark green bars, vertical near the tail, becoming more diagonal towards the forward portion of the body. The flanks are also peppered with dark spots. The fins of the male are larger and greenish-yellow in colour, and his tail fin is tipped with red.

The female's fins are clear to pale yellow.

Breeding. *Tank: 24″×8″×8″. pH: 6·6-6·8. Hardness: 80-120 p.p.m. Temperature: 78°F. Spawns: in floating plants. Method: standard for panchax group. Eggs: 100-150. Hatch: in 10-12 days. Food 1st week: brine shrimp. 2nd week: Cyclops, sifted Daphnia.*

The species is easy to breed, and fairly prolific. The procedure follows precisely that described under *A. lineatus*, p.287.

Pachypanchax playfairi – Golden panchax

E. Africa   ♂ 3"   ♀ 3"   Community, with medium-sized fishes
DIET: All foods   SWIMS: Upper half of tank

This is a most attractive fish, rather more chunky than most panchax, and the snout is shorter. The scales in larger specimens do not lie absolutely flat. They are inclined to stand slightly on edge, giving the appearance that the fish is suffering from dropsy, but this is a perfectly natural formation, and therefore nothing to worry about. The species is peaceful enough in its smaller sizes, but when large it should be kept with medium-sized fishes.

The fins of the female are clear to pale yellow, except that a dark oblique bar appears in the lower rays of her dorsal. When in breeding condition her belly is greyish and well distended.

Breeding. *Tank: 24"×8"×8". pH: 6·6-6·8. Hardness: 80-120 p.p.m. Temperature: 78°F. Spawns: in floating plants. Method: standard for panchax group. Eggs: 80-150. Hatch: in 10-12 days. Food 1st week: brine shrimp. 2nd week: Cyclops, sifted Daphnia.*

The fish are easy to breed, and prolific spawners. They are not so particular about acid water as are most other panchax. Nevertheless, spawns seem larger and greater in number when the water is on the acid side, and fairly soft. They breed in top weed like other members of the group, and after a few days the parents should be removed to prevent egg-eating.

Pachypanchax homamolotus

W. Africa   ♂ 2"   ♀ 2¼"   Community
DIET: All foods   SWIMS: Upper half of tank

This beautiful fish is of medium size, and striking colour, and is peaceful and adaptable.

Our colour plate needs no description, and from it sexing is obvious.

Breeding. *Tank: 24"×8"×8". pH: 6·6-6·8. Hardness: 80-120 p.p.m. Temperature: 78°F. Spawns: in floating plants. Method: standard for panchax group. Eggs: 50-80. Hatch: in 10-12 days. Food 1st week: infusoria, brine shrimp. 2nd week: microworms, fine dried food, sifted Cyclops, etc.*

Cynolebias bellotti – Argentine pearl

Argentina   ♂ 2"   ♀ 1¾"   Community
DIET: Live food, may be trained to take dried food
SWIMS: Mid-water to lower half of tank

A superb little fish, never common in Europe, partly because it is not easy to breed, requires very soft water, and rarely lives longer than one year. It is peaceful, but males may sometimes become aggressive towards one another when breeding approaches.

The male and female are dissimilar. Her body is olive to yellow in colour, and numerous thin, wavy bars of a brownish shade cross her flanks and appear in her fins.

The male is gorgeous. His back is deep mauve, paling to a lavender-green on the sides. His dorsal and anal fins are not only larger than his mate's, but deep

♀

♂

mauvish-green in colour. The tail is lavender-green, and has a maroon-red border. The whole of his body and fins are sprinkled with silver-blue dots, and his flanks are crossed by thin, whitish vertical bars.

Breeding. *Tank: 24″×8″×8″, or smaller. pH: 6·0-6·4. Hardness: 10-50 p.p.m.   Temperature: 74-78°F.   Spawns: in peat or mud.   Method: buries eggs over a period.   Eggs: 50-75.   Hatch: in 12-16 weeks.   Food 1st week: infusoria, brine shrimp. 2nd week: brine shrimp, microworms.*

The breeding tank need only be small, and the bottom covered to a depth of 1½″ with waterlogged sieved peat. No plants are necessary. It is filled with very soft brown peaty water and a pair are placed therein during the morning. In a few minutes the male displays his beauty to his mate, and, with fins spread, flutters round and about her head; then suddenly the pair dive side by side into the peat, sometimes disappearing from view. With fins locked, a few eggs are laid, and the fish reappear. Some minutes later, diving once again into the peat, more eggs are laid. At the end of the day the female is quite slim and spawned out. Both parents are now removed. In a day or two the water should be carefully siphoned off, and the peat left just damp. Evaporation slowly takes place, and the peat gradually dries out, but it should be kept at a temperature of 74°F. After 3 or 4 months soft water is gently poured on to the peat, and some infusoria introduced. Providing that all has gone well, the eggs begin to hatch after this very long period of incubation, and the fry must be fed little and often with minute food.

This is one of the species that lives only a year in nature. The pools they inhabit dry out, and the adult fish die off; but the eggs remain in the mud until the rainy season allows them to hatch out some months later. The fry grow and spawn before the drought in the following year.

Cynolebias nigripinnis

Argentina ♂ 1¼" ♀ 1" Community
DIET: Live food, may be trained to take dried food
SWIMS: Mid-water

Related to the foregoing, this little fish is smaller, and even more beautiful. They are peaceful, but are particular as to conditions, preferring old, acid water tinged brown with peat.

The first impression given by the male is of a starry night in December, for his whole body and fins are a velvety blue-black like the night sky, and he is covered with shining silver-blue spots like a galaxy of stars. His mate is rather more drab, being a brownish-grey, and her sides and fins are patterned by wavy dark bands.

Breeding. *Tank: 12"×8"×8". pH: 6·0-6·4. Hardness: 10-50 p.p.m. Temperature: 74-78°F. Spawns: in peat or mud. Method: buries eggs over a period. Eggs: 50-75. Hatch: in 12-16 weeks. Food 1st week: infusoria, brine shrimp. 2nd week: brine shrimp, microworms.*

The fish is not easy to breed and rear, but the procedure follows exactly that of *C. bellotti.*

Jordanella floridae – *Flagfish*

Florida   ♂ 2"   ♀ 2"   Community, when small
DIET: All foods   SWIMS: Mid-water to lower half of tank

An attractive, rather stumpy-bodied fish, though inclined to be aggressive, especially as spawning-time approaches. It is therefore advisable to keep it with species of similar size. It likes to browse on soft algae.

The male has longer fins, which are bluish in colour and well sprinkled with red dots. His sides glow with scales of many hues, blue, red, and yellow being equally distributed, and these are separated by thin lines of red. The female is not so colourful. She may be recognized by a black dot preceded by a white fleck in the last rays of her dorsal fin. Both fish have a large black dot in the centre of each side, but this is more clearly seen on the female.

Breeding. *Tank: 24"×8"×8". pH: 7·0-7·2. Hardness: 100-150 p.p.m. Temperature: 76°F. Spawns: in depression in sand. Method: deposits eggs over several days, which male fans. Eggs: 100-150. Hatch: in 6 days. Fry wriggling: 2 days. Freeswimming: 9th day. Food 1st week: brine shrimp, microworms. 2nd week: brine shrimp, Cyclops.*

The fish is easy to breed, and the males are aggressive drivers. The tank should therefore be thickly planted with bunches of feathery plants to afford the females some refuge. The male drives the female towards the base of a clump of plants where side by side they deposit and fertilize their eggs, usually in fanned-out depressions in the sand. The process continues spasmodically over several days, after which the female should be removed. The male now fans the eggs, which hatch in 5-6 days, after which he guards his babies and protects them from attack. The young grow quite quickly, and as soon as they are free-swimming the male should be taken out.

♂   ♀

Pterolebias peruensis – Peruvian long fin

Peru   ♂ *2¾"*   ♀ *2½"*   *Community*
DIET: All foods   *SWIMS: Mid-water*

Of fairly recent introduction, this is an attractive species. It is one of those fishes which lays its eggs in mud, and during the dry season the parents die off. The eggs lie buried even though the mud may dry out and crack, but with the next rainy season they hatch, and a new generation grows up. Their lives are necessarily short, and because of this, and the length of time required to raise youngsters, the species is unlikely to become cheap. They prefer soft brown peaty water, and although we call them community fish they are better kept on their own; even then, in their constant driving, males may nip the tails of females.

The general colour is fawny-brown and numerous vertical bars crossing the body. In some lights there is a bluish sheen on the gill-plate and a reddish tinge in the tail. The eye is a beautiful blue-green. The pectorals are large, as are also the anal and caudal fins of the male. The dorsal and anal are striped, and the male's large forked tail is peppered with blue dots. The fins of the female are rounded.

Breeding. *Tank: 24"×8"×8". pH: 6·6-6·8. Hardness: 50-80 p.p.m. Temperature: 80°F. Spawns: in plant thickets, or peat. Method: see below. Eggs: 70-120. Hatch: in approximately 3 months. Food 1st week: brine shrimp, Cyclops. 2nd week: sifted Daphnia, grindal worms.*

The tank need only be half-filled with dark brown peaty water, and a good layer 1" thick of crumbled waterlogged peat should cover the bottom. The tank should be placed in a subdued light, and a pair introduced. The male is an ardent driver, and soon the fish, trembling side by side, lock fins and, raising a cloud of peat, deposit a single egg in the soft fibre, the process being repeated many times a day for several days. After 10 or 12 days the parents should be removed, and the spawning tank left severely alone. According to temperature, the eggs hatch in 6 to 13 weeks. The young fry may be seen after this time, and measure ¼" in length.

They should be fed copiously, and will then grow quickly.

Another method, said to resemble more the natural conditions, is to remove the parents after spawning and gently siphon off the water, leaving the peat just damp. If the tank is covered with a piece of glass the peat dries out slowly. After 8 weeks a small quantity of soft water which abounds with infusoria is poured gently on to the peat.

In nature these fish live in shallow pools, many of which evaporate during the dry season. When the pool becomes completely dry the parents die, but the eggs they have laid sink into the soft mud forming the bottom of the pool. Even though the mud appears to be completely dry, and through shrinkage numerous cracks appear, the warmth and early morning dews create sufficient moisture to keep the eggs at the right humidity, so that the embryo inside never becomes completely dehydrated. Various leaves and decaying water plants settle on the mud, dry out, and partly disintegrate. But with the coming of the rains several weeks later the pools begin to fill with soft rain-water, and the dried leaves and bits of plant produce a most favourable breeding medium for the infusoria (much like the aquarist's method of culturing infusoria in crumbled dried lettuce-leaves). The infusoria are thought to attack the egg-shells (which are once again lying in shallow, soft mud) and, biting through the outer shell, assist in releasing the now fully formed young fish who, on emerging, find ample food among the abundant infusoria. The fry grow rapidly, and later take to mosquito larvae and other natural foods. They attain full size and breed before the next dry season, which will end their lives.

RIVULUS

This genus comprises fishes from the West Indies, Venezuela, Guyana, and Eastern Brazil. All have long tubular bodies, and most have a habit of hanging motionless in the water just below the surface plants. But in spite of their immobility they can dart suddenly, and may even jump out of the water—hence the advisability of keeping the tank covered. The tail is often allowed to drop, giving the back an arched outline. The fishes are generally not brightly coloured, but are none the less attractive in somewhat subdued hues. All females carry a spot in the upper portion of the tail base. A few are as colourful as their male counterparts.

The fishes prefer small live food, but may be trained quite quickly to take the dried product. The genus is not safe with small fishes, but is unhappy if kept with ones that are too large and boisterous. *Rivulus* should be housed with species of their own size who do not disturb their tranquillity.

They breed in much the same way as the panchax group, spawning among floating plants just beneath the surface. They prefer old, slightly acid water.

Rivulus cylindraceus

Cuba   ♂ 2″   ♀ 1¾″   Community
DIET: All foods   SWIMS: Upper half of tank

Typical of the genus is this species, with a long, cylindrical body.

The male is attractive, though not gaudy. His back is brown to olive. A serrated dark brown line starting on the gill-plates extends well into the tail fin. Just above this line the body is tinged with a greenish sheen. Below this line the belly and throat are yellowish-orange; red and green spots embellish his flanks. His dorsal fin is yellowish-green, the top edged with white. The anal fin is yellowish, with red blotches and dots. The tail is greenish-yellow, with a cloudy black border. The female's fins are pale yellow, and she shows the typical 'Rivulus spot' in the upper rear part of the caudal peduncle.

Breeding. *Tank: 24″×8″×8″.   pH: 6·8.   Hardness: 80-100 p.p.m.   Temperature: 78°F.   Spawns: over a period.   Method: lays eggs in floating plants.   Eggs: 100-150.   Hatch: in 10-14 days.   Food 1st week: brine shrimp. 2nd week: microworms, sifted Daphnia.*

The species is easy to breed, and the males are vigorous drivers. The tank should be filled with old, acid water, and planted thickly with Indian ferns. At the surface there should be a good layer of *Riccia* or lesser bladderwort. The male drives the female into the floating plants and, placing himself along her side, tilts her over as he presses her upward. One egg is laid and fertilized. The process is repeated at intervals over the next five or six days. During this time the parents should be well fed on chopped frozen shrimp which has been well thawed out. If their appetites are satisfied they are less likely to eat their eggs. After five or six days the parents are removed, the eggs hatching between 10 and 14 days after laying. The young are fairly large, and will take brine shrimp from the outset.

Rivulus harti

Venezuela, Trinidad ♂ 3½" ♀ 3¼" *Community, with larger fishes*
DIET: *All foods* SWIMS: *Upper half of tank*

This is one of the larger *Rivulus*, and consequently a little more dangerous than most of the genus. It is a prodigious jumper.

The body is greyish-green with numerous thin horizontal stripes from gill-plate to caudal peduncle. These stripes are formed of red dots. The male's fins are greenish-yellow, sprinkled with red dots. His tail has a border of brownish-black. The female is duller, and the red spots on her tail are less bright. Her fins are clear. The spot in her tail is not clearly defined, but can be seen as a dark shading.

Breeding. *Tank: 24"×8"×8". pH: 6·8. Hardness: 80-100 p.p.m. Temperature: 78°F. Spawns: over a period. Method: lays eggs in floating plants. Eggs: 100-150. Hatch: in 10-14 days. Food 1st week: brine shrimp. 2nd week: microworms, sifted Daphnia.*

The species is a prolific breeder, but not over-popular. The procedure is identical to that of *R. cylindraceus*.

Rivulus strigatus – Herring-bone rivulus

Northern S. America   ♂ *1¾"*   ♀ *1½"*   *Community*
DIET: *All foods*   SWIMS: *Upper half of tank*

Here we have the smallest and most beautiful of the *Rivulus,* and the most peaceful. Unfortunately, it is a little timid, and inclined to hide its beauty in the top back corners of the aquarium, lurking under the leaves of floating ferns. It is easily bullied by larger fishes, so should be kept with small species. Old, acid water is preferred, and a slightly higher temperature is needed—say 80°F.

The forward portion of the body and back is brownish and well covered with red spots. The hinder part bears an arrow-head or herring-bone pattern of bright red and beautiful blue-green. The dorsal and anal fins are yellowish-orange tipped with red and sprinkled with red dots and streaks. The tail bears wavy lines of red and blue-green; it is yellowish on the upper and lower edges.

The female carries the same colours, less brightly, and the herring-bone pattern is not so clearly defined. Her 'Rivulus spot' is present, but apt to become merged with the streaks of colour in her tail, and this makes it less obvious.

Breeding. *Tank: 24"×8"×8". pH: 6·8. Hardness: 80-100 p.p.m. Temperature: 80°F. Spawns: over a period. Method: lays eggs in floating plants. Eggs: 100-150. Hatch: in 10-14 days. Food 1st week: brine shrimp. 2nd week: microworms, sifted Daphnia.*

This species, being shyer and more temperamental, is not quite so easy to induce to spawn, but given peace and quiet the fish will soon settle in their new surroundings and breed. This follows the procedure given under *R. cylindraceus.*

Chapter Seventeen

Loaches

FAMILY COBITIDAE

These fish, which include the loaches and botias, come from Malaya, Sumatra, Java, Borneo, and Thailand. They are quaint, rather long-bodied fishes, and they are usually to be found at the bottom of pools on the mud, or in some cases beneath it. They therefore provide the aquarist with excellent aquarium scavengers. Most are exceedingly fast swimmers, and their activity is inclined to stir up sediment, and tends to make the water cloudy. To avoid this their aquarium should be kept clean, and occasionally the mulm should be siphoned out of the tank. The majority of this family have barbels for feeling about the bottom in their search for food. They have no teeth in the jaw, and are thus unable to bite other fishes. Generally speaking, they are peaceful, but a few of the botias chase one another, often making a series of clicking noises during this pursuit. Rarely, however, is any damage done.

Some members of the family are equipped with two bony spikes under the eyes and in front of each gill-plate. The spikes when erected are very sharp; they curve backward and appear formidable weapons, though they seldom seem to be used in aggression. Normally they lie flat and harmlessly against the cheek, where they are inconspicuous. When a botia is held in a net the large spines are immediately projected at right angles from the face, and are very liable to get hooked into the mesh; sometimes this has to be cut before the fish can be released. When it is necessary to catch botias a net of plain cotton or nylon is preferable to one of mesh material.

Acanthophthalmus myersi

Thailand ♂ 5″ ♀ 5″ *Community*
DIET: All foods SWIMS: Lower half of tank

Similar in shape to *A. semicinctus*, but the bars, which are more golden, entirely encircle the blueish, chocolate-coloured body. The belly is silver-blue, and the transverse bars are wider on the lower flanks, tapering as they reach the back. There is a dark spot in the dorsal fin, and the caudal fin is black with a colourless edge.

Males are slimmer than females, this being more noticeable when looking down on them from above. The fish is an excellent scavenger.

Acanthophthalmus semicinctus – Kuhli loach

Malaya, Java, Borneo, Sumatra, Thailand   ♂ *3½"*   ♀ *3½"*   *Community*
DIET: *All foods*   SWIMS: *Lowr half of tank*

These are fascinating, snake-like little fishes with long tubular bodies. The popular name covers several distinct species, but is derived from only one, *A. kuhli*. This is because originally all *Acanthophthalmus* were considered to belong to one species with variable local markings. The fish is an excellent scavenger, but is not easy to catch in a planted aquarium. It is peaceful, and pleasing to watch.

The majority are of a pinkish-grey colour turning to brown on the back; chocolate-brown bars cross the body from top to bottom. In *A. semicinctus* these bars do not reach as far as the belly, but end about half-way down the flanks. Other species have variations in the length, thickness, and shape of these chocolate bars, thus making identification difficult. The dorsal fin is set well back, the last rays ending a little in advance of the first rays of the anal fin.

Sexing is extremely difficult. Occasionally an adult female looks plump.

Breeding.   *Has been achieved in aquaria, but few precise details are available.*

305

Acanthopsis choirorhynchos – Horse-face loach

Thailand, Indo-China, Indonesia ♂ 6″ ♀ 6″ *Community*
DIET: *All foods* SWIMS: *Lower half of tank*

The quaint fish have proved themselves to be at home in an aquarium. In spite of their size, they do not seem in the least aggressive; on the contrary, they are very shy. They make excellent scavengers, not only clearing up food which lies on the sand, but burrowing beneath it to forage out any particles which have worked their way between the crevices. Moreover, they keep the sand well loosened, and are amusing to watch. Mouthfuls of sand are taken in, every particle of food is sifted and swallowed, then the cleansed grains are shot backward out of the gills like a miniature sand-blaster.

The eyes are placed well up on the head, so that the fish while resting on the bottom has a clear all-round view.

In its native haunts *A. choirorhynchos* lives in swift-running streams with sandy or gravel bottoms, and its coloration is in keeping with its surroundings. The belly is silverish, the back and sides are sandy-grey. Regularly spaced brown spots appear along the back. A thin line runs from the lips upward to the eye, and thence from the top of the gill-plate to the base of the tail. Equally spaced along this line are brown dots. The fins are clear, except for a few small dots. The mouth, which is undershot, is equipped with short barbels. The spotted sandy colour is such a good camouflage that the fish is quite difficult to see. When disturbed it will dive beneath the sand, remaining buried for long periods, then only raising its eyes sufficiently to reconnoitre.

The Pan-American pilot who first brought it to the authors had nicknamed it 'Horse-face.' This undoubtedly fits, in an uncomplimentary manner, since it has a long nose and an elongated jaw.

There is no indication of sexual characteristics.

Noemacheilus species

India, Burma, Indonesia, Thailand   ♂ 3"   ♀ 3"   Community
DIET: All foods   SWIMS: Lower half of tank

This is a large genus with numerous species coming from most of South Asia. All are good scavengers, and peaceful. The body is elongated, and the fishes swim with snake-like movements. They have small mouths which are provided with short barbels enabling them to feel around the sand, mud, or gravel for particles of food.

Generally speaking, these fishes are sandy-grey in colour with brown markings. Some have spots, others bars; yet others are mottled to fit in with the locality in which they are found. In the species illustrated the only splash of colour is a dull

307

red spot at the base of the front rays of the dorsal fin.

Sexing is difficult. Adult females are slightly plumper than males.

Breeding. *Tank: 24"×8"×8". pH: 7·2. Hardness: 120-150 p.p.m. Temperature: 78°F. Spawns: in plant thickets. Method: scatters adhesive eggs. Eggs: 100-150. Hatch: in 36 hours. Fry hang on: 1 day. Free-swimming: 3rd day. Food 1st week: brine shrimp. 2nd week: microworms, sifted Daphnia, fine dried food.*

The authors have bred *Noemacheilus* loaches. For example, a pair was placed in a well-planted tank, and were observed swimming swiftly side by side over the sand and along the back of the tank. Periodically the pair would rise together to swim over a bunch of short plants, while eggs were being laid and fertilized. After two hours the pair were removed, and numerous largish eggs were seen among bunches of plants and scattered over the sand. Over 100 fry were reared.

BOTIAS

Most botias are attractively coloured, though quite a few have different markings in different localities. Others appear to develop more vertical stripes with age, thus making true identification somewhat difficult at present.

All the botias are similar in shape, having a somewhat arched appearance over the back, mainly brought about by the sloping shoulders which drop to the head and low, pointed nose. The fishes have short barbels on the lips, assisting them to feel for food when grubbing around the bottom of the tank.

All are equipped with formidable spines which are instantly raised at right angles to the cheeks whenever these fishes are alarmed. They come from rivers where the water is slightly alkaline, pH 7·4. Most dislike acid water, which may even cause death. They grow fairly large, and should only be kept with fishes of a similar size. They are very fond of chopped shrimp, chopped garden worm, and boiled cod roe, but will take dried food.

Breeding. *Relatively few details are available.*

♀

Botia almorhae – Yellow-fin botia

Thailand   ♂ 4¹/₂"   ♀ 4¹/₄"   Community, with larger fins
DIET: All foods   SWIMS: Lower half of tank

Typical of the *Botia* shape, this species is not colourful. It is a dull grey all over, and has a large oval-shaped blotch in the caudal peduncle. In males the sides are streaked with numerous faint vertical bars which do not entirely cross the body. The female occasionally shows a few of these bars, but they are less pronounced, and not so numerous. In both sexes the fins arc faintly tinged with yellow. The species should be kept only with fishes of similar size.

Botia horae – Cream botia

Thailand   ♂ 2³⁄₄"   ♀ 3"   Community
DIET: All foods   SWIMS: Lower half of tank

This *Botia* is not so large as most, and is peaceful with smaller fishes.

The body is a pale cream, the belly white. The tail fin is well sprinkled with dark spots. The most prominent feature for identification, however, is the thin black line which runs from the tip of the snout right over the top of the back, and ends by completely encircling the caudal peduncle. This line is just visible in our illustration of the upper fish, but does not show on the lower one, since it follows the curve of the back.

In males the rear portion of the flanks are crossed by three or four irregular vertical black stripes. The female does occasionally show a few of these bars, but they are much fainter, and usually not more than two or three in number. Sometimes her anal and ventral fins are tipped with bright orange.

Botia lohachata

India   ♂ 4" ♀ 4" Community, with medium-sized fishes
DIET: All foods SWIMS: Lower half of tank

The body is a silverish-gold with intense black markings. These run forward from the eye through the nose and mouth and over the rest of the body in perpendicular bars. In females the bars form themselves into letter Y's, but in some males they appear more like V's. Between these markings there are shorter black bars. The dorsal and caudal fins are also barred. The fish is a good scavenger and fairly active.

Botia lucas-bahi

Thailand   ♂ 54"   ♀ 5½"   Community, with larger fishes
DIET: All foods   SWIMS: Lower half of tank

This attractive *Botia* grows large. It has a habit of excavating a depression in the sand, which it considers its own private domain, and refuses to share with other fishes.

The body is yellowish-green, liberally spotted along the lower half. The back is crossed by numerous vertical bands formed of brown spots. The head and forward portion of the back bear horizontal stripes, again formed by numerous small brown spots. The dorsal fin has a splash of red on the outer edge, sometimes wholly or partly margined with black. No indication of sex has been noted.

Botia macracantha – Clown loach

Sumatra, Borneo ♂ *4½"* ♀ *4½" Community*
DIET: *All foods* SWIMS: *Lower half of tank*

We now come to what is probably the most striking of all the *Botia*, which, though medium to large in size, is extremely peaceful.It will live happily with fishes like *Barbus tetrazona, Barbus nigrofasciatus,* etc. Unlike the Thailand botias, it is not unhappy in slightly acid water. Like all the genus, it enjoys chopped shrimp or cod roe, but will quickly learn to take dried food. These fish are very subject to *Ichthyophthirius* (white spot disease), and most imported specimens develop it shortly after arrival. They should not be heavily treated with methylene blue, as since they are scaleless fish, this dye if used strongly will penetrate the skin and kill the specimens. As the species is generally expensive, the aquarist naturally does not wish to take risks with chemical treatment. Perhaps the safest cure in this case is additional heat, coupled with strong aeration, slowly raising the temperature to 90°F.

The body is a golden-yellow, but at times has a tint of orange. Three broad, blue-black bands run obliquely across the flanks.

The colour somewhat resembles *Barbus tetrazona.*

When one of these botias is placed in a community tank which contains a single male tiger barb the authors have noticed that the barb immediately begins to take an interest in the clown loach, following it about wherever it goes. This would seem to indicate that fishes are able to recognize colour, particulary in those cases where it closely resembles their own. The entirely different shape of the loach does not seem to matter to the tiger barb.

Females are deeper-bellied than males.

313

Botia modesta – Blue botia

Thailand   ♂ 5½"   ♀ 6"   Community, with larger fishes
DIET: All foods   SWIMS: Lower half of the tank

Although of pleasing colour, this *Botia* grows quite large, and should only be kept with fishes of similar size. Like *B. lucas-bahi*, it digs a depression in the sand for private occupation, and will chase away any fishes that try to share its abode. Nevertheless, it is not pugnacious, and does not attack unless provoked; even then it inflicts no bodily harm on its opponent. It will often chase one of its own species, and during the pursuit will make clicking noises, which can be heard quite clearly ten or twenty feet away.

The body is a pale blue all over. A darker blue band crosses the end of the caudal peduncle. The dorsal is a pale blue, all the other fins being golden yellow.

A colour variety sometimes known as *B. pulchripinnis* has a pale green body, and bright red fins and tail. Both are shown in our plate.

Sex is indicated by the bulging belly of the female.

314

Botia strigata – *Striped botia*

Thailand, Sumatra   ♂ 3″   ♀ 3″   *Community*
DIET: All foods   SWIMS: Lowr half of tank

Shorter and more chunky than its near relations, this *Botia* does not grow so large, and is peaceful even with quite small fishes.

The body is yellowish, the belly pale cream. The sides are crossed by numerous vertical bars of a chocolate-brown colour tinged with grey. Quite often several thin bars lie so close together that they form a broader band, then there is a space before more thin bars form themselves into a further band. Possibly this marking has a relation to sex. In our illustration the fish on the right is more evenly striped, slighty deeper-bodied, and plumper; it is probably a female. In both sexes all the fins are crossed by curving bars of a chocolate-grey colour. This species does not seem to entrench itself in a depression in the sand as do some other members of the family. One indication of sex may be the more rounded belly of the female.

FAMILY GYRINOCHEILIDAE

At one time these fishes were considered to be members of the family Cobitidae, but are now classified separately. Only a few species (and onc genus) are known, mostly from Thailand. They are remarkable in that they do not 'breathe' like other fishes, which take in water through the mouth and pass it out over the gills. Above the regular branchial opening used for 'exhaling' is a supplementary one for 'inhaling'. They lack pharyngeal teeth. The mouth is provided with sucker lips which have rough folds on the inner surfaces, enabling them to attach themselves firmly to rocks or leaves, even in fast-running streams. Although these fishes have a swim-bladder, it is small and inadequate to work hydrostatically; only by swimming actively are they able to leave the bottom of the stream.

Gyrinocheilus aymonieri – Sucking loach

Thailand   ♂ 3"   ♀ 3"   Community
DIET: All foods   SWIMS: Lower half of tank

Above is shown a species of this interesting genus. It is a queer little fish with a long tubular body; in comparison with its size, the fins are large. These are no doubt provided to overcome the disadvantage of being unable to float by means of the swim-bladder. The under side of the snout forms the upper lip. The fish is shy, and makes quick darts for cover at the slightest sign of danger. These darts carry it a few feet forward, and then it sinks back on to the sand, being unable to remain for long in mid-water. Frequently it attaches itself to plant leaves or the glass walls of the aquarium, adhering firmly by its sucker lips. It feeds mainly on algæ, and therefore is most useful to the aquarist who is bothered by an excess of this vegetable growth. Nevertheless, it will eat dried food which has sunk to the bottom; even small pieces of chopped shrimp and so forth are taken, providing these do not require mastication.

The back and sides are brownish-yellow, paling beneath. A brown line extends from the snout through the eye to the base of the tail. Equidistant along this line, both above and below it, appear blocks of the same colour. The tail is flecked with spots, the other fins being clear. There is no clue to sex.

Breeding.   *The fish has not been bred in captivity.*

Chapter Eighteen

Catfishes

ORDER SILURIFORMES

At the mention of the word catfishes the mind of the average aquarist immediately jumps to the genus *Corydoras*. But there are, of course, several other catfishes, such as talking catfish, glass catfish, sucking catfish, electric catfish, upside-down catfish, and bubble-nest-building catfish, all of which belong to separate families.

FAMILY BAGRIDAE

This family comprises several found in the Far East. They are longer and slimmer than the *Corydoras*, and also have larger fins and longer barbels. They lack the armoured 'scales' common to the *Corydoras*.

Leiocassis siamensis

Thailand   ♂ 6"   ♀ 6"   Community, with larger fishes
DIET: All foods   SWIMS: Lower half of tank

This very striking catfish from Thailand is rarely found in aquaria, but it may become popular with the owners of large tanks. It is not aggressive, though it will on occasions chase for a short distance any fishes which annoy it. This action is sometimes accompanied with one or two short grunts which seem to warn off the intruder, who is never viciously attacked or harmed. *L. siamensis* enjoys chopped shrimp, small lumps of boiled cod-roe, small worms, and even dried food. It is continually scavenging the bottom for any particles of food left by other fishes. Unfortunately, it is rather inclined to excavate a pit in the sand where it likes to take a quiet rest. Around the nose and mouth it is equipped with eight barbels which give the face a rat-like appearance. In the first rays of the dorsal and pectoral fins there are hard, sharp spines. The adipose fin is extremely long.

The body is a light creamy colour, sometimes diffused with pale pink. It is crossed by several bands of dark grey to black, making a conspicuous contrast. These black bands enter most of the fins.

The female is much deeper and broader than the male, and her tail fin has a reddish hue.

Breeding. *Few details available.*

Mystus vittatus

N. India, Burma, Sri Lanka, and Thailand ♂ 5″ ♀ 5″
Community, with larger fishes
DIET: *All foods* SWIMS: *Lower half of tank*

Though large, this is an interesting catfish. As it is quite a fast swimmer, it should not be kept with very small fishes. Although it will not eat them, it scares them by its bulk, particularly when moving at speed It has a habit of sitting under low-leafed plants, and, by vigorously waving its body and fins, shifts the sand until it has formed a depression large enough in which to lie. This disturbance in a well-laid-out tank can be annoying. Nevertheless, the fish is a useful scavenger.

The sides are fawny-brown. Two lightish gold lines pass along the body. These run from behind the gill-plate, one above and the other under the lateral line, to the base of the tail. The fins are brownish.

The female is much deeper-bellied and broader than the male.

Breeding. *Few details available.*

318

FAMILY CALLICHTHYIDAE

A family of South American catfishes which have large heads, tapering bodies, and are covered with smooth, overlapping armour plates. The first ray of the dorsal, adipose, and pectoral fins is hard. They have four longish barbels.

Callichthys callichthys – Bubble-nest-building catfish

N.E. South America ♂ 4½" ♀ 5" Community, with medium-sized fishes
DIET: All foods SWIMS: Lower half of tank

Though it grows rather large, this is an interesting and unusual catfish. It is peaceful, and a good scavenger, but rather shy.

The overall colour is blackish grey-brown. The overlapping scales tend to give a herring-bone pattern along the sides.

The female is generally larger than the male, deeper under the belly, and much more diamond-shaped when viewed from above. The male is widest by the gill-plates, and then tapers towards the tail.

Breeding. *Tank: 24"×12"×12". pH: 7·2-7·4. Hardness: 150-180 p.p.m. Temperature: 76°F. Spawns: under floating leaf. Method: builds bubble-nest. Eggs: 100-150. Hatch: in 4 days. Fry hang on: 1 day. Free-swimming: 6th day. Food 1st week: brine shrimp, microworms. 2nd week: grindal worms, fine dried food.*

319

The tank was planted merely to make the fish feel at home, and to keep the water cleaner. A large leaf was cut off from a pond lily and allowed to float in the breeding tank. A few hours later the male was noticed to be upside down under the leaf, placing bubbles beneath it with his mouth. The female took no interest whatsoever. So vigorously did the male busy himself in trying to build a nest that he pushed the lily leaf from one end of the tank to the other. This action caused most of the bubbles to slip out and escape.

The authors then made (and thoroughly recommend) a more stable but artificial spawning platter. A 4″ square cut from a piece of slate ⅛″ thick. At opposite sides two tiny holes were bored. Through each of these a piece of catgut or nylon was threaded and tied to form a loop. A ½″ wooden slat was pushed through the loops so that the slate platform hung from it. The piece of wood was placed across the top of the tank and the square of slate slipped along so that it was wedged tightly in one of the front corners of the aquarium. The tank was then topped up so that the under side of the slate platform hung just below the surface of the water. The lily-pad was removed, and the male fish immediately turned his attention to the artificial slate platform. In spite of his vigorous actions the slate remained firm, and soon a large nest of bubbles was built beneath it. Every now and then the male would cease his building activities to pay attention to the female. During his courtship he serenaded her with audible grunts. At length both fish swam up and under the slate. Here, circling round each other, they laid and fertilized eggs while in an upside-down position. Spawning continued for two hours, after which the female was removed, as she was now being driven away by her mate. The large eggs were clearly visible among the bubbles in the nest. The male then spent all his time replenishing the bubbles and guarding the eggs. If a finger was dipped into the tank this normally timid fish immediately made an attack.

The eggs hatched in four days, the young falling to the bottom and becoming difficult to see among the grains of sand. The male did not attempt to eat the fry. On the contrary, he attacked any object which entered the tank. The babies were fed copiously with brine shrimp and microworms. A few days later, when the fry had reached ¼″ in length, the male was removed. Nearly 200 young were raised to maturity.

Hoplosternum species

N.E. South America   ♂ 4½"   ♀ 5"   Community, with medium-sized fishes
DIET: All foods   SWIMS: Lower half of tank

In comparison with the previous species, this fish has a larger, flatter head. The back is not so arched, and the dorsal fin appears longer and shallower.

The body is a dull grey-brown, and is sprinkled lightly with small dark dots. The eyes are much smaller, and, due to the flatness of the head, appear to be rather upwardly inclined. A close examination of our plates will show the main differences.

When viewed from the top females are much wider-bodied than males.

Breeding.   *As described under C. callichthys, p.319.*

321

Hoplosternum littorale – Hoplo

N. South America   ♂ 3¾"   ♀ 4"   Community, with medium-sized fishes
DIET: All foods   SWIMS: Lower half of tank

This genus has a higher, more arching back than the *Callichthys*.

The body is a dull brown, and the sides are speckled with small dark brown spots.

Sexing adult fish is easy, as the female is much wider when viewed from above, whereas the male is more torpedo-shaped; also the front rays of his pectoral fins are tinged with yellowish-brown.

Breeding. *Tank: 24"×12"×12".   pH: 7·2-7·4.   Hardness: 150-180   p.p.m. Temperature: 76°F.   Spawns: under floating leaf.   Method: builds bubble-nest.   Eggs: 100-150.   Hatch: in 3 days.   Fry hang on: 1 day.   Free-swimming: 5th day.   Food 1st week: brine shrimp, microworms. 2nd week: grindal worms, fine dried food.*

The breeding procedure is exactly the same as for *C. callichthys*. At this time the normally peaceful and rather shy male becomes aggressive. Once possessing eggs or young, he has no hesitation in attacking any threatening object in the vicinity.

Hoplosternum species

N.E. South America   ♂ 4¹/₂"   ♀ 5"   Community, with medium-sized fishes
DIET: All foods   SWIMS: Lower half of tank

This species is very similar to the foregoing *Hoplosternum* species in most respects; the body, however, is liberally covered with large brown to black spots.

The males appear slimmer than females, and the front rays of his pectoral fins are golden-brown, brightening towards the tips to orange. The rays of this fin are much longer and stronger than those of the female.

Breeding. Tank: 24"×12"×12". pH: 6-8. Hardness: 150-170 p.p.m. Temperature: 78°F. Spawns: under floating leaf or slate pad. Method: builds bubble-nest. Eggs: 150-200. Hatch: in 3 days. Fry hang on: 1 day. Free-swimming: 5th day. Food 1st week: brine shrimp, microworms. 2nd week: small grindal worms and fine dried food.

The fish, normally peaceful, become aggressive when protecting eggs or fry. Chopped earthworm will condition adults into spawning condition.

FAMILY CORYDORAS

There are innumerable species of *Corydoras*, the majority of which come from northern South America. Most are short and chunky in shape, with high, arching backs and flattish bellies. They do not possess scales. Instead their bodies are covered with bony plates which overlap. These are so hard that few fishes are tempted to attack them, and fortunately *Corydoras* themselves are extremely peaceful. Their lips are equipped with barbels, enabling them to feel about on the bottom in their constant search for food. It is because of this that they have become known as the scavengers of the aquarium. Not only do they eat any food which falls to the sand, but they will dig strenuously between the grains to a depth of half an inch to reach some tit-bit which has settled in a crevice. Neither do they spurn particles of food which are no longer in their first freshness. On the contrary, they seem to enjoy and wax fat upon them.

All *Corydoras* have an adipose fin, the first ray of which is hard-spined. This feature is also present in the first rays of the pectoral fins and the dorsal fin. They have movable eyes, which periodically roll upward as if they were giving a wink. From time to time they make a quick dash to the surface, gulp a mouthful of air, and dive to the bottom again. The air inhaled is stored in a branchial cavity and used as required.

Nearly all the genus prefer alkaline water and a temperature between 68° and 78°F. They do not like excessive heat, so if any aquarist is considering raising the temperature of his tank to, say, 95°F. in an effort to cure an attack of white spot, it is advisable to remove the *Corydoras* before doing so. Care, however, should be taken to isolate these, so as not to transfer the disease. Fortunately, *Corydoras* seem practically immune from white spot, very probably because their bony plates protect them from the burrowing parasites.

Corydoras species – Gold-line catfish

North-eastern S. America   ♂ 2½"   ♀ 2½"   Community
DIET: All foods   SWIMS: Lower half of tank

Not so commonly seen, this catfish is rather like *C. aeneus* overleaf, but the body is darker in colour, and there is an arching gold line. This starts behind the upper portion of the gill-plate, passes under the dorsal and adipose fins, and ends in the caudal peduncle.

From a top view females are more diamond-shaped than males.

Breeding. *Tank: 24"×12"×12". pH: 7·2-7·4. Hardness: 150-180 p.p.m. Temperature: 76°F. Spawns: on plant leaves. Method: standard for Corydoras. Eggs: 200-350. Hatch: in 6 days. Fry hang on: 1 day. Free-swimming: 8th day. Food 1st week: brine shrimp, microworms. 2nd week: grindal worms, fine dried food.*

Corydoras aeneus – Bronze catfish

Trinidad, Venezuela   ♂ 2½"   ♀ 2½"   Community
DIET: All foods   SWIMS: Lower half of tank

Perhaps this is the commonest of all the *Corydoras*, and one of the hardiest. It is an excellent scavenger, and keeps the surface of the sand loose. Unfortunately, it is somewhat shy, and tends to hide beneath the backgrond foliage.

It has a greeny-golden-coloured body. The curved edges of the bony plates divided by the lateral line give a faint herring-bone pattern on the sides.

Females are deeper and wider-bodied than males.

Breeding. *Tank: 24"×12"×12". pH: 7·2-7·4. Hardness: 150-180 p.p.m. Temperature: 76°F. Spawns: on plant leaves. Method: standard for Corydoras. Eggs: 200-350. Hatch: in 6 days. Fry hang on: 1 day. Free-swimming: 8th day. Food 1st week: brine shrimp, microworms. 2nd week: grindal worms, fine dried food.*

This is one of the easiest *Corydoras* to breed.

326

Corydoras arcuatus – Arched catfish

Guyana, Amazon ♂ *2¹/₂"* ♀ *2¹/₂"* *Community*
DIET: All foods SWIMS: Lower half of tank

A most attractive catfish, having a pearly-white body adorned by an arching black line which passes through the eye. This marking follows the curve of the back, passes under the dorsal and adipose fins, and ends in the caudal peduncle.

Sexing is obvious when viewed from above.

Breeding. *Sexing and breeding follows that described in Chapter 12.*

Corydoras elegans – Elegant catfish

Upper Amazon, Peru, Ecuador   ♂ 2¹/₄"   ♀ 2¹/₄"   Community
DIET: All foods   SWIMS: Lower half of tank

The name is misleading, as this 'cat' is not particularly elegant. It is a typical *Corydoras* shape, but of rather dull colouring.

The lower sides are silver-grey. A darker grey band tapers from front to rear. It starts immediately above the gill-plates, and runs just below the line of the back to the upper portion of the caudal peduncle. Green highlights appear on the gill-plates. The dorsal fin has an oblique black bar running across its centre, the upper portion being speckled. In males the top of the adipose fin is black.

Females are deeper-bodied than males, and appear wider when seen from above. With the exception of the dorsal, their other fins are clear.

Breeding. *Tank: 24"×12"×12".   pH: 7·2-7·4.   Hardness: 150-180   p.p.m. Temperature: 76°F.   Spawns: on plant leaves.   Method: standard for Corydoras.   Eggs: 200-350.   Hatch: in 6 days.   Fry hang on: 1 day.   Free-swimming: 8th day.   Food 1st week: brine shrimp, microworms. 2nd week: grindal worms, fine dried food.*

328

Corydoras hastatus – Dwarf catfish

Amazon   ♂ 1½"   ♀ 1½"   Community
DIET: All foods   SWIMS: Mid-water

We now come to one of the smallest catfishes, with an entirely different mode of living from the other species. It does not grub about continually on the sand, but often hovers in mid-water, fins quivering rapidly. Periodically it makes short darts to a new position, where it resumes its hovering action.

The body is olive-grey with a thin dark stripe along the sides. This ends in a large spot at the base of the tail, made even more conspicuous by being bordered on the outer edge by a crescent of white. The other fins are clear.

Adult females are considerably plumper than males.

Breeding.   *Follows the standard pattern.*

Corydoras julii – Leopard catfish

N.E. Brazil ♂ *2½"* ♀ *2¾"* *Community*
DIET: All foods *SWIMS: Lower half of tank*

Of all the *Corydoras* this is probably the most attractively marked.

Though not brightly coloured, its distinctive pattern makes it conspicuous. The overall body colour is a light creamy-grey. The head and forward portion of the body is spotted; some of the spots form irregular lines. The upper portion of the hindquarters is also spotted, but here these markings often form themselves into vertical stripes. Along the centre of the sides, starting in a line below the dorsal fin and ending at the base of the tail, is a horizontal black stripe. Above and below this stripe are two thinner lines formed by rows of black dots. These three lines are made more prominent as the space between them is devoid of dots. The caudal, ventral, and dorsal fins are spotted. In addition, a large black blotch appears in the upper part of the dorsal fin.

Sexing is best done from above, females being broader than males.

Breeding. *Tank:* *24"×12"×12".* *pH:* *7·2-7·4.* *Hardness:* *150-180 p.p.m. Temperature: 76°F.* *Spawns: on plant leaves.* *Method: standard for Corydoras.* *Eggs: 200-350.* *Hatch: in 6 days.* *Fry hang on: 1 day.* *Free-swimming: 8th day.* *Food 1st week: brine shrimp, microworms. 2nd week: grindal worms, fine dried food.*

Corydoras melanistius

Guyana, Venezuela ♂ *2½"* ♀ *2½"* *Community*
DIET: All foods SWIMS: Lower half of tank

This species closely resembles *C. melanistius brevirostris* (p.332), except that the spots on the body are smaller, and the tail fin is quite clear. It has all the attributes of the family, being peaceful, a good scavenger, and long-lived.

The body is silver-grey. From behind the gill-plates to the base of the tail small black dots are evenly sprinkled. An oblique black bar runs over the forehead. It passes through the eye and crosses the forward part of the gill-plate. Another large black blotch is splashed across the highest portion of the back and spreads into the front lower part of the dorsal. The rest of this fin and the adipose are lightly speckled.

Females are rounder under the belly than males, and appear more diamond-shaped from a top view.

Breeding. *Tank: 24"×12"×12". pH: 7·2-7·4. Hardness: 150-180 p.p.m. Temperature: 76°F. Spawns: on plant leaves. Method: standard for Corydoras. Eggs: 200-350. Hatch: in 6 days. Fry hang on: 1 day. Free-swimming: 8th day. Food 1st week: brine shrimp, microworms. 2nd week: grindal worms, fine dried food.*

331

Corydoras melanistius brevirostris

Northern S. America ♂ *2¾"* ♀ *2¾"* *Community*
DIET: All foods *SWIMS: Lower half of tank*

One of the most strikingly marked catfishes, this species has large black spots on a greyish body. A thick black line runs over the forehead and crosses the eye. A black bar adorns the upper portion of the back and continues into the lower front rays of the dorsal. The adipose fin is tipped with black. A few spots appear on the anal, but the tail is heavily covered with large black spots which form themselves into vertical bars.

Females are deeper and wider-bodied than males.

This fish is also known as *Corydoras wotroi*.

Breeding. *Tank: 24"×12"×12". pH: 7·2-7·4. Hardness: 150-180 p.p.m. Temperature: 76°F. Spawns: on plant leaves. Method: standard for Corydoras. Eggs: 200-350. Hatch: in 6 days. Fry hang on: 1 day. Free-swimming: 8th day. Food 1st week: brine shrimp, microworms. 2nd week: grindal worms, fine dried food.*

Corydoras myersi

Ecuador, Peru   ♂ *2¹/₂"*   ♀ *2¹/₂"*   *Community*
DIET: *All foods*   SWIMS: *Lower half of tank*

Though not very often seen, this is another pleasant little catfish.

The body colour is brownish to dull gold. A rather broad brownish-grey band starts at the back of the head, runs under the dorsal and adipose fins, and ends in the upper portion of the caudal peduncle. Just below this band is another one which is less clearly defined; it is narrower, and displays a golden sheen. The tip of the dorsal fin is more rounded than it is in other *Corydoras*.

Viewed from above, adult females are more diamond-shaped than males.

Breeding. *Tank: 24"×12"×12".   pH   7·2-7·4.   Hardness: 150-180   p.p.m. Temperature: 76°F.   Spawns: on plant leaves.   Method: standard for Corydoras.   Eggs: 200-350.   Hatch: in 6 days.   Fry hang on: 1 day.   Free-swimming: 8th day.   Food 1st week: brine shrimp, microworms. 2nd week: grindal worms, fine dried food.*

Corydoras paleatus – Mottled or peppered catfish

S. Brazil ♂ 2½" ♀ 2¾" Community
DIET: All foods SWIMS: Lower half of tank

This catfish vies with *C. aeneus* for the distinction of being the commonest species of the genus. Not that this in any way detracts from its usefulness. It is peaceful, a wonderful scavenger, not so shy as some others, is long-lived, easy to breed, and often becomes a firm favourite with its owner. It enjoys sitting in the front of the aquarium, where it amuses onlookers with frequent winks of the eyes.

The body colour is olive green. Patches of blackish-green mottle the flanks. The gill-plates shine with a metallic green in certain lights. The front rays of the dorsal are olive; the tail fin is peppered with faint spots. Otherwise the fins are clear.

Females are rounder below than males, and viewed from above are more diamond-shaped. The males have a very sharp-pointed dorsal fin.

Breeding. *Tank: 24"×12"×12". pH: 7·2-7·4. Hardness: 150-180 p.p.m. Temperature: 76°F. Spawns: on plant leaves. Method: standard for Corydoras. Eggs: 200-350. Hatch: in 6 days. Fry hang on: 1 day. Free-swimming: 8th day. Food 1st week: brine shrimp, microworms. 2nd week: grindal worms, fine dried food.*

Corydoras punctatus – Spotted catfish

N.E. Brazil   ♂ 2½"   ♀ 2¾"   Community
DIET: All foods   SWIMS: Lower half of tank

This is a pretty catfish, though rarely seen. It is somewhat like *C. julii*, the main differences being that the spots on the body are more clearly defined and spaced farther apart; also the large black blotch in the dorsal fin appears in the centre and not at the upper tip, as in *C. julii*. A study of our two plates will show the differences.

Sexing is not easy until the fish are adult. Then the females are deeper and wider in the body.

Breeding.   Tank: 24"×12"×12".   pH: 7·2-7·4.   Hardness: 150-180   p.p.m. Temperature: 76°F.   Spawns: on plant leaves.   Method: standard for Corydoras.   Eggs: 200-350.   Hatch: in 6 days.   Fry hang on: 1 day.   Free-swimming: 8th day.   Food 1st week: brine shrimp, microworms. 2nd week: grindal worms, fine dried food.

The species breeds easily, often developing a reddish hue from under the belly to the anal fin as the spawning urge approaches. The procedure follows that described in Chapter 12, but the authors have noticed that males with well-developed sharp-pointed dorsal fins are the best drivers. Those lacking this feature often prove to be difficult to breed. The cause may be a deficit of hormones, since there seems to be some connection between fin-development and virility.

335

Corydoras reticulatus – Mosaic catfish

Lower Amazon ♂ *3"* ♀ *3"* *Community*
DIET: *All foods* SWIMS: *Lower half of tank*

This is an attractively marked catfish. It grows slightly larger than most others.

The head and upper flanks are laced with irregular lines giving a mosaic appearance. A black zig-zagging line runs from the centre of the flanks to the base of the tail. The lower sides are covered with thin vertical stripes. There is a golden-green sheen over most of the body. The dorsal and tail fins are sprinkled with lines and spots.

Sexing is difficult until the fish are mature; then the female is deeper-bodied and broader from a top view.

Breeding. *Tank:* 24"×12"×12". *pH:* 7·2-7·4. *Hardness:* 150-180 p.p.m. *Temperature:* 76°F. *Spawns: on plant leaves. Method: standard for Corydoras. Eggs: 200-350. Hatch: in 6 days. Fry hang on: 1 day. Free-swimming: 8th day. Food 1st week: brine shrimp, microworms. 2nd week: grindal worms, fine dried food.*

FAMILY DORADIDAE

These are spiny catfish from South America. They are equipped with bony plates, each bearing its own spine. The front ray of the dorsal is hard and sharp. The pectoral fins are large, and the front rays are also hard. Just above these is a row of razor-like spines on the sides of the fish. The adipose fin, however, is soft-rayed. The mouth has long barbels.

Acanthodoras spinosissimus – Talking catfish

Amazon   ♂ 4"   ♀ 4"   Community, with medium-sized fishes
DIET: All foods   SWIMS: Lower half of tank

♀

♂

This is rather an ugly-looking fish, but popular because of its habit of emitting grunting sounds when irritated by a stick or when lifted out of the water in a net. Even so, the popular name has made it more famous than many other fishes which make louder and more frequent noises. It is rather lethargic, and is inclined to hide away under the sand. Worse still, it is shy, and rarely occupies the front of the tank. It is covered with hard plates, each equipped with vicious spines. The inner edges of the pectoral fins are serrated. When caught in a net the spines are erected, and become so entangled in the mesh that the net may have to be cut before the fish can be released. It is therefore advisable to use a plain material rather than a mesh net for this species.

The body is a very dark brown to chocolate; the fins are mottled in the same colour. It is quite a good scavenger, and will take any food. It seems to live for years.

Breeding.   *As far as is known, the species has not been bred in captivity.*

FAMILY LORICARIIDAE

This family consists of the sucking catfishes, their mouths being placed on the under side of the head. The lips form a sucking disc by which the fishes attach themselves firmly to the glass sides of the aquarium, plant leaves, or rocks. When they are determined to hang on quite an effort is required to remove them. The back is covered with bony plates, but the belly is soft and vulnerable. They inhabit most of north-eastern South America.

Hypostomus plecostomus – Plecostomus catfish

Venezuela, Guyana ♂ *10″* ♀ *10″ Community*
DIET: Algae and other foods SWIMS: Lower half of tank

Aquarium specimens rarely exceed 10″ in length, but they grow twice this size in their natural state. So great has been the demand for this fish that quite recently exports have been limited to preserve the species.

The fins are huge. From a side view the dorsal and tail appear like sails; so do the pectorals and ventrals when seen from above. All the fins have hard front rays. These are erected when the fish is caught or handled, and sometimes get wedged in a mesh net. The mouth is immediately beneath the tip of the snout, the large lips forming a most efficient sucker. There are two barbels. The back is armour-plated for protection. A row of fine spines runs from behind the eye to the adipose fin. *H. plecostomus* may therefore be kept with larger fishes.

The colour is a sandy grey, closely speckled with darker spots. Four faint bars cross the body obliquely, two fairly close together under the dorsal, one under the andipose fin, and one in the caudal peduncle.

A number of related species are also available.

Breeding. *Few details available.*

♂

Loricaria parva – Whip-tail loricarid

Paraguay ♂ 4″ ♀ 4″ Community
DIET: Algae and other small foods SWIMS: Lower half of tank

Not a common fish, but it deserves greater popularity than it receives. The body is long and tapering, being widest at the pectoral fins. The species is a good algae-eater, cleaning the glass and plant leaves of this unsightly vegetable matter; also it will eat cod-roe, bits of shrimp, and even dried food.

The back and the fins are brown with mottled dark markings. The tail has an elongated ray on the top half only.

Mature females are thicker than males.

Breeding. *Eggs are laid on a flat rock, and guarded by the male. Up to 200 eggs may be laid, and they hatch after about a week. Fine dried foods appear suitable for the young.*

Otocinclus affinis – Sucking catfish

S.E. Brazil ♂ 1¾" ♀ 1¾" Community
DIET: Algae and other foods SWIMS: Mid-water

To the aquarist who is troubled with an unsightly overgrowth of algae any of the *Otocinclus* will prove to be a boon, since they feed almost entirely on this growth. Like all vegetable-eaters, they are continuous feeders. When imported the containers in which they travel are dark, so no algae develop. For this reason the fishes usually arrive in poor condition due to under-nourishment. Moreover, they are very prone to *Ichthyophthirius* (white spot disease), and in their weak condition very few arrivals escape infection. All newly purchased *Otocinclus*, therefore, should be rigidly quarantined for at least ten days. During this time they should be kept at 82°F. and treated with a pale solution of methylene blue. Due to their smallness, they should only be kept with species of comparable size.

So efficient are these fishes at clearing algae that they will clean plants, rocks, the sides of the aquarium, and even turn upside down to eat any spores growing on the surface of the water. If algae are not present in the tank they should be scraped from other aquaria and fed to the fish. Failing this, they require a substitute of boiled lettuce or spinach. There are several species of *Otocinclus*, all rather similar. But perhaps the commonest is *O. affinis*, which is fawn, sprinkled with brown spots.

Ripe females are considerably fatter than males.

Breeding. *The female lays single eggs on rocks and the glass walls of the tank. These hatch in 48 hours, and the fry cling on for a further 2 days before dropping to the bottom in search of nourishment. This should consist of fine soaked dried food, mashed microworms, and scraped algæ.*

Otocinclus vittatus – *Striped sucking catfish*

S.E. Brazil   ♂ 1½"   ♀ 1½"   Community
DIET: Algae and other foods   SWIMS: Mid-water

The species resembles *O. affinis*, but a dark black line starts on the lips, runs through the eye, passes along the sides, and ends in a large dark blotch at the base of the tail. All other details regarding *O. affinis* apply here.

FAMILY MALAPTERURIDAE

The one species in this family is described below.

Malapterurus electricus – Electric catfish

W. Africa ♂ *10"* ♀ *10"* *Non-community*
DIET: Protein *SWIMS: All depths*

This is not a species for the ordinary aquarist, but it always receives attention when in a tank on its own in a public exhibition, for it is capable of giving quite severe electric shocks when disturbed and touched. Like the electric eel, the discharges tend to run out if too frequently set off, but after a period of rest the body becomes recharged. *M. electricus* is somewhat sluggish, often resting on the sand at the bottom of the tank, but it gets more lively at dusk or when fed. It lives mainly on smaller fishes, which it stuns with an electric shock and swallows. Some victims, if not eaten, may recover.

The body is suede-grey and, like this material, has a matt surface. As the fish swims and turns the inner flank becomes wrinkled and folded. A few dots appear on the sides. There is a whitish area in the caudal peduncle, and a black bar runs across the base of the tail. Another forms a crescent in the centre of this fin. The dorsal has a darker area at its base. The mouth is equipped with several pairs of barbels.

343

FAMILY PIMELODIDAE

This family is very similar to the Bagridae, but inhabits South America.

Microglanis parahybae – Bumble-bee catfish

Northern S. America ♂ 3" ♀ 3" Community, with larger fishes
SWIMS: Lower half of tank

It has a large mouth, and will swallow small fishes so quickly that only a bulging stomach shows evidence of what has happened. The first ray of the dorsal and the pectoral fins are hard, sharp spines. All are erected stiffly when the fish is caught in a net or attacked by larger species. The trailing edge of the pectorals is serrated. Small hooks at the tips of these fins often catch so firmly in fine mesh nets that the material may have to be cut before the fish can be released. When lifted from the water the species sometimes makes a buzzing sound similar to that of a bee smothered with a cloth. Viewed from above, the head is round and large, the body tapering from the pectoral fins to a point at the tail.

The colouring is striking. The body is nearly jet-black, but in places there are one or two patches of pinkish grey. The first of these forms a band over the back of the head and runs down behind each gill-plate. Another appears on the flanks below the outer edge of the dorsal. One is to be seen on the forward portion of the adipose fin. There is yet another on the caudal peduncle; behind this two more show on the upper and lower edges of the base of the tail. The dorsal is black, but the outer edge is clear, and a colourless semicircle appears through the centre of this fin. The ventrals and pectorals are black; the tips of the latter are colourless. The anal fin is black, but has a clear patch in its centre. The tail has a black border near its outer edge, though the tips of the rays are clear. There are three pairs of barbels. One pair protrudes from the upper lip; these are longish, and are marked with alternate patches of black and white. A similar pair projects from the lower lip. The third pair also appears below the mouth, but these are shorter and colourless.

Sexing is difficult as both fish are similarly marked. At maturity females are deeper and rounder-bellied than males.

Breeding. *Few details available.*

Pimelodella gracilis
Amazon, Brazil ♂ 5" ♀ 5" Community, with larger fishes
DIET: All foods SWIMS: Lower half of tank

Another long-whiskered catfish, which grows large, so should not be kept with small fishes.

The body is pale blue-grey, and a blue-black line runs from behind the gill-plate to the base of the tail. The fins are grey.

The female is much deeper-bodied than the male.

Breeding. *Not known to have been bred in aquaria.*

FAMILY SCHILBEIDAE

Etropiellus debauwi – Congo glass catfish

Zaire ♂ *1¾"* ♀ *1¾"* *Community*
DIET: All foods SWIMS: Mid-water

This fish was first imported about five years ago; it has proved to be extremely hardy, and appears to be quite long-lived. The original specimens still thrive happily in our tanks without showing any signs of ageing. The species is extremely active, constantly swimming in mid-water from one end of the tank to the other, and never seems to rest. They are absolutely peaceful, and will take any food.

The body is remarkably transparent. A broad black stripe runs from behind the gill-plate to the fork of the tail. Above this a thinner one follows the line of the back, and ends on the outer edge of the upper lobe of the tail. A third travels from the pectoral fins along the lower portion of the body, and terminates above the last rays of the long anal fin. The intestines are enclosed in a silvery sac, the swim-bladder being clearly visible. The eyes are large. The dorsal fin, which consists of only two or three rays, sticks up like a spike just behind the head. Two short, stubby barbels protrude from the tip of the snout. Some fish appear deeper just below the pectoral fins. These may be females.

Breeding. *Few details available.*

FAMILY SILURIDAE

This family comprises the glass catfishes, featured by their long, transparent bodies, antennae-like barbels, minute dorsal and long anal fins. They come from Java, Sumatra, Thailand, and West Africa.

Kryptopterus bicirrhis – Glass catfish

Sumatra, Java, Thailand   ♂ 3½"   ♀ 3½"   Community
DIET: All foods   SWIMS: Mid-water

For many years this species was the only glass catfish kept by aquarists. It is hardy, very transparent, and once settled down will take any foods. Unfortunately, it is shy, seeking out a favourite shady spot beneath a large leaf at the back of the tank. Here it hovers, tail tilted downward and fins quivering, to keep afloat in mid-water. At feeding time it darts out, snatches a mouthful, and returns at once to its favourite haunt. It rarely swims actively about the aquarium, but when disturbed will dash to some other place of cover. The mouth is large; small fry up to ½" in length will be devoured. Two long, hair-like barbels, resembling antennae, project from the tip of the snout. The dorsal fin consists of a single short spine. This appears just behind the head, and looks like a hair. The anal fin runs practically the whole length of the under side of the body.

In some lights the fish appears silvery; in others it is colourless. At times light striking through the transparent body is split up into the colours of the spectrum, as if the rays had passed through a prism. When kept in darkish tanks the species develop brown stripes, which run lengthwise along the body. At these times the fish is not nearly so transparent.

Breeding.   *Few details available.*

347

FAMILY SYNODONTIDAE

Nearly all come from tropical West Africa. They have armour-plated backs and hard spiny rays to their fins. The eyes are set higher up and closer together than in most other fishes. When grubbing about on the bottom they turn the normal way up. A number of sensitive barbels assist them in their search for food. While swimming from one spot to another they roll over, and proceed belly upward. Frequently they rest in this position under large plant leaves.

Synodontis nigriventris – Upside-down catfish

Zaire ♂ *2″* ♀ *2″* *Community*
DIET: All foods *SWIMS: Lower half of tank*

First imported in the 1950s, this fish caused quite a stir because of its habit of swimming upside down. In shape it closely resembles the *Corydoras*, but is considerably more spiny. The front rays of the dorsal and pectorals are hard and sharp. When the fish is caught in a net these spines are stiffly erected and become firmly hooked into the mesh, which may need cutting before release is possible. It is therefore better to use a net of plain material than one of fine mesh. The head and forward portion of the back are covered by a bony armour. Just above the pectoral fins this bony plate forms a long, sharp spine which lies against the fish's sides. From the lips protrude several pairs of barbels, the upper ones being quite long. When lifted from the water the fish makes croaking grunts.

The general colour is greyish, but the body, fins, and barbels are mottled with dark mauve blotches. The caudal peduncle bears broad mauve bars. The belly is

348

mauvish black. The back is lighter than any other part. This feature is unusual, as normal swimming fishes are dark on the back and lighter in the belly.

A fish looking up from below sees the light-coloured belly of another fish above it against a background of light entering the surface of the water. The same fish looking down on one below sees the dark back against the bottom. Because *S. nigriventris* swims upside down its colour pattern has to be reversed to bring about the usual camouflage.

Females are rounder and deeper-bellied than males.

Breeding.   *Few details available.*

Synodontis shoutedeni

Equatorial W. Africa   ♂ 6"   ♀ 6"   Community, with larger fishes
DIET All foods   SWIMS: Lower half of tank

This upside-down catfish is greyish, mottled with dark mauve patches. The fins are longer and more pointed. The bony plating which covers the head and fore-part of the back carries a similar spine just above the pectoral fins. The shield of armour is clearly seen on the bottom fish in our plate. The species is not aggressive, but, knowing it is well protected, it will not hesitate to chase away other large fishes which annoy it. Such attacks do not mean harm, but serve merely to drive off the offender. There are two antennae-like barbels on the upper lip; four smaller ones, each provided with side branches, project from the bottom lip. The adipose fin is very long at its base, but the rays are short. The points of the tail tend to curve inward.

The fish does not swim upside down nearly as much as *S. nigriventris*, and consequently its belly is not so dark.

Chapter Nineteen

Labyrinth Fishes

SUB-ORDER ANABANTOIDEI

These fish, popularly known as the labyrinth fishes or anabantoids, are equipped with an auxiliary breathing apparatus which enables its possessor to gulp a mouthful of air from above the surface of the water. On descending they force this air into a special compartment known as the labyrinth, which is situated in the head. From this store of air, oxygen is extracted and passed to the blood-stream. The imprisoned air lasts for a considerable time when the fish is inactive, but if it is excited or nervous, or should the metabolism be speeded up by additional heat, the store of air in the labyrinth is used at a faster rate. When this occurs the fish frequently returns to the surface for fresh supplies. On gulping more air through the mouth and forcing it into the labyrinth the used store, now depleted of oxygen, is forced out through the edge of the gill-covers. These fish are therefore able to live in dirtier, fouler, and warmer water than can most others. Nevertheless, it is a mistake to think that they do not extract dissolved oxygen from the water in which they live. On the contrary, they use up nearly as much of this gas as do other fishes.

If several labyrinths are added to an aquarium already stocked to capacity their presence will cause a shortage of oxygen. But it will be the species not equipped with an auxiliary breathing apparatus that will die first.

Most are beautiful. The larger species are rather aggressive, but their colours and the interesting method of reproduction have made them firm favourites among aquarists. This method ('bubble-nesting') is described in Chapter 12.

Sexing is not difficult, as males are usually much more colourful, and have longer points on the dorsal and anal fins. Furthermore, females bulge just behind the pectoral and ventral fins.

Anabas testudineus – Climbing perch

India, Sri Lanka, Indonesia, Philippines ♂ 5½" ♀ 6"
Community, with larger fishes
DIET: All foods SWIMS: Lower half of tank

In its natural habitat this fish grows to between 12" and 15" in length, and is used for food. Aquarium specimens, however, rarely exceed half this size. The species has received a fair amount of publicity on account of its ability to come out of water and travel overland to other ponds. It has been nicknamed the 'climbing perch,' since it will ascend banks and even the lower branches of trees. On each gill-plate there is a spine. When these are extended the fish, by waggling its head, is able to

hook first one and then the other spine on to some plant or object, thereby making a forward progression. When on land the pectoral fins are held rigid and used as front legs. These, as will be seen in our plate, keep the belly off the ground, and enable clumsy steps to be made. The picture was taken as the specimen was walking along a branch of a tree. Such rambles are not a necessity; the fish is more at home in the water. *A. testudineus* is not vicious or aggressive with fishes of its own size. On the contrary, it is inclined to hide behind tall plants at the back of the aquarium, Indian ferns being particularly favoured.

The back is a pale mauvish-blue. The sides and belly are silvery-yellow. There are two black spots; one appears immediately above the pectoral fins, the other shows up in the base of the tail. All the fins are a rich golden yellow.

The female is larger than the male. She is considerably deeper-bodied, and thicker just behind the pectoral and ventral fins.

Breeding. *Tank: 24″×12″×12″. pH: 6·8-7·2. Hardness: 120-150 p.p.m. Temperature: 80°F. Spawns: in floating plants. Method: eggs float at surface. Eggs: 100-150. Hatch: in 24 hours. Fry hang on: 2 days. Free-swimming: 4th day. Food 1st week: infusoria, brine shrimp. 2nd week: fine dried food, microworms.*

The tank should contain some sand; plants should be provided in case one of the fish becomes too aggressive. The other can then avoid head-on attacks by dodging round the clumps of foliage. *A. testudineus* does not build a bubble-nest (see Chapter 12). The parents go into the usual embrace, and the small eggs rise to the surface of the water. Since the pair do not look after their eggs they may as well be removed.

Belontia signata – Comb-tail

Sri Lanka ♂ 5" ♀ 5" Community, with larger fishes
DIET: All foods SWIMS: All depths

This is not a colourful species, and it grows too large for the average aquarist. Kept with other fishes of its own size, it behaves moderately well. The popular name is derived from the extending rays of the tail fin, which give the appearance of a toothed comb.

The groundwork of the body is grey. Each scale, however, is edged with dull red, and this gives a network formation. Irregular wavy bands of dull red cross the sides from top to bottom. All the fins are a rusty hue, the edges being clear.

The male is usually larger than the female, and not so thick in the region behind the ventrals and pectorals. His dorsal and ventral fins are longer and more pointed than those of the female, and the extending rays of his tail are also slightly longer.

Breeding. *Tank: 30"×15"×15". pH: 6·8. Hardness: 100-150 p.p.m. Temperature: 80°F. Spawns: in typical embrace. Method: eggs float among bubbles in poor nest. Eggs: 300-400. Hatch: in 48 hours. Fry hang on: 2 days. Free-swimming: 5th day. Food 1st week: infusoria. 2nd week: brine shrimp, microworms.*

The tank should be filled with water to a depth of 8-10". Clumps of plants should be set here and there to protect the female in case the male becomes too aggressive. He will blow a few bubbles, but they do not form into a nest, as described in Chapter 12. After the usual embrace the floating eggs are massed together among the bubbles. Parents tend their young, but once the fry are free-swimming the adults should be removed.

Betta picta – Mouth-brooding betta

Thailand, Malaya, Indonesia   ♂ *2"*   ♀ *1¾"*   *Community*
DIET: All foods   *SWIMS: Mid-water*

Though not over-colourful, this is an attractive fish. Its outstanding feature is that it is a mouth-breeder, the hatching being done in the mouth of the male. *B. picta* is not aggressive, but when kept in numbers males occasionally chase females.

The colouring is not brilliant, and, as in most bettas, the intensity varies considerably. When content the fish is a mauvish-brown all over. A dark line runs from the lips through the eye and across the gill-plate. Should the fish be disturbed, caught, and put into a jar, it turns a more greyish colour, and faint bars appear vertically on the sides.

Sexing is easy, since the male has a dark maroon lower edge running the entire length of his anal fin. Females show no sign of this coloured border. This masculine feature remains when the fish is in full colour, or when it is put in a jar and lacks its normal hues.

Breeding.   *Tank: 24"×8"×8".   pH: 6·8-7·0.   Hardness: 120-150 p.p.m.   Temperature: 80°F.   Spawns: in typical embrace.   Method: male incubates eggs in his mouth.   Eggs: 80-100.   Hatch: in 15-18 days.   Food 1st week: brine shrimp. 2nd week: sifted Cyclops, fine dried food.*

The tank need be only lightly planted to make the fish feel at home. Sometimes they will start to lay their eggs in a few hours. But if the female is not ripe spawning will not take place for several days; even so, the male will not harm her. When spawning occurs the fish embrace in the usual *Betta* fashion. Immediately afterwards, as the pair separate, the male picks up the dropping eggs; but instead of blowing them out into a nest he retains them in his mouth. The pair embrace

353

repeatedly, and each time the male collects and stores the eggs. After spawning the female may as well be removed, as she takes no further part in the rearing of the young. During the next 10-12 days the male's jaw and gill-plates are somewhat extended, and it is obvious that he is carrying the eggs. When all the eggs have hatched in his mouth, the male releases the fry into the surrounding water. Although he rarely eats the fry once they are free-swimming, the risk can be entirely eliminated if he is removed: the babies in the breeding tank are safe without his protection.

Red betta

Blue betta

Red female betta

Black betta

Betta splendens – Siamese fighting fish

Thailand, Cambodia, Indonesia ♂ 2¾" ♀ 2½" *Community*
DIET: *All foods* SWIMS: *All depths*

The original wild specimens of these fish, although colourful, were generally darkish. Here and there the iridescent scales shone with jewel-like spots, and their fins were much shorter.

The modern aquarium-developed *B. splendens* is so different that it is hardly recognizable as being the same fish. It may be a brilliant cornflower blue, a vivid red, a bright green, a black, or a cream with red fins. These self-coloured fish are the most prized in shows and exhibitions, but there are numerous beautiful individuals which blend two or more hues in one. Generally speaking, such specimens are more common and cheaper. When not in perfect colour bettas are a dull, indistinct hue, but have a dark line running from the lips through the eye to the base of the tail. Females in particular often appear thus, but once excited the overall colour spreads and the line fades. It is unfair to assume that any *Betta* showing the lateral bar will always remain so; the slightest excitement will bring out the true colour, and he may well be a superb specimen.

In Thailand these fish provided sport, much the same as cock-fighting did in England before becoming illegal. Large sums of money were waged by owners and onlookers as two male fish of different hues were placed in a bowl or tank of water to fight. This continued either to the death, or until one of the owners would admit defeat in order to save his fish from the *coup de grâce*, and so be able to stage a return match at a later date. Some fish after many bouts acquired a reputation comparable to professional boxers of today.

On facing each other unacquainted males will spread their gorgeous fins and waggle their bodies in aggressive threats. As the pair approach the gill-plates are extended and the gill membranes protrude fanwise round the throat, much like the feathers of a fighting-cock. With a lunge a combatant will bite and rip off a strip of one of the opponent's fins. In like manner the attacked fish will retaliate, and in a short while the gorgeous fins of both will be hanging in frayed rags and tatters. Eventually one becomes so damaged that he is unable to manoeuvre quickly. When this happens his opponent, being at an advantage, is able to twist and turn, and thereby inflict damage more easily. Occasionally in nature a badly beaten fish will retire before he is killed, but in a confined space he is unable to get away, and will have to fight to the death. The victor will recuperate surprisingly well. Most of his fins which are torn will knit together again; but the rays will thicken where they rejoin, and scars will show; he will never again be a perfect exhibition specimen. Fins which are torn too short may not reattain full length.

In spite of the fighting prowess of these fish the beginner need not be deterred from having one in his tank, for it will not battle with other fishes. It is true that *B. splendens* is not partial to other anabantids, and will occasionally chase them, but since most labyrinths prefer to swim away and avoid a fight, no damage is done. A male *Betta* may safely be kept with several females. They will not attack him, or fight to the death among themselves, though they will often squabble and tear one another's fins. Two males reared together from birth may also live fairly peacefully, but this depends mainly on their individual temperaments.

Sexing is easy, as the females have much shorter fins, and are considerably thicker in the region behind the pectorals and ventrals.

Breeding.   Tank: 24"×8"×8".   pH: 6·8-7·0.   Hardness: 150-180 p.p.m.   Temperature: 80°F.   Spawns: in typical embrace.   Method: standard for bubble-nest-builders.   Eggs: 150-250.   Hatch: in 3 days.   Fry hang on: 2 days.   Free-swimming: 6th day.   Food 1st week: infusoria. 2nd week: infusoria, brine shrimp.

Only females well filled with roe should be tried for breeding. If unready to spawn they may be killed by the male.

The method of reproduction is fully described under 'Bubble-nest-builders' in Chapter 12. After spawning the female should be removed immediately. Once the fry are free-swimming the male may be taken out.

Colisa chuna – Honey gourami

India   ♂ 1½"   ♀ 1¼"   Community
DIET: All foods   SWIMS: All depths

One of the smallest gouramis, this peaceful fish grows to only two-thirds the size of the dwarf gourami. When young, or not in breeding condition, it is a rather drab creamy colour, but a male under excitement is striking. His dorsal fin becomes a golden yellow and the body darkens, his anal fin is gold turning to copper, and the shorter rays of this fin bear a dark blue-black border which stretches backward across the fin, narrowing as it does so. Females are similarly coloured, but not nearly so brightly.

The male builds a bubble nest at the surface of the water, using any plant to help anchor his nest. Males are not too aggressive, but occasionally a female not too full of roe may be killed. Generally speaking, they are easy to breed. Females should be removed after spawning, and the male when the young are free-swimming.

Breeding.   *Tank: 24"×8"×8".   pH: 6·4-6·8.   Hardness: 30-50 p.p.m.   Temperature: 80°F.   Spawns: in typical embrace.   Method: standard for bubble-nest builders.   Eggs: 80-120.   Hatch: in 48 hours.   Fry hang on: 2 days.   Free-swimming: 5th day.   Food 1st week: infusoria, 2nd week: infusoria, yolk of egg. 3rd week: infusoria, brine shrimp.*

When showing off and exciting the female the male has a curious habit of turning from the horizontal to the perpendicular, nose upward, so that he looks as if he is floating on his tail.

Colisa fasciata – *Striped gourami*

India   ♂ 4³/₄"   ♀ 4¹/₂"   Community
DIET: All foods   SWIMS: All depths

Although this is an attractive and extremely colourful fish, it has had to yield its place in the aquarium to its smaller cousins. It is hardy, peaceful, and easy to feed.

Male and female are very different in colour, she being as drab as he is gorgeous. She is a dull reddish-brown with a dark line running from the gill-plate to the base of the tail. Her fins are brown with a rusty-coloured edge. The back of the male is brown. The sides are more of an orange tinge, and are crossed by several thin, slightly oblique blue bars. The lower portions of the gill-plates are a bright blue. His dorsal is tipped with orange-red, the centre portion being more blue-green. The anal fin is blue, the outer tips of the rays being bright red; the trailing point of this fin is edged with red. The tail is orange with red dots. His ventrals take the form of long, thin filaments (commonly known as feelers); they are bright orange-red.

Breeding.   *Tank: 24"×12"×12".   pH: 6·8-7·0.   Hardness: 150-180   p.p.m. Temperature: 78°F.   Spawns: in typical embrace.   Method: standard for bubble-nest-builders.   Eggs: 150-250.   Hatch: in 3 days.   Fry hang on: 2 days.   Free-swimming: 6th day.   Food 1st week: infusoria. 2nd week: infusoria, brine shrimp.*

The tank should be planted merely to make the fish feel at home.

357

Colisa labiosa – Thick-lipped gourami

Burma ♂ 2¾" ♀ 2½" Community
DIET: All foods SWIMS: All depths

Here we have another pleasing gourami, not too large for the average aquarium, yet big enough to be able to occupy a tank with other medium-sized fishes. The lips are not particularly thick, but are bordered by dark markings above and below which make them appear wider than they actually are.

The male is normally a chocolate-brown, but has blue vertical stripes on his sides. Blue appears in his dorsal, ventral, and caudal fins; the two former are edged with red, and are longer and more pointed than those of the female. Red streaks appear in his tail. His ventrals are bright red. At breeding time, however, the male turns much darker, sometimes nearly black. The edges of the dorsal and anal fins are then bordered by a golden-orange which stands out conspicuously and makes him appear a real beauty.

Colour and length of fins is a sure indication of sex. But with all fishes equipped with feeler-like ventrals the females are always thicker and more rounded in the area above these fins, and behind the pectorals, than are the males.

Breeding. *Tank: 24"×12"×12". pH: 6·8-7·2. Hardness: 150-180 p.p.m. Temperature: 80°F. Spawns: in typical embrace. Method: standard for bubble-nest-builders. Eggs: 150-550. Hatch: in 48 hours. Fry hang on: 1 day. Free-swimming: 4th day. Food 1st week: infusoria. 2nd week: infusoria.*

The species produces a bubble-nest, but sometimes incorporates into the structure a few bits of plant or duckweed, *Riccia* being preferred. The male takes mouthfuls of air from the surface, and instead of spitting out bubbles forces the air through his gills, exuding a mass of very fine bubbles which float to the surface. At other times he will build underneath the leaves of floating ferns. Nests are frequently constructed in a corner of a community tank, where spawning takes place. The young have little chance of survival in such a spot, so the nest and spawn should be drawn into a large jar and removed. When these fish are deliberately spawned in a breeding tank the procedure prescribed in Chapter 12 should be followed.

Colisa lalia – Dwarf gourami

India   ♂ 2"   ♀ 2"   Community
DIET: All foods   SWIMS: All depths

Of the four *Colisa* mentioned in this book, this is undoubtedly the most beautiful; it is also one of the smallest, and is very peaceful. Its brilliance is best revealed when the fish is in the front of the tank and illuminated by light coming from over the viewer's shoulder. Unfortunately, it is shy, and is inclined to lurk round the darker parts of the aquarium.

The female cannot compare with her mate in appearance. She is a silvery colour, and faint bluish stripes occasionally glisten on her flanks. All her fins are clear. The male is superb, and this is not only at breeding-time.

Sex is easy to determine because of the colour differences. Furthermore, males have longer and more pointed tips to the dorsal and ventral fins. Females are thicker in the belly above the ventrals and behind the pectorals.

359

Breeding. Tank: 18"×10"×10". pH: 6·8-7·2. Hardness: 150-180 p.p.m. Temperature: 80°F. Spawns: in typical embrace. Method: standard for bubble-nest-builders. Eggs: 100-150. Hatch: in 48 hours. Fry hang on: 2 days. Free-swimming: 5th day. Food 1st week: infusoria, yolk of egg. 2nd week: infusoria.

The tank should be planted to make the fish feel at home, as they are inclined to be scarey. Some *Riccia* or other small floating plants should be included, as these are used to reinforce the bubble-nest blown by the male.

After laying her eggs the female should be removed. Once the fry are free-swimming the male may be taken out, as the young will not require his protection. The babies are minute, and need extremely fine food. Unless the stomachs of the fry are kept well filled they die in great numbers during the first week or two. When ⅛" long they can be fed brine shrimp; later sifted Daphnia may be given.

Helostoma temmincki – *Kissing gourami*

Malaya, Indonesia, Thailand ♂ 6" ♀ 6" *Community, with larger fishes*
DIET: *All foods* SWIMS: *All depths*

In nature these fish grow to 12", and are an important food fish. In aquaria they rarely exceed 6". The deep body is a golden cream, but laterally compressed, so that seen from a side view they look more bulky than when seen head on. They have gained wide publicity from their 'kissing' habit. The fish approach each other with their rather protruding thick lips turned back, so that they look somewhat like tiny rubber rings. The two place their lips together, and stay in that position for several seconds. Occasionally the authors have tried with a thin stick to part a pair which have just locked themselves together, but the fish could not be separated until they themselves decided to break apart. Why they unite their lips is probably part of a threat display rather than a sign of attention. On occasions they will attempt to suck on to the sides of other fishes; frequently they will adhere to the glass walls of the aquarium, where they eat some algae. Only when large do they tend to become a little aggressive, and should then be kept with bigger species.

These fish have tremendous appetites, and are often unknowingly starved by their owners. They adore dried food that floats, and will take 7 or 8 feeds of this daily. Constant meals prevent a hollow appearance which is frequently noticeable over their foreheads.

Since male and female are alike, sexing can be told by the thickness of the female's body in the area above the ventrals and behind the pectorals.

Breeding. Tank: 30"×15"×15". pH: 6·8-7.2. Hardness: 150-180 p.p.m. Temperature: 80°F. Spawns: in typical embrace. Method: eggs float at surface. Eggs: 300-350. Hatch: in 24 hours. Fry hang on: 2 days. Free-swimming: 4th day. Food 1st week: infusoria. 2nd week: infusoria, fine dried food.

The species is often considered difficult to spawn, but this is because breeding is usually attempted long before the fish are mature. From 5″ in length upward they breed readily. They go into the usual embrace, and eggs are exuded and fertilized. These float to the surface, but are not housed in a nest, as the parents do not construct one. Some bits of floating plant help to hide the spawn, but if the adults are well fed they are not inclined to eat their eggs. As soon as the female is slim both parents may be removed. The large number of fry require an abundant supply of infusoria over the next few days. Some feeds of fine yolk of hard-boiled egg should also be given.

A less common green variety is sometimes available in the trade.

♀

♂

Macropodus cupanus-dayi – Spear-tailed paradise fish

Sumatra, Malaya ♂ *2¾″* ♀ *2¾″ Community*
DIET: *All foods* SWIMS: *All depths*

Though inclined to be a little shy, this is a pleasant, easy to breed, peaceful fish.

The colouring is dull reddish-brown, though at times it has a purplish hue. Two dark bands traverse the body from the head to the base of the tail. The dorsal and anal are reddish-brown, the outer portions being more red. The trailing points of these fins are edged with electric blue. The tail is spear-shaped, with its centre rays protruding some distance beyond the others. This fin is edged in electric blue.

The female has shorter fins than the male; her belly is deeper and wider, particularly in the area behind and below the pectorals. Sexing is not easy until the fish have attained maturity.

Breeding. *Tank: 24″×8″×8″. pH: 6·8-7·2. Hardness: 150-180 p.p.m. Temperature: 80°F. Spawns: in typical embrace. Method: standard for bubble-nest-builders. Eggs: 100-150. Hatch: in 48 hours. Fry hang on: 2 days. Free-swimming: 5th day. Food 1st week: infusoria, yolk of egg. 2nd week: infusoria, brine shrimp.*

Provided the female is full of roe, *M. cupanus-dayi* is one of the easiest of the labyrinths to breed. The male builds a nest. He is not too aggressive, and rarely harms the female. They embrace in the usual fashion. Eggs are blown into the nest, after which the female may as well be taken out. The male tends the eggs. Once these have hatched he may be removed. The fry grow rapidly, and are breedable in 5-6 months.

Macropodus opercularis – Paradise fish

S.E. China, Korea ♂ *5"* ♀ *4½"* *Community, with larger fishes*
DIET: All foods *SWIMS: All depths*

Once king of the aquarium, this fish has recently lost favour owing to its size and somewhat aggressive nature, but kept in a large tank with medium-sized fishes it is still a popular beauty. It is extremely hardy, and will stand low temperatures.

Male and female are normally similar in colour, but the male has longer fin-tips than his mate. The female is considerably deeper and thicker in the body behind and rather below the pectorals. When breeding, the male's colour is greatly intensified, while the female is inclined to become more drab.

There are a number of tank-bred varieties.

Breeding. *Tank:* *24"×12"×12".* *pH:* *6·8-7·2.* *Hardness:* *150-180 p.p.m. Temperature: 78°F. Spawns: in typical embrace. Method: standard for bubble-nest-builders. Eggs: 250-350. Hatch: in 48 hours. Fry hang on: 2 days. Free-swimming: 5th day. Food 1st week: infusoria, yolk of egg. 2nd week: brine shrimp, microworms.*

The fish conform to the standard pattern of bubble-nest-builders. The female should be given some protection while the male is building his nest. This may be accomplished either by plant thickets round which she can dodge, or she may be placed inside a large jar floating in the tank. The pair embrace, and eggs are blown into the nest. After spawning the female should be removed. The male tends the eggs. When the fry are free-swimming he also should be transferred to another tank.

Sphaerichthys osphromenoides – Chocolate gourami

Malaya, Sumatra ♂ 2¼" ♀ 2¼" Community
DIET: All foods SWIMS: All depths

This is shy, and rather touchy as to water conditions. It is imported in large numbers from the Far East, but even with modern air travel losses are frequently very high. Those which arrive alive are somewhat weakened, and are very prone to *Ichthyophthirius* and gill infections. Quite a number refuse to eat, and die. The price is therefore never cheap. Nonetheless, once acclimatized it lives well in the aquarium, proving to be a quiet, very peaceful, attractive fish. It seems to prefer soft peaty water with a pH of 5·0 and a hardness of under 5 p.p.m. It should only be kept with smaller, non-aggressive species.

In keeping with its retiring nature, the colouring of *S. osphromenoides* is subdued. The body is a brownish-grey. Crossing the flanks are creamy-grey stripes. One of these, just behind the head, is vertical. At the back of this lies a horizontal one, but two more vertical ones cross the hind-quarters. In front of the dorsal there are two very tiny bars, only ⅛″ long, and another in the upper part of the caudal peduncle. The dorsal is brownish-grey. The anal fin has a dark edge, and in the male the banded pattern across the hind-quarters extends into this fin. Nevertheless, sexing is difficult unless the fish are in full colour.

The species is extremely fond of gnat larvae and blood worms. It will take *Daphnia, Cyclops*, and white worms. When trained it will consume even good dried food; but its mouth is small, and food should be graded accordingly.

Breeding. *Tank: 24″×10″×10″. pH: 5·0-6·0. Hardness: less than 5 p.p.m. Temperature: 77-86°F. Spawns: after a brief display. Method: mouth-brooder. Eggs: up to 80. Fry free-swimming in 2-3 weeks. First food: infusoria. Then newly hatched brine shrimp. Once thought to be a livebearer, it is now known to be a mouth-brooder. After spawning, the eggs are collected by the male, and incubated in his mouth for about 2-3 weeks. The fry must be fed on tiny foods, such as infusoria and perhaps brine shrimp. Up to 80 eggs are produced; the female may also mouth-brood.*

Trichogaster leeri – Lace gourami

Malaya, Sumatra, Thailand   ♂ 5″   ♀ 4½″   Community
DIET: All foods   SWIMS: Upper half of tank

Sometimes known as the pearl, or mosaic, gourami, this attractive fish grows to a good size, and is usually extremely peaceful. On occasions, however, a frustrated male may make aggresive darts at other fishes, and may chase them for a few seconds. It is fairly hardy, but occasionally suffers from gill infections. These cause it to gyrate erratically before sinking to the bottom to die. All newly acquired specimens should be quarantined and treated with a broad-spectrum parasite remedy.

In colour and finnage male and female are similar until they reach maturity, then the rays in the male's dorsal begin to lengthen until it extends well over the centre of the tail. The hind portion of his anal fin also grows; frequently on the trailing edge the rays protrude as short filaments. Now he starts to develop an orange-red throat and chest, this being particularly brilliant during courtship. His feeler-like ventrals are bright red; the female's are only a yellowish-orange.

Breeding. Tank: 24"×12"×12". pH: 6·8-7·2. Hardness: 120-150 p.p.m. Temperature: 80°F. Spawns: in typical embrace. Method: standard for bubble-nest-builders. Eggs: 150-200. Hatch: in 48 hours. Fry hang on: 2 days. Free-swimming: 5th day. Food 1st week: infusoria, yolk of egg. 2nd week: brine shrimp, fine dried food.

The fish are easy to spawn, and the male rarely, if ever, harms the female. He builds a large bubble-nest, frequently under the leaves of floating ferns; this he reinforces with bits of plant. Sometimes he even tears leaves from stalks of *Myriophyllum*, biting and tugging quite hard to break them off. Eventually the female is coaxed or driven under the nest, where the usual embrace takes place. The floating eggs are carefully stowed in the centre of the nest. After spawning the female may as well be removed. The male tends the eggs, continually blowing more bubbles to maintain the home. Although he looks after his young, it is as well to remove him once they are free-swimming. Then, siphoning through a fine nylon material, the water should be lowered to a depth of 6". This reduces pressure, and prevents the fry from sinking into the depths. The babies are very small, and are usually produced in great numbers. Food must be abundant, and later, when they are 1" long, they will enjoy numerous meals of floating dried food, white worms, and mosquito larvae.

Trichogaster microlepis – *Moonlight gourami*

Thailand   ♂ 5"   ♀ 4½"   Community
DIET: All foods   SWIMS: Upper half of tank

The species was first introduced into Britain by the authors in 1953. In shape and temperament it strongly resembles the lace gourami, but has a more turned-up snout, and the rear portion of the body from dorsal to tail is longer. It is extremely peaceful and hardy, beautiful and breedable, yet difficult to raise. Dried food is much enjoyed.

The first impression is that of a pearly fish. But, this popular name having already been appropriated by *T. leeri*, the wife of one of the authors suggested as an alternative 'moonlight gourami'. This has proved to be entirely suitable, since in some lights the fish is a cold steel-blue, while in others it takes on a pale, elusive

gold. The eye is black, surrounded by gold. If kept in a dark tank a black line appears on the sides from nose to tail, but this marking disappears entirely in well-lighted aquaria.

Sexing is possible only in adult fish. The ventral feelers of the male and the forward edge of his anal fin become bright orange. The rays of his dorsal also grow, to make this fin longer and more pointed than that of the female. Her ventrals are colourless, and the body just above these is thicker and deeper than in the male. Frequently her snout is not so upturned as that of her mate.

Breeding. *Tank: 30″×15″×15″. pH: 6·8-7·0. Hardness: 120-150 p.p.m. Temperature: 80°F. Spawns: in typical embrace. Method: standard for bubble-nest-builders. Eggs: 300-350. Hatch: in 48 hours. Fry hang on: 2 days. Free-swimming: 5th day. Food 1st week: infusoria, yolk of egg. 2nd week: infusoria, brine shrimp.*

The tank should be provided with bunches of plants, round which the female may take refuge while the male builds his nest; not that he is vicious, but he seems to prefer to keep her at a distance during the construction period. The surface of the water should be covered with young floating ferns. These the male utilizes when blowing his bubble-nest. So vigorous is he in this work that he will even tear up stalks of *Myriophyllum* and *Hygrophila* and push them into the nest to reinforce it. Eventually, when all is ready, he allows the female to swim under the nest. Then, embracing her in the usual labyrinth manner, eggs are laid and fertilized. Coating each with a bubble, he blows them into the nest. When spawning is finished the female should be removed. The male continues to tend the eggs. Once the fry are free-swimming he should be removed from the breeding tank, and then

367

the water be lowered to a depth of 6". The minute babies must be fed copiously. Even so, many die off, and a spawn of 350 may easily be reduced in a month to a mere dozen or so. The exact cause of this mortality is not clear, but the authors are still investigating and trying out ways to counteract this trouble.

Trichogaster pectoralis – Snakeskin gourami

Thailand, Cambodia, Indonesia ♂ *4½"* ♀ *4½" Community*
DIET: *All foods* SWIMS: *All depths*

Though this fish grows to a foot or more in length in its native haunts, when confined to the average big aquarium it rarely exceeds 5". Even so, its large size prevents it from becoming more popular. It is extremely peaceful, somewhat shy, and not particularly colourful.

The body is an olive grey-brown with a broken black line running from gill-plate to caudal peduncle. Somewhat faint fawn-coloured bars cross the flanks obliquely. The fins are clear, but tend to become yellowish on the outer edges.

The male is usually slightly larger than the female. His dorsal and anal fins are longer and more pointed. Both sexes have somewhat blunter-shaped heads than most gouramis.

Breeding. *Tank: 30"×15"×15". pH: 6·8-7·0. Hardness: 100-150 p.p.m. Temperature: 80°F. Spawns: in typical embrace. Method: standard for bubble-nest-builders. Eggs: 300-500. Hatch: in 48 hours. Fry hang on: 2 days. Free-swimming: 5th day. Food 1st week: infusoria. 2nd week: brine shrimp, fine dried food.*

The species is easy to breed and very prolific. Parents do not harm their young.

♂

♀

Trichogaster trichopterus – Three-spot gourami

India, Malaya, Sumatra, Thailand   ♂ 5½″   ♀ 6½″
Community, with larger fishes   DIET: All foods   SWIMS: All depths

Being extremely hardy, attractively coloured, and obtainable very cheaply, this fish is often sold to beginners. This is all very well when it is young and small, but it grows quickly, and becomes far too large for the average aquarist. Furthermore, it often turns spiteful with smaller fishes, and sometimes becomes a bully and a nuisance. Kept with medium-sized species it generally behaves itself, and is then quite a favourite. Like all gouramis, it enjoys floating dried food.

The body is a pale silvery blue, and is crossed vertically by numerous wavy bands of a darker hue. These bands usually slant forward at the base. There is a large dark blue spot in the centre of the body, and another at the base of the tail. The belly has a yellowish-green tinge, and the dorsal, anal, and caudal fins are spotted in the same colour.

On reaching maturity the female becomes deeper and much thicker than the male, particularly in the area behind the pectorals and ventrals. Her dorsal fin is not so long and pointed as that of her mate.

There is a brown variety of this fish which when large is even more aggressive than the blue.

Breeding. *Tank: 24″×12″×12″. pH: 6·8-7·2. Hardness: 120-150 p.p.m. Temperature: 80°F. Spawns: in typical embrace. Method: standard for bubble-nest-builders. Eggs: 250-950. Hatch: in 48 hours. Fry hang on: 2 days. Free-swimming:*

369

5th day.   Food 1st week: infusoria, yolk of egg. 2nd week: infusoria, brine shrimp.

These are the easiest labyrinths to breed, and are so prolific that they are always obtainable cheaply. The tank should be well stocked with clumps of plants, as the male while building his nest is inclined to bully the female. Eventually the pair embrace beneath the bubbles, and the lighter-than-water eggs float. Some spread over the surface, but this does not seem to matter, as they nearly always hatch out. After spawning the female should be removed, or she may be damaged by her mate. The male keeps guard. After hatching he also should be taken out of the tank. The free-swimming fry appear in great numbers just below the surface of the water. Unlike most gouramis, the babies are so hardy that few die; they grow quickly, and are over 1″ in length in six weeks.

Trichogaster trichopterus sumatranus – Blue gourami

This fish is derived from the former. It is similar in all respects, except for its mottled coloration.

Trichopsis pumilus – Sparkling gourami

Java, Borneo ♂ *1″* ♀ *1¼″* *Community*
DIET: All foods *SWIMS: All depths*

This beautiful little fish vies with the dwarf gourami in colour. Unfortunately, it is so small that much of its beauty is overlooked. It undoubtedly has a future, for besides being colourful it frequently makes a grating noise, especially when courting. Surprisingly, this sound, coming from such a small fish, is clearly audible at a distance of 20 feet.

Male and female are similarly coloured, and sexing is therefore difficult. As the fish are small it is not easy to notice her fuller, deeper belly. A curious thing is that one day a male is so brilliant that any novice could pick him out, but the next day even an expert might fail to see any difference between a pair.

Breeding. *Tank: 24″×8″×8″. pH: 6·8-7·0. Hardness: 120-150 p.p.m. Temperature: 80°F. Spawns: in typical embrace. Method: bubble-nest under leaf. Eggs: 50-100. Hatch: in 72 hours. Fry hang on: 2 days. Free-swimming: 6th day. Food 1st week: infusoria. 2nd week: infusoria, brine shrimp.*

This little fish has another claim to fame. It is a bubble-nest-builder with a difference: building its nest under a small leaf, growing horizontally a few inches above the sand.

As sexing is so difficult, five or six fish should be placed in a breeding tank. This should be planted with a few *Cryptocoryne beckettii* and one or two stalks of *Hygrophila polysperma*. In a short time a male will select a female and pay court to her. Quivering his fins in front of her, he will display himself, and make the grating noise previously referred to. The other fish in the tank will be constantly driven away from the selected spawning-site. Once it has become obvious which is the true pair the remainder should be removed. The couple now left alone play up to

371

each other. The grunting becomes more frequent as they search for and decide upon a certain leaf under which the male builds his bubble-nest. This is so small that it is often difficult to detect; but a few tiny bubbles at the surface of the water gives the astute aquarist a clue, for these have slipped from under the leaf and risen to the surface.

Therefore look for the nest below a leaf which is situated directly under the tell-tale surface bubbles. Now the nest may be seen densely packed beneath a leaf measuring only 1″ long by ¼″ wide. If spawning is witnessed the aquarist will see the fish locked in the typical anabantid embrace. On breaking apart the male picks up the falling eggs, and any which have reached the sand. These he coats with a bubble, and blows them into the nest. When spawning is over it is as well to remove the female, but she should be placed apart from others, so that when next required for spawning the aquarist knows full well where he has a guaranteed female.

The eggs are rarely noticeable, but in two days the tail of the fry may be observed hanging downward from under this same leaf.

The male often transfers the fry to the under side of another leaf until they become free-swimming. At this stage it is best to remove him, once again taking care to place him in a tank where he may be identified immediately when required for a further spawning.

It is surprising how even experienced aquarists can fail to notice obvious sex differences in some species of fish. The authors have to admit that this was the case with *T. pumilus* when this book was first published.

The fins were carefully scrutinized to see if those of the male were longer, more pointed, or more colourful; and though these appeared so at certain times, it was not an infallible guide.

The fishes bred easily enough, but we had to wait and catch, from a tank containing many, one pair that were showing signs of courtship.

Scrutiny continued, until one day the obvious was noted—so obvious that it was remarkable that it had been missed so often before.

Females have a row of reddish-brown dots forming a single horizontal line along the middle of the flanks. Males not only possess this same line, but have another row of dots more widely spaced, forming a second somewhat arched line above the original.

♂

Trichopsis vittatus – Croaking gourami

Thailand, Malaya, Indonesia   ♂ 2"   ♀ 1¾"   Community
DIET: All foods   SWIMS: All depths

Though famed as the croaking gourami, this fish usually makes less noise, and not so often, as the previous species.

The body is a rusty red. A dark line passes from the lower lip through the eye across the gill-plate. The fins are long, the pectorals of the male having particularly long, feeler-like filaments. His dorsal, anal, and tail are also longer and more pointed than those of his mate. All the fins are rusty brown.

The female is thicker and deeper-bellied.

Breeding. Tank: 24"×8"×8". pH: 6·8-7·0. Hardness: 120-150 p.p.m. Temperature: 80°F. Spawns: in typical embrace. Method: standard for bubble-nest-builders. Eggs: 100-150. Hatch: in 48 hours. Fry hang on: 2 days. Free-swimming: 5th day. Food 1st week: infusoria. 2nd week: infusoria, brine shrimp.

The male builds a bubble-nest at the water surface. After spawning female should be removed. The male guards the eggs, but once the fry are free-swimming he may be taken out.

Chapter Twenty

Cichlids

FAMILY CICHLIDAE

This is a large family of spiny-rayed fishes, most of which come from Central and South America. Many hail from Africa, and at least two species are found in India and Sri Lanka. The family is intelligent, mating, breeding, and caring for their young in a more advanced manner than do other fishes. Most cichlids are highly coloured and have gorgeous finnage. Many of them prefer slightly alkaline water.

LARGE AND MEDIUM CICHLIDS

Aequidens curviceps – Sheepshead acara

Amazon ♂ *3¹/₂"* ♀ *3¹/₂"* *Community, with medium-sized fishes*
DIET: *All foods* SWIMS: *Lower half of tank*

This fish is just too large to be classified as a dwarf cichlid, but it is a border-line case. It is not harmful with medium-sized species, is only aggressive at spawning-time, and, like the dwarfs, does not tear out plants.

A. curviceps is attractively coloured, with a bluish tinge. A few short, dark bars come and go over the forward part of the back. The dorsal fin is blue; it has a yellow tip, and is edged with red. The anal is yellowish, and the tail has an orange border.

Males have longer points to the ends of the dorsal and anal fins. Females are thicker through the body just above the ventral fins.

Breeding. *Tank: 24"×8"×8". pH: 7·0-7·2. Hardness: 150-180 p.p.m. Temperature: 80°F. Spawns: in flower-pot. Method: standard for dwarf cichlids. Eggs: 150-250. Hatch: in 3 days. Fry wriggling: 3 days. Free-swimming: 7th day. Food 1st week: brine shrimp. 2nd week: microworms, fine dried food.*

Breeding follows the procedure given in Chapter 12.

375

♀ ♂

Aequidens latifrons – Blue acara

Central America   ♂ 6″   ♀ 6″   Community
DIET: All foods   SWIMS: Lower half of tank

This fish is not suitable for the aquarist with small tanks, but may be kept with other large cichlids.

The colour is a greeny-blue. In the upper portion of the flanks it is liberally spangled with shining scales of light blue; these markings turn browner towards the belly. As with many cichlids, vertical bars running across the body come and go according to the fish's mood. A large dark spot appears in the upper portion of the body about half-way between the eyes and tail. The fins are orange with blue spangles.

Males have longer points to the dorsal and anal fins. Just behind and below the pectorals they are not so thick or deep-bodied as females.

Breeding. *Tank: 30″×15″×15″. pH: 7·0-7·2. Hardness: 150-180 p.p.m. Temperature: 80°F. Spawns: on rock. Method: standard for large cichlids. Eggs: 300-500. Hatch: in 3 days. Fry wriggling: 3 days. Free-swimming: 7th day. Food 1st week: brine shrimp. 2nd week: microworms, fine dried food.*

The species is a prolific breeder, caring tenderly for its young. *A. latifrons* will often spawn again when the first brood has reached ¾″ in length and is still in the tank. The breeding procedure follows that described in Chapter 12.

♀   ♂

Aequidens maroni – Keyhole cichlid

Guyana, Venezuela   ♂ 4"   ♀ 4"   Community, with larger fishes
DIET: All foods   SWIMS: Lower half of tank

Though the species has no bright colours, it is one of the pleasantest cichlids. It is quiet and peaceful, does not tear out plants, but is rather shy.

The overall tone is deep brown with darker patches coming and going according to the fish's moods. A bar of deeper hue runs across the face. A nearly black spot appears high on the flanks about two-thirds of the distance between head and tail. Occasionally a vertical bar, widening towards its base, emerges below the spot, and looks like the keyhole of a mortice lock—hence the name. Sometimes this feature is adorned by a golden outline. The fins are pale brown.

Sexing is difficult, except when the female is full of roe. At this time she is obviously thicker than the male behind and below the pectoral fins. In both sexes the trailing points of the dorsal and anal are long. These extremities in aged specimens sometimes curl inward, nearly wrapping the tail.

Breeding. *Tank: 24"×12"×12". pH: 7·0-7·2. Hardness: 150-180 p.p.m. Temperature: 80°F. Spawns: in flower-pot. Method: standard for medium cichlids. Eggs: 200-300. Hatch: in 4 days. Fry wriggling: 3 days. Free-swimming: 8th day. Food 1st week: brine shrimp. 2nd week: microworms, Cyclops.*

The fish do not breed regularly. They may spawn two or three times in quick succession, and then desist for several months. In order to obtain another spawn quickly it is best to remove the flower-pot in which the eggs are laid to a bare tank. Apply aeration close to the eggs, and add methylene blue to the water (see Chapter 12). Once the fry are hatched the flower-pot should be returned to the parents in the hope that they may spawn again within 10 days. Do not feed the babies until they are free-swimming.

Aequidens portalegrensis – *Green acara*

S.E. Brazil ♂ *5½″* ♀ *5½″* *Community, with larger fishes*
DIET: *All foods* SWIMS: *Lower half of tank*

This is perhaps the commonest of the genus, mainly because it is a prolific breeder, and aquarists who spawn it have plenty of young fish to give away. Although the species is fairly peaceful, it is not safe with small fishes, and requires a good deal of room.

The general body colour is greenish, but the scales sparkle here and there with a bluish tinge. A dark spot appears in the centre of the flanks and at the base of the tail. Sometimes a horizontal stripe runs from the eyes to the caudal peduncle. Frequently numerous vertical bars cross the body, but these can disappear at will. The fins are greenish-yellow, the lower half of the tail being liberally spotted with bluish-green.

Male and female are very similar, but he is brighter, and has more spots in the tail. The female is wider behind and below the pectoral fins.

Breeding. *Tank: 36″×15″×15″. pH: 7·0-7·2. Hardness: 150-180 p.p.m. Temperature: 78°F. Spawns: on flat rock. Method: standard for large cichlids. Eggs: 250-450. Hatch: in 3 days. Fry wriggling: 3 days. Free-swimming: 7th day. Food 1st week: brine shrimp. 2nd week: microworms, fine dried food.*

Probably the easiest and most prolific of all cichlids to breed. So attentive are the parents, and so great is the number of fry produced, that it is unnecessary to remove the eggs for safety or to obtain more frequent spawnings. Thus a large tank is recommended, so that the babies may attain ½″ in length before it becomes necessary to transfer them to a larger home. The parents would spawn in an aquarium only 24″×12″×12″, but the family would soon require larger quarters. In a big aquarium the adults may spawn again even though the first batch, now ¾″ long, are still in the tank.

Astronotus ocellatus – Oscar

N.E. South America   ♂ 12″   ♀ 12″   Non-Community
DIET: Mostly protein   SWIMS: Lower half of tank

This is the giant of aquarium cichlids. It requires a very large tank, particularly since it is difficult to sex until nearly full grown. This means that several may have to be reared in order to obtain a pair. It is not generally aggressive, but needs space.

Unlike most cichlids, the scales do not shine. The texture more resembles brown suede mottled with greyish markings and splashed here and there with vivid reddish-orange patches. A ring of this colour adorns the base of the tail. The fins are dusty brown, but at any time the fish may take on a much darker hue.

Sexing is possible only with large fish, and when the female becomes thick with roe. Sometimes the behaviour of a pair gives a clue to their sex.

Breeding. *Tank: 48″×15″×15″, or larger. pH: 7·0-7·2. Hardness: 150-180 p.p.m. Temperature: 80°F. Spawns: on flat rock. Method: standard for large cichlids. Eggs: 500-600. Hatch: in 3 days. Fry wriggling: 2 days. Free-swimming: 6th day. Food 1st week: brine shrimp, microworms. 2nd week: Cyclops, sifted Daphnia.*

Cichlasoma biocellatum – Jack Dempsey

Brazil   ♂ 7"   ♀ 6"   Non-community
DIET: Mainly protein   SWIMS: Lower half of tank

A gorgeous fish, but much too large and aggressive to be kept in community tanks. It tears out plants.

Colour varies considerably when young, but as the fish ages it becomes a blue-back with shining scales of bottle-green. A black spot appears in the centre of the flanks, and another at the base of the tail. The fins are the same colour as the body, but the dorsal is edged with red.

The male is more brightly spangled, and the trailing point of the dorsal fin is longer than that of his mate.

Breeding.   Tank: 36"×15"×15".   pH: 7·0-7·2.   Hardness: 150-180   p.p.m. Temperature: 80°F.   Spawns: on flat rock.   Method: standard for large cichlids.   Eggs: 300-500.   Hatch: in 3 days.   Fry wriggling: 3 days.   Free-swimming: 7th day.   Food 1st week: brine shrimp, microworms. 2nd week: sifted Daphnia, Cyclops.

This is one of the species where males may kill females before mating, so care must be taken to prevent fatalities. Once in agreement they spawn readily, and make devoted parents, following precisely the procedure outlined in Chapter 12.

Cichlasoma cyanoguttatum – Texas cichlid

Texas, Mexico ♂ 9" ♀ 9" *Community, with large fishes*
DIET: All foods SWIMS: Mid-water

A mild-mannered cichlid, but one which grows far too large for the average aquarist.

The body is a pearly grey crossed by several vertical bars of a darker hue. A black, triangular spot appears at the base of the tail. The head, body, and part of the fins are liberally speckled with pale blue dots.

Longer points to the dorsal and anal fin of the male determine sex.

Breeding. *Tank: 36"×15"×15". pH: 7·0-7–2. Hardness: 150-180 p.p.m. Temperature: 78°F. Spawns: on flat rocks. Method: standard for large cichlids. Eggs: 350-500. Hatch: in 3 days. Fry wriggling: 3 days. Free-swimming: 7th day. Food 1st week: brine shrimp, microworms. 2nd week: sifted Daphnia, Cyclops.*

♀

♂

Cichlasoma festivum – *Festive cichlid*

Amazon ♂ *6"* ♀ *5"* *Community, with large fishes*
DIET: All foods *SWIMS: Mid-water*

One of the quietest and most peaceful cichlids. It does not tear out plants. The name is misleading, for the colouring is not bright or festive. Nevertheless, the fish is smart because of its oblique dark line. This runs dead straight from the lips diagonally upward through the eye, crosses the upper flanks, enters the dorsal fin, and ends in the pointed tip.

The general body colour is greenish-grey, with a yellowish tinge. Faint vertical bars of grey appear on the sides. There is a dark spot on the upper portion of the caudal peduncle. The fins are yellowish-green speckled with brown dots. The lower half of the gill-plate in both sexes is pale blue.

Sexing is difficult, as both fish are similarly marked. On reaching maturity the male develops slightly longer points on the dorsal and anal fins. These, however, are not exaggerated. The female when full of roe is thicker behind and below the pectoral fins than her mate.

Breeding. *Tank: 24"×12"×20" high. pH: 7·2-7·4. Hardness: 150-180 p.p.m. Temperature: 80°F. Spawns: on 'Vitrolite' bar or leaf. Method: remove eggs, and hatch in separate tank. Eggs: 250-350. Hatch: in 4 days. Fry wriggling: 4 days. Free-swimming: 9th day. Food 1st week: infusoria, brine shrimp. 2nd week: brine shrimp, sifted Cyclops.*

These fish may spawn in a community tank providing they are not disturbed by

382

other big, aggressive species. Even so, it is better to give them quarters of their own, for when the eggs are removed and hatched separately a good pair will spawn every ten days for months on end. The breeding tank should be nearly as high as it is long, but need not be particularly wide from front to back. It should have a 2″ layer of sand on the bottom, and be planted to make a permanent home. The fish will spawn on a long, wide leaf like that of *Echinodorus intermedius*, but this is difficult to set correctly after transfer. The authors prefer to use a long piece of opaque Perspex. This should be 18″ long by 3″ wide by ¼″ thick. It is pushed 1″ into the sand, and leant against the side of the tank nearly reaching the surface of the water. Here it stands, 10 degrees off perpendicular, and is opaque enough to appear solid and strong to the spawners, who prefer it to transparent glass. In a few days the pair make half-hearted attempts to clean this bar with their mouths. Shortly afterwards the female presses her protruding ovipositor against the bar and, moving slowly upward, deposits a row of eggs upon it. The male moves in and fertilizes these. Spawning continues until a patch 3″ long by ¾″ wide, containing about 350 eggs, is laid.

During the spawning period, which lasts about 1½ hours, the aquarist should prepare a small hatching tank 24″×8″×8″. It should be quite bare, and filled to a depth of 4″ with alkaline water of the same pH, hardness, and temperature as that in the tank where spawning is taking place. Five drops of 5 per cent. methylene blue and an aerator stone attached to an air-line are placed in the water in the hatching tank. When spawning is completed the Perspex is transferred and placed on its side lengthwise in the little aquarium, so that the eggs face the viewer. The aerator is pushed under the bar in order to allow the bubbles to rise about ¾″ in front of the patch of eggs, thus creating water circulation. In 48 hours eyes appear in the eggs. Hatching occurs two days later, and the wriggling fry hang from the bar by a sticky thread attached to their heads. They remain in this state, absorbing the yolk-sac for food, until strong enough to break the thread. This occurs 3 days later, when they fall to the bottom. In a further 72 hours they rise in a cloud and become free-swimming. Now the strength of the methylene blue is reduced by changing three-quarters of the water in the tank. It will then be too weak to kill the infusoria and brine shrimp with which the fry should now be fed. After 10 days sifted *Daphnia* and *Cyclops* will be taken.

Fishes that spawn on bars and leaves usually take their food in mid-water, and do not readily grub about at the bottom of the tank. For this reason microworms are not a good food to feed the fry. They will seize the slowly sinking worms, but once these reach the bottom of the aquarium they are mostly ignored. Here the worms will die and cause pollution. As stated before, this type of cichlid should be given food that hops about in mid-water, and also some of the dried product that floats.

Cichlasoma meeki – Fire-mouth cichlid

Central America ♂ *4½″* ♀ *4″* *Community, with larger fishes*
DIET: All foods *SWIMS: Lower half of tank*

Looks belie this gaudy cichlid. It gives the impression of being very savage, but actually it is fairly mild-mannered when kept with large fishes. Nevertheless, two males may have occasional squabbles, and when the breeding urge approaches the protective instinct gives *C. meeki* a natural aggressiveness. At thsese times it will dig pits in the sand, tear out plants which may obstruct its view, and make determined charges at any fishes which approach its selected territory.

The general body colour is olive, but the scales shine in rows of blue dots. The outstanding feature is the vivid scarlet throat and belly. A black line runs from the eyes to a large spot on the flanks. Faint vertical bars appear at times on the sides. On the lower edge of the gill-plate is a prominent diamond-shaped black spot which is edged with silver-blue. The fins are reddish, but adorned with flecks and stripes fo blue. The upper edge of the dorsal is scarlet. The lower edge of the ventrals and anal is bluish-black. The female is similarly coloured; but her dorsal and anal fins are not so long or pointed. She is usually smaller.

Breeding. Tank: 24″×12″×12″. pH: 7·0-7·2. Hardness:120-150 p.p.m. Temperature: 80°F. Spawns: in flower-pot. Method: standard for medium cichlids. Eggs: 200-250. Hatch: in 4 days. Fry wriggling: 3 days. Free-swimming: 8th day. Food 1st week: brine shrimp. 2nd week: microworms, fine dried food.

The species is easy to breed. It deposits eggs inside a flower-pot. Male and female should now be returned to their normal tanks. An aerator is placed near the eggs in the flower-pot and 5-7 drops of methylene blue added to the water. Do not feed until the fry are free-swimming.

♂

Cichlasoma nigrofasciatus – Convict cichlid

Honduras, Nicaragua   ♂ 4"   ♀ 3½"   Non-community
DIET: All foods   SWIMS: Lower half of tank

This is not a large cichlid, but aggressive enough to be unsafe with any small or medium-sized fishes. It is a frequent spawner, and if kept in a community tank causes havoc by tearing out plants and incessantly digging pits in the sand.

Long before maturity the fish can be easily sexed, as it is one of the species in which the female is more colourful than the male. He is a dark mauvish-black, the body being crossed by vertical bars. The foremost of these is inclined towards the head at an angle of 45 degrees. A dark blotch appears at the base of his tail. His dorsal bears shades of green, and when mature this fin and the anal grow longer points than those of the female. She is usually smaller, and flecks of gold adorn her lower sides and belly. Her dorsal and anal fins are bluish-green, and at mating-time she is round underneath and thicker than her mate.

Breeding. *Tank: 24"×12"×12".   pH: 7·0-7·2.   Hardness: 150-180   p.p.m. Temperature: 80°F.   Spawns: in   flower-pot.   Method: standard   for   medium cichlids.   Eggs: 250-350.   Hatch: in 3 days.   Fry wriggling: 3 days.   Free-swimming: 7th day.   Food 1st week: brine shrimp. 2nd week: microworms, fine dried food.*

An easy and prolific breeder. Spawning follows the pattern described in Chapter 12. It is best to remove the male and allow the female to tend the eggs.

385

♂

Cichlasoma severum – Severum

Amazon   ♂ 6"   ♀ 5½"   Community, with larger fishes
DIET: All foods   SWIMS: Lower half of tank

In spite of the name (meaning 'severe'), this is not a very aggressive cichlid if kept with fishes of its own size. Like any member of its family, it may become quarrelsome at breeding-time. It also pulls out plants.

When young the fish is a pale brown with a few vertical bars. But on reaching maturity the male has a greenish tinge, and along his flanks reddish-brown spots form themselves into horizontal but slightly arched stripes. The most outstanding feature is a slightly curved upright bar a little in front of the caudal peduncle. This bar links together a large spot in the rear portion of the anal fin with a similar one in the dorsal fin. When fully grown the fins of the male become brownish, and are sprinkled with spots of red and blue. His dorsal and anal fins grow long points; these extend back far enough to reach the outer edge of the tail.

The female is duller, and her fins are shorter.

Breeding. *Tank: 30"×15"×15". pH: 7·0-7·2. Hardness: 150-180 p.p.m. Temperature: 80°F. Spawns: on flat rock. Method: standard for large cichlids. Eggs: 300-350. Hatch: in 3 days. Fry wriggling: 3 days. Free-swimming: 7th day. Food 1st week: brine shrimp. 2nd week: microworms, fine dried food.*

The species is not such a ready breeder, but when spawning occurs it follows the procedure described in Chapter 12.

Etroplus maculatus – *Orange chromide*

India, Sri Lanka ♂ 3″ ♀ 3″ *Community, with medium-sized fishes*
DIET: All foods *SWIMS: Lower half of tank*

A very striking fish, different in colour from most cichlids. Except at breeding-time, it is not aggressive with medium-sized fishes. Usually it does not pull out plants.

When young, or in an unfavourable situation, the fish is a dull buff with a black spot in the centre of the sides. But when happy, or in courting dress, the species is very beautiful. The whole body turns a brilliant golden-yellow, the sides being sprinkled with rows of carmine dots. These are more abundant in the male. The fins are gold to orange, the dorsal bearing numerous red dots, but the ventrals and lower edge of the anal turn jet-black. The spot on the side of the body fades to pale blue.

Sexing, according to most books, is extremely difficult, but the authors do not agree with this. An obvious and infallible colour mark seems to have escaped notice in the past. In the tail fin of the female there are two white bands, one running parallel to the upper edge, the other parallel to the lower. These white markings are always plainly visible whether she is in full colour or not. They are completely absent in the male.

Breeding. *Tank: 24″×8″×8″. pH: 6·8-7·2. Hardness: 120-150 p.p.m. Temperature: 80°F. Spawns: in flower-pot. Method: standard for medium cichlids. Eggs: 200-250. Hatch: in 3 days. Fry wriggling: 3 days. Free-swimming: 7th day. Food 1st week: infusoria, brine shrimp. 2nd week: microworms, fine dried food.*

Once a male has mated the pair should be kept apart from other orange chromides so that they may be easily identified again. This is because the species is very likely to mate for life and spawn frequently. Should a strange female be offered to the original male he may kill her in a few minutes.

If possible several fish should be placed together in a large tank, when one pair will soon mate up and keep all the rest away from their selected spawning-site. Once this occurs the pair should be removed to a breeding tank. They spawn in a flower-pot, following the procedure described in Chapter 12. After the parents have been removed they should not be placed with other chromides, or fighting may result. When the female is ready to breed again she will start digging pits in the sand. The pair should then be reuinted in a breeding tank once more.

The young grow rapidly to ¾″ in length. At this stage the weaker ones may be killed off by their stronger brethren, so the aquarist is advised to keep a close watch and remove any which are being attacked. Even so, the young are more difficult to rear than most cichlids.

Etroplus suratensis – Silver chromide

Sri Lanka ♂ *3″* ♀ *2¾″* *Community, with medium-sized fishes*
DIET: All foods *SWIMS: Lower half of tank*

This fish resembles the foregoing in shape, but is of a quite different colour.

The body is greyish-black covered with rows of tiny silver dots, giving the first impression that the fish is in an advanced stage of *Ichthyophthirius*. About three-quarters of the way along the flanks in the upper half is a striking spot which is oval in shape and encircled by gold. The dorsal fin is dull gold edged with black. The ventrals are long and prominent; the forward rays are light yellow. The anal fin has a greenish tint.

Breeding. *The procedure follows that of E. maculatus.*

Geophagus cupido – Cupid cichlid

N.E. South America ♂ 3½″ ♀ 3½″ Community
DIET: All foods SWIMS: Lower half of tank

A rather attractive little cichlid which, generally speaking, is not aggressive.

The upper half of the body is a pale mauvish-olive, the lower portion being a greenish-gold. The most striking markings are a short, thin line from the top of the head to the hind portion of the eye and a broader, more intense, line which runs from the top of the eye down to the lower jaw.

Breeding. *No obvious external sexual characteristics; is said to be a mouth-brooder (see G. jurupari overleaf).*

Geophagus jurupari

Amazon ♂ 4½" ♀ 4½" *Community, with medium-sized fishes*
DIET: All foods SWIMS: Lower half of tank

An uncommon but very likeable cichlid. The head is long and pointed; the lips are prominent. The eye is large, and situated well up on the head. The dorsal is high and long; the body narrow and elongated. The species seems to be peaceful. It is not shy, and is amusing to watch. Using its pointed snout as a shovel, it scoops up mouthfuls of sand, sifting particles of food, and shooting out the refuse in showers from the gill-plates, making it a good scavenger.

The overall colour is greyish-olive; faint bars cross the flanks vertically. A black spot appears in the upper portion of the base of the tail. The flanks are adorned with numerous horizontal rows of tiny greenish-gold dots. On the face the rows of dots form gold stripes, which run downward at an angle of 45 degrees. Dots of similar colour appear in the rear portion of the dorsal, ventral, and tail fins. The first rays of the anal are pale yellow.

Males develop longer points on the dorsal and anal fins.

Breeding. *Spawning may occur in a community tank, for the species is a mouth-brooder. The pair circle round each other just above the sand, the female depositing eggs which are immediately fertilized by the male. She now picks up the eggs and incubates them in her mouth, occasionally spitting out a few and grabbing them again instantly. After spawning it is best to remove the female to a separate breeding tank. Incubation takes about 10 days, during which time the mother refuses all food. Once the young are free-swimming they will take brine shrimp. For further details see Pseudocrenilabrus multicolor, p.408.*

Hemichromis bimaculatus – Jewel cichlid

Central Africa   ♂ 4"   ♀ 3¾"   Non-community
DIET: All foods   SWIMS: Lower half of tank

A very beautiful but vicious cichlid. It will attack its own species as well as other fishes larger or smaller than itself.

When young or not excited it is a dull olive, with three black dots showing up on the sides. However, when it wears courting colours it is beautiful. Now the head and belly turn a fiery red; the scales on the flanks and gill-plates sparkle like blue-green jewels—hence the popular name. All the fins are edged with brilliant red, and shine profusely with blue-green spots. The black dot in the centre of the body disappears entirely.

The male is even more jewelled than the female, particularly in the regions of the gill-plates, the flanks, and the tail fin. His is not necessarily the brightest red; indeed, at times the female is so brilliant that the uninitiated might consider her to be the male.

Breeding. *Tank: 30"×15"×15". pH: 7·0-7·2. Hardness: 120-150 p.p.m. Temperature: 80-82°F. Spawns: in flower-pot. Method: standard for medium cichlids. Eggs: 250-300. Hatch: in 3 days. Fry wriggling: 3 days. Free-swimming: 7th day. Food 1st week: brine shrimp, microworms. 2nd week: microworms, fine dried food.*

The species is not difficult to breed, providing that a pair get on well together. But the aquarist is advised to watch for some little time, and to intervene if one fish is being bullied too fiercely. After spawning the male should be removed. Once the fry are free-swimming the female may also be taken away. The young grow rapidly, and soon develop aggressive tendencies. They will kill each other unless given plenty of plants and rocks round which they may dodge and take refuge. Spawns may be large, but it is not every aquarist or pet shop that will buy the surplus of such vicious fish.

391

Melanochromis auratus – Malawi golden cichlid

Lake Malawi   ♂, ♀, *to 4″*   *Community, with other cichlids*
DIET: *All foods*   SWIMS: *All levels*

Many of the comments referring to the care and breeding of *Pseudotropheus zebra* also apply to this species. When young, this fish is bright yellow, and gains black stripes as it gets a little older. At maturity the male changes colour noticeably and becomes black with pale or golden stripes running along its body, whilst the females retain the black stripes on yellow or white of the juveniles.

Another aggressive, territorial cichlid, that needs to be kept with other rock-dwelling rift lake cichlids or 'mbuna' as they are known.

Breeding.   *See Pseudotropheus zebra, p.412.*

392

Oreochromis (Sarotherodon) mossambicus – Tilapia

E. Africa   ♂ 7"   ♀ 7"   Community, with large fishes
DIET: All foods   SWIMS: Upper half of tank

Most tilapia are mouth-breeders, but grow too large for the average aquarist. We show one species, which is perhaps the smallest. For a large fish, it is surprisingly fond of dried food. With mouth open and head tilted upward, it ploughs through the floating particles and gathers in mouthfuls.

The fish is greenish-grey, with a dull gold edge to the outer border of the tail fin. At times this edge has a reddish tint, and a thin red margin appears on the dorsal fin. Three faint vertical bars cross the rear portion of the flanks. Occasionally, when stimulated, a few white patches occur in the forward upper portions of the body, and the lower part of the male's gill-plate.

The dorsal and anal fins of the male are slightly longer and more pointed than those of the female, and the dull gold in his tail is a little more pronounced.

Breeding. *Tank: 30"×15"×15". pH: 7·0-7.2. Hardness: 150-180 p.p.m. Temperature: 78°F. Spawns: in depression in sand. Method: mouthbreeder. Eggs: 100-150. Hatch: in 14 days. Food 1st week: brine shrimp, microworms. 2nd week: sifted Daphnia, fine dried food.*

The tank should be planted to make the fish feel at home. The pair fan a depression in the sand and then, head to tail, circle just above it. Eggs are laid and fertilized, then after spawning the female should be removed. The male picks up the eggs and incubates them in his mouth for about 14 days before the young appear.

393

Angel fish   *Black lace angel*

Pterophyllum scalare – Angel fish

Amazon   ♂ 5"   ♀ 5"   Community
DIET: *All foods*   SWIMS: *Mid-water*

The elongated dorsal and anal fins of this graceful fish have earned it the popular name 'angel fish.' Because of its exotic appearance, nearly every aquarist likes to have at least one in his collection. This is one of the cichlids which does not tear out plants or dig pits in the sand. Angels are generally peaceful, but grow rapidly, and soon become out of proportion to other small species. However, if their owner has a larger tank they may be transferred, and will easily grow to maturity. They will eat all types of food, including the dried product.

Angels are sometimes temperamental, and get scared after being moved, and then refuse to eat. But they must not be coddled or kept in a quiet place, as this merely increases their nervousness when they have to be approached. It is far better to place them in a community tank with other less excitable fishes, preferably where people are continually passing. Here they soon settle down, behave normally, and feed well. Once this happens they become very tame, and will eat out of their owner's fingers. Some even allow him to pick them out of the water and replace them without fright. Such specimens will breed readily. The nervous ones are often too scared to mate.

The normal angel is so well-known that a full colour description is unnecessary. It suffices to say that the body is silvery with vertical black bars which adorn the fins and flanks. There is a glowing red in the upper half of the eye. The ventrals are pale blue; they are very long, and curve back in graceful, unbroken points. On good specimens the upper and lower rays of the tail extend in filaments three times the length of this fin.

Black angel

Just after the Second World War M. Carels, the renowned fish-breeder of Ghent, Belgium, produced a strain of angel fish which were normal-coloured in the front part of the body, but jet-black from the third bar to the tip of the tail. Some of these fish were exported to America, and very probably from this stock was developed the black lace angel. In this the body and markings are darker, making the lighter parts appear like network seen through black lace. Further line breeding produced the pure black angel, in which the whole body and fins are jet-black.

Veil-tailed angel

Sexing has always been considered difficult. Various writers have drawn attention to minute differences in the first short rays of the dorsal fin. Others have stated that the distance between ventral and anal fins indicates sex. Still others refer to the angle of this portion of the body. But the authors, after scrutinizing thousands of angels, failed to detect the vague difference referred to; yet a pronounced feature which we have found true has always been overlooked, or never mentioned. This is a characteristic which is clearly visible on all fishes bearing long, feeler-like ventral fins. The body of the female bulges noticeably behind and below the pectorals, or—what amounts to the same thing—above and behind the ventrals, as shown in Fig. 21. In this region the females are convex, while males are concave.

To those following this system for the first time the angel should be viewed from head on, preferably while it is feeding at the water surface, as then it has its head inclined upward. Now the bulge shown in Fig. 21 should be clearly visible on a female. In this area a male appears as though he had been pinched between thumb and forefinger.

Once having observed the difference it is no longer necessary to see the fish head on. A side view is quite satisfactory, since the bulge on a female catches the light and shines slightly. On the other hand, the dent in the male casts a weak shadow. True, after a large feed both sexes are thicker, but the method still applies, as at all times females will bulge considerably more than males. By this system the authors are able to sex angels when the overall length from tip of nose to end of tail is only 2″. So far the method has proved to be infallible. Time and again a couple of youngsters of 1½" body diameter have been placed in a breeding tank, and when 8 months old have spawned, proving them to be a true pair.

Just prior to breeding the bulge on the female is very pronounced. The two fish face each other, jerk their fins, and kiss. At this time her ovipositor protrudes about ⅛"; it is nearly as wide as it is long, and almost square at the extremity. The corresponding organ of the male is shorter, thinner, and much more pointed.

Two other species of angel fish exist, though they are rarely seen in aquaria. These are *P. eimekei* and *P. altum*.

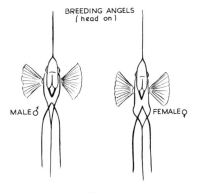

BREEDING ANGELS
(head on)

MALE ♂   FEMALE ♀

Fig. 21

Breeding.   *Tank: 24"×12"×24" high.   pH: 7·0-7·4.   Hardness: 150-180 p.p.m. Temperature: 78°F.   Spawns: on tall leaf or "Vitrolite" bar.   Method: remove eggs and hatch in separate tank.   Eggs: 300-400.   Hatch: in 3 days.   Fry wriggling: 4 days.   Free-swimming: 8th day.   Food 1st week: infusoria, brine shrimp. 2nd week: brine shrimp.*

A proved pair should be housed in a tank of the dimensions given above. This is well-planted, and becomes their permanent home. They should be given slate or Perspex pieces on which to spawn. The procedure follows exactly that described under *Cichlasoma festivum*, except that angels cleanse the area thoroughly with their mouths until every speck of sediment and algae has been removed. If the slate or Perspex is taken out, and the eggs hatched in a separate tank with methylene blue, a good pair of angels will spawn every 8 days for 18 months or more without a break. Should it be left where it is the parents take turns in fanning the eggs. Provided the eggs do not fungus, and that the parents do not tire of their duties and eat the spawn, it is a wonderful sight to see the adults with their fry, and to watch how they look after them and gather them into a tight ball as dusk approaches. When they raise their young the parents are unlikely to spawn again until the babies are 8 to 10 weeks old.

Symphysodon aequifasciata – Pompadour or discus fish

Amazon ♂ 7" ♀ 7" *Community, with medium-sized fishes*
DIET: Mainly protein SWIMS: Mid-water

Most superb of all fresh-water tropicals is an adult pair of discus. They are worthy of a large tank, and special care and attention. Though not aggressive, they should not be kept with small fishes, neither should they be placed among large, savage species which may damage them. Recently there have been more importations of young pompadours, but even so the price is high. The majority of these youngsters caught in the wild are infected with minute organisms. These multiply, especially where chills and frequent changes of water occur, and bring about the death of the fish.

When small discus are quite drab, having brownish flanks crossed vertically by several dark bars. Up to 2" in length, the body is slightly elongated. After this stage it becomes deeper, the fish being greater in measurement from top to bottom than from nose to tail. On reaching 6 to 7 months old flecks of blue appear about the head and gill-plates. These markings extend with age until they spread over most of the back, as well as in the region of the anal fin. The fins become darkish blue on the inside, splashed with streaks of pale blue and orange. The outer portions turn pale blue and orange. The borders are bright red, though the first short rays of the dorsal and anal are tipped with white. The ventral fins are long; they are red with orange tips. The body turns mahogany colour. Sometimes there is a golden hue; at other times a reddish one is noticeable.

Sexing is regarded as extremely difficult.

Breeding. *Tank: 36"×15"×15". pH: 6·4-7·0. Hardness: 50-80 p.p.m. Temperature: 80°F. Spawns: on long leaf or piece of slate. Method: parents fan eggs. Eggs: 150-250. Hatch: in 3 days. Fry wriggling: 4 days. Free-swimming: 7th day. Food 1st and 2nd weeks: mucus secretion exuded by parents.*

Though this fish has not been bred by the authors, below is given an authentic breeding account.

The tank is filled with slightly acid water, and planted as a permanent home for the parents. The vegetation includes *Sagittaria*. After some love play the adults select and clean a tall, broad leaf. On this the female deposits her eggs in rows, and as they are laid the male fertilizes them. The spawn is fanned by the parents. The young, stuck by a thread to the leaf, wriggle violently. The parents now move the babies to a new site, washing them in their mouths during the transfer.

During this period the adults secrete a whitish mucus over their bodies, which provides the fry with their first food. Indeed, they will take nothing else, and may be seen pecking furiously from the sides and upper portion of the backs of their parents. Although other minute foods have been tried, the babies will not thrive on any alternative diet. Thus the best hope of raising the fry is to leave them with their parents. Occasionally the spawn is eaten, but this risk is inevitable. Once the youngsters are 3 to 4 weeks old they may be removed and fed on brine shrimp, sifted *Daphnia*, and finely scraped raw heart. They grow rapidly, and, unlike the imported specimens, appear healthy and hardy.

DWARF CICHLIDS

Apistogramma agassizi

Guyana   ♂ 3"   ♀ 2¾"   *Community*
DIET: All foods   SWIMS: Lower half of tank

A very beautiful, peaceful little fish, with an outstandingly long dorsal fin and an elongated tail.

The overall body colour is a pale olive-gold with scales of sparkling blue. The dorsal fin is golden with an edge of deep red. The oval tail is pale yellow with a a bright yellow streak near the outer edge of the upper half. The lower portion is decorated with a purplish-blue streak, beneath which is a golden area.

The male is much more colourful than the female, and his fins are larger and longer.

Breeding. *Tank: 24"×8"×8". pH: 7·0-7·2. Hardness: 120-150 p.p.m. Temperature: 80°F. Spawns: in flower-pot. Method: standard for dwarf cichlids. Eggs: 80-150. Hatch: in 3 days. Fry wriggling: 3 days. Free-swimming: 7th day. Food 1st week: brine shrimp, microworms. 2nd week: microworms, fine dried food.*

The tank should be well planted, and provided with a flower-pot or slate structure, as described in Chapter 12.

400

Apistogramma ornatipinnis – Ornate dwarf cichlid

Guyana ♂ 3" ♀ 2¾" Community
DIET: *All foods* SWIMS: *Lower half of tank*

This is one of the prettist dwarf cichlids, and is very peaceful.

The general body colour is reddish-brown, but large patches of blue adorn the sides. A black line starting about the head curves downward through the eye to the lower edge of the gill-plate. Behind this the throat is a vivid blue. The dorsal fin is blue, the first rays being black. The outer edge is bright red. The ventral fins are brilliant orange; the anal is bluish, with streaks of red and blue. The tail is spotted in its centre, the upper and lower edges being bright orange-red. The outer edge of the male's tail is concave, giving him the appearance of having two short points in the upper and lower lobes.

The female is less gaudy. Her body bears several broad, vertical bars of blue-black. A black line runs from the eye to a spot in the caudal peduncle. The colouring of her fins is similar to the male's, but more subdued.

Breeding. *Tank: 24"×8"×8". pH: 7·0-7·2. Hardness: 120-150 p.p.m. Temperature: 78°F. Spawns: in flower-pot or slate structure. Method: standard for dwarf cichlids. Eggs: 250-300. Hatch: in 3 days. Fry wriggling: 3 days. Free-swimming: 7th day. Food 1st week: infusoria, brine shrimp. 2nd week: brine shrimp, microworms.*

Like most dwarf cichlids, the species is short-lived, and spawning should be attempted before the parents get too old.

Apistogramma pertense

Guyana   ♂ 2"   ♀ 16"   Community
DIET: All foods   SWIMS: Lower half of tank

A quiet, inoffensive little fish which may be kept in community tanks with other small species.

The general body colour is greenish-grey, developing a yellowish tinge in maturity. A black line runs from the eye to the base of the tail and ends in a spot of the same colour. Faint vertical bars cross the flanks. the head and gill-plates are flecked with scales of shining blue. The fins are yellowish, but the first rays of the dorsal are black.

The dorsal and anal fins of the male are longer and more pointed than those of the female.

Breeding.   *Tank: 24"×8"×8".   pH: 7·0-7·2.   Hardness: 100-120 p.p.m.   Temperature: 78°F.   Spawns: in flower-pot.   Method: standard for dwarf cichlids.   Eggs: 100-120.   Hatch: in 3 days.   Fry wriggling: 3 days.   Free-swimming: 7th day.   Food 1st week: infusoria. 2nd week: brine shrimp, microworms.*

The species is not quite so prolific as most.

♂ ♀

Haplochromis wingati – Nigerian mouthbrooder

Cental Africa ♂ 4" ♀ 3¾" Community,. with larger fishes
DIET: All foods SWIMS: Lower half of tank

Another mouth-breeder, though rather more aggressive than *Psudocrenilabrus multicolor*. The male has a beautiful bluish-green sheen, the female being less coloured and more golden.

Like *P. multicolor*, a pair fan a depression in the sand and then in a head-to-tail position circle round each other, the female laying eggs and the male fertilizing them. The female stops every now and again to pick up the eggs, which she retains in her mouth.

For incubating, hatching, and feeding, see *P. multicolor*.

Nanachromis nudiceps

Central Africa   ♂ *3¼"*   ♀ *3"*   *Community*
DIET: All foods   *SWIMS: Lower half of tank*

Introduced into Britain by the authors in 1952, this rather long-bodied dwarf cichlid caused quite a sensation. The somewhat protruding jaw gives it an aggressive appearance, but it is quite peaceful, though occasionally a male will ill-treat a female if she does not respond to his advances.

The long, slender body is bluish, but in certain lights it shows duck-egg green, while at other times it takes on a purplish hue. The lengthy dorsal fin is bluish and edged with red. The anal is mauve. In males the tail is adorned in the upper half with purplish-brown streaks. The absence of colour in this fin of the female is the first identification of sex in young fish.

Breeding. *Tank: 24"×8"×8".   pH: 7·0-7.2.   Hardness: 100-120 p.p.m.   Temperature: 80°F.   Spawns: in flower-pot or slate structure.   Method: standard for dwarf cichlids.   Eggs: 80-120.   Hatch: in 3 days.   Fry wriggling: 3 days.   Free-swimming: 7th day.   Food 1st week: brine shrimp. 2nd week: brine shrimp, microworms.*

The species breeds readily, and the young are not difficult to raise.

Nannacara anomala

Northern S. America ♂ 2¼" ♀ 2" *Community*
DIET: *All foods* SWIMS: *Lower half of tank*

Though not one of the most colourful dwarf cichlids, the species is very prolific, and therefore one of the commonest.

The body is an olive green splashed with blue highlights here and there among the scales. The dorsal fin is edged with red.

The female is less colourful; her dorsal, anal, and ventral fins are not so long and pointed as those of the male.

Breeding. *Tank: 24"×8"×8". pH: 7·0-7.2. Hardness: 150-180 p.p.m. Temperature: 76°F. Spawns: in flower-pot. Method: standard for dwarf cichlids. Eggs: 75-120. Hatch: in 3 days. Fry wriggling:: 3 days. Free-swimming: 7th day. Food 1st week: brine shrimp, microworms. 2nd week: microworms, fine dried food.*

The species often breeds in a community tank of medium-sized fishes. If no flower-pot is present the pair will spawn in a depression in the sand, and guard their eggs. The authors have frequently raised families in this manner. Even so, it remains remarkable that the parents are able to guard both the eggs and hatched fry throughout the hours of darkness as well as during the day. Perhaps the most surprising thing of all was what in a large community tank, measuring 36"×15"×15", well stocked with fishes, no special food could be given solely to the babies, since all the other fishes present would have intercepted it. Nevertheless, the ever-attentive parents must have ensured that their offspring were nourished for the fry grew to maturity in this community tank.

Papiliochromis (Microgeophagus) ramirezi

Venezuela   ♂ 2½"   ♀ 2½"   *Community*   DIET: *All foods*   SWIMS: *Lower half of tank*

This truly gorgeous little fish is peaceful, and does not tear out plants. The species seems to do better in slightly acid soft water. It may be easily identified, as the top edge of the dorsal fin is concave.

The colour is not easy to describe, since it varies from blue to mauve; at times the belly is purplish-pink. The eye is red. A black stripe runs from the nape of the neck through the eye down to the lower edge of the gill-plate. The sides bear dark vertical bands which are most pronounced towards the head, and become fainter near the tail. The flanks are adorned with sacales of shining blue. The dorsal, anal, and caudal fins are orange with blue dots. The first rays of the dorsal are jet-black, the tips being separated like the teeth of a comb. The second ray is elongated. The first rays of the ventrals are black, the third and fourth rays being bright blue.

Sexing is difficult until the fish are fully mature. Only then will it be noticed that the male is the more brightly coloured; the black spike in his dorsal is longer, and his anal is more pointed. The female becomes rounder and deeper when full of roe.

Breeding. *Tank: 24"×8"×8". pH: 6·5-6·8. Hardness: 80-100 p.p.m. Temperature: 80°F. Spawns: in flower-pot. Method: standard for dwarf cichlids. Eggs: 80-100. Hatch: in 3 days. Fry wriggling: 3 days. Free-swimming: 7th day. Food 1st week: infusoria. 2nd week: brine shrimp, microworms.*

Sometimes the species hollows out a depression in the sand where it spawns. Should this occur, remove the female. The male fans and guards the eggs; he should be transferred once the young are free-swimming.

♀ ♂

Pelvicachromis guntheri

West Africa ♂ 6" ♀ 6" Community, with larger fishes
DIET: All foods SWIMS: Lower half of tank

In its smaller sizes it is moderately peaceful, but becomes aggressive with age.

At breeding-time the male is beautiful. The upper flanks are golden-olive, barred vertically and horizontally by bright bands of olive-green. The lower flanks and belly are suffused pink. The male's dorsal is edged with burnished gold, and black blocks adorn the lower areas of this fin for three-quarters of its length; in between, the fin is green-gold at first, turning to silver-pink in the centre, shading off to blue, and finally green-gold again at its tip. The ventrals and anal are silver-blue, and a blue-green stripe appears along the upper lip. The female is similarly coloured, but less brightly, and she lacks the colour and black markings in the dorsal fin. The male who incubates the eggs in his mouth, the babies being nearly ¼" long when they first appear. At the first sign of danger they scramble hurriedly into the mouth of either parent for protection.

Breeding. *Tank: 24"×12"×12". pH: 7·0-7.2. Hardness: 120-150 p.p.m. Temperature: 78°F. Spawns: in depression in sand. Method: male incubates eggs. Eggs: 30-50. Hatch: in 2 to 3 weeks. Free-swimming immediately on leaving the male's mouth. Food 1st week: microworms, grindal worms. 2nd week: grindal worms, dried food.*

Pseudocrenilabrus (Hemihaplochromis) multicolor
– Egyptian mouthbrooder

Egypt ♂ 3″ ♀ 3″ *Community*
DIET: All foods SWIMS: Lower half of tank

For those aquarists with small tanks who wish to witness the incubation of eggs in a fish's mouth, and to watch how the babies seek refuge in their mother's jaws, this is the fish to keep. In its larger sizes the species occasionally becomes aggressive, but it will breed when only 1½″ long. At this size it is normally safe with other small fishes.

The males are considerably the more colourful. Their scales shine with bluish-green, body and fins being covered with red dots. A bright orange-red patch adorns the tip of the anal fin. Females are less colourful; they have a yellowish tinge, and lack the red patch in the anal.

Breeding. *Tank: 24″×8″×8″. pH: 7·0-7·4. Hardness: 150-180 p.p.m. Temperature: 78°F. Spawns: in depression fanned in sand. Method: female incubates eggs in mouth. Eggs: 25-75. Hatch: in 14-16 days. Free-swimming: immediately on leaving the mother's mouth. Food 1st week: brine shrimp and microworms. 2nd week: sifted Daphnia and dried food.*

A pair will often spawn in a community tank. After fanning a slight depression in the sand, they circle each other head to tail. Eggs are laid and fertilized. The female then picks up the spawn in her mouth. She now refuses all food, and her lower jaw begins to get deeper. After a week her appearance is noticeable. Her jaw protrudes, and her normal rounded chin becomes angular and square; her belly through lack of food shrinks, and she looks all head. Her jaw also expands sideways, and viewed from the front the eggs may be seen in the cleft of her jaw plates. It is now best to remove her in a jar to a small breeding tank. Catching and transferring her, if done calmly, rarely upsets her. She should be watched daily from now on, and soon tiny eyes will be seen in the eggs in her jaws. About a week later she may be noticed swimming with 20 or 30 babies near her. If disturbed the young will jostle each other in their frantic attempts to reach the safety of the interior of her mouth.

Commercial breeders keep several females in one tank with a few males. When the females are seen to be carrying eggs each is caught and placed in a jam-jar, several of which are floated in a bare aquarium. As each produces her babies the mother is caught in a small net and the fry tipped into the tank. To ensure that the mother has not got a few babies still in her mouth she is returned to th jar, which should be floated in the original tank for an hour. If no more fry appear she may then be tipped out.

Pelvicachromis pulcher – Dwarf rainbow cichlid or krib

Central Africa   ♂ *3¾"*   ♀ *3"*   *Community*
DIET: All foods   *SWIMS: Lower half of tank*

The authors received the first specimens of this beautiful fish in 1953. Nearly every aquarist who saw them gave advance bookings for young when bred. The species has proved to be one of the most popular dwarf cichlids ever. It is peaceful, does not tear out plants, eats any food, and breeds easily. Moreover, it is one of those species in which both sexes are equally brilliant; if anything, the female at spawning-time is the prettier.

The general body colour is a golden-green, though the back is an olive-brown. The lower portion of the gill-plates and throat is a brilliant blue. A red patch appears in the belly of the male. His ventrals and anal fins are edged with peacock blue; the dorsal has a blue-green border. In adult males the top half of the tail is tinted with orange, and clear black spots numbering from one to seven appear in this region. The female is similarly coloured, but the reddish area in the abdomen spreads nearly to her back. Her dorsal has a golden edge, and 1, 2, or 3 black spots appear in the rear portion of this fin. The ventrals are bluish-red, but her tail remains almost clear.

Sexing adults is obvious. However, in young fish 1″ long, male and female can be distinguished. This is because the females show the black spot in the rear part of the dorsal. At this stage the corresponding fin of males is clear. In a few weeks he will develop these dorsal markings, but, as if to avoid confusion, he simultaneously shows the arcing orange area in the upper half of the tail. Though at first this is faint, it is unmistakably there. Females never bear this orange arc in their tails.

Breeding. *Tank: 24″×8″×8″. pH: 7·0-7·2. Hardness: 120-150 p.p.m. Temperature: 80°F. Spawns: in flower-pot or slate structure. Method: standard for dwarf cichlids. Eggs: 50-250. Hatch: in 3 days. Fry wriggling: 3 days. Free-swimming: 7th day. Food 1st week: brine shrimp. 2nd week: microworms, sifted Cyclops, a little fine dried food.*

This is a species where our slate structure is better than a flower-pot. Young fish will spawn every month and produce about 50-75 eggs. Older specimens breed less frequently, but families may be larger. The authors' best single spawn was 224 raised to maturity.

Pelvicachromis species – Medium rainbow cichlid

Nigeria   ♂6", ♀ to 5½"   Community, only with large fishes
DIET: All foods   SWIMS: Lower half of tank

Numerous other species of *Pelvicachromis* (formerly *Pelmatochromis*) are now available, although their taxomony is not fully agreed upon as yet.

411

Pseudotropheus zebra – *Zebra cichlid*

Lake Malawi   ♂, ♀ to 4"   Community, with other cichlids
DIET: All foods   SWIMS: All levels

This is one of the most familiar of the several hundred species of cichlids which originate from the East African rift valley lakes. It occurs in a wide variety of colour forms, which can make identification and sexing difficult. The zebra cichlid, like so many other rift valley cichlids, can be aggressive, and is best kept with other related cichlids in a large aquarium containing plenty of rocky refuges.

Breeding.   *The female mouth-broods the eggs and fry for up to four weeks. There are usually 30-40 fry, which can be fed on normal fry foods. See also Pseudocrenilabrus multicolor.*

Chapter Twenty-one

Some Other Tropical Fishes

FAMILIES ATHERINIDAE AND MELANOTAENIDAE

These two families are becomingly increasingly popular with aquarists. Many of their species are marine. A few, however, do come from fresh water, and several of these are described in this chapter. The rainbow fishes or silversides, as they are called, are attractive, peaceful, and swift swimmers, having the ability to leap from the water when frightened. They have two dorsal fins and long, narrow, laterally compressed bodies. The eyes are large; the mouth is small. All prefer the addition of some salt to the water or at least hard, alkaline water.

♂

♀

Bedotia geayi – Madagascar rainbow

Madagascar   ♂ 2¼"   ♀ 2"   Community
DIET: All foods   SWIMS: Mid-water

The aquarist does not get many fishes from Madagascar with which to adorn his tank, but here is one species that he will certainly be proud to own. It is quietly colourful, peaceful, lively, and of a pleasing elongated shape.

The species has a double dorsal; the anterior one set midway along the body is rarely raised, the posterior one is kept well displayed, and gives the fish a torpedo-like appearance. As will be seen from our colour plate, the male has longer, more pointed, colourful fins. In adult specimens the caudal fin has a brilliant red semicircle round the outer edges.

Breeding. *Tank: 24"×8"×8".   pH: 6·8-7·0.   Hardness: 50-80 p.p.m.   Temperature: 78-80°F.   Spawns: over a period.   Method: eggs suspended on sticky threads catch in plant thickets.   Eggs: 50-100.   Hatch: in 6 days.   Fry hang on: 1 day.   Free-swimming: 8th day.   Food 1st week: infusoria. 2nd week: infusoria, brine shrimp.*

Keep adults well fed; they will ignore the eggs and spawn for several days. Eyes of embryos visible on fourth day. Remove adults before first fry hatch; other eggs will be in varying stages of development. Feed infusoria for a fortnight as late-hatching fry require it. Young grow quickly, reaching ½" in 3 weeks.

♀

♂

Melanotaenia fluviatilis – Australian rainbow fish

Australia ♂ 5" ♀ 4½" Community
DIET: All foods SWIMS: Upper half of tank

This is a considerably larger fish than some of the other two *Melanotaenia*. It is deeper-bodied and more laterally compressed. The fins, too, are much longer in this species, particularly those of the male, his posterior dorsal and anal fin tips often reaching well beyond the caudal peduncle.

The fish is a silver-blue or golden-green, according to the light striking the flanks. The fins are yellow flecked with reddish-brown spots, and have dark edges. Although the fish grows to 5" in a four-foot-long aquarium, it is perfectly peaceful and does not molest fishes measuring ½" upward. There is a large scale on the gill-plate of both sexes, and this carries a delightful reddish-gold spot. Males are generally larger than females, and the fins much longer and more pointed.

Breeding. *Tank: 24"×8"×8", or larger. pH: 6·6-6·8. Hardness: 50-80 p.p.m. Temperature: 78°F. Spawns: in plant thickets. Method: scatters semi-adhesive eggs. Eggs: 200-300. Hatch: in 48 hours. Fry hang on: 2 days. Free-swimming: 5th day. Food 1st week: infusoria. 2nd week: infusoria, brine shrimp.*

This species is not difficult to spawn. It requires a tank 24"×8"×8" or larger, filled with rain-water and thickly planted. No salt need be added. Unlike the two previous species, they do not seem to spawn over a period of days. After spawning the parents must be removed.

♂   ♀

Melanotaenia maccullochi – Australian rainbow fish

Australia   ♂ 3″   ♀ 3″   Community
DIET: All foods   SWIMS: Upper half of tank

Very active, peaceful fish which, when in suitable surroundings, show considerable colour. They will take any food, and are easy to breed. Slightly alkaline water with a pH of 7·0-7·4 and of medium hardness is preferred. When unduly scared these fish are inclined to jump, so their tank should be kept tightly covered.

The body has a greenish-golden sheen, and is crossed horizontally by numerous thin brown stripes. The fins are reddish—more so on the outer edges—and are sprinkled with fine dots. There is a bright red spot on the gill-plates.

The male is a little more colourful than his mate; his fins are of a more pronounced orange-red. The female is deeper-bodied at spawning-time, and the light catching her abdomen makes her look more silvery in this region.

Breeding. Tank: 24″×8″×8″. pH: 7·0-7·2. Hardness: 180 p.p.m. Temperature: 78°F. Spawns: over a period. Method: scatters semi-adhesive eggs. Eggs 100-150. Hatch: 6-7 days. Fry hang on: 2 days. Free-swimming: 9th day. Food 1st week: infusoria, brine shrimp. 2nd week: microworms, sifted Daphnia.

The breeding tank should be thickly planted, particularly with fine-leaved foliage. An addition of one teaspoonful of salt to each gallon of water may induce spawning. The male chases the female, and the pair, trembling side by side, scatter rather large, pale yellow eggs among the plant fronds. In their excited dashes some of the spawn gets disturbed and falls to the bottom. Provided the parents are well fed, they ignore the eggs, so the pair may be left together for 2 or 3 days. Over this period spawning often continues. They should be removed before the eggs hatch, as they will eat the young fry.

Melanotaenia nigrans – Dark-striped Australian rainbow fish

Australia ♂ 3½" ♀ 3¾" Community
DIET: All foods SWIMS: Upper half of tank

In outline it is long and slim. The stripes running horizontally along the sides are blacker, and the edges of the dorsal and anal fins are darker. Sexing is not difficult, as the male has longer fins, is brighter-coloured—with beautiful sheens of blue, yellow, and green—and considerably slimmer than his mate.

Breeding. *Tank: 24"×8"×8". pH: 7·0-7·2. Hardness: 180 p.p.m. Temperature: 78°F. Spawns: over a period. Method: scatters semi-adhesive eggs. Eggs: 100-150. Hatch: 6-7 days. Fry hang on: 2 days. Free-swimming: 9th day. Food 1st week: infusoria, brine shrimp. 2nd week: microworms, sifted Daphnia.*

For breeding the procedure is the same as that described under *M. macullochi.*

Telmatherina ladigesi – Celebes rainbow fish

Celebes (Sulawesi) ♂ 2¼" ♀ 2" Community
DIET: All foods SWIMS: Mid-water

A beautiful fish, but very susceptible to changes of water. This should be alkaline, with a pH of 7·2-7·4, to which has been added one teaspoonful of salt to every gallon. When the fish are purchased the buyer is strongly advised to take enough water with the specimens to house them comfortably for several days. Should this be very different in pH and hardness from that on the aquarist's premises the fish must on no account be transferred, or death is liable to occur. Before they are removed to another tank the water must be altered gradually; this is best done by changing a small cupful daily. Even so, they will not thrive under very acid conditions. Once in a situation to their liking they are not difficult to keep.

The body is a lovely translucent gold. The pectoral fins are set rather high up on the body, and from behind these to the base of the tail is a brilliant pale blue stripe. The posterior dorsal and anal fins have separate split rays, the foremost being black. The rest of these fins, pectorals, and tail are tinged with gold, though in the tail the colour is strongest on the outer edges of the upper and lower lobes.

Sexing presents no problem, as the dorsal and anal fins of the male grow extensions, the front rays forming separate filaments. The female's fins are quite normal.

Breeding. *Tank: 24"×8"×8".   pH: 7·2-7·4.   Hardness: 180-200 p.p.m.   Temperature: 78-80°F.   Spawns: over a period.   Method: eggs with sticky threads catch in plant fronds.   Eggs: 80-100.   Hatch: in 5 days.   Fry hang on: 2 days.   Free-swimming: 8th day.   Food 1st week: infusoria. 2nd week: brine shrimp.*

A pair should be placed in a breeding tank in which numerous separate stalks of *Myriophyllum* are planted close together, or left floating. Male and female tremble side by side among the feathery foliage, and large, clear eggs may be seen hanging on threads in the fronds. These plant stems with the eggs attached should be gently removed and floated in a bare breeding tank contaning water of the same composition and slightly tinted with methylene blue, or a similar anti-fungal treatment. Spawning continues over several days, and each morning the new eggs should be transferred. When the stalks are separate there is no difficulty in lifting out each one. But when they are planted in bunches to extract a single stem is difficult. It usually results in uprooting the whole clump, and at the same time losing sight of the precious eggs.

FAMILY CENTRARCHIDAE

Though not really tropicals, a few species of sunfishes are kept by some aquarists. Generally speaking, they prefer slightly lower temperatures and a good deal of light. They come from the south-eastern states of the U.S.A., and have two nostrils on each side of the snout. Two of the smaller species are described here.

Elassoma evergladei – Pygmy sunfish

South-Eastern U.S.A. ♂ *1"* ♀ *1"* *Community*
DIET: *Live foods* SWIMS: *Lower half of tank*

This sunfish generally fares rather better than *Mesogonistius chaetodon* in a community tank. It does not mind an average temperature of 76° to 78°F. and, being a little more agile, is better able to get its share of live food.

The normal colour is a dull grey. The male has larger and darker fins than his mate. In breeding garb he turns black, and his sides sparkle with greenish-gold dots.

Breeding. *Tank: 24"×8"×8". pH: 7·2. Hardness: 150-180 p.p.m. Temperature: 78°F. Spawns: in nest. Method: lays adhesive eggs. Eggs: 50-70. Hatch: in 48 hours. Fry hang on: 1 day. Free-swimming: 4th day. Food 1st week: infusoria. 2nd week: brine shrimp, microworms.*

The breeding tank should be planted normally, but contain some floating pieces of *Myriophyllum* and *Riccia*. These are gathered by the male and used to build a rough nest at the bottom of the aquarium. The pair enter their home and, quivering side by side, deposit and fertilize small, clear eggs. After this the female should be removed. The male then guards and fans the spawn. Once the young are free-swimming the male should be taken away, as he is liable to eat the fry.

Mesogonistius chaetodon – Poor man's angel

Eastern U.S.A. ♂ *2½"* ♀ *2½" Community*
DIET: *Live foods* SWIMS: *Mid-water*

Rather a quiet fish, which swims with an independent, stately air. The fins are kept well-spread in alkaline water to which has been added a teaspoonful of salt per gallon. It prefers live food, and is not easy to feed in a community tank, being beaten to the post by quicker-moving fishes. It is not aggressive, and is inclined to be thrust aside and made unhappy by other species. Furthermore, it prefers a lower temperature than most inhabitants of a community tank. The popular name is no longer true. Since angels are now so easily bred and plentiful, their price has dropped considerably, leaving *M. chaetodon* more expensive, at least in Britain.

The body is a creamy buff with thin black stripes crossing the flanks vertically. Sexing is difficult, as male and female look alike.

Breeding. *Male guards the eggs (see Elassoma evergladei).*

FAMILY CENTROPOMIDAE

It comprises species of very transparent little fishes which inhabit salt, brackish, and fresh water. The majority are found in Malaya, Borneo, and Thailand, though some species come from India and Burma. Quite a few have been imported, and do well in the home aquarium. All have double dorsals.

Chanda buruensis

Tropical Far East ♂ *2″* ♀ *2″* *Community*
DIET: All foods SWIMS: *Upper half of tank*

A hardy, transparent fish which is attractive and peaceful. The body is more elongated than in the better-known *Chanda lala*. It does well in pure fresh water, but has no objection to small additions of salt. It feeds near the surface, and enjoys live food like *Daphnia* and *Cyclops* or floating fruit-flies. Nevertheless, it learns to accept a dried product which does not sink too rapidly. The species is nearly colourless, but the translucent scales produce reflected highlights in all the colours of the spectrum. The body is most transparent.

When full of roe females are considerably thicker than males.

Breeding. *The authors have not bred this species, but it is likely to follow the method described under C. ranga overleaf.*

♂

♀

♀

Chanda ranga – *Glass fish*

India, Burma, Thailand   ♂ *1½"*   ♀ *1½"*   *Community*
DIET: Small live food   *SWIMS: Upper half of tank*

The most popular of the glass fishes is this somewhat chunky little beauty. Compared with *C. buroensis*, it is shorter, deeper-bodied, and has a wider expanse of finnage. The eyes are large. Although the fish looks delicate, it is in fact quite hardy. It prefers alkaline water to which has been added one teaspoonful of salt per gallon.

The body is more or less colourless, but has a faint tinge of gold. Adult males have a slightly orange tint, and the trailing edges of their dorsal and anal fins are bordered with a thin line of electric blue. Both sexes show thin vertical bars across the body. At times the glassy flanks reflect the light in prismatic colours, pale blue being predominant.

Breeding. *Tank: 24"×8"×8".* *pH: 8·0-8·6.* *Hardness: 280-300 p.p.m.* *Temperature: 80"F.* *Spawns: in floating plants.* *Method: scatters tiny eggs at surface of water.* *Eggs: 100-150.* *Hatch: in 12 hours.* *Fry hang on: 1 day.* *Free-swimming: 2nd-3rd day.* *Food 1st week: infusoria. 2nd week: brine shrimp.*

The breeding tank should contain plants of feathery foliage like *Myriophyllum,*and have a 1" layer of *Riccia* floating at the surface. After much driving male and female tremble side by side. Then he presses her to a horizontal position beneath the *Riccia*, where the minute eggs are deposited. After spawning the parents may be removed, and the tiny fry fed with very small infusoria. In some cases the parents will continue to spawn over a period, and if well fed do not molest eggs or fry. Youngsters may be trained to take fine dried food.

♀

♂

Chanda wolffii – Glass fish

Thailand ♂ *2"* ♀ *2" Community*
DIET: *All foods* SWIMS: *Upper half of tank*

First imported by the authors from Thailand in 1955, this fish took very happily to aquarium life. Much the same shape as *C. ranga*, it lacks colour, but has a good spread of finnage which it keeps erect at all times. The species enjoys dried food, so is not difficult to keep. Our specimens are absolutely peaceful. It is said that *C. wolffii* grows to 8″ in its native rivers, but aquarium specimens are unlikely to exceed 3″.

Occasionally an individual fish will show a white spot on the body or fins. This, however, is not *Ichthyophthirius* or any infectious disease. On closer examination these rather large, somewhat creamy spots look more like air bubbles beneath the skin.

So far sex is not apparent.

Breeding. *Breeding has not been achieved by the authors, but it would seem that the procedue would follow closely that of* C. ranga.

423

FAMILY CHANNIDAE

This family, which includes the genus Ophiocephalus, is commonly known as the snake heads, and is closely related to the anabantoids. Compared with these, the snake heads possess a simpler form of suprabranchial cavity which permits them to breathe air from above the surface of the water. They come from Africa, India, Burma, Indonesia, Thailand, and Southern China. In shape their bodies are long, cylindrical, and snake-like, with biggish heads and extremely large mouths well-equipped with sharp conical teeth. They grow to a large size, and are commonly used for food in their native lands. None of the snake heads is safe in a community tank; they even fight among themselves, and often the victors devour the vanquished.

All are too dangerous, and grow too large, for the average aquarist, so we do not consider it worth while to illustrate and describe the numerous species. Though they differ in colour and markings, all are similar in habit. For this reason we are taking a typical example, if only to warn the aquarist of what to expect.

Channa asiatica – Snake head

S.E. Asia   ♂ 12"   ♀ 12"   Non-community
DIET: Meat, fish, and other protein   SWIMS: Lower half of tank

The pair illustrated above were only 3" long when photographed. They were then being fed on medim-sized earthworms and full-grown female guppies. At the time of writing, six weeks later, they are 8" in length, and are feeding on chunks of horsemeat the size of grapes, as well as disposing of any unwanted fish up to 3" in length. Given a large tank, they may be expected to grow to 18″ or more.

They are most attractively coloured, and get more beautiful as they increase in size. The general body hue is brown to chocolate, the back and sides being crossed by short bars. The dorsal and anal fins are bluish with a white edge surrounding both. The tail is brownish; it is peppered with red dots, and has a red border. As the fish grows patches of blue appear round the jaws. Flecks of the same colour adorn the body, and the blue in the fins is intensified.

Breeding. *Tank: 30″×15″×15″. pH: 6·8-7·0. Hardness: 100-150 p.p.m. Temperature: 80°F. Spawns: above plants. Method: eggs float. Eggs: 100-150. Hatch: in 3 days. Fry float: 7-10 days. Food 1st week: Daphnia, white worms. 2nd week: fine minced meat, chopped earthworms.*

The tank should be well-planted to afford hiding-places until the pair are acquainted with each other. They come side by side in plant thickets just below the surface of the water. They waggle their bodies close together, and large amber eggs are laid and fertilized. These float to the surface, and the male guards them zealously. Now the female should be removed. Once the fry are swimming about the male should be taken out. During the first few days the young fish float near the surface, and have difficulty in swimming at lower depths. But after a week or ten days they lose this buoyancy and stay near the bottom of the tank, frequently rising to gulp air at the surface of the water. In nature during droughts the fish bury themselves in mud and worm their way deeper as their surroundings tend to dry up. So long as they can keep damp they are able to breathe in little or no water by means of their suprabranchial cavity.

SLEEPERS, FAMILY ELEOTRIDAE

This family, often called 'sleepers', may be distinguished from others in that the two ventral fins are separate and distinct; they never form a disc-like sucker. These fishes are found in most coastal areas of the tropics. They generally inhabit brackish water, but some ascend the rivers till they reach fresh water, though they frequently return to tidal areas for spawning.

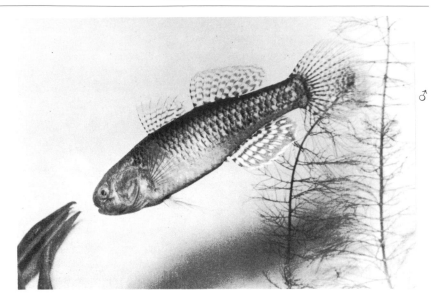

Dormitator maculatus – *Spotted sleeper*

Coastal areas round Gulf of Mexico and Northern S. America ♂ *5″* ♀ *5″*
Community, with medium-sized fishes DIET: *All foods* SWIMS: *Lower half of tank*

This is a quiet though somewhat sluggish fish.

The body is brownish-grey, rather heavily spotted. Faint bars appear horizontally on the gill-plates and vertically on the rear of the flanks. A shiny blue spot is to be seen just behind the upper edge of the gill-plate. The double dorsal fin is a brownish-grey, flecked with two rows of spots. The large, round anal fin bears shiny blue spots, and has an edging of the same colour. The eyes look opaque and appear mauvish-blue in certain lights.

The female is less colourful, and deeper in the belly than her mate.

Breeding. *Tank: 24″×8″×8″. pH: 7·2-7·4. Hardness: 160-200 p.p.m. Temperature: 80°F. Spawns: in flower-pots or slate structure. Method: lays tiny adhesive eggs. Eggs: 100-150. Hatch: in 4 days. Fry hang on: 3 days. Free-swimming: 8th day. Food 1st week: infusoria. 2nd week: brine shrimp.*

Very small adhesive eggs are attached to the inside of a flower-pot or the perpendicular walls of the slate structure (see Chapter 12). On completion of spawning the female should be removed. The male guards and fans the eggs, but it is best to take him away when the fry are free-swimming. The tiny babies require large quantities of small infusorians.

Mogurnda mogurnda

N. Australia   ♂ 4″   ♀ 4¼″   Community, with larger fishes
DIET: All foods   SWIMS: Lower half of tank

A rather sluggish species which is unsafe with smaller fishes.

The body is browish, but flecked with spots of red, yellow, blue, orange, and purple. The mosaic pattern resembles a gaudy Persian carpet. The fins are brownish, sprinkled with maroon dots.

The male's fins are larger, and he has more coloured dots on his flanks. The female is considerably thicker and more swollen at breeding-time.

Breeding. *Tank: 24″×8″×8″. pH: 7·2-7·4. Hardness: 160-180 p.p.m. Temperature: 78°F. Spawns: in flower-pot or slate structure. Method: adhesive eggs stuck to perpendicular surface. Eggs: 100-150. Hatch: in 5 days. Fry hang on: 3 days. Free-swimming: 9th day. Food 1st week: infusoria and brine shrimp. 2nd week: microworms and sifted Daphnia.*

Large brown, oval-shaped eggs are deposited and fertilized a few at a time until a patch about 1¼″ diameter appears. They are thick-shelled and opaque. At one end sticky fibres attach them to a vertical surface, where they hang overlapping one another. Once spawning is completed the female should be removed. The male guards and fans the eggs. As he does so the current he creates in the water wafts the spawn up and down like waving fronds of seaweed. As soon as the young are free-swimming the male also should be removed.

GOBIES, FAMILY GOBIIDAE

This is the largest family of gobioid fishes, and may be distinguished by the ventral fins, which are joined and form a sucking disc. With this the fishes are able to adhere to plants, rocks, and other flat surfaces. Many species are found in fresh-water far inland; others inhabit brackish water in coastal areas. The majority are smallish and colourful.

Brachygobius doriae – Wasp goby

Malaya, Java, Borneo, Thailand ♂ 1¼" ♀ 1¼" Community
DIET: Live food SWIMS: Lower half of tank

An attractive little goby which is quite safe in a community tank of small fishes. It seems hardy, but is not very lively, and spends much of its time resting or making little hops on the sand. Small live food is preferred, but some dried will be taken. At feeding-time it will swim up regardless of bigger fishes and make sure that it receives its share.

The body is a creamy-yellow crossed with black bands. These are alternately broad and narrow, the latter crossing only the upper half of the body.

Males are slightly brighter-coloured; females have deeper, rounder bellies.

Breeding.   *Eggs are laid under a shady ledge. They hatch after four days, and the fry grow slowly, feeding on normal fry foods.*

Brachygobius xanthozona – Bumble bee

Malaya, Thailand   ♂ 1¾"   ♀ 1¾"   Community
DIET: Live food   SWIMS: Lower half of tank

The commonest of the black-and-yellow-banded gobies, which has been imported for years in large numbers. It may be recognized by the very broad black bands that cross the body, the interspaces being bright gold. Though labelled 'community,' it occasionally nips the fins of smaller fishes. Furthermore, when housed with other species it is difficult to feed. It rarely eats anything but live food. As it is slow in movement, it seldom gets a good share of white worms or *Daphnia*, as these are gobbled up by the other inhabitants while this goby is making up its mind to seize a particular tit-bit.

At times the yellow areas on the flanks turn an orange-red; these are probably males in courting dress. But the authors have never succeeded in breeding the species, though it is said to spawn inside a flower-pot and take 5 or 6 days to hatch.

Breeding.   *Few details available.*

Gobius vaimosa baleati – Rhino-horn goby

Sri Lanka   ♂ 1½"   ♀ 1¼"   Community
DIET: All foods   SWIMS: All depths

An attractive little goby with a distinctively shaped dorsal fin, which resembles the horn of a rhinoceros, and led us to give it the popular name above.

The fish is peaceful, and quite lively for a goby; it swims about sedately, and never seems in any hurry. The body is pale yellow, somewhat faintly mottled in the hind-quarters. A striking black bar crosses the body and continues upward into the dorsal fin; another crosses the forehead, and after passing through the eye slants to the lower edge of the gill-plate. The front rays of the dorsal are vivid yellow.

The male is slightly brighter than the female, and his fins are longer and more pointed.

Breeding.   *Few details available.*

Stigmatagobius species

Sri Lanka   ♂ 4"   ♀ 4"   Community, with medium-sized fishes
DIET: All foods   SWIMS: Lower half of tank

This fish seems peaceful, even though it has a large mouth. It spends most of its time on the sand, but periodically does swim quite a distance before taking a short rest. It appears to enjoy any food, and is an excellent scavenger. When seen head on its drooping mouth gives it a lugubrious expression. Suddenly the lower lip is dropped, and a mouthful of sand is scooped up, exactly like the grab of an excavator. The rather transparent mouth makes visible the sand which is being sifted; this is spat out when the particles of food have been extracted. The ventral fins form a perfect sucking disc for anchoring the fish to objects; this is clearly depicted in our illustration. The eyes are high up on the head, as though supported on minute stalks. This suggests that the species may at times leave the water, climb on to a rock, and peer round, but so far this action has not been observed in our specimens.

The colour is sandy grey. A prominent black line runs through the eye to the lower jaw. Brownish-grey spots appear in a broken line along the sides. The fins are large and clear, the caudal being longish and oval in outline.

Females appear to be thicker than males.

Breeding.   *No details available, but see S. sadanundio overleaf.*

♀   ♂

Stigmatagobius sadanundio

Thailand, Java ♂ 3½″ ♀ 3″ *Community*
DIET: All foods *SWIMS: All depths*

A new, prettily marked, active goby, first imported into Britain by the authors in 1955. Although it grows to 4″, it is quite peaceful with smaller fishes, being more inclined to dart at its own kind than at strangers. *S. sadanundio* does not stay at the bottom of the aquarium like most gobies, but swims about at all depths, frequently taking short spells of rest. Its sucker-disc ventrals enable it to cling with ease to plants, rocks, or the glass sides of the aquarium.

The general colour is grey, with a few dark spots sprinkled over the body and on the fins. Shining pearly spots light up the fins so that at times they gleam like jewels.

The male is easily distinguishable by his more colourful markings, and by the much larger, longer, and more pointed fins. The trailing edge of his dorsal is split into pointed filaments. At breeding-time the female is thick, deep, and round; she literally bulges with eggs.

Breeding. *Spawning has been reported, but few details are available on care of the eggs and fry.*

432

KNIFE FISHES, FAMILIES GYMNOTIDAE AND NOTOPTERIDAE

The Gymnotidae hail from the north of South America and are distantly related to the characins. Their long, compressed, tapering bodies resemble a thin blade or stiletto, so they have been nicknamed the knife fishes. Somewhat similar in shape, but distinct from the South American species, are those belonging to the family Notopteridae, which comes from Indonesia, Burma, and Africa. The knife fishes have been erroneously called eels, but they are not even related to eels.

FAMILY GYMNOTIDAE

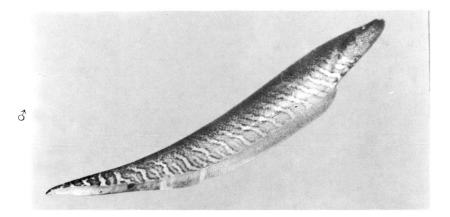

♂

Gymnotus carapo – Striped knife fish

N. South America ♂ *12"* ♀ *12"* *Non-community*
DIET: *Protein* SWIMS: *Lower half of tank*

These unusual fishes are hardy and interesting, but they grow too large for all except those who specialize in keeping oddities. They are unsafe in community tanks, the mouth being large enough to swallow smaller fishes. When kept on their own they will eat pieces of meat, shrimp, aged guppies, etc. *G. carapo* is nocturnal in habits, and generally lethargic during daylight. The long, flat, tapering body hangs motionless in the water, the head slanting upward at an angle of 25 degrees, the long ventral fin beneath the body rippling to ensure stability. The fish occasionally moves forward or backward with equal ease.

The colour is a brownish-grey. Numerous wavy pale grey stripes cross the body slantwise. These stripes are wider and farther apart towards the tail.

As far as is known, the species has not been bred in captivity.

433

Hypopomus artedi – *Knife fish*

Guyana ♂ 12" ♀ 12" Non-community
DIET: Protein SWIMS: Lower half of tank

Very similar to the foregoing, but the body is a brownish olive-green. The sides are speckled with irregular dark spots and bear a faint horizontal line in the centre.

We have no record of the fish having ever been bred in captivity. It is sometimes placed in the family Rhamphichthyidae.

FAMILY NOTOPTERIDAE

Xenomystus nigri – *African knife fish*

W. Africa ♂ 6" ♀ 6" Community, with medium-sized fishes
DIET: All foods SWIMS: Lower half of tank

As will be seen from the photograph, the African knife fish is not so long and narrow in outline as the typical South American knife fish. The colour is a uniform dark grey.

Our specimens are only 4" long, but they do not as yet appear aggressive in a community tank of medium-sized blind cave tetras, black mollies, etc.; and they have soon learned to come forward and eat dried food, though they also like chopped shrimp and cod-roe. They are rather shy, and prefer to swim in the background. Unlike the South American knife fishes, *X. nigri* swims about continually, often with the head tilted downward.

Breeding. *Few details available.*

434

FAMILY MORMYRIDAE

Gnathonemus petersi – Elephant nose

West Africa ♂, ♀ *to 10"   Species tank*
DIET: *Tubifex, small earthworms, bloodworms* SWIMS: *Mid to lower levels*

This fish requires plenty of hiding places, in a dimly lit tank. It can be aggressive, especially towards others of the same species, but needs careful feeding with the correct types of food.

Breeding.   *Little information available.*

FAMILY MASTACEMBELIDAE

The spiny eels are found in the Far East. Some species hail from India, others from Burma and Thailand. The body, extremely long and thin, is covered with minute scales. It is eel-like in appearance and movement. The head is long and narrow, the snout being sharply pointed with a fleshy proboscis tipped with nostrils; this organ is movable, and is poked in and around the sand in search of food. The fish has a second pair of nostrils more normally situated. The mouth is tiny, with minute teeth in the jaw.

Some species have separate dorsal, anal, and caudal fins. Others have a single median fin, which is all three combined as one. Many Mastacembelidae grow 9" to 30" in length. These large ones can swallow small, thin fishes, so are unsuitable in the average aquarium. One species, however, *M. pancalus*, is a desirable novelty.

Mastacembelus circumcinctus – Large spiny eel

Thailand ♂ 7"   ♀ 7"   *Community, with larger fishes*
DIET: *Live foods* SWIMS: *Lower half of tank*

Some years ago the authors received a number of species from Thailand. Although several were identical, others had slightly different markings. Some were without doubt *M. circumcinctus*. All grew 7" to 8" in length, and were somewhat quarrelsome, while their yellowish-brown bodies have vertical stripes. Some others were speckled; large brown spots adorned the dorsal fins. They ate the same foods as *M. pancalus*, but, having larger mouths, were able to eat small garden worms, which they seized with relish. Females appeared thicker than males.

435

Mastacembelus pancalus – *Spiny eel*

Madras   ♂ 4″   ♀ 4″   Community
DIET: Small live worms   SWIMS: Lower half of tank

This is the smallest member of the genus; it is harmless, uncommon, attractive, and breedable. A disadvantage is that it is extremely difficult to catch. When approached it dives into the sand and, as the net gets near, it shoots to another place beneath the sand. When several have to be caught it necessitates removing the plants and taking the sand out in small handfuls until each fish is captured. The species devours *Hydra*, but it will be seen that to transfer a few to an infested tank means wrecking the aquarium to get them out again. There are less troublesome ways of clearing *Hydra*.

M. pancalus has been much maligned. It is said to hide in the sand with only its head showing, in order to pounce upon and swallow any unwary fish approaching too closely. This is not true. The mouth is so small that it can swallow only white worms, blood worms, glass worms, and *Daphnia*, as well as a few *Hydra*. Even these are sucked in lengthwise. The fish soon becomes tame, and at feeding-time, will emerge from its hiding-place and take white worms from its owner's fingers. Any worms which fall to the bottom—even those which bury themselves in the sand—are soon searched out by this fish.

The colour is a sandy grey-brown. Thin stripes cross the body vertically. A brown stripe runs from the pointed snout through the eye to the gill-plate, and then continues as a row of distinct dots. Another more widely spaced row of dots appears along the upper flanks. The fins are clear except for minute specks. The dorsal, caudal, and anal fins are all separate.

The fish gets its popular name from a row of short sharp spines along the back, which can be raised at will. Females are distinguishable from males by greater thickness of body.

Breeding. *Tank: 24"×8"×8". pH: 7·0-7·8. Hardness: 150-180 p.p.m. Temperature: 80°F. Spawns: among floating plants. Method: deposits adhesive eggs. Eggs: 50-100. Hatch: in 3 days. Fry hang on: 2 days. Free-swimming: 6th day. Food 1st week: infusoria, brine shrimp. 2nd week: sifted Daphnia, microworms.*

Thanks to Wing-Commander Lynn, the authors can claim to have been the first to breed any of this genus in captivity. Lynn was fishing in a small pond in India, and, although he saw many species of fishes, all attempts to catch them with a *Daphnia* net proved futile, so mosquito netting was placed in the pond and allowed to sink. Waders then crossed the pool from the far bank, and in doing so had to push aside fronds of floating hornwort. On reaching the net it was pulled in as though seining. Various fishes were captured, among them being *M. pancalus*.

The authors tried unsuccessfully to breed these in flower-pots laid on the sand and among bunches of rooted plants. It was only after Lynn explained how these fish were caught that the key to their breeding was realized. Had the fish been in the mud the mosquito netting sinking on top of them would have trapped none. But if they were lurking in the floating hornwort they would, on being disturbed, have dived downward for safety: in this case they plunged into the net.

Since the fish lives and feeds on the bottom, why was it lurking in floating weed? Perhaps for spawning purposes? To test this theory a breeding tank was set up and covered with a 1" layer of hornwort. Immediately our specimens swam into it and wriggled together, half supported in the fronds of the plants. Eggs were laid, fertilized, and hatched in 3 days. The young did not have long, pointed snouts; these developed after about a month. The parent fish completely ignored the eggs and fry. Later, for experiment, newly born guppies were placed in the tank, but proved to be too big to be swallowed, and were of no interest to the adult spiny eels.

FAMILY NANDIDAE

The family is comprised of several genera which come from three different parts of the world. One group hails from the Far East, another from central West Africa, and the third is found in Guyana and the Amazon.

Most of the family have large mouths, and are not safe if kept with small fishes. The dorsal and anal fins usually consist of two portions, the fore-part being spined with hard rays, the hind portion bearing soft rays. The dorsal also extends to a great length along the back. The soft-rayed part of both the dorsal and anal projects beyond the normal outline of these fins, and is often transparent. At first glance these fishes look as though they have lost their tails.

♀ ♂

Badis badis – Dwarf perch

India   ♂ 2¾″   ♀ 2½″ Community, with medium-sized fishes
DIET: Live foods   SWIMS: Lower half of tank

These are the smallest of the family, but even so they are not safe in the same tank with small fishes. When several are kept together they are liable to squabble, and not infrequently one is killed. They are hardy, but not active, and have a habit of remaining for a time stationary in mid-water, then suddenly they will make a short dart to another position. Occasionally they will take a good dried food.

Mostly these fish are a chocolate-brown colour with darker bars. Like chameleons, they can vary their colours rapidly to suit their surroundings; occasionally they show off in most distinguished colours and patterns. The bars on the body form themselves into chains of red with red and brown links. The fins may take on a pinky-blue or brown hue. Unfortunately, these fish rarely stay in superb colour for long. Males often look hollow-bellied, but ripe females are thick and deep just above the ventral fins.

Breeding. *Tank: 24″×8″×8″.   pH: 7·0-7·2.   Hardness: 120-150 p.p.m.   Temperature: 80°F.   Spawns: in or under flower-pot.   Method: male fans eggs.   Eggs: 80-100.   Hatch: in 48 hours.   Fry wriggling: 2 days.   Free-swimming: 5th day.   Food 1st week: infusoria, brine shrimp. 2nd week: brine shrimp, microworms.*

The species is very easy to breed. Spawning takes place in a flower-pot which has had its base knocked out. The pot is placed on its side on the sand, with the larger end facing the front of the aquarium. Bunches of plants should be placed in the tank to afford protection to the female. Eventually the male coaxes her inside the pot, where she lays her eggs. Usually they are deposited high up, so that when spawning she turns on her side, or even upside down. After laying a few eggs she moves away, and the male comes in and fertilizes them. The process continues until about 100 eggs are laid, when the female should be removed. The male fans and guards the spawn. Once the babies are free-swimming the male may be taken out. Growth is slow. When the youngsters reach about 1″ in length squabbles break out, and the smaller and weaker ones are often killed.

The species will spawn in a community tank if given a flower-pot, and it is surprising how many young can be raised—mostly due to the care of the male, who drives off any fishes which would otherwise eat the fry.

♂

Polycentropsis abbreviata – African leaf fish

Nigeria ♂ 3″ ♀ 3″ Non-community
DIET: *Live foods* SWIMS: *Mid-water*

Those aquarists who specialize may like this fish. It is not safe in a community tank, as it has a very large mouth capable of swallowing fishes half its own size. It hangs about inactively in the water. The soft-rayed portions of the dorsal and anal fins, also the tail, are so transparent that *P. abbreviata* at first glance seems to have lost the rear portion of its anatomy: hence the name implying abbreviation. It will eat worms, bluebottles, and water insects if these are large enough to be worth while swallowing.

The colour varies from yellowish-brown to dark brown, and is mottled with darker blotches.

Breeding. *The fish is occasionally bred, though this has not been achieved by the authors. The male is said to blow a nest of bubbles under floating plants such as Indian ferns. Among the*

439

bubbles the female deposits single eggs which are fertilized by the male. Spawning continues until 80-100 eggs are laid, after which the female should be removed. Hatching occurs in 3-4 days, and the fry will take brine shrimp, sifted Daphnia, and small white worms. The male should be taken out once the fry are able to look after themselves.

♂

Polycentrus schomburgki – Leaf fish

Northern S. America   ♂ 3"   ♀ 3"   Community, with larger fishes
DIET: Live foods   SWIMS: Lower half of tank

Although kept by some aquarists with large fishes, *P. schomburgki* is not to be recommended to the average amateur, as it is unsafe with the usual species kept. It requires live food, and, although it will eat worms and water insects, small fishes are much preferred.

The body is oval in shape, and is a brownish-grey in colour, though this can change to a near-black. The sides are irregularly spotted, and at times dark vertical bars appear. A black line in the form of an arrowhead, with its point at the pupil of the eye, shows up on the side of the head. The fins are brownish, but are edged with white. The soft-rayed parts of the dorsal, anal, and tail fins are transparent.

Females are deeper and thicker than males, and usually they are paler in colour.

Breeding. *Tank: 24"×12"×12". pH: 7·0-7·2. Hardness: 120-150 p.p.m. Temperature: 78°F. Spawns: in flower-pot. Method: male fans eggs. Eggs: 80-100. Hatch: in 4 days. Fry wriggling: 3 days. Free-swimming: 8th day. Food 1st week: brine shrimp, microworms. 2nd week: microworms, sifted Daphnia.*

Spawning takes place in a flower-pot laid on its side among plant thickets. The procedure follows that described under *Badis badis* (p.438).

FAMILY ORYZIATIDAE

Oryzias javanicus – Rice fish

Malaya, Java   ♂ 1½"   ♀ 1½"   Community
DIET: *All foods*   SWIMS: *Upper half of tank*

Rather similar to *Oryzias latipes*, but it has a more pointed nose and the head is flatter on the top, followed by an arching back, giving the appearance of having a dip in the neck. It is peaceful.

The general body colour is silvery-grey, and it has an electric-blue spot above each eye which is very striking. The body is semi-transparent, and the swim-bladder is clearly seen through the fish's sides.

The female is considerably deeper-bodied and wider in the belly.

Breeding.   Tank: 24"×8"×8".   pH: 6·8-7·0.   Hardness: 50-80 p.p.m.   Temperature: 78-80°F.   Spawns: in clear water above plants.   Method: eggs attached by fine thread, catch on plants.   Eggs: 50-100.   Hatch: in 8-10 days. Food 1st week: infusoria. 2nd week: infusoria, brine shrimp.

For breeding procedure see *O. latipes* overleaf. The family Oryziatidae is closely related to the killifish (Cyprinodontidae).

Oryzias latipes – Golden medaka

Java, Malaya, China, Japan, Korea ♂ *1½"* ♀ *1½"* *Community*
DIET: All foods SWIMS: Upper half of tank

Often known as the rice paddy fish, it is not common in Europe, though it does appear from time to time. Although not striking in appearance, it has a pleasant disposition, is quiet and not aggressive, and is extremely easy to breed.

The general body colour is a light golden-yellow, the fins being slightly paler.

The female may be distinguished by her smaller fins and deeper belly.

Breeding. *Tank: 24"×8"×8". pH: 6·8-7·0. Hardness: 50-80 p.p.m. Temperature: 78-80°F. Spawns: in clear water above plants. Method: eggs attached by fine thread, catch on plants. Eggs: 100-150. Hatch: in 8-10 days. Food 1st week: infusoria. 2nd week: infusoria, brine shrimp.*

The breeding tank should be placed where it will receive good light, and set up with several bunches of feathery plants. Two males and three or four females may be used. The males chase the females over thickets and, trembling side by side, she expels eggs while he fertilizes them. The eggs often appear in little bunches of five or six, and are attached to her vent by a slender thread. Females may often be seen swimming around with the bunches of eggs still attached, but these eventually get brushed off on to the plants. In a day or two numerous bunches may be seen caught in the foliage, mostly near the top of the stems. The parents if well fed do not eat the eggs, and rarely touch the hatching fry.

Some breeders prefer to leave the parents in the original breeding tank for only 5 or 6 days, and then move them to another aquarium, where spawning continues.

442

The method eliminates the chances of the fry being eaten, or being pushed about at feeding-time. As many as 100 fry appear every fortnight. Alternatively, eggs attached to pieces of plant may be floated in battery jars, where they hatch.

FAMILY PANTODONTIDAE

Pantodon buchholzi – Freshwater butterfly fish

Tropical West Africa   ♂ and ♀ to 4"   Community, not with small fish
DIET: Live and dried food, at surface   SWIMS: Surface regions

This unusual-looking fish spends most of its time at the water surface. Consequently, some floating vegetation, as well as a good-fitting lid, is necessary. It usually adapts well to a diet of flaked foods, or live foods such as small crickets can also be offered. Although generally peaceful, it should not be trusted with very small fish.

Breeding.   *Eggs are laid at the water surface, and float until they hatch after 48 hours. The fry require very small live food, and are difficult to rear.*

FAMILY PERIOPHTHALMIDAE

The mud skippers, as this family of gobioid fishes is called, form one of the most remarkable groups. The eyes are large, and are supported on short stalks at the top of the head. They can be projected, so that while the body remains submerged the eyes break the surface to view the landscape, or they may be withdrawn beneath the surface of the water. Thus, Periophthalmidae are able to spy out mosquitoes and other insects. Then, leaping along the surface of the water, they capture their prey. Furthermore, they are able to breathe atmospheric air. The powerful muscles of the pectoral fins allow them to raise themselves as though on short legs, crawl out of the water, and travel quite a distance over land. On these escapades small snails and insects are searched for and devoured. When alarmed in their native pools or streams the fishes often evade danger by leaping on to land. Alternatively, when on shore they may jump back into the water. These fishes are able to walk on land much more efficiently than the climbing perch, which has only a clumsy waddling movement.

♂   ♀

Periophthalmus species – Mud skipper

Tropical Far East, W. Africa ♂ *5"* ♀ *5"* *Non-community*
DIET: *All foods* SWIMS: *In shallow water, and crawls on land*

This most interesting and amusing oddity requires a special housing. It needs plenty of room, shallow water, and sloping sandy banks or rocks so that it may climb out of the water. The atmosphere must be warm and damp. Without warmth and moisture the fish will get too dry.

The general colour is a brownish-grey speckled with darker spots about the face and neck. The edge of the anterior dorsal fin is black. Beneath this is a white band, the rest of the fin being a mauvish-blue. The anterior dorsal is traversed by a blue line edged above and below with white.

Breeding. *The mud skippers have not been bred in captivity.*

444

Chapter Twenty-two

Brackish-water Fishes

There are several fishes which will live in aquaria that contain sea-water, or half sea and half fresh water, or which can be slowly acclimated until they will live in fresh water. Even so, most prefer the addition of salt, and alkaline conditions. They come from several families. Few such fish have been bred in the aquarium.

FAMILY MONODACTYLIDAE

Monodactylus argenteus – Malayan angel or mono

Indian Ocean ♂ 5″ ♀ 5″ Community, with larger fishes
DIET: All foods SWIMS: Mid-water

This moderately peaceful fish is a swift swimmer. As it flashes round the aquarium the compressed sides, covered with minute scales of gleaming silver, shine brightly.

A black line from above the head runs downward through the eye. Another curves at a slightly different angle behind the gill-plate into the thorax. The dorsal and ventral fins are a brilliant gold.

Females appear to be thicker in the region below the ventral fins. The species may be acclimatized to fresh, brackish, or sea-water, and does well in all.

♀

♂

Monodactylus sebae – *Striped finger fish*

West African coastal areas   ♂ 5″   ♀ 5″   *Community, with larger fishes*
DIET: All foods   SWIMS: All depths

An attractive fish, though a little aggressive once settled in. It inhabits fresh, brackish, or pure salt water.

In comparison to *M. argenteus*, the fins are longer and the body shorter. There are no bright colours, but the contrasting black bars on a pure silver ground are sufficient to arrest the eye.

The species will eat any fresh food, and is soon trained to accept a good dried product.

Sexing is not obvious.

446

FAMILY SCATOPHAGIDAE

Scatophagus argus – Scat

Indonesia ♂ 7" ♀ 7" Community, with larger fishes
DIET: All foods SWIMS: Mid-water

Usually imported in small sizes, few of these attractive fish grow to maturity. The body is round and laterally compressed. The fins when well-spread stand up smartly.

The majority of scats are an olive green, but are coloured with darker olive spots. A perpendicular line always runs through the eye. There is a prettier variety popularly called the tiger scat in which the spots form themselves in vertical broken bars. The upper portion of the head and back glows with red which sometimes intermingles with the bars and appears again in the forward rays of the ventral and anal fins. The hind portions of the dorsal, anal, and tail are a chrome yellow.

Females are thicker in the belly region, and usually slightly less colourful than males.

FAMILY SYNGNATHIDAE

The pipe-fishes are found in most tropical waters in the Far East, some living in fresh water, others in brackish. The long, thin body is covered with bony plates, the skeleton being external. Most resemble the well-known sea horses, having a snouted head and long tail. Moreover, like sea horses, the male carries the eggs in a pouch situated in the abdominal region.

447

Syngnathus species – Pipe-fish

Indonesia, Thailand ♂ 6″ ♀ 6″ Community
DIET: Small live food SWIMS: All depths

Our plate shows a trio of pipe-fishes imported from Singapore, but others almost identical have been received from Thailand. The species will live in fresh, brackish, or salt water, though brackish seems preferred. They are peaceful, but rather difficult to feed.

448

FAMILY THERAPONIDAE

Therapon jarbua

Shores of Indian Ocean ♂ *4″* ♀ *4″ Community, with large fishes*
DIET: All foods SWIMS: Lower half of tank

Though somewhat quarrelsome, this fish is common enough to be seen in many salt- and brackish-water aquaria. It can grow very large, but in normal tanks rarely exceeds the above dimensions.

The body is silver. Black rings encircle the fish horizontally like contour lines. In the front rays of the dorsal there is an intense black patch. Three stripes cross the tail from front to back.

Females are thicker and deeper than males.

FAMILY TETRAODONTIDAE

There are numerous puffers: a few inhabit fresh water, but many live in brackish or salt water. They are able to inflate themselves with air until they look like miniature balloons. At the same time small spines are erected over most of the body. Inflation is done for protection. In the first place, it scares an aggressor: the puffer becomes too large a mouthful for some jaws, and the spines turn its normally soft, flabby exterior into a prickly, less edible meal. When lifted from the water a puffer usually performs this act, and makes a croaking sound as the air is sucked in. If returned to the tank the fish is so buoyant that it floats upside down momentarily, then, deflating itself quickly, it dives for safety. The genus *Tetraodon* have strong, parrot-like beaks of bone just beneath the lips, and the powerful mandibles enable the fish to break off pieces of coral, crush up snails, and sometimes slice through the shells of medium-sized crabs. Nevertheless most puffers are not really aggressive, but may nip fins.

Tetraodon fluviatilis – Puffer fish

Shores of Indian Ocean, Philippines ♂ 3″ ♀ 3″ Community, with larger fishes
DIET: Mainly protein SWIMS: Mid-water

This species is the commonest seen in home aquaria. It is hardy, attractive, and not too aggressive, and does well in fresh or brackish water or in pure sea-water.

The back and upper sides are a beautiful golden-green, but well covered with sizeable brown spots which occasionally form themselves into rings. The belly is silver-white.

Sexing is difficult. It is shown in illustration in Chapter 23.

Tetraodon species – Freshwater puffer

Thailand ♂ 3″ ♀ 3″ Non-community
DIET: Mainly protein SWIMS: Lower half of tank

We show here one of the fresh-water puffers that are available in the trade.

It will eat fish, meat, prawn, earthworm, etc., ignoring dried food and small white worms.

450

Though slow in movement, when tried in a community tank of medium-sized fast-swimming fishes it was able to make a stealthy approach and a final dart, usually upward, at a fish, its beak taking a clear semi-circle out of the unfortunate target.

The body is green with mottled brown markings, but set off with a bright red eye, and a similar bright red spot towards the tail.

FAMILY TOXOTIDAE

The archer fishes, as they are commonly called, have received great publicity. This is because they have specially shaped jaws, a groove inside the mouth, and a long tongue, enabling them to squirt drops of water at flies and other insects well above the surface. The accuracy of their aim is phenomenal. They can hit a fly 3½-4½ feet away, nearly always scoring a bull. Occasionally they fire at insects on the wing, and, though marksmanship is not a hundred per cent efficient, should they miss, repeated shots follow in such quick succession that the target is usually hit. The impact occurs with such force that the insect may be lifted a foot or more into the air.

451

Toxotes jaculator – Archer fish

Shores of Indian Ocean to Philippines   ♂ 4½"   ♀ 4½"   Community
DIET: Most foods   SWIMS: Upper half of tank

This species seems to be the commonest, and most exported. It thrives well in an
aquarium, and is hardy and peaceful. Despite shooting down insects, it will readily
take pieces of meat, fish, shrimp, crab, etc.

The body is a silver-grey crossed vertically by five short black bars. The dorsal,
anal, and ventrals are black, the pectorals white, and the tail dark grey.

Females appear to be deeper and rounder in the belly.

Chapter Twenty-three

Tropical Marine Aquaria

Though fresh-water fishes have been kept in aquaria for many years, comparatively few aquarists have ventured into the marine side of the hobby. In the past this has been understandable, as little was known about sea-water or the beautiful coral fishes. The majority of aquarists do not live near the coast, and acquiring sea-water was difficult and expensive. Although certain marine biological stations were prepared to sell and send sea-water great distances, the weight made costs high, and to ensure arrival in a pure condition special containers were necessary. Furthermore, if the water became quickly fouled replacements were not immediately at hand, and expenses were reincurred.

Today it is possible to buy salts which when mixed with fresh water produce artificial sea-water in which most tropical marine fishes and even invertebrates will thrive. Formerly, marine fishes were extremely difficult to catch and transport. But, with the advent of the aqua-lung and the expansion of air-freight services, they are becoming increasingly plentiful, and many now cost no more than their fresh-water cousins.

The sight of a well-set-up marine tank, sparkling with crystal-clear water, enhanced by a background of various shapes of coloured coral, and containing half a dozen or more of the most striking coral fishes, is literally breath-taking. Even the most colourful fresh-water fishes rarely compare with the gaudy brilliance so artistically blended in the little marine beauties.

Marine fishes are a little more delicate than most fresh-water fishes, although modern aquarium equipment and good-quality stock means that marine fishkeeping is far simpler than it was a few years ago.

The following hints may prove useful:

Size of tank:
Minimum recommended size is about 30 gallons, but preferably a little more, since the maintenance of stable conditions will be easier in a larger tank. Filled aquaria are *heavy*—a 3 ft set-up tank may weigh 200 to 300lb, so it will need a firm, even base or stand.

All-glass tanks are to be preferred, as metal-framed tanks corrode in sea-water. In fact, metals are best avoided when keeping marine fishes, since not only is corrosion a problem but the metals which dissolve into the water can be poisonous to the fish.

Water Quality:
Marine organisms need constantly filtered, vigorously aerated sea-water with a pH

between 8·0 and 8·3, a specific gravity of 1.020-1.022 and a constant temperature around (77°F). The nitrite and ammonia levels should be at (or close to) zero. A number of high-quality salt mixes are available, enabling aquarists to produce perfect sea-water for aquarium use.

Filtration, aeration:
A method to maintain satisfactory conditions in a marine tank is via an undergravel filter. The filter bed should consist of a layer of washed cockleshell (to maintain an alkaline pH), on top of which is placed a layer of unwashed coral sand (the biological filter). Separate the two using a gravel tidy. Use 10lb cockleshell and 10lb coral sand per square foot of tank bottom. Do not turn the filter off for extended periods; provide vigorous aeration at all times. Additional filtration and aeration can be provided using a power filter.

Lighting:
Provide about 100 watts of white fluorescent lighting for each 50 gallons of water. Invertebrates will often need more than this, as will seaweeds.

Stocking:
Compatibility can be a problem in marine tanks, so decide early on if you want a fish only or a mixed fish-invertebrate tank, and discuss suitable tank inmates with your local dealer. Stock only with pollution-tolerant fish (e.g., damsels) until the nitrite-ammonia peak has subsided. Then gradually increase to a maximum of 1″ of fish per four gallons of water over six months. After 12 months this may be increased to 1″ of fish to two gallons. Provide plenty of rocky refuges for the fish.

Feeding:
Good-quality flaked, tablet, freeze-dried and frozen foods are an ideal diet for most marine fish. Feed 2 to 3 times per day, with only as much as can be consumed in a few minutes. Feed invertebrates twice a week; anemones and most crustaceans on tablet or gamma-irradiated frozen foods, filter feeders on a liquid invertebrate food. Vitamin and trace element supplements are available.

Water changes, water quality:
Every 2 to 4 weeks, check the specific gravity, pH, ammonia and nitrite content of the tank water. Afterwards change 20 per cent of the tank volume and replace with fresh salt water at the correct specific gravity and temperature. Tank water may be removed via a siphon tube, along with any debris which has accumulated on the tank floor.

Diseases:

Marine organisms, just like any others, are subject to diseases. Incorrect tank care (especially poor water-quality and overcrowding) will increase the susceptibility of most marine fish to disease. However, proper tank care is not the only factor in preventing disease outbreaks in a marine aquarium. Unless you are sure of the health status of new stock, all new fish (and invertebrates) should be quarantined in a separate tank for at least two weeks. *Quarantine* of new stock and *proper aquarium care* will go a long way to preventing disease outbreaks. Would-be marine hobbyists should note that some disease treatments are toxic to marine invertebrates or the helpful bacteria in the filter. Consequently only 'safe' remedies should be used in a set-up marine tank, especially if invertebrates are present. For this reason beginners are recommended to start with a fish-only system, concentrating on a small number of relatively hardy fishes.

NATIVE MARINE AQUARIA

Many of the fish and invertebrates which inhabit the coastline and rock pools of Britain and temperate North America can also be kept in a suitably set-up aquarium. The above hints also apply to temperate marine aquaria, but less light will be required and, of course, no heating. In fact, most temperate marine creatures prefer quite cool conditions, and hence it is wise to site this type of aquarium in a suitably cool position in the home.

SURGEON FISHES, FAMILY ACANTHURIDAE

Common throughout the warm oceans of the world. They are generally vegetarian.

Paracanthurus hepatus – Regal tang

Indo-Pacific   ♂ 10"   ♀ 10" (usually smaller)   Community
DIET: Algae, soft lettuce, suitable dry food   SWIMS: All depths

A beautifully coloured fish, which may lose some of its colour with age. Can be kept in a small shoal with other similar-sized fishes.

TRIGGER FISHES, FAMILY BALISTIDAE

Generally colourful though somewhat aggressive fish which can grow quite large. Common throughout tropical oceans.

Balistoides niger – Clown trigger

Balistoides conspicillum is sometimes referred to as *Balistoides niger*. It is another rather aggressive fish, which can only be kept with similarly robust fish.

Rhinecanthus aculeatus – Picasso trigger

Indo-Pacific   Length: to 12"   Community, with robust fishes
DIET: Most foods   SWIMS: All levels

A quite hardy but aggressive fish that grows rather large. Easy to feed, but may attack smaller fishes.

ANGEL FISHES AND BUTTERFLY FISHES, FAMILY CHAETODONTIDAE

Small to medium-sized fishes that are common around tropical reefs. Although beautiful, some species are delicate and difficult to feed, and can be a little aggressive among themselves. The juveniles of some angel fishes have very different markings to that of their adult form. Many species require quite large tanks and are not recommended for the beginner.

Other species suitable for the home aquarium include the collared butterfly *Chateodon collare*, the threadfin *Chateodon auriga*, the moon butterfly *Chateodon lunula*, and various dwarf angel fishes, the *Centropyge* species.

Chaetodon species – Butterfly fishes

Indonesia, Polynesia ♂ 5″ ♀ 5″ Community
DIET: *Mainly protein* SWIMS: *All depths*

Chaetodon species are spread throughout most tropical seas. Most have disc-shaped, compressed bodies and a pointed snout. They can be somewhat choosy about food, and like white worms and small pieces of chopped prawn and various small live foods. Since they are often slow movers, they frequently lose the tit-bit, which is grabbed by faster-moving fishes.

Holacanthus ciliaris – Queen angel fish

West Indies, Florida   ♂ 8"   ♀ 8"   Community
DIET: Mainly protein   SWIMS: All depths

This beautiful fish grows to 20" or more in the ocean, but smaller specimens are better for the marine aquarist. The species is somewhat quarrelsome, and, being equipped with a savage spine on the lower edge of the gill-plate, can inflict wounds on other fishes.

Coloration is truly regal, blue and gold, and the head is crowned with a dark blue coronet, while the dorsal and anal fins bear flowing trains.

Marine Fishes

| *Amphiprion* | *A. ocellaris* | *Pomacentrus* | *Heniochus* | *Tetraodon* |
| *ephippium* | | *coeruleus* | *acuminatus* | *fluviatilis* |

Heniochus acuminatus – Wimple fish

Indian Ocean ♂ *4″* ♀ *4″* *Community*
DIET: All foods SWIMS: *Lower half of tank*

This attractive fish is similar to the fabulous and delicate Moorish idol (*Zanclus*).

The long, pointed dorsal fin is kept mostly upright and contrasts magnificently with the shorter, rounded anal fin. The species is extremely docile; it does not attack other fishes, but swims around minding its own business, which seems to be a constant search for food. However, should any fish take a sly nip at it, it quickly retaliates, as if to stand for no nonsense, then immediately resumes its former occupation.

The clear-cut black-and-white body is enhanced by bright yellow in the rear portion of the lower rays of the dorsal fin and tail. The pectorals are pale yellow, but the ventral fins are solid jet-black. The fish is pictured above. A relatively hardy fish.

Pomacanthus annularis – *Blue ring angel*

Indian Ocean, Polynesia   ♂ 6"   ♀ 6"   Community
DIET: Shrimp, white worms, etc., and some algae or vegetable food
SWIMS: Mid-water

This is a very beautiful fish of disc-like shape, with compressed sides. Unfortunately, it grows rather large, and may become quarrelsome. It likes some vegetable food. If seaweed is not available blue angels will enjoy picking at lettuce leaves. These can be anchored with a piece of string to a stone or a bit of slate so placed that the leaf appears to be growing upward in the water.

The fish grows to a great size in nature, but small specimens are best in a marine community tank. The body, as will be seen from our colour plate, is vividly striped with brilliant blue lines.

461

BATFISHES, FAMILY EPHIPHIDAE OR PLATACIDAE

Hardy fish, which may venture into river estuaries in tropical regions. Tall juvenile fish develop a more disc-shaped body with increasing age.

Platax orbicularis – Batfish

Indo-Pacific   Length: to 24"   Community
DIET: Most foods   SWIMS: All levels

Less attractive than many tropical marine fishes, this fish will grow fast yet remain gentle. Best kept in a shoal, if space permits.

DAMSEL FISHES, FAMILY POMACENTRIDAE

This is a large family of marine coral fishes, and they often live in small groups around coral reefs. They are generally hardy, colourful and hence popular for the home aquarium—but they can be a little aggressive in small tanks. They are excellent first fish for the beginner in this branch of the hobby. Certain species can be bred in the aquarium.

Butterfly-fish   *Sergeant-major*

Abudefduf species – Sergeant-majors

Tropical oceans   ♂ 2½″   ♀ 2½″   *Community*   DIET: *Most foods*   SWIMS: *Mid-water*

The genus *Abudefduf* is widespread, and there are many species, quite a few of which have been nicknamed 'sergeant-majors.'

They are hardy, will eat most foods, but are a little aggressive, though unlikely to do much damage to other fishes of similar size. They are full of life, and nearly always on the move. The sergeant-major pictured right above is at first inclined to hide behind clumps of coral, but it soon settles down and becomes bolder, even to the extent of occasionally monopolizing the most prominent portion of the tank, thus taking the eye off other more colourful species.

♀

Dascyllus aruanus – Striped damsel

Indonesia ♂ 2" ♀ 2" Community
DIET: Most foods, likes some seaweed or algae SWIMS: All depths

Though not brilliantly coloured, no fish could be more striking.

D. aruanus is a little aggressive—more so with its own kind than with others. However, it settles down quickly, and claims its own special place. At feeding-time it dashes out, and soon becomes tame. The species is amusing to watch as it swims forward or backward with equal ease through the jagged branches of coral without touching the fronds. It is hardy and easy to keep.

The body is silver, slashed with three broad black bands. A white patch appears on the forehead. The tail is nearly colourless, and often almost invisible. The remaining fins are jet-black. The ventrals have a silver front edge.

Dascyllus carneus – Cloudy damsel

Indian Ocean ♂ 2" ♀ 2" *Community* DIET: *All foods* SWIMS: *All depths*

This little damsel is smaller and stubbier than most, and is less aggressive. It is hardy, and easy to feed, soon learning to take even dried food.

The forepart of the body is dark grey, which shades into a black band, the hind-quarters are grey, but a patch of creamy white appears on the back just below the dorsal fin, and again on the caudal peduncle. The last rays of the dorsal and the tail fin develop a beautiful blue when the fish is in tip-top condition.

Also shown in our plate is a single specimen of *Tetraodon fluviatilis*, the spotted puffer fish.

$\circlearrowleft$

Dascyllus trimaculatus – White-spot damsel

Indian Ocean, Indonesia $\circlearrowleft$ 2" $\circleddash$ 2"   Community
DIET: Most foods, likes some seaweed or algae   SWIMS: All depths

In characteristics and habits this fish is similar to *D. aruanus*. The head is more rounded, and the snout blunter.

The body and fins are jet-black all over, but three large silver-white spots appear, one on each upper flank and one on the front of the head. When this fish is not entirely happy the intense black fades to a dark grey.

Pomacentrus coeruleus – Blue damsel

Indian and Pacific Ocean $\circlearrowleft$ 2½" $\circleddash$ 2½"   Community
DIET: Shrimp, fish, meat, etc., and some dried food   SWIMS: Lower half of tank

A brilliant, beautiful damsel. It is hardy and lively, but a little snappy with its own kind.

The whole body is a brilliant royal blue. The fins and tail are a rich yellow. When unhappy the blue turns darker, and may even become black.

CLOWN FISHES OR ANEMONE FISHES,
FAMILY POMACENTRIDAE

These small, colourful marine fishes are also hardy and popular with marine hobbyists. In the wild many species usually live in association with anemones. Clown fishes are not killed by the stinging cells on the anemone's tentacles because their skin has a special coating. They receive some protection from predators while within the tentacles of their host anemone, and the latter may benefit in return by sharing some of the food brought to it by the clown fish.

Some clown fish can be kept without an anemone, and even bred in the aquarium.

Amphiprion bicinctus – Dark clown fish

Indian Ocean, Red Sea   ♂ 3"   ♀ 3"   Community
DIET: All foods   SWIMS: All depths

The clown fishes make some of the best inhabitants of the marine aquarium. They are most attractive in colour and behaviour, hardy, reasonably cheap, friendly, and easy to feed.

A. bicinctus has a black back, but shades to yellow on the face and belly. Two silver blue bands slash the body, and these are so clear and clean that they seem to be painted on. All the fins are yellow.

Clowns enjoy chopped shrimp, white worms, and most good dried foods; they soon become tame, and will eat from their owner's fingers.

Amphiprion ephippium

Indian Ocean, Red Sea   ♂ *1³/4"*   ♀ *1³/4"*   *Community*
DIET: All foods   SWIMS: All depths

A pleasing little clown fish with a deep, stumpy body that is somewhat laterally compressed. Except for the one white band over the head, the fish is red all over.

It is friendly, attractive, easy to keep, and will take all the usual foods, including the dried product.

Amphiprion ocellaris – Clown fish

Indian Ocean, Polynesia, Red Sea   ♂ *2³/4"*   ♀ *2³/4"*   *Community*
DIET: Shrimp, fish, meat, some dried food   SWIMS: All depths

One of the commonest of the clowns, and probably the most popular coral fish kept today. It is hardy and cheap. Having a happy disposition, it is not aggressive, and several will live happily together. The fish swims with an exaggerated waggle. It has an inquiring nature, and will investigate objects. When a little scared it will face the danger and, waggling its body more intensely, swim up and down like a professional boxer ducking and rising to prevent being a stationary target. Clowns soon become tame, and rush to greet their owner in the hope that they will receive a tit-bit.

468

DRAGON FISHES OR SCORPION FISHES, FAMILY SCORPAENIDAE

A large family, frequently found on rocky shores and around coral reefs in tropical seas. They are predators which lie in wait for their prey; invertebrates and other fishes. Their fins carry poisonous spines, which can inflict serious wounds, even causing death.

Pterois volitans – Dragon fish

Red Sea, Indian Ocean, Polynesia ♂ *and* ♀ *8 to 10″*
Community, with other similar-sized fish
DIET: *Small fishes, shrimps, worms, etc.* SWIMS: *All depths*

Weird and wonderful, this fish always creates a stir. The head is large, and the body tapers towards the tail. But the outstanding features are the long, spiny-rayed dorsal and pectoral fins, which bear poisonous spikes. These can cause the death of other fishes, and the aquarist who has inadvertently run one of the spines into his flesh will experience a badly swollen, aching arm. However, it is not only the poison of *P. volitans* which makes it dangerous; it will pursue and swallow any fish which is capable of passing through the large mouth.

The colour is as dangerous-looking as the thorny appearance. The body and each spine is coloured with alternate bands of pale and darker brownish pink.

PIPEFISHES AND SEAHORSES, FAMILY SYNGNATHIDAE

Several species are available, and all are slow, delicate feeders. They prefer relatively still tank conditions, and cannot be mixed with larger fish or more aggressive feeders.

$\female$

Hippocampus species – Sea horse

Warm and temperate seas ♂ *6".* ♀ *6" Community, with small fishes*
DIET: Small live food SWIMS: *All depths*

The sea horses, of which there are many species, come from most warm seas where branching coral abounds. Like the pipe-fishes to which they are related, they have a bony armour on the outside of the body.

They swim in an upright position, and resemble prancing horses. Locomotion is by means of the dorsal fin, which vibrates very rapidly, and reminds one of a small boat being driven along by an outboard motor.

All have long, prehensile tails, with which they anchor themselves to branches of coral, and very often to each other.

Unfortunately, sea horses are slow and somewhat difficult to feed, requiring small food. The faster fishes get there first, and usually snatch their food from under their snouts; moreover, the authors have found that they usually get bullied.

470

Sea horses have little or no defence, and other fishes bite the dorsal fin away, sometimes right down to the flesh; this prevents them from swimming, and the wounds eventually cause death. In our opinion they should be housed on their own, and not kept with coral fishes.

Breeding. *Mating is unusual: the pair come together face to face, the female then inserts her ovipostor, in the male's abdominal pouch and places her eggs therein.*

These the male fertilizes and hatches, his abdomen expanding as growth increases. Eventually he gives birth to fully formed young sea horses, about ½" in length.

INVERTEBRATES FOR THE TROPICAL MARINE AQUARIUM

A wide range of invertebrates, including corals, anemones, fanworms, mussels and clams, starfish, prawns, shrimps and hermit crabs, are now available in aquarium shops, and can be kept in a suitably set-up aquarium. To consider the care of more delicate marine invertebrates (e.g., corals) is beyond the scope of this book, but a number of quite hardy invertebrates can be kept (even by the beginner) with fish such as damsels, clownfish and the like.

Small prawns, shrimps and hermit crabs are ideal additions to the tropical marine aquarium, so long as it does not contain any larger predatory fish like triggers or dragon fish. These crustaceans are useful scavengers, and at least one species (the cleaner shrimp, *Hippolysmata*) is said to remove parasites from co-operative fishes.

Small to medium-sized anemones can be kept with a range of fishes, so long as the tank is not too small and the light levels quite high. Anemones usually contain tiny algae cells in their bodies, which need bright light to survive. In the absence of suitable light conditions, these algal cells (or zooxanthellae) gradually die, and so does the anemone. Small, slow-moving fishes in a small tank may fall prey to an anemone.

Starfish and even clams can also be kept. Most starfish are scavengers, while clams are filter-feeders and require fine suspended matter two or three times a week. Clams may also have algal cells within their bodies (like anemones), and hence also require bright light.

Starfish and even clams can also be kept. Most starfish are scavengers, while clams are filter-feeders and require fine suspended matter two or three times a week. Clams may also have algal cells within their bodies (like anemones), and hence also require quite bright light.

FINAL COMMENTS

Marine fishes (and invertebrates) are a little more delicate and do require special care. Beginners must first keep relatively hardy varieties before venturing on to keeping delicate fishes and corals. Even so, with patience it is quite possible to breed some tropical marine fish in the home aquarium.

471

A Classification of Living Fishes

Fishes are an extremely numerous and diverse group of vertebrate animals. They dominate the waters of the world through a variety of morphological, physiological and behavioral adaptations, some of which have been described elsewhere in this book.

Fishes, in one form or another, have been around for about 400 million years, and during this time they have evolved and developed so that now they live in just about every watery habitat of the world—from ponds on the tops of mountains, down to the ocean depths; in desert springs and tropical jungle streams, and even in underground caves!

Below is indicated one of the current systems for classifying fish. There are of course other systems, and anyone interested in finding out more about fish classification should consult one of the relevant texts mentioned elsewhere in this book.

The fish alive in the world today can be divided into three main groupings:

1. Agnatha or 'jawless fishes', which includes the lampreys and hagfish. There are about 50 living species of these fish, none of which are really relevant to aquarists. The agnathans are important in another sense, in as much as their ancestors gave rise (many millions of years ago) to the two other major groupings of fishes, the Chondrichthyes and the Osteichthyes.
2. Chondrichthyes, or 'cartilaginous fishes', include the sharks, rays and skates, as well as the lesser-known ratfish and chimeras. This grouping contains perhaps 700 living species, most of which are of no relevance to aquarists. The sharks within this group are, however, popular with sports fishermen and film-producers!
3. Osteichthyes, or 'bony fishes', are today's dominant fishes. There are in the region of 20,000 species alive in the world today, a little over half of which live in freshwater.

These bony fishes are further divided into the following four sub-groups:
(**a**) Dipneusti or 'lung fishes', with five living species (*Neoceratodus* from Australia, *Protopterus* from Africa and *Lepidosiren* from South America).
(**b**) Crossopterygii or 'fringed-finned fishes', of which the coelacanth (*Latimeria chalumnae*) is the only living species. It was a close relative of the coelacanth that gave rise, again many millions of years ago, to amphibians—from which came reptiles, birds, mammals and Man!
(**c**) Brachiopterygii or 'bichirs'. There are 11 living species in this grouping, which includes *Polypterus* and the reed fish (*Calamoichthys*).
(**d**) Actinopterygii or 'ray-finned fishes'. This grouping, which contains the vast majority of the 20,000 or so species bony fishes alive in the world today, contains

most of the fish which Man eats, catches for sport, farms on fish farms—or keeps in aquaria and ponds for ornamental purposes.

Within the above-mentioned major taxonomic groupings, the fish are divided into smaller and smaller groupings by scientists until we get to the family, genus and species level.

Most species of plants and animals (including fish) have a two-word scientific name. This scientific name is universal in its application, and means that scientists from different countries can refer to the same species, but without confusion. Thus by way of an example, the bronze catfish has the scientific name *Corydoras aeneus*. This means that it is placed in the genus *Corydoras* (along with some other *Corydoras*), yet it has the unique species name of *aeneus*. Aquarists should try to familiarize themselves with the scientific names of their fish, as they will find it useful when trying to obtain information from text books and the like.

Where there is some uncertainty or disagreement of the correct current scientific name, a compromise between the most up-to-date and the most familiar to aquarists has been provided. In a small number of instances, alternative names have been provided, and in one or two situations the fish described have actually been classified a stage further than species level—to sub-species.

Throughout the text, $\male$ refers to male fish and $\female$ to female fish.

Appendix Two

Unit Conversion Table

Wherever possible in this book Imperial/British units have been quoted. However, the following information may prove useful.

To convert	Into	Multiply by
°dH (water hardness)	ppm Ca CO$_3$	17·9
°C	°F	(°Cx1.8) + 32
°F	°C	(°F−32) × 0·556
centimetres	feet	0·033
centimetres	inches	0·39
centimetres	yards	0·011
cubic centimetres	cubic inches	0·061
cubic inches	cubic centimetres	16.4
cubic metres	cubic yards	1·31
cubic yards	cubic metres	0.77
feet	centimetres	30.5
feet	metres	0.31
gallons (US)	gallons (UK)	1.20

To convert	*Into*	*Multiply by*
gallons (UK)	litres	4.55
gallons (UK)	gallons (US)	0.83
gallons (US)	litres	3.79
grams	pounds	0.0022
inches	centimetres	2.54
kilograms	pounds	2.21
kilograms	tons (metric)	0.001
kilograms	tons (UK)	0.00098
kilograms	tons (US)	0.0011
kilometres	miles	0.62
litres	gallons (UK)	0.22
litres	gallons(US)	0.26
litres	pints (US)	2.11
metres	feet	3.28
metres	yards	1.09
miles	kilometres	1.61
pints (US)	litres	0.47
pounds	grams	453.6
pounds	kilograms	0.45
square centimetres	square inches	0.16
square inches	square centimetres	6.45
square kilometres	square miles	0.39
square metres	square yards	1.20
square miles	square kilometres	2.59
square yards	square metres	0.84
tons (metric)	kilograms	1000.0
tons (UK)	kilograms	1016.1
tons (US)	kilograms	907.2
yards	centimetres	91.4
yards	metres	0.91

Note

1 Imperial gallon weighs 10lb

1 US gallon weighs 8.34lb

1 litre water weighs 2.2lb

To calculate the surface area of an aquarium: length × width (in inches) = surface area in square inches.

To calculate the capacity of an aquarium: length × width × water depth (in feet) = capacity in cubic feet. Multiply capacity in cubic feet by 6.25 to obtain capacity in Imperial gallons. Deduct 10 to 20 per cent. from this to allow for gravel and rocks (if present).

Example: 2 × 1 × 1 foot aquarium

Surface area = 24 × 12 inches = 288 square inches

Capacity = 2 × 1 × 1 feet = 2 cubic feet = 13.5 Imperial gallons

Weight of water = 13.5 × 10 = 135lb.

Reading List

BOOKS

Tropical Aquarium Fishes by D Mills & G Vevers (Salamander, 1982).
The Complete Aquarium Encyclopedia edited by J D van Ramshorst
    (Phaidon, 1978).
The Aquarists' Encyclopedia by G Sterba (Blandford, 1983).
How Fishes Live by P Whitehead (Phaidon, 1975).
Encyclopedia of Underwater Life edited by K Banister and A Campbell
    (George Allen and Unwin, 1985).
Fishes – An Introduction to Ichthyology by P Hoyle and J Cech
    (Prentice-Hall, 1982).
Aquarium Systems edited by A D Hawkins, (Academic Press, 1981).
The Fishkeeping Yearbook edited by J Dawes (Robert Royce, 1985).
Making Your Own Aquarium by J Hansen (Bell & Hyman, 1979).
Pocket Guide to Aquarium Fishes by G Vevers (Mitchell Beazley, 1982).
The Cichlid Aquarium by P V Loiselle (Tetra Press 1935).
Rift Lake Cichlids by G S Axclrod (Tropical Fish Hobbyist 1979).
A Fishkeeper's Guide to Fish Breeding by C Andrews (Salamander, 1986).
Marine Tropical Aquarium Guide by F de Graaf (T.F.H. 1982).
Keeping Marine Fish by G Lundegaard (Blandford, 1985).
Marine Aquarium Keeping by S Spotte (Wiley-Interscience, 1973).
A Fishkeeper's Guide to Marine Fishes by D Mills (Salamander, 1985).
The Seashore and Shallow Seas of Britain and Europe by A C Campbell
    (Hamlyn, 1976).
Starting with Marine Invertebrates by J G Walls (T.F.H., 1974).
The Marine Aquarium Manual by M Melzak (Batsford, 1984).
Brackish Aquariums by M Gos (T.F.H., 1979).
A Fishkeeper's Guide to a Healthy Aquarium by N Carrington
    (Salamander, 1985).
Fish Pathology by H H Reichenback-Klinke (T.F.H., 1973).
Encyclopedia of Live Foods by C Masters (T.F.H., 1975).

MAGAZINES

Aquarist & Pondkeeper, Buckley Press Ltd, 58 Fleet Street, London EC4Y IJU.
Practical Fishkeeping, EMAP National Publications, Bretton Court, Bretton,
    Peterborough.
Tropical Fish Hobbyist, T.F.H. Publications Ltd, 4 Kier Park, Ascot, Berks
    SL5 7DS.

INDEX

All scientific names marked with an * are those of plants; names not so marked are those of fishes. Illustrations normally appear on the same page as their relevant text, but where there are illustrations apart from their text, these are italicized.